CONTRADICTIONS: FINANCE, GREED, AND LABOR UNEQUALLY PAID

RESEARCH IN POLITICAL ECONOMY

Series Editor: Paul Zarembka
State University of New York at Buffalo
USA

Recent Volumes:

RESEARCH IN POLITICAL ECONOMY VOLUME 28

CONTRADICTIONS: FINANCE, GREED, AND LABOR UNEQUALLY PAID

EDITED BY

PAUL ZAREMBKA
State University of New York at Buffalo, USA

Emerald

United Kingdom – North America – Japan
India – Malaysia – China

Emerald Group Publishing Limited
Howard House, Wagon Lane, Bingley BD16 1WA, UK

First edition 2013

British Library Cataloguing in Publication Data
A catalogue record for this book is available from the British Library

ISBN: 978-1-78190-670-5
ISSN: 0161-7230 (Series)

CONTENTS

LIST OF CONTRIBUTORS

Wladimir Andreff	Centre d'Economie de la Sorbonne, University Paris 1 Panthéon Sorbonne, Paris, France
Zak Cope	School of Politics, International Studies and Philosophy, Queens University Belfast, Belfast, Northern Ireland
Cecilia Beatriz Escobar Meléndez	Department of Economic Sciences, University of Athens, Greece
Jean-Guy Loranger	Economic Department, Université de Montréal, Montréal, Québec, Canada
Jie Meng	Institute of Economics, School of Social Sciences, Tsinghua University, Beijing, People's Republic of China
Tony Norfield	Economics Department, School of Oriental and African Studies, University of London, London, UK
José A. Tapia Granados	Institute for Social Research, University of Michigan, Ann Arbor, USA
Julian Wells	Department of Economics, Faculty of Arts and Social Sciences, Kingston University London, Kingston upon Thames, United Kingdom

CRISIS AS UNEXPECTED TRANSITION ... TO A GREED-BASED ECONOMIC SYSTEM

Wladimir Andreff

ABSTRACT

Analyzing how the post-Soviet transition interacts with the crisis of market finance exhibits a new "greed-based economic system" in the making. Asset grabbing is at its core and hinders capital accumulation. All the various privatization schemes have triggered off asset grabbing, asset stripping, and asset tunneling. A global contagion of such behavior has spread the power and cohesion of managers/shareholders (oligarchs) worldwide. Financial asset grabbing is less straightforward, though much widespread, and operates in financial markets through new financial products, securitization, firms buying their own shares, hedge funds, stock price manipulation, short selling, and the distribution of stock options.

Shadow banking, and more generally a global informal economy, results from grabbing strategies in financial markets that breach the formal rules of capitalism. In alleviating and circumventing the rules, the oligarchy paves the way for economic malpractices and crime, calling capitalist laws into question.

Contradictions: Finance, Greed, and Labor Unequally Paid
Research in Political Economy, Volume 28, 1–48

ISSN: 0161-7230/doi:10.1108/S0161-7230(2013)0000028003

In such context, systemic greed underlies unconstrained maximization of relative wealth, for which asset grabbing is a rational means, in a winner-take-all economy. At the present stage of our research, a greed-based economy cannot yet be theoretically defined as a transition either to a new phase of capitalism or to another different system.

Keywords: Asset grabbing; privatization; financial markets; shadow banking; systemic greed; winner-take-all

The current financial crisis is often analyzed as beginning in 2007 and the focus is on subprime mortgage loans and Lehman Brothers bankruptcy. However, the first forewarning signs of a deep crisis in globalized financial markets emerged in the late 1980s. In 1987, a stock market crash spread internationally from the United States after which the savings and loans system collapsed in 1989. Boyer (2011) underlines that with the October 1987 crash the ghost of the 1929 crisis reappeared and Fed had already made a decision to widely open its finance to traders seriously hit by falling stock market prices. Though the crisis worsened after 2007–2008, it was indeed maturing over a twenty-five-year lapse of time.

Centrally planned economies exhibited signs of crisis in the late 1980s as well (Andreff, 1985; Chavance, 1987). The crisis deepened between 1987 and the 1989, the year symbolic milestone – the Berlin wall – collapsed. Combining negative rates of economic growth, open inflation, foreign trade deficit and debt, and newly emerging unemployment, the Soviet Union and Eastern Europe for the first time fell into an extreme economic slump. In the very same year 1987 reforms were launched that triggered off the final countdown for the former Soviet system, from *perestroika* and *glasnost* in the USSR to the first calls for privatization programs in Poland and Hungary. Thus, 1987–1989 were actually revealed as years of a dramatic breakdown in the global economy: planned economies were imploding, on the one hand, while, on the other hand, a phase of accelerated capitalist globalization,[1] fuelled by liberalization, privatization, and market finance development, was coming across serious turbulences. It must be stressed that the fatal crisis in Soviet economies and the first significant indices of a crisis in global capitalism occurred simultaneously. This was more than chronological coincidence; no doubt, simultaneity had deeper foundations. From 1987 to 2012, every year somewhere in the world has witnessed a series of significant financial crises, stock market crashes, economic recessions, and tremendous bankruptcies (see Table 1).

Neo-liberal euphoria claimed a supposed final "victory" of capitalism over communism (*The end of history* by Fukuyama). From 1990 to 2006, this claim of victory has hidden that market finance was sliding into a global crisis. Neo-liberal economists focused instead on hindrances to post-Soviet transition to a market economy – using the mainstream wording. In the 1990s, the predominant Washington consensus drove economic policies and reforms, definitely broke up the former centrally planned system, promoted

Table 1. A Nonstop Global Crisis from 1987 on.

1987:	U.S. stock market crash spreading to European stock exchanges
1988–1989:	Final deep economic recession in East European centrally planned economies
1988–1989:	Revolving bankruptcies of U.S. savings and loans; collapse in 1989
1988–1993:	Economic recession of the Japanese economy
1990–1993:	Deep transformational recession in PTEs (Post-Soviet transition economies), which lasts longer in CIS countries (Commonwealth of Independent States) (up to 2000 in Ukraine)
1992:	U.S. economic recession, financial crisis in Estonia, sterling pound, Italian lira, and Spanish peseta crises
1993:	The European monetary system implodes
1994:	Financial crises in Bulgaria and Russia
1994–1995:	*tequila* financial crisis in Mexico
1995:	Barings Bank's bankruptcy, financial crises in Latvia and Lithuania
1996:	Financial crisis in Kyrgyzstan
1996–1997:	Financial crises in Bulgaria and the Czech Republic
1997:	Financial crises in Asia (Hong Kong, South Korea, Indonesia, Malaysia, Philippines, Thailand, Vietnam) and Albania
1998:	Asian crisis spreads to Australia and Chile, financial crises in Kyrgyzstan, Russia, Slovakia, Ukraine, U.S. stock market crisis, LTCM (Long Term Capital Management) speculative funds bankruptcy
2000:	Stock market crash, the Internet speculative bubble bursts out (e.crash), financial crisis in Turkey
2001:	Enron, WorldCom, Parmalat, etc., fraudulent bankruptcies
2001–2002:	Financial crisis in Argentina
2001–2003:	Global FDI recession in the aftermath of 9/11, collapse of trans-border mergers and acquisitions in a bad stock market mood
2006:	Increasing repayment defaults on subprime mortgage loans
2007:	Subprime mortgage loan crisis
2008:	Global financial crisis starts up with Lehman Brothers, AIG, Merrill Lynch, etc., bankruptcies
2008–2009:	Global FDI recession
2009–2012:	Global economic recession (except in a few emerging countries)
2010:	Flash stock market crash (May 6)
2010–2012:	Euro zone crisis

post-Soviet transition economies (PTEs), and aligned most developing countries (DCs) on to liberalization and privatization programs. Along with it, an ideological watchword spread throughout the world: neo-liberal capitalism is the best recipe for macro- and microeconomic governance in all post-1989 economies. However, the Washington consensus overshadowed that market finance crisis and post-Soviet transition were evolving in an interaction between them. That both could have come out from a same process of mimetic contagion remained unspeakable to neo-liberal analyses and unacknowledged in most heterodox economic approaches.

Without denying some similarities between the current crisis and post-1929 years as regard the downturn of real estate and financial markets, and overall recession, the two crises cannot be further compared. The following differences in 1929 were basic: no collapse or transition of an alternative centrally planned economic system had occurred; no regional or international integration had gathered PTEs together with long-lasting capitalist economies as it happened with the European Union's eastward enlargement; globalization through foreign direct investment (FDI) and global finance had not gone as far as nowadays; the tertiary and financial sectors were not as significant in the whole economy as today; and a phase of regulated capitalism had not prevailed beforehand.

Thus, it seems realistic to hypothesize that the current crisis of global capitalism structures and institutions is deeply rooted in the interactions between post-Soviet transition and the turmoil of market finance. Would not a deepening crisis of "financialized" capitalism and the collapse of planned economies, combined together in globalization, pave the way for an overall transition toward a radically new economic system?[2] In any case, this hypothesis is not one of a sudden and sharp break up of capitalism. Rather, our assumption points more at an evolutionary change which preserves a vast range of capitalism's institutions while new informal rules incongruent with capitalism emerge before being formalized into new institutions.

No mainstream analysis had approached the current financial crisis as interacting with PTEs transformation so far. A number of analyses contend that:

a. Intense speculation and excess risk-taking have fueled major drifts in finance-dominated capitalism and have inflated financial bubbles; the latter have burst out in repeated crises that no substantial systemic reform was capable to prevent;
b. PTEs transformation has met various dysfunctions, distortions, and "leeways" compared to neo-liberal IMF- and World Bank-sponsored

transition programs; the outcome of this transformation is not a full-fledged market economy aligned on to Western economies.

However, even heterodox economists have usually neglected to analyze the interactions between (a) and (b) in depth. Most of them do not show that the aforementioned drifts and "leeways" in PTEs transformation together with the crisis of market finance are part and parcel of an overall evolutionary change that affects all the different areas of the global economy. Those elements that seemingly lay the ground for a new economic system in the making are dealt with here as follows:

Asset grabbing: assets which were previously accumulated in the public sector are grabbed through privatization without fuelling capital accumulation, on the contrary, hindering it (Section 'Privatization: asset grabbing versus capital accumulation').

Financial asset grabbing is indirect and results from betting in financial markets (Section "Asset grabbing in financial markets: Risk taking and rash betting").

Cheating with the formal rules of capitalism in view of grabbing assets and financial payoffs has become a usual game in a sort of global shadow economy (Section "Cheating with the Rules of Capitalism and the Global Shadow Economy").

Infringing the laws and institutional rules of capitalism makes the dominant oligarchy sure to win all financial bets with certainty (Section "Circumventing and Perverting Institutional Rules of Capitalism").

Systemic greed uses asset grabbing, instead of capital accumulation, as its major means for wealth and enrichment maximization without constraint, in a winner-take-all economy beneficial to oligarchs (Section "The Hypothesis of Systemic Greed: A Transition to a "Greed-Based Economic System").

PRIVATIZATION: ASSET GRABBING VERSUS CAPITAL ACCUMULATION

Privatization, though at the core of neo-liberal capitalist views and policies, paradoxically triggers off a process of wealth acquisition that differs from and hinders capital accumulation as soon as privatization is achieved by means of asset transfers. The latter translate into grabbing previously accumulated capital in the public sector when a buyer does not pay the full price for assets coming into his/her possession.[3] Privatization is a unique window of opportunity that will never come back again to grab or strip an enterprise's assets at cut-price. The one who has easily grabbed assets often stakes[4] them, partly or entirely, on lucrative nonproductive activities, that is, he/she rarely uses all his/her cheaply grabbed capital to invest in real production. Thus, asset grabbing erects itself as an obstacle to capital accumulation.

Privatization, in a macro sense, may result from a swifter growth in the private sector as compared with the public sector and/or a rapid increase in the number of *de novo* start-ups. If so, its momentum relies on capital accumulation to make profits and on profit-making for capital accumulation, business as usual in capitalism. However, microeconomic privatization transfers existing assets from state ownership to private owners. Here the logic is one of property and asset redistribution. If state-owned property is given away for free or underpriced, the economic momentum relies on asset grabbing (Frye & Shleifer, 1997) by individuals or groups who are privileged by the techniques chosen for transferring property. Such grabbing is predatory. Predation for predation per se is not a foundation of capitalism. While it has characterized specific phases of capitalism as a tool for primary accumulation in a Marxian sense, at the dawn of capitalism and in colonization episodes, both are outdated since the emergence of global capitalism (Andreff, 1976). If, after being grabbed, assets are used otherwise than for capital accumulation in production and trade – for speculation, financial bets, games, squandering, asset flight abroad, laundering misappropriated assets, this is not a founding feature of capitalism. These asset uses point at the basic traits of a wealth acquisition system relying on the redistribution of existing assets instead of the creation of new real economic value.

First privatization programs were launched before the crisis in developed countries and DCs, and then spread to over 28 PTEs in the 1990s and to China after 1997. Still, asset grabbing through privatization is not over; the Greek government initiated a €50 billion privatization program in April 2011. If such an economic policy were to be sustained in the long run, asset grabbing would not end up until all the public assets are exhausted, that is, the entire public sector being wiped out.

Privatization Financial Deals: Property Leverage and Cut-Price Asset Sales

Privatization resorted to increasingly predatory transfer techniques. At the very beginning, the standard privatization program, as recommended by the

IMF (Hemming & Mansoor, 1988), was usually splitting the stockholding equity of would-be privatized companies into four "slices" before selling them; each slice was doomed to be acquired by specific buyers. In the French 1986–1988 privatization program, a maximum 20% of all stocks were to be sold in international stock markets; a minimum 10% of stocks were preserved at a cut discount for the firm's employees; 15–30% of stockholding equity were to be acquired by a hard core of controlling shareholders each of whom was allowed to acquire between 0.5% and 5% of all stocks – the hard core eventually was chosen by the government; the remaining slice consisted in stocks publicly offered in the domestic stock market to the resident population.

A point is rarely made that such capital sharing provided advantageous *property leverage* to core shareholders.[5] By buying 15–30% of all stocks, they were able to monitor all the decisions over total stockholding equity (a 3.3–6.6 lever). Core shareholders "borrowed," so to say, property rights from employees and small shareholders for free in view of reaching the profitability objectives they had fixed, as monitoring owners, to privatized firms. When stock prices fell during the October 1987 crash, 20% of small shareholders sold their depreciated stocks in companies which were out of their control anyway. Core shareholders and institutional investors acquired these stocks at low price in the market. Thus, first playing on property leverage and then skimming off depreciated stocks in the market, a small group of core block-holders grabbed assets in leveraging people's savings. It was all the more so that those 80% small shareholders who had kept their stocks went on behaving as sleeping partners in privatized companies. Deprived from their property rights and happy with it (!), they kept passive. As regards core shareholders, they actually made short-term financial rather than strategic real investment motivated by synergy between their business and a privatized company (Cartelier, 1992). At the end of the day, foreign investors appeared to be the major winners in French privatization, just like in PTE privatization.

In France and DCs, the government refused to embark on a privatization program à la Thatcher where the equilibrium price was to be found by the stock market itself after an initial public offering (IPO). A *fixed price*[6] IPO technique was adopted. A privatization commission fixed a range of potential stock prices, topped with a maximum price and downward blocked by a minimum price, after having audited a public enterprise to be privatized. The minister for privatization has nearly always opted for a price higher than the minimum assessed by the commission, though quite lower than any expected stock market price. Such crystal clear and *systematic asset underpricing* (Andreff, 1992a, 1999) was a precondition for the French privatization success story since it triggered off an excess demand for stocks of privatized companies. A low initial price facing an excess demand favored an overnight market price hike after privatization. This made privatization popular to savers and, by the same token, enriched core shareholders. The latter grabbed assets at a higher initial stock price offered to them than to regular savers, though still at a discount price, and then bought further stocks at depreciated prices after the 1987 crash.

The government's choice resulted in a tighter cross-ownership between core shareholders of different privatized companies, and between them and different firms, banks, and insurance companies. Cross-ownership was accompanied with increased interlocking directorates across major companies in French capitalism. Cronyism was denounced with regard to the gathering of shareholders in the hard cores. Interest groups often used crony relationships to grab assets. Thanks to increasingly present institutional investors in hard cores, the financial sector grabbed more and more assets this way. After 1995, the hard cores and a number of cross-ownership relationships were dissolved so that the share of core shareholders fell down to an average 20% of stockholding equity in CAC40[7] companies, that is, down to a level that secures a company's monitoring (Andreff, 1996) without a too heavy and useless capital immobilization.

Discount-price asset grabbing was even more extensive when privatization proceeded with over-the-counter *non-market sales* of assets. Then asset pricing resulted from bargaining between the government and private rescuers, and in any case the outcome was underpricing. International consultants who often advised the rescuers were used to widely propagate the idea that the economic value of firms in PTEs and DCs was nearly zero due to supposedly obsolete physical assets. Arthur Andersen took the opportunity of being involved in PTE privatization drives, before the Enron scandal, in view of training its staff at downward-biased value auditing in favor of the rescuers and inside dealers (Andreff, 2007).

In various DCs, asset sales were integrated into *debt-equity swaps* (Bouin & Michalet, 1991). Chesnais (2011) contends that debt equity tendering was a sort of testing ground for future securitization. The rescuers bought in the secondary market of a given DC, at (at least 50%) discount, debt equities issued in hard currency. Afterwards, these equities were redeemed for stocks of would-be privatized enterprises. The latter were thus acquired half-price or less. This was again discount-price asset grabbing. Given the inflationary impact of such swaps and a limited number of potential rescuers in DCs, the government was used to manage these deals with the least possible transparency. Discount-price selling of a nation's assets was held against the government whenever transnational corporations (TNCs) or foreign rescuers succeeded in a debt-equity swap.

Asset Tunneling Bad Practices

Spontaneous privatization in PTEs was a specific grabbing by a manager or a managerial group which relied on stripping and tunneling state-owned assets to his/her private satellite company. Extremely low transfer pricing in trading contracts signed between the satellite company and a state-owned enterprise was used on purpose. The radical uncertainty linked to transition fueled these bad practices. Thus *managers became stock owners* of their company's assets. The distinction between managers and owners vanished, and did not make sense any longer since a group of *stockholding managers* had emerged, often coined *oligarchs*. Spontaneous privatization was tolerated by governments, though illegal and corrupted because it enabled oligarchs to swiftly grab assets; in the transition context an ideology supporting the view that assets would only be efficiently managed in private ownership, whoever the owner, was pushed forward. A priori unpopular, spontaneous privatization became definitely hated by the population when oligarchs, facing the radical uncertainty of transition, started transferring assets to tax havens, buying casinos and soccer teams abroad and were involved into money trafficking. Besides, privatization was a top-down political and administrative process widely open to collaboration (Blasi, Kroumova, & Kruse, 1997) and corruption between the managers of state-owned firms and privatization local authorities. Inside dealing was more the rule than exception. When the future identity of asset owners becomes blurred, privatization generates considerable uncertainty that makes managers eager to loot assets.

Asset acquisition with credit leverage, the so-called leverage buy-out (LBO) became *management-employee buy-out* (MEBO) in PTE privatization. Managers and employees acquired assets of their own company with cut-price leveraging on bank loans. They often benefited from a discount indexed on their seniority in the company. MEBO privatization was a government excuse to give assets away for free. The discount applied on to already undervalued prices that were beforehand calculated by those managers eager to acquire the company's assets. The repayment of bank loans and interest payment were tax free. Adopting MEBO privatization circumvented the opposition of managers and employees to their company's privatization and enabled managers to grab assets at cut-price or for free. After MEBO privatization, managers usually bought their employees' equities at over-the-counter low prices (Frydman & Rapaczynski, 1994).

Mass privatization proceeded with giving away companies' equities or vouchers redeemable into stocks to all the population at a negligible price. The first experience with mass privatization evidenced a success story in British Columbia in 1986: 86% of the province population was willing to acquire five shares at an estimated $6 value each. However, a number of buyers rapidly sold their equities. Most stocks concentrated into the hands of a small group of owners (Andreff, 1992a): for the latter, this obviously was cut-price asset grabbing. Nevertheless, the World Bank promoted mass privatization as its most favored method in PTEs and praised it to the skies in the Czech Republic – and for a while in Russia – where it was adopted as the first priority privatization technique (Boycko, Shleifer, & Vishny, 1995).

Mass privatization was implemented by creating privatization investment funds. Citizens deposited their privatization vouchers (acquired for free or nearly so) in the funds which were promising "fantabulous" returns, much higher than the current 15% global norm for shareholder value growth.[8] Many funds were financial pyramids indeed. They were undertaken in all PTEs by promoters, who becoming wealthy at a rocket speed, then flew away to tax havens. Albania, a distinguished World Bank good guy, was plagued in 1997 with sixteen Ponzi schemes offering up to a 100% return per month; they collected $1.2 billion, that is, 50% of the Albania's GDP value at the moment. Half Albanese government members were involved as promoters of financial pyramids; they had to resign and some of them were sued for illicit enrichment. The subsequent financial crisis destroyed over 30% of all domestic enterprises (Andreff, 2007). Most fortunes built up thanks to Ponzi schemes remained unpunished in other PTEs.

With mass privatization asset grabbing was used on a large scale and concentrated assets in the oligarchs' hands. In Russia, a big majority of privatization voucher holders sold them overnight at discount price[9] to new, rich, and forthcoming oligarchs. This did not happen without a series of embezzlements and fraudulent losses of millions of privatization vouchers (Freeland, 2000). Assets were also grabbed through selling stocks over-the-counter since a stock exchange still did not exist; such sales went on even after a stock exchange had been set up (Andreff, 2005). This equity trading did escape any regulation, just like any over-the-counter trade in developed capitalisms. In mass privatization, one can never know who the next owner would be. The Czech Republic, a country which privileged mass privatization, has much suffered from asset looting.

The World Bank eventually abandoned its program of swift privatization in PTEs (2002) after many sharp criticisms about the so-called *loans for shares* scheme, which relied on bank loans with manufacturing assets as collateral (Andreff, 2005). This scheme was a forerunner to inventions that occurred in financial markets in the 2000s. It was implemented in Russia in 1995 and definitely discredited privatization deals in this country where they eventually were nicknamed predations.[10] The idea was that a bank *can grab assets through lending money to clients who are not capable to repay the loan.* The deal was as follows: the heavy fiscal deficit of Russian government was covered in 1995 by loans from a few major Russian commercial banks; the loans were guaranteed by collateral allocated on auction. The collateral consisted in stocks of the best state-owned enterprises still not privatized. If in September 1996 the government would not be able to repay the loans, each bank could either sell the stocks deposited as collateral or keep them as its own property, and thus takeover the "crown jewels" of Russian manufacturing industry. The Russian government, indeed, was not able to repay in due time and all the banks opted for keeping stocks as their own. Some banks were both applying for stocks and organizing the auction; consequently, they colluded on guaranteeing the loans, crowding out competitors, and winning the auction. The latter turned out to be insider dealing with conflicts of interests; it enabled a dozen of bankers/oligarchs, connected to President Yeltsin, to grab the best of Russian industrial assets for peanuts (Hedlund, 2001). This deal was soon qualified infamous and naked grabbing, including by the World Bank (Birdsall & Nellis, 2002). It had nothing to do with the usual rules of capitalism, but later on it inspired other bankers elsewhere in the world.

Stockholding Managers: Shareholder Value and Wealth Concentration Act 1

Managers swiftly reached the minimum percentage[11] of shares necessary to hold the decision-making power and stand as core shareholders in privatized companies (Andreff, 1995). They formed a monitoring group of managers/owners or stockholding managers, or insiders/outsiders in the principal-agent model wording, a model which is definitely disqualified for analyzing privatized companies by the very emergence of this group (Andreff, 2000). Oligarchic managers/owners emerged also in Western capitalisms at nearly the same time with allocating stock options to managers (Section "Asset grabbing in financial markets: Risk taking and rash betting"). Then managers became highly sensitive to shareholder value and, as stockholders, started having vested interest in property gains derived from stock price increase.

Moreover, managerial entrenchment (Filatochev, Wright, & Bleaney, 1999) using more or less legal practices in privatized firms in PTEs basically relied on managers controlling the stock purchases and sales by other stockholders than themselves. Thus, managers secured their position as major stock buyers in their own company and in some other firms (of which they consequently became outsiders). This strategy created "reciprocal institutional cross-ownership" (King, 2001) materialized in fast-increasing interlocking directorates across privatized companies that paved the way for new self-controlled industrial-financial groups. Stockholding managers joined the bankers of these groups in a new oligarchy.

Privatization is key factor of growing inequalities in wealth, revenues, and power distribution (Birdsall & Nellis, 2002). In Russia in 1995, revenues derived from property rights were as high as 45% of overall household incomes, while wages reached only 40% and social transfers 15% (Silverman & Yanowitch, 2000). In PTEs, 1–2% of new rich[12] concentrate in their hands a major part of national income, savings, and property (Guriev & Rachinsky, 2005). In Russia and the CIS, 2 million people (0.7% of the population) own all the new private property, and 2% of rich Russians save 54% of overall savings (Andreff, 2007). Wealth concentration in Central Eastern Europe, though a little bit lower than in Russia, primarily benefits to those who were able to grab assets at discount prices or for free during the privatization drive.

Global Mimetic Contagion of Asset Grabbing Practices

Asset grabbing has spread from PTEs to developed capitalisms. Mimetic contagion was fuelled first by an increasingly global economic competition resulting from PTEs foreign trade reorientation to the West. Investing in PTEs, including through trans-border mergers and acquisitions of privatized firms, a number of Western companies were confronted to asset grabbing, sometimes suffering from it, often directly or indirectly benefiting from it. At the dawn of transition, privatization through asset sales to foreigners was forbidden or restricted by law, but it became predominant by the end of the 1990s, in particular in the banking sector: in 2003, 90% of banks settled in the Baltic States were foreign-owned, 95% of Slovak banks, 87% of Czech banks, and 77% of Hungarian banks. These banks were dramatically exposed to cross-border lending contagion in multinational banking (Derviz & Podpiera, 2011). Western competitors seriously felt the competitive pressure of these newly privatized firms, not strong in terms of profitability but from financial payoffs they were able to derive from assets acquired for free or peanuts. Competition grew even harsher in the 2000s when firms based in PTEs, BRICS,[13] and emerging countries started investing significantly abroad, namely in Europe.[14]

The impunity[15] of asset grabbing practices in PTEs provided incentives for TNCs and banks from developed capitalisms to mimic the behavior of newly privatized firms and banks owners. International relocation of asset grabbing moved first to tax havens. Then grabbing practices were imported to the most developed core capitalism, once a way out of impunity had been found there (Section "Cheating with the Rules of Capitalism and the Global Shadow Economy"). Discount-price asset grabbing, over-the-counter stock trade, LBO, bad loan securitization, inside dealing, lending to insolvent clients and Ponzi schemes, all have thrived throughout the entire global economy. Mimetic contagion is not a one-way avenue: banks from PTEs also mimicked Western bankers with excess risk-taking. In fact, most banks in PTEs fell into insolvency between mid-2007 and mid-2009 whether they were affiliates of multinational banks in dire financial straits or not (Dietrich, Knedlik, & Lindner, 2011).

The very existence of an alternative Soviet system until 1989 was compelling capitalism and its power elites to demonstrate their higher economic efficiency through the enforcement of capitalist formal rules and institutions. Capitalist elites had an incentive to invest in production and trade, including the competition with the opponent Soviet system; at that time they did not undertake massive capital flight to financial markets. The co-existence of two opposing systems was a hard stick to capitalist discipline, but this factor of economic discipline faded away in 1990 (Andreff, 2010). Since then, many drifts beyond the formal rules have spread cross-border throughout the two systems with deregulation, globalization, and "financialization" of the economy. A leveling off the playing field ideology minimized all the constraints that hinder naked competition (Dore, 2000) and facilitated mimetic contagion of asset grabbing practices.

ASSET GRABBING IN FINANCIAL MARKETS: RISK-TAKING AND RASH BETTING

Assets grabbed in PTEs privatization were often invested in financial markets with very ill-considered risk-taking although it was more acceptable than the radical uncertainty of transition. Investment achieved in French, British, and DCs' privatizations did not remain immobilized when a 15% profitability norm was not fulfilled. New opportunities emerged to make money in speculating and betting on the new complex products provided by market finance. Finance took over the global economy and was glutted with fund outflows from PTEs that were looking for portfolio investment abroad.

New Financial Products and Securitization: Indirect Grabbing and Risk Transfer

Subprime mortgage loans innovated – not really since Russian bankers had the same idea earlier – by *lending to insolvent clients*. The purpose was to artificially inflate the housing demand, though with taking a rash risk.[16] Then American banks transferred the risk on to other holders through securitization of bad loans because, contrary to Russian banks, they could not rely on collateral of a similar size and quality. In case of nonrepayment, they could at best seize foreclosed houses, which had been financed with subprime loans. The seizure would grab assets depreciated by the collapse of the real estate market. However, this cannot be compared with the Russian banks' loans for shares scheme in terms of asset grabbing magnitude. The return on despoiling American poor was much lower than the one of capturing the crown jewels of Russian manufacturing industry.

A liar loan to a poor American did not require that he/she exhibited and justified revenue big enough to repay the loan. Nevertheless, this was a means for banks to grab real assets at extremely low prices in case of nonrepayment; thus, a liar loan was also coined a predatory loan. Lending to insolvent clients was a bank's strategy and not only, as assumed in mainstream economics, a result of a weak incentive for banks to correctly assess the borrower creditworthiness, or of a simple relaxation in borrower selection criteria. Furthermore, there is also a strategic dimension involved: when banks wittingly lend to insolvents, they urgently need either substantial collateral to hedge against tremendously high risk (Russian banks) or to get rid of such risk through securitization (American banks).

Bad loan *securitization* enables a bank to clean off its balance sheet and, by the same token, circumvent capital ratio regulation, transfer the risk to portfolio investors who buy its securities, and immediately recover liquid assets that will be used to finance liar loans again. A bank gives up its too risky assets to a structured investment vehicle (SIV), which is an off-balance sheet vehicle that finances its asset purchase by issuing securities on the market. The bank is interested in selling bad loans at higher price than their cost, thus making a certain profit and passing on to security buyers the burden of risk holding and the hope of making money from it. Here *grabbing financial payoffs and liquid assets* occur. These gains are not reinvested in the real economy; instead they are poured again in rash risky financial bets such as subprime mortgage loans followed by their securitization, and so on and so forth.

Compared to the aforementioned financial gains, seizing real estate and houses is of no interest per se for a bank except that, in case of crisis, seized houses happen to be *real asset grabbed without any risk* since the risk is held by portfolio investors who beforehand have bought the corresponding securities. This process is at odds with capital accumulation; it is rather a double predation by banks that is detrimental to both subprime borrowers (who lose their houses) and portfolio investors in securitized bad loans who are stuck with bad-quality securities though classified AAA by credit rating agencies. Asset grabbing becomes crystal clear when a financial institution advertises, then recommends and sells a given financial product to its clients while selling it short on its own. For instance, the Paulson and Co hedge fund co-operated with Goldman Sachs to create a collateralized debt obligation (CDO) labeled Abacus. Then the fund's managers betted on a market price fall of Abacus while they were selling it to portfolio investors. Thus a financial institution *grabs liquid assets on its clients' future losses*. Other wealth is grabbed by selling low-quality securities; this grabbing is detrimental to portfolio investors and actually despoils them. Goldman Sachs grabbed enough assets to commit itself to paying the SEC, in July 2010, a $550 million compensation for having cheated its clients – an amount which represented a two-week profit of the bank in 2009 (Raufer, 2011). New financial products have become increasingly sophisticated and nontransparent with regard to the incurred risk holding; this pertains to futures, derivatives, collateralized mortgage obligations (CMO), CDOs, CDO squared, and synthetic CDO. All are predatory in a sense since they transfer the risk to portfolio investors without actually transferring them a quality asset. Portfolio investors are cheated. With credit default swaps (CDS), only the estimated risk of the portfolio is transferred and hedged against with credit derivatives. Derivatives grew as risk exacerbating tools for speculation, since a financial institution which has initially granted a credit is more interested in expanding this activity rather than checking the quality of its bad debts. The tools used for transferring the risk have mushroomed to such extent that nobody knows who holds what any longer.

Hidden risks only reveal themselves when a crisis bursts out. Then, those financial institutions which hold excess risk must actually repay with their own assets or possibly go bankrupt or eventually are bailed out by the government. During a crisis, their own *depreciated assets are grabbed at discounted prices* by other financial institutions with lower risk exposure (the acquisition of Bear Stearns by JP Morgan for $10 a share instead of $170 two months earlier). The occurrence of a crisis materializes an asset grabbing process of big-risk holders, which was only potential as long as the financial euphoria was lasting.

Securitization, just like privatization, involves moral hazard. With securitization, a financial institution which issues a junk security, knowing that it will distribute a nonrepayment risk, relaxes its credit selection criteria since the increased risk will be circulated to and held by security investors. Similarly with privatization, a rescuer does not know the exact value of assets which are on sale and the magnitude of the real risk he/she is going to take. Moreover, he/she cannot check the risk, and the privatization administration cannot either. *Inside dealing* is a means for circumventing moral hazard, hence its high frequency in both securitization and privatization.

Finance Actually Grabs Enterprises

The objective of increasing shareholder value means that a growing share of production must go to stock owners (Dore, 2000), including stockholding managers. The latter use the growth in shareholder value as a predatory instrument to grab the real economy. Grabbing proceeds at a rate which is the difference between the 15% profitability norm for stockholding companies and the normal profit rate (a proxy of which is the rate of economic growth, about 4% in the pre-2007 global economy). Predation is more important for companies which are not listed at the stock exchange because they are assessed to be more risky businesses so that the profitability requirement is in the range of 25% (Morin, 2011). A company usually cannot provide such high return on its own assets, except if it has taken risks which are not associated to its current business, and are often hidden speculative risks.

When a company *buys its own stocks*, this reduces the overall number of existing equities since the stocks that have been bought show up on both sides (assets/liabilities) of the balance sheet and thus can be removed.

The removal enables the company to distribute more dividends at year end to those stockholders who have kept their stocks. In fact, the company dips into its cash the money required to buy equities which will be removed. This is obvious predation in favor of stockholders. Buying its own stocks does not provide fresh cash to the company. On the contrary, stockholders draw personal wealth from the company. Far from financing the companies, the stock market taps them. Estimated €19.4 billion assets have been taped this way in 2007 at the Paris Stock Exchange, and $630 billion at the New York Stock Exchange (Mouhoud & Plihon, 2009). Capital that companies raise from stockholders through issuing stocks is smaller than the overall money paid by companies to stockholders through buying back their stocks and distributing dividends. Companies which significantly buy their own stocks invest less in the real economy: asset grabbing hinders capital accumulation.

Cheap credit facilitates those LBOs which target the takeover of a company' property, with up to 90% of the overall stockholding equity value borrowed to financial institutions (a lever of 10). Most LBOs and MEBOs practically are predatory and, if leverage is high, risky deals. Investment funds often undertake such operations to grab, after privatization and/or restructuring, important payoffs from re-selling previously acquired companies, making a 30–100% surplus value. An LBO triggers off the company's debt repayment which, together with risky financial investments and buying its own stocks, pushes up the company's shareholder value. Those who have succeeded in grabbing assets benefit from this growth in value. Nothing in that encourages a company toward investing in the real economy.

Hedge funds have become a major failing during the current financial crisis because they bet on rash, risky, and illiquid assets while their growing debts are in liquid assets. However, they grab assets on a predatory mode by means of LBO, private equity, and company delisting (Aglietta, Khanniche, & Rigot, 2010). Thus, the company is withdrawn from the stock market and falls under the monitoring of a speculative fund in favor of which a raid has been designed. The funds dismantles and restructures the acquired company, revalues dividends up to the norm of shareholder value growth, and strips some assets – an asset stripping that proceeds through cut-price asset sales rather than illegal asset transfers as in PTEs. Hedge funds aim at realizing substantial financial payoffs whatever the market situation, and they sell short when assessing that the market situation will worsen, typically a strategy that fuels the crisis.

Betting in Financial Markets: Rash Risk-taking and Stock Price Manipulation

Trade in financial markets has actually evolved to *betting* for a potentially unlimited number of betters and amounts of monies with which to bet (Jorion, 2011). At the stock exchange, the game no longer boils down to foreseeing who will win a beauty contest, as meant by Keynes. Rather, it consists in the player reacting to credit ratings with decisions that guarantee him/her of making a *winning bet with certainty*; this includes for him/her to bribe the beauty contest jury (the credit rating agencies) or even change the rules of the game so as to secure its winning certainty (Section "Cheating with the Rules of Capitalism and the Global Shadow Economy"). Big betters (banks, hedge funds, oligarchs), rather than foreseeing the winner, get into a position of winning without risk by manipulating the market. For other betters, bets in financial markets have become a leisure that competes with casinos, lotteries, horse race betting, games of chance, and sport gambling (Dore, 2000). These players are most often losers in financial markets. Through laddering[17] and spinning,[18] a bank can manipulate stock market prices. IPO privatization served as a laboratory for experiments with laddering and spinning. Goldman Sachs was a major actor of market manipulation that inflated the Internet bubble in resorting to laddering when it participated in IPOs; it was fined $40 million for that in 2005 (de Maillard, 2011). In other IPOs, it also utilized spinning. Big betters' activism destabilizes both the stock market and stockholding companies. It suffices for them to acquire a percentage of the stockholding equity in a company, and then wage a campaign against incumbent management so as to trigger a stock price fall; afterwards they launch a proxy fight across shareholders for company's monitoring, and finally leave the battle ground with pocketing a surplus value when the stock price rises again after the fight.

Apparently rash risk-taking expands far beyond the stock market. Lending money without securing beforehand that debtors can repay – lending to insolvent clients – is high risk-taking of the kind that one only accepts in games of chance. This is far beyond a normally acceptable risk to a capitalist, an entrepreneur or an investor in the real economy. Before the crisis, lending to insolvent clients was considered in capitalism as a thoughtless and excessive practice; bankers refrained themselves from using it, audits and credit rating agencies were created to avoid it. Nowadays, since such practice is so widespread, something basic has changed: the risk itself is traded as a financial product. Risk is no longer a constraint to decision-making but instead it is a product offered in financial markets that opens wide avenues for substantial financial payoffs. The riskiest bets are the most profitable and do attract people who are prompted by greed, that is, in particular oligarchs. When profitability of risky assets rises to a much higher level than normal returns on nonrisky assets, then a mimetic behavior spreads everywhere, and all investors rush to acquire the same risky assets. Such high risk-taking was mimicked across American banks, but once confidence vanished in financial markets it was at the roots of their bankruptcies (e.g., Bear Stearns, Lehman Brothers and so on).

Banks, hedge funds, and oligarchs look for *eliminating any chance in financial games they play* in such a way as to win all the time. A same strategy can be seen in either trader compensation indexed on stock market payoffs, never on losses, or in stock price manipulation[19] by institutional investors and financial betters. Market finance has created new products characterized by a permanent assurance of high payoffs produced by increasing risks which in principle must never materialize. Various innovations facilitate stock market manipulation, namely, day trading – speculative betting in real time, dark pools,[20] and flash trading. In any case, leverage is there to increase the magnitude of winning bets. Losses are left to uninitiated players/investors. When losses happen to affect professionals in finance as in 2008, then the default risk generalizes by contagion, and systemic risk is at the corner.

More subject to open criticism is the behavior of go-go fund managers who speculate in view of drawing gigantic payoffs from very swift bets and flash traders who never hold any asset longer than a few seconds and achieve 70% of all transactions in U.S. securities (Barton, 2011). Infinitesimal variations in financial market prices or indices multiplied by a huge mass of mobile finance make abundant returns. In order to grab the latter, finance professionals buy and sell what they do not own: they acquire call options to buy an asset at an option price when speculating on price increase in the near future; they can also acquire put options to sell when expecting a price fall. Betting with a risk limited to the option price and a nearly 100% probability of winning has become the new meaning, subverted by market finance, associated wth the verb "to invest." A high return requirement is never adjusted downwards. No return lower than without-risk return is accepted any longer (Artus, Betbèze, de Boissieu, & Capelle-Blanchard, 2009). The search for high returns induces a *mimetic behavior* which spreads across finance professionals, thus speculative bubbles happen to inflate, and then crash.

Short Selling and Credit Rating Agencies

Short selling[21] enables one to achieve financial payoffs through *speculating on falling asset price* – I win my bet on others' losses. It exacerbates decreasing market price tendencies and translates into substantial losses for others (portfolio investors, indebted states), losses which are the counterparty for payoffs grabbed by short selling betters. A number of oligarchs' fortunes were made in short selling. George Soros fortune skyrocketed when he speculated on a falling exchange rate of the sterling in 1992. American banks became used to pocket significant profits with short selling, whereas hedge funds spread their business in speculative betting on banks' falling stock prices since 2007.

Credit rating agencies that deliver AAA ratings to new financial products usually are at the same time stakeholders in the securitization of these products. Building up a new financial product is intertwined with its rating (Aglietta, 2008). Conflicts of interests[22] are therein! However, the role of rating agencies is less underlined as regards *downgrading* an asset, debtor, or country rating. When agencies downgrade a rating, they send a crystal clear signal to financial markets, meaning that it is time to speculate on the price fall of an asset/institution/country debt and therefore sell short. A downgraded rating is the green light awaited for by all potential asset grabbers to make substantial speculative gains on a deceasing asset price. Rating agencies look like a referee whistling the kick-off of a *definitely winning downward speculative game*. Betters (banks, hedge funds) immediately react with short selling. Those assets easily grabbed in privatization deals or otherwise (speculation, swindling, fraud) concentrate abundant money at the oligarchs' hands which is available for bets on falling stock and other financial market prices or rates (and on raw material prices as well).

Stock-Options and Managers/Oligarchs

A stock-option is a right allocated to a manager of buying stocks below market price since the purchasing price (exercise price) is fixed in advance and remains constant. If the market price rises, a stock-option holder will be able to buy stocks at the exercise price and resale them at a quite higher market price, pocketing a surplus value. This does not incur any risk of losing money for the holder because, if the stock market price falls lower than the exercise price, the holder will not exercise his/her option. From the very beginning, stock-options were aimed at aligning managerial interests on to the owners' objective (the shareholder value growth) but, at the end of the day, they turned out to be a civilized[23] manner for managers to tunneling assets toward their own property and stripping small shareholders. "Multiplying the forms of managerial remuneration tightly indexed on stock market price variations, and the skyrocketing wealth of top decision makers and the finance sector exhibit colluding interests among these social groups, which is detrimental to wage earners" (Boyer, 2011). Let us rather talk about cohesion, beyond collusion, of interests within and across a new social group of oligarchs, that is, stockholding managers and other asset grabbers. Just like in PTEs, a new category of insiders/outsiders emerged beyond any possible understanding of the principal-agent model. The probability of inside dealing within this new dominant social group is high, in particular when it aims at bringing about circumstances of financial gain certainty.

Since stock-options make managerial compensation pending on the outcome of stock market bets, this drives the managers to take rash risks in view of inflating the stock market price of their company. Thus, managers often play a game of targeting short-term payoffs rather than long-term shareholder value increase. They leave no room for chance, thanks to privileged insider information, and are not sanctioned if they fail. Therefore, it is a game in which "heads I win, tails you lose" rules, a statement also heard to stigmatize trader remuneration and bad loan securitization. Issuing new financial products, bad debt securitization, taking the shareholder value as the managerial yardstick, hedge fund management, speculation, price manipulation, and short selling are what drive daily decisions made by managers, whereas most stockholders are left remote from the theater of operations. Stockholders have discovered that they have hired extremely well-paid managers who eventually work exclusively on their own and grab without risk an important share of the bank's or firm's wealth. Lordon (2009) suggests that managers have moved "in the other camp," joining stockholders in their logic. Asset profitability, indexed bonuses, and stock-options stand in the background of this move. He correctly coins (p. 284) managers as grabbers. In fact, the delineation between the two camps has changed. Nowadays major owners (core shareholders) are tightly involved in corporate governance while stockholding managers are co-owners, so there is just one camp, the oligarchs' one, where seeking to grab assets prevails over capital accumulation.

Using financial markets to supervise companies' management has transformed the corporate governance regime and reinforced the power of an oligarchy which circulates throughout listed corporations and investment banks in order to extract nonshared profit and tunnel it outside the company with stock-option surplus values, golden parachutes, and preferential allocation of stocks when a merger or acquisition occurs. All this is not without its embezzlements and collusion between firms' insiders and the finance sector decision makers. This oligarchy resembles closely to the one which has emerged in PTEs. Boyer (2011) points at a *de facto* alliance between managers of big stockholding companies, financial institutions, in particular investment banks, and wealthy citizens who got rich very swiftly. Indeed, the new oligarchy is a motley crew: bankers, CEOs, and managers benefiting from stock-options, merging industry-finance oligarchs, and heads of institutional investors, all are both insiders and outsiders; in addition, traders, speculators as well as some crooks, *maffiosi* and criminals close the list (and the league) of so-called oligarchs. They are broadly similar and cohesive due to a common swift enrichment based on immediate grabbing of assets first, then revenues, and all other wealth they are capable to grab in the short term.

Some analyses differentiate between oligarchs, high-flying managers, professional and casual racketeers, appraisers, audits, and organized crime families (de Maillard, 2011). However, as pointed out by Akerlof and Romer (1993), it is not easy, or even impossible, to delineate those who take rash risks in view of making huge financial gains from those adopting systematic strategies of naked looting. Thus, there is no serious means for introducing distinctions within our above-defined category of oligarchs since they all grab assets in some way.

Wealth Hyper-Concentration, Act 2

The emergence of oligarchs in the past two decades highly *concentrated revenues and even more property* in emerging countries, PTEs, and developed capitalisms. The number of billionaires in dollars in the world more than doubled within ten years, from 4.5 million individuals in 1996 up to 9.5 millions in 2006, with an increasing proportion of Russian, Chinese, East European, and emerging country oligarchs. In 2006, ninety-five thousand people had a $13,000 billion property at disposal that is one quarter of all wealth produced in the world (Morin, 2011); this is a statistical proxy for the global oligarchy. These people do not represent more than 0.00016% or a 0.16 millionth of world population. Such wealth hyper-concentration lies in the background of *revenues'* hyper-concentration. Revenues from property are half the overall income of the 0.01% richest French people (Pech, 2011). Among the revenues derived from capital, the share of dividends has increasingly crowded out real investment financing; this provides an additional proof that asset grabbing prevails over capital accumulation. As to Landais (2007), when taxed income of 90% French people increased by 4.6% from 1998 to 2006, the highest percentile taxed income increased by 19.4%, the one of the 0.1% richest families (35,000 families) by 32%, and for the 0.01% richest (3,500 families) by 42.6%.

CHEATING WITH THE RULES OF CAPITALISM AND THE GLOBAL SHADOW ECONOMY

Speculative bubbles, financial crashes, and panics give rise to all sorts of incentives to cheat, swindle, and fraud with one watchword: run for your own life in the overall mad rush (Kindleberger, 1989). Contrary to this defensive attitude, rigging and faking practices that emerged with market finance and in PTEs are offensive and geared toward systematic enrichment of cheaters. A shadow economy and all its fake transactions were enshrined in centrally planned economies (Andreff, 1993); likewise fraud and faking grew up as enshrined to market finance and PTEs since 1987–1990. With liberalization, nothing refrained market finance any more from opting for a functioning that emancipates from capitalist legality. Wealth grabbing through predatory activities, some of which criminal, has thrived across PTEs and then, by contagion, throughout the entire global economy.

Cheating on New Financial Products and Shadow Banking

If some bank intends to transform an excess risk associated with holding bad debts into a normal risk, one way-out is to *cheat* and hide its insolvency risk in derivatives and securities which are transferred to unaware investors. The very same banker (Milken) who invented junk bonds later on had the idea of securitizing bad debts by combining them with more robust loans into one single security which is divided into tranches (de Maillard, 2011). The latter were sold to portfolio investors without disclosing any information about the extremely high risk contained in the security they bought. This is the cradle of CDOs which were forged by merging junk bonds and mortgage-backed security (MBS). Maintaining *nontransparency* on the most risky inputs of a security is not economic crime[24] per se, but for sure it is cheating about the product quality – a way of cheating that resembles to that which characterized planned deliveries by Soviet enterprises. In capitalism, commercial cheating is usually sanctioned with some financial penalty when disclosed. However, new financial products create a context for huge asset grabbing through cheating on quality. MBS, ABS, CDO, and CDS are toxic products, contagious in terms of systemic risk. They also are, to some extent, illicit products. The same applies to high-yield bonds, the new high-return securities that were launched in 2009. Several lawyers consider subprime mortgage securitization as an *innovative swindling* which scatters and externalizes bad loans off the balance sheets of financial institutions (Raufer, 2011) so as to alleviate their need of own assets. With SIV, profitability of financial products is artificially inflated in a nontransparent way.

It is not by chance that the 1998 Russian financial crisis has triggered off the emergence of shadow banking which escapes existing regulation. When Russian banks defaulted, Western banks and their clients in turn found themselves in dire financial straits. They transferred all risky business to nonregulated banking activity. They undertook swaps with clients and other banks, and contracted short-term transactions on derivatives with other banks without bookkeeping them. This book-cooking actively cheated regulators from removing the highest risks from balance sheets so that nobody could correctly assess them.

Later on, the originate-to-distribute model adopted by Western banks gave rise to high risks then transferred through securitization vehicles. The banks hedged against high risks in the derivatives market, and thus shadow banking thrived. Hedge funds which have a similar balance sheet structure compared to banks, but without the same prudential constraints, look like a sort of "unchartered banks." Off-balance-sheet vehicles, conducts, and SIV can also be assimilated to shadow banks (Aglietta et al., 2010). A crucial element of shadow banking lies in dark pools, which are informal and nonregulated platforms trading about 44% of overall financial transactions, of course invisible to market regulators. Sales of financial assets are achieved there in total discretion and nontransparency, a favorable context for insider dealing.

Fraudulent Fake Accounting

Fraudulent accounting often conceals predatory practices. Cooking the books and cheating with accounting rules are useful tools for success in asset grabbing. Managers have high incentives to disclose fallacious information to small shareholders. It suffices them to exploit insider information asymmetry. Those managers compensated with stock-options have incentives to do all they can to push up the company's stock market price, in particular to invent imaginative accounting (Stiglitz, 2010). They are used to disclosing high-profit data that will propel stock prices up. Audits often suggest appealing clients with dubious practices that exhibit a company's fallacious image. Firms hire highly paid audits to deliver a loose assessment of the company and look at book-cooking and financial manipulations with blind eyes, which help preserving their AAA ratings. Otherwise bankers and portfolio investors would fly away and never invest in a number of firms if their real balance sheets were disclosed. Arthur Andersen was a world champion of fake accounting when working with Enron, Worldcom, Sunbeam, Waste Management, Global Crossing, Halliburton, Qwest, Dynegy and, Colonial Realty (de Maillard, 2011; Lambin, 2011; Roche, 2011). Fake accounting is more profitable than accounts' supervision in the auditing business, so the former evolved into a routine. This looks like the routine of former Soviet state-owned enterprises which were used to release fake statistics to central planners, a practice somewhat lasting in many PTE firms, now for tax avoidance.

The number of fraudulent bankruptcies has grown without entailing any state intervention, which means that infringing the rules of capitalism implicitly becomes an accepted mode of governance; only a few are cracked down. Genuine white collar criminality is condemned[25] but still goes on; this has nothing to do with the formal rules of capitalism any more. Mass accounting frauds are not isolated issues, but rather are prototypes of a new economic system in the making. Nowadays, fraud is integrated by managers as one mode of management, if not regular, at least systematically resorted to in case of financial straits. Absence of accounting and of financial transparency characterize all the new rich in PTEs, from financial traders to oligarchs acquainted with political power. The behavior is quite similar between those audits which analyzed Enron and maintained a favorable assessment, until bankruptcy, and central planners who were used to validate the rigged data delivered by state-owned enterprises, until the collapse of planned economies. The purpose was to cheat and mislead portfolio investors here and central planners there. In both cases, account dressing shows up a picture as if a new wealth were created that indeed does not exist. Systemic rules are circumvented until the point where a genuine informal or shadow global economy emerges.

Financial Pyramids

Outlawed since 1920 in the United States, Ponzi schemes[26] re-emerged as mass swindling during PTE privatization. They were used for the enrichment of a few who leveraged on gullible people savings, in a time when, according to its propagandists, the rate of return was promised to be exceptional in emerging capitalism. This was revealed to be a contagious practice since at the same moment Ponzi schemes suddenly sprang up again in the United States. Madoff's financial pyramid was designed as a global network continuously pumping out liquid savings like machinery (and machination) geared toward permanent liquid asset grabbing. Among Madoff's victims were found hedge funds and big banks whose confidence was close to naivety or, more probably, connivance. Even Russian oligarchs and Latin-American drug-dealing *maffiosi* were abused by Madoff (Aglietta et al., 2010). Asset grabbers had been in turn grabbed from their own assets! *Competition across oligarchs* does not exclude that some dupe others.

Subprime loans are a *variant of a financial pyramid* since it is a scheme whose solvency is not guaranteed by revenues. When house buyers sign up their loan, they do not have at hands revenues or assets to repay the debt (they can go on paying interests if and only if housing market prices are rising). A borrower thus enters an attractive low-cost credit system relying on a promised purchase of real estate whose value must increase faster than his/her credit cost. What the borrower does not see is that he/she is enrolled in a diabolic spiral which only works as long as the real estate bubble inflates. When borrowers pay their interests on subprime loans, the bankers capture a speculative surplus value resulting from price inflation in the real estate market. Many practices, without being Ponzi schemes properly speaking, are similar to financial pyramids, as it was exhibited in the Enron scandal. However, a financial pyramid crushes down as soon as the number of entering participants stops growing or confidence fades away.

Small-scale Ponzi schemes – as Madoff's (an estimated $65 billion predation) – drive their initiators to be sued in court. If a similar scheme is built up at the whole banking system scale, as it ensues from subprime loans, then it cannot be sued. It is definitely beyond the rules of capitalism since a *global, systemic, and tolerated fraud* contravenes such rules; underneath the global fraud, a number of individual frauds are swarming such as offering loans to borrowers who are not eligible. The registered number of suspected financial frauds grew up from 1,318 in 1996 to 63,173 in 2008 in the United States (de Maillard, 2011). Most suspicions refer to predatory lending, that is, loans whose ultimate aim is asset grabbing. When fraud happens to be the norm to such an extent, and no longer exception, actually capitalism rules no longer prevail. Capitalism cannot be defined by the permanent violation of its own rules. In addition to breaching trust, illegal enrichment, insider dealing, and price manipulation, banks and financial institutions are increasingly blamed for intentional mistakes, fraud, and from time to time economic crime. Those who are blamed are not only marginal rule cheaters like Madoff, but the biggest banks in the world. Fraud as a system, is this capitalism future? Or is it a transition to another economic system run under different rules, even though they are informal?

Tax and No-Regulation Havens and Tax Evasion

TNCs, oligarchs, and big fortune holders, for the sake of tax optimization, play on all cords of tax evasion and avoidance. Offshore financial centers keep secrecy and facilitate avoiding most regulations and tax rules, and often they allow for some criminal activities such as money laundering. They are tax and no-regulation havens hosting all the economic actors who wish to dissimulate transactions that contravene the formal rules of capitalism.

Capital flight, facing the radical uncertainty of transition, plagued all the PTEs, in particular those where the state was sharply weakened (Russia), and was geared toward tax havens. Russian and Chinese billionaires are among the most important clients in tax havens (Rusal, the world leader in aluminum industry, owned by Oleg Deripaska, is listed at the Hong Kong stock exchange) where shadow banking is also located. Tax havens are used to launder the fortunes of oligarchs through absolutely nontransparent or fictitious companies and to pay the least possible taxes. They are refuges for assets grabbed in developed capitalisms and PTEs. Once grabbed in the harsh global competition battlefield, assets are harbored in tax havens, that is, platforms for secure and nonregulated enrichment.

Hedge funds, hundreds of insurance companies, and thousands of non-transparent companies are settled in tax noncooperative financial centers. Absence of protection of minority shareholders also attracts big TNCs there. Toxic financial products leaning against subprime loans are deposited and many securitization structures (SIV) are registered in tax havens. Big developed countries support these offshore centers that facilitate hiding the disreputable methods – and reprehensible by usual rules of capitalism elsewhere – of their oligarchs. Money laundering is often shielded against police inquiries since these places are also judicial havens.

Financial Criminality and Organized Crime

In all the previous bad practices, there is a risk that financial actors who infringe the rules fall into economic delinquency and crime where they are going to meet organized crime (Mafia, traffickers, and dealers). The first area for such meeting is located in PTEs where economic reforms have created financial markets that do not finance new investments in the real economy but enable cunning managers to deal and fly away with others' money (Stiglitz, 2002). Stiglitz adds that they would have been sentenced as crooks or white collar criminals in the United States. In Russia, one businessman out of six has been prosecuted for having committed a recognized economic crime in the past ten years. When organized crime reached its climax in Russia in 1998, it took over 50% of all commercial banks, 60% of state-owned enterprises, and 40% of private firms (UNODCCP, 2001, p. 1). The size of the Russian criminal economy sounds smaller today because a part of it melted away into the formal economy.

The drifts of financial capitalism also lead to merging legal, shadow, and criminal activities. Borderlines are blurred and fluctuating across these three areas of activity and depend on the changes that may occur in the formal rules of capitalism. For instance, 130 American savings and loans have laundered an estimated $5 billion of Mafia's money and these deals are not alien to their bankruptcy. In 2008, when deprived from liquidities, several banks absorbed important flows of criminal money and some were financially saved by this dirty money inflow. Among others, American Express Bank, Western Union, HSBC, and Banco Santander are spotted for their involvement in money laundering (Raufer, 2011). Economic crime that helps basic capitalist institutions, is it still capitalism? Is not the entire economic system falling over into perverting its own rules to such extent that the whole system itself is changing? In the United States, the insidious penetration of organized crime in finance utilizes unsponsored ADRs (American Depositary Receipts).[27] The latter is instrumental to issuing a company's stocks without the company's consent and without warning it, and then develop over-the-counter shadow trade in the stocks. Is this looting, predation, or naked robbery? None of them sticks to the rules of capitalism.

Three banks share all the specific ADR market: Citibank, Deutsche Bank, and Bank of New York-Mellon. The latter accepted to pay $26 million to the U.S. federal justice and $14 million to Russian customs for finding a way out from a litigated laundering of funds coming from Russia, a deal which was discovered by the FBI and the U.S. Internal Revenue (Junghans, 2011).

With unsponsored ADRs, the most influential bankers in the world became aware of how efficient the methods of organized crime are. Then, they made the decision to adopt and adapt them to their business. No banker has received a penal sentence so far. Those guilty of fraud are rewarded twice, by financial payoffs and by impunity. Fraud impunity obviously fuels the contagion of economic swindling and crime.

A *global shadow economy* has developed in the past quarter of a century. With post-Soviet transition, the size of the shadow economy reached its climax in PTEs – up to 42% of GDP in Russia and 49% in Ukraine (Andreff, 2007). In any period of systemic transition, borderlines between legal, informal, and illegal business are porous and blurred. Is not the swift growth of a global shadow economy – with deep intertwining between the legal and the fraudulent – a reliable index of transition to a post-capitalist system? Just like any shadow economy, the global one generates illegitimate inequalities and worsens the risk of a recurring and continuous crisis.

CIRCUMVENTING AND PERVERTING INSTITUTIONAL RULES OF CAPITALISM

A firm or a bank cannot accumulate deficits and debts for long without going bankrupt in capitalism. This fundamental institutional arrangement has not been strictly implemented during PTE transition and is less and less enforced in global finance. Circumventing and perverting formal institutions are a means for asset grabbers to achieve their winning bets with certainty. If such means do not suffice for securing substantial financial gains and asset grabbing without risk, oligarchs then resort to state capture and lobbying. Once the state is captured, they attempt to obtain a marked change by breaking up the old formal rules.

Soft Budget Constraint, Bad Loans, and Systemic Risk

A soft budget constraint (SBC) characterized the very existence of planned economies (Kornaï, 1980). Enterprises never went bankrupt because, when being in the red, they were bailed out by the single state bank that was a branch of the public revenue department. One priority task of transition was to harden the SBC, but this appeared to be not that easy and did not show up as a clear result from economic liberalization and dismantling the state bank (Andreff, 2007). Hardening a SBC was revealed to be unexpectedly complex due to tight connections[28] between firms and banks, and the government pressure on banks asking them to grant loans to private and public enterprises whatever their degree of creditworthiness and indebtedness.

An SBC emerges when a firm meets *ex ante* a possible – *a fortiori* certainty about – *ex post* negotiation of a new finance, credit, subsidy, or bail out. SBC has been lasting in PTEs even after banks were no longer allowed to *ex ante* commit themselves to bailing out any firm. However, a bank *de facto* has incentives to provide new finance to an indebted firm as soon as it fears that its initial investment in it is going to be irrecoverable. The correlation between banking credit to enterprises and their payment arrears strengthened all over the 1990s (Berglöf & Roland, 1998). Facing their resulting loan portfolio deterioration, the government bailed the banks out, which meant to them that their budget constraint was kept soft and they could afford lending to insolvent enterprises again and again. If, in case of bad loans, a bank knows that the government will bail it out *ex post*, it has an incentive "to gamble on resurrection" (Roland, 2000), and it does not liquidate its too risky assets. This behavior in turn increases the probability of a bank being bailed out *ex post*. Then the *state is captured* by banks. The size of big banks (too big to fail) and, indirectly, the overall magnitude of their bad debts spread over a great number of big firms (too many to fail), increasing the probability of contagion and systemic risk; this makes the state being captured by the banks even more necessary. In such circumstances, one bank's bankruptcy must have such high costs that it is preferable that the loans be renewed (Mitchell, 1998).

In order to avoid such bank behavior in PTEs, the government should have intervened *ex ante* to prevent banks from gambling on resurrection. This could have been done with tight control over the banks or bigger initial bank capitalization. This undone, the government was compelled afterwards to take over bad debt management and financial cleaning of the banks' balance sheets in all PTEs. Then, the state authorities arranged bilateral debt rescheduling between one bank and one firm, wrote off bad loans, recapitalized the banks, revoked some bank licenses, or closed them down. More often they created a hospital bank to consolidate bad debts. A similar solution was adopted for the management of bad debts of the U.S. savings and loans by creating a Resolution Trust Corporation in 1989, for avoiding a Crédit Lyonnais bankruptcy in 1993 with the creation of the *Consortium de réalisation*, for rescuing the Anglo-Irish Bank through transferring its bad debts to the National Asset Management Agency in 2008, or in launching a Orderly Restructuration Fund to save banks in Spain in 2009.

SBC and its consequences are found outside PTEs (Kornaï, Maskin, & Roland, 2003). It was a core issue in the U.S. savings and loans bail outs[29] and the banking crisis in Asia. As regards the biggest banks in the world, the certainty of being bailed out by the state has phased out their fear of lending to insolvents and then passing bad debts on to all the finance business through securitization. The 2008 financial crisis has strengthened the banks' belief that it will be the same again and again, since a number of them have been actually bailed out by the government. Consequently, taxpayers took on losses while bankers got public money. Some U.S. banks even sold the great bulk of CDS they were holding on the U.S. government; then it was obvious that they were speculating on their own government failure. The banks are too big to fail but big enough for jeopardizing government finance. The plan for rescuing U.S. banks in 2009 extended the state guarantee, confirmed their SBC, and provided them a new encouragement to take ill-considered risks. A few bankruptcies and banking concentration have made the "too big to fail" threat even more significant, have worsened state capture by big banks, have shortened contagion circuits, and have paved the way for a next crisis sequence.

State capture by banks easily drifts into having a *political* dimension. Those banks which are too big to fail also are too powerful on political grounds, and the normal rules of capitalism are suspended to protect their stockholders and those investors who buy their securities (Stiglitz, 2010). With the financial crisis, the rules which do not suit to bankers' strategies are changed.[30] The international financial oligarchy has succeeded in convincing the governments to transform excess debts of private banks into public debt. When it increases its public debt, a state deliberately subordinates itself to those who hold huge extra money (Jorion, 2011), that is, asset grabbing oligarchs.

From Informal Rules to Capturing the State in View of a Change in Formal Rules

Social acceptance of informal, sometimes purely illegal practices as new functioning rules, the state being captured through lobbying (Hanson & Teague, 2005), and oligarchs dominating the economy (Guriev & Rachinsky, 2005) have characterized Russia and most PTEs in the past twenty years. A similar situation has emerged in developed countries and the global economy.

Oligarchs, banks, and investment funds are the major *winners from deregulation*. No regulator or supervising authority actually reacted after witnessing that banks were increasingly lending to too risky investors. The banks neglected and then contravened prudential rules. Hedge funds circumvented with complete impunity those rules that they considered did not fit with their business. Regulation of derivatives was rejected.

Facing the *formal rules* of capitalism, oligarchs succeeded in *circumventing*, *manipulating*, *avoiding* their enforcement, or having them *abolished*. SIVs were held by banks without sticking to the own asset requirements (Orléan, 2009). Repealing the Glass-Steagall Act[31] enabled investment banks to collect savings deposits, exposing them to financial bets and fraudulent practices. The oligarchs' objective is to divert common rules to their exclusive benefit in such a way as to win financial bets every time with certainty. They modify the rules during the game in financial markets and then the non-initiated suffer from disproportionate losses. A consensus was reached in the highest finance and political authorities that the rules in force have ceased to be enforceable; this argument is utilized as an excuse by oligarchs for manipulating them. Hedge funds which are submitted to few information disclosure constraints have vested interests in manipulating the regulation authorities and are quite free to do so. This is what they did before 2008 and again when they attempted to prevent political decision makers to regulate their activity after 2008 (Aglietta et al., 2010). Through manipulating formal rules, the oligarchy secures the self-fulfillment of its own prophecies in terms of financial payoffs and asset grabbing.

Instead of formal rules that do not fit with their grabbing strategies, oligarchs elaborate on *informal practices*, sometimes illegal, which make them sure of winning all the financial bets they undertake. Much widespread informal rules at work in PTEs flooded into developed capitalisms. Then the very concept of fraud, meant as breaching a beforehand-established norm, becomes blurred. Fraud does not mean any longer getting over *ex ante* clearly defined prohibition, but refers to predatory behavior witnessed *ex post*. The great bulk of asset grabbing is based on the fuzziness that now plagues the rules of capitalism.[32] When the violation of a formal rule is not sanctioned, or the sanction is not significant enough, the point is reached where social acceptance and validation of an informal practice start-up. The risk of being sanctioned for unfair operations in financial markets has vanished these days, as the CDS business exhibits it.

Deregulation brought incentives to commit frauds in unknown proportions and opened a period of lax law and rule enforcement, leading to a partial criminalization of finance with regard to the formal rules of capitalism. But the same frauds should not necessarily be considered as criminality in a context of mushrooming informal rules specific to systemic transition periods.[33] Getting rid of constraining norms, oligarchs can grab assets in an illicit, fraudulent, or criminal way without bearing any sanction when informal rules are spreading throughout the economy. They can legally follow up the same (previously informal) practices if the latter once happen to be formalized in a new institutional arrangement alien to the formal rules of capitalism. The current compensation norms of CEOs and traders, and banking bonuses which would have been deeply shocking or even forbidden in some countries in the 1990s ended up as being informal, and then formal rules. Lending to insolvents or toxic financial products started up as informal practices but then was increasingly accepted as the rule of the game. Step by step, frauds not only became tolerated but increasingly appeared legitimate to many economic actors. Then the situation was ripe for oligarchs to attempt obtaining that their informal practices be validated by the state and some formal rules. Those tricks, frauds, and crimes that are used for asset grabbing became systemic and opened an avenue which drives out of the economic system of the rules of capitalism as fraud, predation, and despoilment started to be acknowledged and accepted as usual modes of economic governance. The previously sanctioned predatory methods ceased to be sanctioned. The economy entered an era of "legal swindling," an oxymora that exhibits the exit from capitalist legality on a path toward new formal rules alien to capitalism.

Finally, oligarchs do capture the state in view of having *new formal rules* passed by Parliament or adopted by other authorities, thus ratifying and validating their former informal practices. The networks linking financial oligarchy to political power are mobilized to influence mapping out new rules and laws, and their enforcement. Russian big firms and banks maintain good relationships with the Kremlin. The best "national champions" of Russian industry are under the control of few oligarchs who are openly welcome to the Kremlin. In China, big companies are financially supported by the state and managed by a narrow circle of businessmen well acquainted with or introduced to the Communist party. In the United States, the industry of auditing agencies has devoted $15 million to lobbying in 1998–2000 in order to influence the house members and senators in favor of deregulation (Stiglitz, 2003).

Oligarchs' lobbying aims at promoting rules that favor financial bet winners and open opportunities for asset grabbing. Updating the banking sector regulation (Frank-Dodd Act) has reshaped it in accordance with the bankers' expectations so that speculation, the most profitable banking activity, is not only safeguarded but also optimized. Proactive lobbying has ensured that no regulation would prevail over financial products that are aimed against subprime loan securitization. The net capital rule or Pickard regulation, set up in 1975, delineates the highest allowed rate of leverage (a maximum multiplier of twelve) for investment banks. Under pressure of the biggest banks, the SEC admitted a twice higher rate and tolerated bigger leverage (Lordon, 2009). By early 1998, LTCM had a leverage multiplier of 25 and the Carlyle Capital's was 30 before it went bankrupt early 2008.

THE HYPOTHESIS OF SYSTEMIC GREED: A TRANSITION TO A "GREED-BASED ECONOMIC SYSTEM"

Kornaï (2000) raised the question to know whether transition in PTEs paved the way for a third economic system, neither capitalism nor socialism. If so, the new system should be coined both post-capitalist and post-socialist. In the past quarter of a century, such a supposedly third economic system did not really emerge in either PTEs or developed capitalisms. Instead a more likely transition period opened up. During a systemic transition, by definition, the structures and formal institutions of two systems do coexist in a same economy. On the one hand, the structures and institutions of the old system are in a phase of destruction while those of a new system are in a phase of creation. A part of the economy does not function any longer in accordance with the formal rules of capitalism – we coin this a "greed-based economic system." The contention here is that the current transition promotes wealth maximization without constraint instead of profit maximization under constraint; it fuels the creation of a fast-growing segment in the economy that functions according to winner-take-all rules. The latter are much more nonegalitarian than the wage-earners' domination by capitalists. The transition to a greed-based economic system is progressing step by step insofar as the new rules take time to spread from privatizations and financial markets to other patches of the entire global economy. This is an evolutionary transition, transformation, or mutation.

Enrichment Maximization without Constraint

A number of analyses since 2008 have implicitly or explicitly contended that enrichment does not meet any constraint any more. Thus, without actually conceptualizing it, they point to an hypothesis of *greed* not only being rational from an individual standpoint but also making itself a system, greed becoming *systemic*. If this assumption were to be verified in the long run, it would bring with it the roots of another system than capitalism. Let us call it a greed-based economic system. In such system, any oligarch's objective is first to maximize his/her enrichment in absolute terms and second, even more so, to maximize it comparatively with and detrimentally to others by eliminating all the constraints through the violation of capitalism rules. Comte-Sponville (2004) wrote, about capitalism, that "no law forbids egoism"; paraphrasing him, one would say that, in a greed-based economic system in the making, no law forbids either greed or addressing incentives to enrich oneself without limit for greedy people.

In the literature, one finds references to a wealth maximization behavior without constraint whereas the capitalism logic is one of profit maximization under some constraints that are accounted for by managers (Morin, 2011). Bankers' and oligarchs' unlimited greed is also referred to (Attali, 2009; Stiglitz, 2010). Even the recent collapse of the financial system did not put an end to greedy behavior. Bankers were immediately eager to use the state money that bailed their banks out to pay themselves huge bonuses in proportion to their huge losses. Shareholder value maximization was caricatured in stating that "greed is good" although the statement was sullied by enterprises' predatory practices undertaken for the sake of greed (Barton, 2011). In fact, there is no caricature in that: greed is the rationale for actors whose strategy is asset grabbing and who are capable to manipulate the formal rules on purpose; greed deeply roots into the newly emerging economic system.

If we grasp all the previous ideas in a nutshell, unlimited enrichment is rooted in three cumulative sources: (a) *maximizing revenues* (profit, interest) *derived from assets, which is typical of capitalism*, (b) *increasing at a forced pace the value of assets invested in the real economy by aligning its growth on a norm for shareholder value growth, which is typical of "financialized" capitalism*, (c) *systematic and continuous asset grabbing* (predation, despoilment) *without reinvesting the grabbed assets into production but investing them instead again and again in financial bets, which is typical of a greed-based economic system*. Taken together, the three enrichment sources point at a *transition period* between "financialized" capitalism and something new.

Greedy strategies can lead their actors to fraud and committing economic crime when greed takes roots as a behavioral norm. In capitalism, greed and enrichment at any rate are not irrational but remain subject to two series of constraints. On the one hand, formal rules of capitalism delineate which enrichment practices are illegal or criminal. On the other hand, capital accumulation constrains a share of profit to be reinvested in real production and the means of production (Marx variant); a sufficient share of overall savings must finance real investment in physical assets and immobilized financial assets (Keynes variant); or a share of nonconsumed income must be preserved for manufacturing production goods (Pareto-Barone variant). Such kind of constraints no longer holds in a greed-based economic system since it is not based on either capital accumulation or real investment or any sort of asset immobilization but on grabbing liquid and illiquid assets. Whatever their liquidity, grabbed assets must be easy to shift, and highly mobile, from one's property to the other and from one financial bet to another. In a greed-based economic system, all nonimmediately consumed financial gains are instantaneously staked in games and financial bets that do not require asset immobilization any longer than a few (fractions of a) second(s). In a sense, maximizing financial and property gains *without constraint* makes it a significant difference compared with the previous phases of capitalism.

A Winner-Take-All Economy

Enrichment maximization being without constraint, a maximum or optimal level of profit or wealth does not exist any longer. The yardstick cannot be wealth maximization in absolute terms any more since the maximum is infinite now. The only possible alternative behavioral norm, in a society where permanent competition and comparison prevail, consists in enriching oneself at a faster pace than others, that is, *maximizing one's relative wealth*. A must is to win and preferably take all possible gains, that is, without leaving anything to others. What is at stake here is to win in privatization and in stock and financial markets in such a way as to get richer than others – or most of them. Thus *asset grabbing is a rational means* to reach this aim because, in putting into my own property an asset grabbed from others, I reduce his/her enrichment in order to increase my own. Economic and social life increasingly turns out to resemble a tournament or a game of chance in which each oligarch rigs the game to win it with certainty. Economic and more basically financial competition sounds like a sporting contest whose winners are those who do not stick to the rules in order to win and make money. "Making money is everyone obsession, making others losing money is an unfortunate collateral damage without significance. Such are the rules of the game" (Roche, 2011).

In the 1990s, Anglo-American capitalism started to be represented as an economic system where the winners take all, a *Winner-Take-All-Society* (Dore, 2000; Frank & Cook, 1996). This society is characterized by a few people holding high revenues and a wide property, that is, a group of oligarchs as above-defined. If one winner takes all in each game, logically a huge majority of the population loses.[34] It is even more so if the winners are repeatedly the same oligarchs who load the dice. With systemic greed and winner-take-all, actually the rational egoism hypothesis underlying mainstream economics is not enough and not relevant. Oligarchs do not restrict themselves to optimize their wealth under constraint according to their own egoist interest. Each of them takes as much as he/she can, including through grabbing others' assets. It is urgently needed that heterodox economists undertake analyzing greedy and rigged strategies of a winner-take-all economy, in particular in the market finance business. A heterodox analysis must even go further since such strategies are rooted as systemic and are, with enrichment maximization without constraint, the second pillar of a greed-based economic system.

The game and betting dimensions are much more significant in the functioning of a greed-based economic system than what is known about capitalism. In capitalism, investing consists in taking a calculated risk with a win uncertainty about net revenues. In a greed-based system, no one invests this way, but instead anyone and everyone bets. Betting boils down to taking a maximum risk to grab assets. In a greed-based economic system, oligarchs manipulate the rules in order to win their rash bets and, as far as possible, take all. This is not betting as a cards player does – or bets in any game of chance – in which the player takes a true risk. An oligarch takes a fake risk because he/she rigs the bet in view of eliminating any real risk for himself/herself and transfers the true risk on to all those who will lose (999/1,000th of the population). A bank which uses for insider dealing an information that it gets before anyone else can be compared to a poker player who can see his/her opponents' cards. Betting with the outcome certainty of a win is crucial for maximizing enrichment and a winner-take-all strategy in which it is instrumental to cheat, rig, and fraud with the rules of capitalism.

Transition to A Greed-based Economic System: Oligarchs and Losers

Identifying the winners in a greed-based economic system is rather easy; they are oligarchs as defined in Section "Asset grabbing in financial markets:

Risk taking and rash betting." The identification of losers is trickier but can logically be derived from identifying the winners. A good example of a winner is Mr. Paulson who has himself structured the Abacus junk product aimed against subprime loans. Then he started betting against the hedge funds and pocketed $1 billion invested by too many greedy people. Goldman Sachs had simultaneously facilitated selling the Greek sovereign debt, securitized a part of it in order to hide how much big it was, and created CDS enabling the bank to speculate on a default of the Greek debt (Roche, 2011). A deep social dividing line and social conflict come out from this: aggressiveness is linked to greed for winners, and in opposition to resentment for losers (Jorion, 2011). A part of the U.S. elites has consciously set up a predation system whose victims primarily are households with a modest way of life. Ponzi schemes (from Madoff to securitization) boil down to loot assets deposited by clients who are the genuine losers. When taxpayers currently pay for covering the bad debts of those banks which have been bailed out by the state and for a distribution of bonuses to bankers, a clash between winners and losers is obvious at a macroeconomic and social level. A gap deepens to the abyssal between globalized elite of oligarchs and the so-called "middle class" which suffers, with less and less complacency, the destroying impact on its income of the elite globalized games.

How to interpret such mutation? Witnessing a swiftly multiplied number of financial bets incites some economists (Davies, 2010) to talk about a *casino economy*. The global shadow economy indeed considers the whole planet as a wide casino where anyone can stake any amount on anything and everything, regardless of the rules, in total nontransparency and with repeated conflicts of interests. Games of chance of the poor and business games of the rich are not without links. However a clarification must be made here: oligarchs are in the position of global casino managers who fix the mechanics of one-armed bandits in such a way as to win the money staked by other players. Among the latter some occasionally win, most of them steadily lose. A bank gets rid of securitized bad loans for money in an attempt, as in a casino, to make up its losses, including with biased bets favoring it, like the subprime loans. The die is cast!

Some proxies for the systemic greed hypothesis are found in the literature, deeply breaking with capitalism of the Roaring Fifties to Seventies. Stiglitz (2002) talked about corrupted crony capitalism, Soros (1998) denounced capitalism of the crooks (he perfectly knows what it is all about!), Orléan (2009) stigmatized a "financialized" capitalism, and Lordon (2009) stressed on deregulation and finance domination. However, *capitalism cannot be defined by the permanent infringements of its own rules*, in particular when infringements start with new informal rules that eventually turn out to be the new formal rules (Section "Cheating with the Rules of Capitalism and the Global Shadow Economy"). Repeated infringements trigger a *slow evolution* – no revolution but a long-lasting crisis since 1987, which is not over yet – affecting simultaneously capitalism and post-communism.[35] Since PTEs have initiated most financial drifts of capitalism earlier than Western bankers and investment funds, the idea of an interacting co-evolution between two economic systems (Chavance, 1999) is worth being revisited in this new context. An interactive evolution can indeed come out with a new phase of capitalism or a new third economic system as above suggested by Kornaï (2000). Here lies the need for further theoretical analysis of what is identified as a greed-based economic system.

Asset Grabbing in Everyday Life: Rigged Betting in Sports

Dore (2000) correctly contends that betting in financial markets has joined other games in *everyday life* activity, on the job and during leisure time. Bets are becoming pillars of the entire economic system. From Playstations to games of chance, many people seek gains from betting in their everyday life, including monetary gains derived from gambling on horse races and the outcome of sporting events. People are so addicted to betting in most Asian countries, the Balkans, Central America, and tax havens that it is now an actual way of life. The sports economy and online sport betting (Andreff, 2012) show up many similarities with the functioning of financial markets. Here again endlessly looking for monetary gains and then rigging the game in order to avoid risk is contagious. Match fixing on a wide scale started developing exactly during the same years when Russian, Chinese, and other PTE oligarchs got rich and new millionaires emerged in some Asian countries. When connected to online betting, as it is nowadays the case, match fixing is a whole industry collecting at least €200 billion per year.

Moreover, with the current financial crisis, a number of financial market players have embarked on a flight to quality and moved liquid assets not only from financial markets to raw material markets but also to the global market of match fixing and betting. The latter is global since those who fix the matches are internationally connected through various global networks (Hill, 2009), just like Russian and Chinese oligarchs and all bankers are. Match fixing, and thus corruption in sports, has a single objective: enrich oneself at the fastest pace and with the highest possible certainty to win. A sort of equivalence with short selling in financial markets is to bet on a team's loss, even on the loss of your own favorite team (the one you are a fan of). Rigging the game has become a highly risky business – due to potential sanctions if caught – but extremely lucrative. Fixed matches are also used as a tool for money laundering by asset grabbers and organized crime. Thousands of online sports betting web sites circumvent any sort of regulation and are accessible from anywhere in the world within a second. Match fixers cannot be discovered and sanctioned, just like oligarchs, bankers, and hedge funds managers accountable for asset grabbing.

Toward a Theoretical Analysis of the Greed-based Economy

The collapse of centrally planned economies and their post-communist transition re-opened a debate in Marxist theory about the sequence of modes of production between capitalism, socialism, and communism as well as controversies in comparative economics about sequencing the market economy, a central planning system, and possibly their convergence[36] into a sort of mixed economy. The above-delineated greed-based economy raises the same issue: what could be its theoretical underpinnings in a historical long-run sequencing of economic systems or modes of production? Asset grabbing instead of capital accumulation, systemic greed, and winner-take-all instead of usual profit making sounds like radical changes; but the theoretical question is to know whether a greed-based economy paves the way to a new phase of capitalism or consists in a transitional form actually breaking up from capitalism, that is, a transition to an unknown post-capitalism in the present state of Marxist theory and comparative economics. Or, perhaps, is it simply a mirage leaving the current global "financialized" capitalism absolutely unchanged? Both empirical evidence and the first step analysis presented in this chapter do not lean in favor of the last hypothesis. Then we are left with a theoretical trade-off regarding the delineated greed-based economy between being either a new phase in capitalist development or a first phase in a possible post-capitalist system. This theoretical alternative obviously cannot be dealt with overnight and receive a clear-cut response without digging deeper and longer into economic theory.

Even though it is not an excuse, identifying a greed-based economy as it has been done here is only a first analytical step. It is not enough since, for instance in the framework of Marxist theory, it would have required to root it in the analysis of social relationships, ownership modes, and productive forces. Our analysis gives an insight into how much asset grabbing is subversive of the current capitalist ownership regime but does not provide an approach in depth, for instance à la Marx, of a transformation in the ownership mode. It is clear that asset grabbing, systemic greed, and winner-take-all trigger off a non-negligible change in social relationships but the latter is not yet qualified in terms of capital–labor relationships since the implications of a greed-based economy for the labor market, wage earning, and exploitation are not yet derived at this stage of our research.

CONCLUSION

Protesting against an economy based on systemic greed remains limited to more or less audible nonoligarchic circles so far, including alter-globalists, indignant citizens, appalled, post-autistic, and heterodox economists. All the losers who make up for 99% of global population must question and challenge such a greed-based economy. The latter adds many worse effects of asset grabbing, predation, cheating, fraud, unjustified enrichment, and economic crime to the well-known harmful consequences of capitalism. More heterodox economic research is urgently needed about it.

NOTES

1. Two reviewers correctly raised the point as to why the current crisis is not traced back here to 1971 or 1974. In a nutshell, in the early 1970s, capitalism had not yet reached its phase of a full-fledged globalization. Moreover, the crisis actually was not global since centrally planned economies were not in a deep slump at the moment.

2. We lean toward coining it a "greed-based economic system" which could be envisaged as either a new phase of capitalism or a more radically new economic system. Further theoretical work should elaborate on this point and go beyond the temporarily adopted wording of a greed-based economic system (Section "Toward a Theoretical Analysis of the Greed-based Economy"). The latter exhibits some common features with the so-called "financialized" capitalism of which it is, so to say, the dark side. In addition, it shows some characteristics derived from PTEs.

3. Following Bajt (1968) and Bettelheim (1970), possession refers to supervising and monitoring capital (i.e., the power of holding all the decision-making over the use of capital, the distribution of earned profits, and capital accumulation). Those who exert the power of possession may or may not have the full ownership of all the company's assets. Property rights does not entirely coincide with effective possession; it is often only partial. A possible "property leverage," mentioned below, arises.

4. Grabbing assets without investing them in real production was so widespread a strategy among the rescuers of privatized companies that the government, in

various PTEs, enacted as a prerequisite to privatization that the rescuers must invest in real production and maintain employment.

5. Just like risk-taker leverage is a ratio between the overall risk taken and his/her own assets, property leverage is a ratio between the overall company stockholding equity, in fact monitored by core shareholders, and the latter's actual share in the overall company's stockholding equity.

6. The first five companies privatized by Thatcher government were sold through a fixed price IPO (Kay & Thompson, 1986). Even with a fixed price IPO, the initial stock price can be lower than the market equilibrium price since some bribed bankers may rig the price; it was the case of 309 IPOs at the New York Stock Exchange, which involved Salomon Smith, Citibank, Crédit Suisse, and First Boston (Stiglitz, 2003).

7. CAC40 is the index of the biggest 40 companies listed at the Paris stock exchange.

8. Harvard Capital, a Czech privatization funds, promised to redeem privatization vouchers into stocks at a 10 times higher value (a 1,000% rate of return). The Russian MMM funds offered 2,000% and attracted 5 million savers. In Romania, 20% of the population were gullible in similar funds.

9. In 1992, privatization vouchers whose nominal value was 10,000 rubles were traded over-the-counter for a bottle of vodka (the price of which was in the range of 5,000 rubles at the time).

10. In Russian language, a play on the words can confuse *privatisatsiya* – privatization – with *prikhvatisatsiya* (derived from the verb *hvatat*, to grab), which means grabbing, predation, or theft. Seen from Russia, the loans for shares scheme showed up as a more civilized predatory transaction than acquiring assets with a *kalachnikov* machine gun at hands with the help of violent entrepreneurship (Volkov, 1999).

11. It is mathematically demonstrated that the lower is this percentage (often quite below 10%) the more dispersed the stockholding equity across a large number of stockholders (Andreff, 1996), what exactly occurred with MEBO and mass privatization.

12. In Romania, 80% of new millionaires originate from the former communist *nomenklatura*, 61% in Russia, over 50% in Poland. Oligarchs (managers/owners) represent between 1% and 10% of new rich depending on the PTE.

13. Brazil, Russia, India, China, and South Africa.

14. Empirical evidence is documented in Andreff (2003) and Andreff and Andreff (2005).

15. Out of all oligarchs involved in the infamous loans for shares privatization, only Mikhaïl Khodorkovski was eventually sentenced to jail, but primarily because he politically opposed the President of the Russian Federation.

16. The standard presentation is: banks gave out loans to subprime investors who wanted to buy houses. The risk of the loans was then partially sold to other investors (investment banks and hedge funds) in form of CDO (credit default options or collateralized debt obligations). Since only the bank had information on actual quality of these loans, this led to moral hazard problem: banks were interested in increasing the number of loans, even if their default probability was high, because their own risk was mostly sold off to investment banks and hedge funds (Hens & Rieger, 2010).

17. Laddering consists in a bank canvassing investors before an IPO with offering them to buy a certain number of stocks at bottom price and asking them to commit buying more stocks some time later when the stock price will be growing. Those bank-connected investors (and the bank itself) will then sell their own stocks at higher price, deriving financial payoffs from speculation without any risk.

18. With spinning, a bank underestimates on purpose a company's stock in an IPO and offers to the company's managers to acquire stocks at underestimated price against their loyalty commitment to the bank.

19. Jorion (2011) provides various examples of stock market price manipulation. One is to swiftly multiply transactions within a same second (quote stuffing). Sergueï Aleynikov, a Russian mathematician who worked with Goldman Sachs was sentenced by stock exchange regulators for borderline (between honest and dishonest) transactions. Stiglitz (2010) sees in blurred and borderline manipulations the origin of banking scandals since the 1990s.

20. A dark pool gathers thousands mortgages consolidated by securitization in a same MBS. Transactions within a dark pool are dealt over-the-counter and are not disclosed.

21. Short selling consists in someone selling right now assets that he/she does not hold in view of buying them forward at lower price.

22. Since the early 2000s, the number of conflicts of interests has sharply increased. A conflict of interests is a situation in which personal interests of an individual are contradictory with his/her duties which precisely consist in protecting those interests he/she is in charge of.

23. Civilized, as compared with the methods utilized in privatized firms in PTEs, that is many (about 20 types of) blatant breaches of the law protecting shareholder rights – such as paying an entrance fee at the general meeting of shareholders, voting with show of hands, faked counting of shareholder votes, not convening small shareholders to the meeting, etc. (Andreff, 2007). That is the reason why stock-options are so rare in PTEs since they are not necessary to seal the power of core stockholding managers there.

24. Nevertheless Michael Milken was sentenced ten years to jail (serving only two) but on other charges of racketing, tax avoidance, and insider dealing. He remains one of the biggest 200 fortunes in the United States today.

25. Namely by de Maillard (2011) and Pons (2006); in the latter one can find a detailed description by a lawyer of all the techniques used for fake accounting, embezzlements, insider dealing, and financial fraud.

26. In 1920, Charles Ponzi attracted enormous investments and paid huge interest for it, but only by using newly arriving investments, thus getting deeper and deeper into debt. At the same time, he financed a luxurious life from this and even bought a private bank. Finally, the whole scheme broke down, and he ended in prison for many years (Hens & Rieger, 2010).

27. Issuing an ADR is rather simple. A bank buys stocks from a financial intermediary who has bought them in the stock market. These stocks are kept as deposit in the bank's balance sheet. Then the bank can issue ADR within the limits of the amount of acquired stocks, although the stockholding company whose stocks are traded usually must allow the bank to do so (then ADR are sponsored). An American exemption to this rule comes out with absent company protection. Thus, a

bank can issue a company's stocks without the company's agreement. Then ADR is unsponsored (Junghans, 2011).

28. Following the privatization drive, banks had significant shares in the stockholding equity of many companies. Moreover big firms created their own banks ("pocket banks"). Connected lending was the rule, though informal. Firms and banks were too connected to fail.

29. The state bailing the U.S. savings and loans out is assimilated to a credit line open by the government on which they have a free drawing right (Akerlof & Romer, 1993). This is clearly an incentive to asset grabbing, if not looting.

30. For instance, the IASB 39 norm of the International Accounting Standards Board which relies on a notion of "fair value" compelled the banks to recapitalize when a part of their assets lost value due to a falling market price. This norm was repealed on April 4, 2009.

31. Passing the Gramm-Leach-Bliley Act in 1999 nullified the Glass-Steagall Act (in force since 1933).

32. It increasingly ensues a legitimacy crisis of the existing economic system in all the nonoligarchic social strata, including among "honest" capitalists who believed in the virtues of the rules that had backed capitalism development in the 19th and 20th centuries as well as their personal fortune expansion, and that informal practices and financial crisis do not obtain any more in the future.

33. Informal rules have been crucial in the transition from planned economies to PTEs. Informal rules offered a way-out to those actors who cannot or do not want to adapt – or stick – to (new) formal rules in PTEs. If informal rules spread over many actors, then they create a shadow or informal economy as the one mentioned in Section "Cheating with the Rules of Capitalism and the Global Shadow Economy". The shadow economy develops until the point where new changes in the formal rules validate the informal rules by formalizing and stamping them. New formal rules are actually enforced after creating the proper supervision and sanction authorities.

34. Except if the gains distribution were at random from one game to the other, but this is precisely excluded by asset grabbing strategies, cheating, rigging, and manipulating the market.

35. A similar hypothesis is implicit in Jorion (2011): "a rarely mentioned hypothesis emerges: were not capitalism and communism struck down by a same illness?" (p. 10) and "capitalism and communism join in a final collapse" (p. 18). And in Pollin (2009, p. 154): "indeed economic development in transition countries has triggered the outgrowth development of the financial sector in developed countries."

36. This follows up a long lasting convergence hypothesis first launched by Tinbergen (1961) that we have criticized as a theoretical dead end (Andreff, 1992b).

ACKNOWLEDGMENTS

I thank for their comments participants to the AEH, FAPE (AFEP), IIPPE Joint Conference: *Political Economy and the Outlook for Capitalism*, Paris, July 5–8, 2012, and two reviewers. All remaining mistakes are of my own.

REFERENCES

Aglietta, M. (2008). *La crise. Comment en est-on arrivé là ? Comment en sortir?* Paris: Michalon.

Aglietta, M., Khanniche, S., & Rigot, S. (2010). *Les hedge funds. Entrepreneurs ou requins de la finance?* Paris: Perrin.

Akerlof, G. A., & Romer, P. M. (1993). Looting: The economic underworld of bankruptcy for profit. *Brookings Papers on Economic Activity*, *2*, 1–60.

Andreff, M., & Andreff, W. (2005). La concurrence pour l'investissement direct étranger entre les anciens et les nouveaux membres de l'Union européenne. *Economie appliquée*, *58*(4), 71–106.

Andreff, W. (1976). *Profits et structures du capitalisme mondial*. Paris: Calmann-Lévy.

Andreff, W. (1985). The external constraint in the economic crisis of eastern European countries. In P. Zarembka & T. Ferguson (Eds.), *Research in political economy* (Vol. 8, pp. 27–93). Greenwich, CT: JAI Press Inc.

Andreff, W. (1992a). French privatisation techniques and experience: A model for central-eastern Europe? In F. Targetti (Ed.), *Privatization in Europe: West and east experiences* (pp. 135–153). Aldershot: Dartmouth.

Andreff, W. (1992b). Convergence or congruence between eastern and western economic systems. In B. Dallago, H. Brezinski & W. Andreff (Eds.), *Convergence and system change. The convergence hypothesis in the light of transition in eastern Europe* (pp. 47–85). Aldershot: Dartmouth.

Andreff, W. (1993). *La crise des économies socialistes: la rupture d'un système*. Grenoble: Presses Universitaires de Grenoble.

Andreff, W. (1995). Le contrôle des entreprises privatisées dans les économies en transition. *Revue Economique*, *46*(3), 763–772.

Andreff, W. (1996). Three theoretical analyses of corporate governance in privatized enterprises. *Emergo: Journal of Transforming Economies and Societies*, *3*(1), 61–74.

Andreff, W. (1999). Residual state property and the privatisation of management: An insight into the french experience. In A. Böhm (Ed.), *Management and privatization of residual state property: The corporate governance implications* (pp. 109–157). Ljubljana: Central & Eastern European Privatization Network, EU Phare-Ace Programme.

Andreff, W. (2000). Privatisation and corporate governance in transition countries: Beyond the principal-agent model. In E. F. Rosenbaum, F. Bönker & H.-J. Wagener (Eds.), *Privatisation, corporate governance and the emergence of markets* (pp. 123–138). London: Macmillan.

Andreff, W. (2003). The newly emerging TNCs from economies in transition: A comparison with Third World outward FDI. *Transnational Corporations*, *12*(2), 73–118.

Andreff, W. (2005). Russian privatization at bay: Some unresolved transaction and governance cost issues in post-Soviet economies. In A. Oleinik (Ed.), *The institutional economics of Russia's transformation* (pp. 213–244). Aldershot: Ashgate.

Andreff, W. (2007). *Economie de la transition. La transformation des économies planifiées en économie de marché*. Paris: Bréal.

Andreff, W. (2010). *La transition postcommuniste comme origine de la crise actuelle du capitalisme mondial, in: 75 ensayos breves de economia critica en homenaje a Benjamin Bastida*. Barcelona: Publicacions i Edidions de la Universitat de Barcelona.

Andreff, W. (2012). *La mondialisation économique du sport. Manuel de référence en économie du sport*. Bruxelles: De Boeck.

Artus, P., Betbèze, J.-P., de Boissieu, C., & Capelle-Blanchard, G. (2009). *De la crise des subprimes à la crise mondiale*. Paris: La Documentation Française.

Attali, J. (2009). *La crise et après?* Paris: Fayard.

Bajt., A. (1968). Property in capital and in the measn of production in socialist economies. *Journal of Law and Economics*, *11*(1), 1–4.

Barton, D. (2011). Capitalism for the long term. *Harvard Business Review* (March). Retrieved from http://hbr.org/2011/03/capitalism-for-the-long-term/ar/1#

Berglöf, E., & Roland, G. (1998). Soft budget constraints and banking in transition economies. *Journal of Comparative Economics*, *26*(1), 18–40.

Bettelheim, C. (1970). *Calcul économique et formes de propriété*. Paris: Maspero.

Birdsall, N., & Nellis, J. (2002). *Winners and losers: Assessing the distributional impact of privatization*. Washington, DC: Center for Global Development.

Blasi, J., Kroumova, M., & Kruse, D. (1997). *Kremlin capitalism: The privatization of the Russian economy*. Ithaca, NY: Cornell University Press.

Bouin, O., & Michalet, C.-A. (1991). *Le rééquilibrage entre secteurs public et privé: L'expérience des pays en développement*. Paris: OCDE.

Boycko, M., Shleifer, A., & Vishny, R. (1995). *Privatizing Russia*. Cambridge, MA: MIT Press.

Boyer, R. (2011). *Les financiers détruiront-ils le capitalisme?* Paris: Economica.

Cartelier, L. (1992). L'expérience française de privatisation: bilan et enseignements. *Revue Internationale de Droit Economique*, *3*, 375–402.

Chavance, B. (dir.). (1987). *Régulation, cycles et crises dans les économies socialistes*, Editions de l'EHESS, Paris.

Chavance, B. (1999). Le capitalisme et le socialisme comme espèces systémiques: Formation, co-évolution, transformation. In B. Chavance, E. Magnin, R. Moramed-Nejad, J. Sapir (dir.), *Capitalisme et socialisme en perspective. Evolution et transformation des systèmes économiques* (pp. 295–315). La Découverte, Paris.

Chesnais, F. (2011). *Les dettes illégitimes. Quand les banques font main basse sur les politiques publiques*. Paris: Raisons d'agir.

Comte-Sponville, A. (2004). *Le capitalisme est-il moral?* Paris: Albin Michel.

Davies, H. (2010). *The financial crisis: Who is to blame?* Cambridge: Polity Press.

de Maillard, J. (2011). *L'arnaque* (2e éd.). Paris: Gallimard.

Derviz, A., & Podpiera, J. (2011). Cross-border lending contagion in multinational banks. In R. W. Kolb (Ed.), *Financial contagion: The viral threat to the wealth of nations* (pp. 327–334). Hoboken: Wiley.

Dietrich, D., Knedlik, T., & Lindner, A. (2011). Central and Eastern European countries in the global financial crisis: A typical twin crisis? *Post-Communist Economies*, *23*(4), 415–432.

Dore, R. (2000). *Stock market capitalism: Welfare capitalism. Japan and Germany versus the Anglo-Saxons*. Oxford: Oxford University Press.

Filatochev, I., Wright, M., & Bleaney, M. (1999). Privatisation, insider control and managerial entrenchment in Russia. *Economics of Transition*, *7*(1), 481–504.

Frank, R. H., & Cook, P. J. (1996). *The winner-take-all-society: Why the few at the top get so much more than the rest of us*. New York, NY: Penguin Books.

Freeland, C. (2000). *Sale of the century: Russia's wild ride from communism to capitalism*. New York, NY: Crown Business.

Frydman, R., & Rapaczynski, A. (1994). *Privatisation in eastern Europe: Is the state withering away?* Budapest: Central European University Press.

Frye, T., & Shleifer, A. (1997). The invisible hand and the grabbing hand. *American Economic Review*, *87*(2), 354–358.
Guriev, S., & Rachinsky, A. (2005). The role of oligarchs in Russian capitalism. *Journal of Economic Perspectives*, *19*(1), 131–150.
Hanson, P., & Teague, E. (2005). Big business and the state in Russia. *Europe-Asia Studies*, *57*(5), 657–680.
Hedlund, S. (2001). Property without rights: Dimensions of Russian privatisation. *Europe-Asia Studies*, *53*(2), 213–237.
Hemming, R., & Mansoor, A. (1988). *Privatization and public enterprises*. Washington, DC: IMF.
Hens, T., & Rieger, M. O. (2010). *Financial economics: A concise introduction to classical and behavioral finance*. Heidelberg: Springer.
Hill, D. (2009). How gambling corruptors fix football matches. *European Sport Management Quarterly*, *9*(4), 411–432.
Jorion, P. (2011). *Le capitalisme à l'agonie*. Paris: Fayard.
Junghans, P. (2011). *Les ADR non parrainés, nouveau trou noir de la finance mondiale*. In X. Raufer (dir.), La finance pousse-au-crime, Paris: Choiseul.
Kay, J. A., & Thompson, D. J. (1986). Privatization: A policy in search of a rationale. *Economic Journal*, *96*(March), 18–32.
Kindleberger, C. P. (1989). *Manias, panics and crashes: A history of financial crises*. New York, NY: Basic Books.
King, L. P. (2001). *The basic features of postcommunist capitalism in eastern Europe: Firms in Hungary, the Czech Republic and Slovakia*. Westport: Praeger.
Kornaï, J. (1980). *The economics of shortage*. Amsterdam: North Holland.
Kornaï, J. (2000). What the change of system from socialism to capitalism does and does not mean. *Journal of Economic Perspectives*, *14*(1), 27–42.
Kornaï, J., Maskin, E., & Roland, G. (2003). Understanding the soft budget constraint. *Journal of Economic Literature*, *41*, 1095–1136.
Lambin, J.-J. (2011). *Quel avenir pour le capitalisme? Débats actuels*. Paris: Dunod.
Landais, C. (2007). *Les hauts revenus en France(1998-2006): une explosion des inégalités*, Ecole d'Economie de Paris, juin.
Lordon, F. (2009). *La crise de trop? Reconstruction d'un monde failli*. Paris: Fayard.
Mitchell, J. (1998). *Strategic creditor passivity, regulation and bank bailouts*. CEPR Discussion Paper Series No. 1780. Centre for Economic Policy Research, London.
Morin, F. (2011). *Un monde sans Wall Street?* Paris: Seuil.
Mouhoud, E. M., & Plihon, D. (2009). *Le savoir et la finance. Liaisons dangereuses au cœur du capitalisme contemporain*. Paris: La Découverte.
Orléan, A. (2009). *De l'euphorie à la panique: penser la crise financière*. Paris: Editions Rue d'Ulm.
Pech, T. (2011). *Le temps des riches. Anatomie d'une sécession*. Paris: Seuil.
Pollin, J.-P. (2009). Système bancaire: rupture ou continuité? In P. Dockès, J.-H. Lorenzi (Eds.), *Fin de monde ou sortie de crise?* (pp. 153–174). Le Cercle des Economistes, Perrin, Paris.
Pons, N. (2006). *Cols blancs et mains sales. Economie criminelle, mode d'emploi*. Paris: Odile Jacob.
Raufer, X. (dir.) (2011). *La finance pousse-au-crime*. Paris: Choiseul.
Roche, M. (2011). *Le capitalisme hors la loi*. Paris: Albin Michel.

Roland, G. (2000). *Transition and Economics. Politics, Markets and Firms.* Cambridge, MA: MIT Press.

Silverman, B., & Yanowitch, M. (2000). *New rich, new poor, new Russia: Transforming politics anda property in East Central Europe.* Armonk: M.E. Sharpe.

Soros, G. (1998). *The crisis of global capitalism.* New York, NY: Perseus Books LLC.

Stiglitz, J. E. (2002). *Globalization and its discontent.* New York, NY: W.W. Norton.

Stiglitz, J. E. (2003). *The roaring nineties.* New York, NY: W.W. Norton.

Stiglitz, J. E. (2010). *Freefall: America, free markets, and the sinking of the world economy.* New York, NY: W.W. Norton.

Tinbergen, J. (1961). Do communist and free economies show a converging pattern? *Soviet Studies, 12*(4), 333–341.

UNODCCP. (2001). *Russian capitalism and money-laundering.* New York, NY: United Nations Office for Drug Control and Crime Prevention.

Volkov, V. (1999). Violent entrepreneurship in post-communist Russia. *Europe-Asia Studies, 51*(5), 741–754.

World Bank. (2002). *Transition – the first ten years: Analysis and lessons for Eastern Europe and the former Soviet Union.* Washington, DC: World Bank.

DID GOLD REMAIN RELEVANT IN THE POST-1971 INTERNATIONAL MONETARY SYSTEM?☆

Jean-Guy Loranger

ABSTRACT

The central hypothesis to be tested is the relevance of gold in the determination of the value of the US dollar as an international reserve currency after 1971. In the first section, the market value of the US dollar is analysed by looking at new forms of value (financial derivative products), the dollar as a safe haven, the choice of a standard of value and the role of special drawing rights in reforming the international monetary system. Based on dimensional analysis, the second section analyses the definition and meaning of a numéraire for international currency and the justification for a variable standard of value based on a commodity (gold). Then follows the theoretical foundation for the empirical and econometric analysis used later. The third section is devoted to the specification of an econometric model and a graphical analysis of the data. It is clear that an inverse relation exists between the value of the US dollar and the price of gold. The fourth section shows the estimations of the different specifications of the model including linear regression and cointegration analysis.

☆The chapter was completed in 2012 and is now published posthumously.

Contradictions: Finance, Greed, and Labor Unequally Paid
Research in Political Economy, Volume 28, 49–88

ISSN: 0161-7230/doi:10.1108/S0161-7230(2013)0000028004

The most important econometric result is that the null hypothesis is rejected in favour of a significant link between the price of gold and the value of the US dollar. There is also a positive relationship between gold price and inflation. An inverse statistically significant relation between gold price and monetary policy is shown by applying a dynamic model of cointegration with lags.

Keywords: Money; value; benchmark; gold; dollar; cointegration

INTRODUCTION

Nowadays most economists reject any connection between money and a particular commodity (gold). They propose state money while ignoring the need for *international currency* to be linked to the real world by a benchmark as a standard of values or prices. Today's economists who follow Ricardo's ideas consider money as a medium of circulation and reject or minimise the store-of-value function which can also be viewed as a reserve-of-purchasing-power. The concept of a store of value is non-existent in a Walrasian general equilibrium for money because if supply and demand are in equilibrium, there will be no excess of money to store or to hoard. The money store-of-value function is also incompatible with an equilibrium circuit of money so frequently postulated by some post-Keynesians. The store-of-value function or the reserve-of-purchasing-power function is at the heart of Marx's circuit of money capital which has been analysed in Loranger (1982a, 1982b, 1982c, 1986).[1] The central question to be examined in this article is whether the world's reserve currency was linked in any way to the real world after its official link to gold was cut in 1971. Most economists reject the idea that the dollar as a reserve currency is linked to a commodity – in particular to gold. Some argue that the US dollar is strong enough to stand by itself and its liquidity is desirable in a time of financial crisis because the quantity of gold is not significant with respect to the quantity of dollars used either in international transactions or as a currency reserve.[2] The latter argument is not convincing because at the time of the gold standard in the 19th century, most transactions were made in sterling instead of gold. The quantity of sterling in circulation or in reserve was far more important than the gold reserve. When questioning the value of one unit of sterling being equal to a quantum of gold, the answer was clear and immediate as the '*de jure*' definition was accepted at the world level. Through the *exchange rate system*, each domestic currency was linked to an international currency and, consequently, linked to a benchmark elected as a general equivalent.

The distinction between a '*de jure*' and a '*de facto*' situation is justified by the change in the exchange rate regime from 1971: except for certain countries, the fixed exchange rate system was abandoned in favour of a variable exchange system. A similar movement followed with the standard of money value; the fixed standard of value for money with respect to gold was replaced by a variable standard of value. *This is the hypothesis to be tested in this article*. From a '*de jure*' viewpoint, there is no link between international currency and a commodity (gold) since 1971. However, from a '*de facto*' viewpoint, the link still exists. An important question to consider is how does the market define a benchmark (fixed or variable over time) and, if it is necessary, can the benchmark be changed or reinterpreted?

Two recent publications invite a rethinking of the problem in terms of money-commodity *The Value of Money* by Patnaik (2009) and *Capitalism with Derivatives* by D. Bryan and M. Rafferty (2006). Patnaik's conclusion is that oil is the money benchmark while Bryan and Rafferty's conclusion is that derivatives are the new 'commodity' (risk as a meta-commodity) benchmark for money. In November 2010, Robert Zoellick, the president of the World Bank said, This new system is likely to need to involve the dollar, the euro, the yen, the pound and a renminbi [yuan] that moves towards internationalisation. The system should also consider employing gold as an international reference point of market expectations for inflation, deflation and future currency values.[3] Robert Mundel (1997) predicted the comeback of gold in the early 21st century when he said, 'More likely, gold will be used at some point, maybe in 10 or 15 years when it has been banalized among central bankers, and they are not so timid to speak about its use as an asset that can circulate between central banks. Not necessarily at fixed price, but a market price'.[4]

Firstly, the intent of this paper is to discuss the value of the US dollar as an international currency reserve and its evolution since the end of the dollar-gold link in 1971. This evolution is characterised by the emergence of financial derivatives after 1972 and the search for a new benchmark linking the dollar to the real world. Four types of commodities are usually recognised as benchmarks:

- Labour power as a commodity. This is the choice of most Keynesian and Marxist economists, although it comes from very different hypotheses.[5]
- Gold as a variable standard of value as proposed by R. Zoellick in 2010 and by R. Mundel in 1997 – it is the preferred hypothesis presented in this paper.

- Special drawing rights (SDR) based on a basket of other commodities as advocated by China, France, Russia, India and Brazil.
- Oil as an alternative standard is the preference of some economists including P. Patnaik.

The second aim is to discuss the definition of a *numéraire* and the concept of a variable standard of value to better understand the value of money linked to a commodity. With the help of dimensional analysis, one can demonstrate the formal correspondence between Walras' and Marx's *numéraire* which is defined as any particular commodity for Walras and a quantum of a certain commodity assumed to be gold in Marx's form IV.[6] Although most economists reject any connection between money and a particular commodity (gold) due to the existence of legal tender money in every country, it will be shown that the reduction of the real world to a dimensionless number (see Section 'The Walras *Numéraire*') is equivalent to showing that money is neutral and has no meaning *per se*. This hypothesis is faulty because it disregards the importance of money's link to the real world. The *de facto* variable standard of value assumed paramount importance once the link between US dollar and gold was officially removed, historically creating a rather exceptional situation for an international reserve currency.[7] A third aim is to show that a strong link exists between the price of gold, the value of the US dollar and other key financial variables (i.e. Dow-Jones [DJ] index, interest rate and inflation). This is achieved by an empirical analysis based on monthly observations from 1971 which was the year that the Bretton Woods Accord ceased to exist. An econometric analysis will validate what can be observed by a simple inspection of the data. Assuming that β is a parameter linking the value of the dollar to gold, the null hypothesis to be tested is $\beta = 0$; that is there is no link between the value of the dollar and the value of gold. Therefore, if $\beta \neq 0$, this shows that the demonetarisation of gold is a myth in theory as well as in reality.

THE MARKET VALUE OF THE US DOLLAR AND ITS NEW FORMS

The Form of the Universal Currency

In ancient times, each empire had the power to create its own money which circulated in other countries and insured its support by conquering the wealth of other nations. Presently, the situation of the dollar is not much different; *however, the form of value is more sophisticated because of the financial innovations that increasingly characterised its sway as an international reserve currency.* Writings on the topic of the 1980's international financial markets certainly showed that these innovations were not as sophisticated as they are today (Loranger, 1982a, 1982b, 1982c). The development of the Eurodollar phenomenon allowed private banks and/or other investors to have access to dollars outside of US financial markets including borrowing on the world market. However, these measures were insufficient because many developing countries were forced to accept structural adjustment plans with strict conditionality because they did not have the necessary creditworthiness. Continuous deregulation starting in the early 1980s with the Reagan administration led to the unlimited development of financial markets, the emergence of many kinds of derivative products and the securitisation of debts (slicing and repackaging debts) and also the rise of securitised lending. By the 1990s, these risk management instruments became a new commodity that could be exchanged on markets in the same manner as other financial products. Therefore, ABS, ABCP, CDO, CDS[8] and so on were developed and traded by Wall Street bankers and their imitators in Europe and in other countries which had the financial strength to issue and sell them. Since many of these products were difficult to price according to their risk factor, the market for them brutally collapsed in 2007 and created the largest financial meltdown at the world level.[9]

Expansion of Financial Derivatives

The notional value of a derivative contract corresponds to the value of the underlying security (shares, bonds, etc.). Since the underlying security is supposed to be related to a physical capital asset, the notional value of a derivative is simply another instrument which, like shares, transcends time and space because it can be bought and sold anytime and anywhere when the value is based on a physical asset located in real time and space. Therefore, the market value of a derivative contract is the amount of money required to purchase it as opposed to purchasing shares or bonds related to physical assets (see Table 1). This is an important advantage for banks, other financial institutions (hedge funds), firms and individuals which gives them the leverage to buy large amounts of notional capital with a small quantity of liquidities or by borrowing instead of reducing their liquidity.[10] Securities can be unbundled, repackaged and sold as a different security where risk is divided and spread between many investors who buy ABS,

Table 1. Importance of Financial Derivatives.

	2001		2004		2007		2009		2011 (1st half)	
(a) Outstanding derivative contracts notional amount December (trillions $)										
OTC (over the counter)	111	82%	220	84%	596	89%	615	90%	642	91%
Organised exchanges	24	18%	47	16%	72	11%	73	10%	65	9%
Total	135	100%	295	100%	668	100%	688	100%	707	100%
Market value	3.8		6.4		15.8		21.6		20	
(b) Distribution of the total OTC (707T) in 2011 by type of contract										
Interest 78%, foreign exchange 9%, CDS 5%, equity-linked and commodity 1.5%, others (unallocated) 11.2%										
(c) Foreign exchange market and daily turnover (trillions $)										
Notional amount (OTC)	16.7	31.5	57.6	49.2	65					
Market value (average December)	0.7	1.9	3.3	2.1	2.3					
Daily turnover (daily average April)	1.5	2.1	3.4	4.1	4.0 (2010)					
Annual turnover (240 days)	360	456	792	960	960					

Source: BIS, Triennial Survey 2010, Quarterly Review I, 2012.

ABCP, CDO and CDS. Bryan and Rafferty's (2006) book is an important contribution to understand the role and development of financial derivatives as a consequence of unlinking the dollar to gold, the beginning of rising uncertainty for the exchange rate and the need to find a new benchmark for the value of the dollar. They considered risk as a 'meta commodity', a hypothesis that I reject,[11] but it is a serious theoretical contribution to the subject of the equivalence problem between money and the real world in the post-1971 international monetary system. Bryan and Rafferty see these financial instruments as a new way to value firms' assets in time and space. They state:

> *The commensuration properties of financial derivatives mean that the logic of capital is driven to the center of corporate policy making. Assets that do not meet profit-making benchmarks must be depreciated, restructured and/or sold. The decision not to do so is now more readily exposed to market scrutiny, as investment bankers use derivatives and derivatives' prices to unbundle the performance of the different assets and liabilities of firms.*[12]

Table 1 shows the importance of the development of derivatives over the last 10 years. Their phenomenal expansion is an indication of the volatility of financial markets and in particular, the uncertainty generated by the floating exchange rate system. It is no surprise that a crisis of exchange rates is developing around the world and a reform of the international monetary system is necessary if one wants to reduce uncertainty around exchange rates (see Table 1c).

A unanimous agreement does not exist for the definition and measurement of derivatives.

According to the Bank of International Settlements (BIS), the notional amount of OTC derivatives contracts and the notional amount of organised exchanges totalled 707 trillion dollars at the end of June 2011. The largest of these transactions is on interest rate. The growth over the seven-year period (2001–2007) is 410% representing an average annual growth of 59%. One observes, however, that the financial meltdown 2007–2009 brutally stopped that growth which increased by only 7.7% from 2007 to 2011[13] giving an average annual increase of only 3%. However, since 2007, the market value of derivatives has increased by 37%.[14] Another interesting characteristic of this phenomenon is that transactions on organized markets have been continuously losing ground and represent only 9% of the total value of derivative contracts in 2011. Because banks make the largest portion of OTC contracts, their power is more concentrated than ever. With foreign exchange contracts representing only 9% of total transactions in 2011, it is interesting to examine this subsector in terms of turnover while considering the idea of taxing this particular type of transaction. Also revealing is the increasing volatility of the value of money and the numerous exchange rate crises that cannot be stopped without reforming the International Monetary System. One observes the rapid growth of notional foreign exchange contracts between 2001 and 2007; however, growth stopped and turned negative (−15%) between 2007 and 2009, moving from 57.6 trillion dollars to 49.2 trillion then resuming its growth over the last two and a half years to 65 trillion. The market value of foreign exchange contracts had an accelerated growth for the period 2001–2007 moving from 0.7 trillion dollars in 2001 to 3.3 trillion in 2007 with a decrease of 30% over the last three years. The impact of the great financial crisis is clearly shown by these figures. The yearly turnover of foreign exchange derivatives is now hovering around 1000 trillion dollars. A Tobin tax of one-tenth of 1% would produce revenues of one trillion dollars. The scale of these transactions may appear to be exaggerated because hedging in financial derivatives (offsetting an existing position) is quite common. Since the world GDP is estimated around 60 trillion in 2009 (IMF, 2010), this is approximately 10 times less than the notional figure of OTC derivative contracts. According to Bryan and Rafferty, it is neither possible nor desirable to eliminate financial derivatives because they are the new vehicles for storing the value of money. They also consider that derivatives are the new standard of value and form of holding wealth which changes in time and space (a variable standard of value). Bryan and Rafferty wrote:

> *... valuation across space, time, and between different asset forms is the stuff of derivatives. Derivative traders.... operate in a world of perceived equivalence but, and this is critical, it is not a fixed equivalence – for if equivalence were fixed, there would be no need for derivatives" (B. & R. p. 36) [Derivatives] are commodities that manage risk. And because risk exposure is so changeable, the market for these risk management commodities has acquired a high level of liquidity (volume and mobility) with many of the characteristics of money.... Derivatives constitute new private global money.* (Bryan & Rafferty, 2006, p. 38)

It would be more accurate to describe derivatives as a new form of money as in bills, credit cards and credit money preferred as a means of exchange and payment in certain situations. Bryan and Rafferty affirm that no difference exists between derivatives and money – with derivatives serving as a benchmark for unknowable fundamental values.[15] In Marxian analysis, abstract labour values are unknowable values and money is the *raison d'être* for revealing those values through the market place.[16] Derivatives play a similar role to the Marxian approach, but the problem with the definition of the standard of value or benchmark for money remains an unresolved problem in the Bryan–Rafferty approach. This new style of trading became necessary because of the uncertainty and risks emanating from the regime of fluctuating exchange rates and deregulation in banking and financial institutions at the world level. The most important cause is the termination of the fixed definition of the US dollar with gold in 1971. In 1972, the Chicago Mercantile Exchange introduced the first derivative in currencies. The Chicago Board of Trade introduced the first derivative in interest rates in 1975 and the Chicago Board Option Exchange (CBOE) was created in 1973 as a market for options that were previously exchanged as OTC (Bryan & Rafferty, 2006, p. 94). These new financial institutions were created to counteract the volatility of exchange rates and other financial instruments (shares, bonds...) after the collapse of the Bretton Woods Agreement.

The Strength of the US Dollar

Since the variable exchange rate regime is the consequence of the abandonment of an official link between the US dollar and gold, what would the value benchmark of the dollar as a currency reserve be? An incorrect response would be to state that the value of a dollar is defined by a basket of strong currencies such as the euro, yen, Swiss franc, sterling pound and so on...which states the tautology: a dollar is a dollar! Sadly, this constitutes standard teaching in many macroeconomic courses. Economists cannot justify a fundamental dimension in economics – money, the medium in which value is determined and expressed by market prices and how it attains its own value with another commodity used as a general equivalent. As mentioned, this mainstream opinion has been challenged by Patnaik (2009). He wrote,

> *A monetary world necessarily requires.... the fixity of the value of what is used as money vis-à-vis some commodity, be it gold or silver or labour power... Fiat money is as much commodity money as money fixed against gold; it is just that the commodities in the two cases are different. The world has never succeeded in getting out of commodity money.* (Patnaik, 2009, pp. 163–164)

Patnaik uses the awkward term 'propertyist', meaning that the value of money is determined not by supply and demand as the monetarists claim, but outside of it. He mentions that Keynes and Marx are both non-monetarist economists because Marx specifies that money is determined from outside by a money commodity and Keynes states that the wage rate is given. More explicitly Patnaik says,

> State backing can at best confer juridical acceptability, but for it to actually function in the economy in a meaningful manner something more is needed and this something is the fact that it has a commodity backing, of the commodity labour power, through the fixity of the money wage rate in any single period. (Patnaik, 2009, p. 164).

In the Marxist approach, it is the labour power of gold miners embodied in the commodity as a general equivalent which reveals the relative value of all other commodities without revealing its own value. According to Patnaik, the stability of the US dollar is now based on the price of oil. As he states,

> *It follows that the present currency arrangement hinges crucially on the stability of the price of the dollar in terms of oil, in the sense at least of the absence of persistent declines in it,*[16] *which is why it can be called the oil-dollar standard. No matter what the "de jure" situation, the world has not moved away from commodity money.* (Patnaik, p. 208)

Patnaik finished his book in June of 2008 just before the beginning of the financial meltdown that had a tremendous impact on the price of oil with wild fluctuations from $140 to a low of $40 and it is now above $100. Patnaik's hypothesis about an oil–dollar standard is not supported by the present economic situation (see Graph 1). However, he has a long-term view about the future of the price of oil. He believes that the United States is an imperialist power and wants to keep control over the production and flow of oil from Middle-East countries (including Iran) and will wage war to retain price control over this resource. Here is the unique advantage for an imperialist power in that even if its financial system is fragile, the US

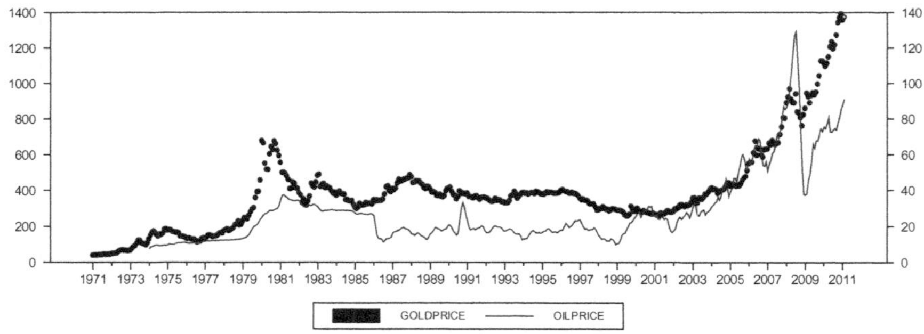

Graph 1. Gold Price and Oil Price 1971–2011. *Sources:* World Gold Council, gold price, London pm fix. Stat Can oil price, table 329–0038.

economy can finance wars and the restructuring of its debt at a near zero interest rate with savings coming from the rest of the world. Any other country in this situation would be declared a failed state – an example being some of the Euro zone countries. This type of crisis will last as long as financial instability continues. As the late H. P. Minsky (1982) would have written, '*It is Happening Again*.'

The next section is devoted to choosing the best variable standard of value between oil and gold and show that oil cannot be a good standard of value as assumed by Patnaik.

Oil or Gold as a Standard of Value

First, define a variable standard of value which is elected to be the general (universal) equivalent for all the other commodities. The word 'elected' means chosen and accepted universally by people around the world.[17] Actually, one could speak instead of Marx's form II (total or expanded form of value) where each commodity is taken as a specific equivalent for other commodities which might be gold, petroleum, etc.

> *On the other hand, the expanded expression of relative value, the endless series of equations, has now become the form peculiar to the relative value of the money commodity. The series itself, too, is now given, and has social recognition in the prices of actual commodities. We have only to read the quotations of a price-list, backwards, to find the magnitude of the value of money expressed in all sort of commodities. But money itself has no price.*[18]

Speculation on certain basic commodities such as oil, potash, aluminium, copper, silver and gold cannot be understood otherwise. Speculators seek to protect the value of their wealth by exchanging money for commodities or for their derivatives which may, for a certain period of time, be considered better stores of value than the dollar. This clearly shows that the US dollar maintains a link with the real world of commodities. Money is not neutral or abstract for speculators.

Comparing the prices of oil and gold between 1979 and 2012, one sees that the price of oil was around $20 a barrel at the end of 1979,[19] while the market price of gold was around $375 an ounce compared to its official price ($46). In March 2012, the price of oil was around $105 a barrel while the price of gold fluctuated around $1650 an ounce which is an increase of 5.25 times for the price of oil compared to an increase of 4.4 times for the price of gold. The question is which of these two commodities would be the best standard of value reflecting successive devaluations of the international currency (US$)? Note in passing that if commodity money like gold has value (labour power of gold miners), its relative value is unknown, but its price is determined by the market or by a general agreement which can be far above its cost price. This means that, without speculation, the price of gold might be much lower. *If stability is a desirable quality for a standard of value, then gold is more stable than oil.* Showing extreme volatility during the great financial crisis, the price of oil moved from $60 in 2007 to above $130 in 2008 and fell back to $40 in 2009 while climbing up again to above $100 by the end of March 2012. The gold price reflects the uncertainty of the US dollar as a reserve currency with its successive devaluations that are close to the inflation rate over the long period.

This can be observed in Graph 2 where the nominal and the real price of gold show somewhat downward sloping curves between 1987 and 2005. To have a clearer picture of the parallel evolution between the price of gold and inflation, one can examine the period between 1983 and 2007 where the data are not affected by the great financial crisis beginning in 2008. The consumer price index in the United States, based at 100 in the period 1982–1983, reached 206 in 2007; hence, the value of the index increased by 2.1 times between 1982 and 2007. The price of gold in mid-1983 was $413 and was $697 in 2007 with its value increasing 1.7 times for the same period. Since the price index is based on the average of 1982–1983, the nominal value and real value of gold are around $413. The real value of gold at the end of 2010 is $557 representing an increase of 35% over the 28-year period with an average annual growth of 1.25%. This observation is in accordance with what many observers note about gold. In the long run, gold is a conservative

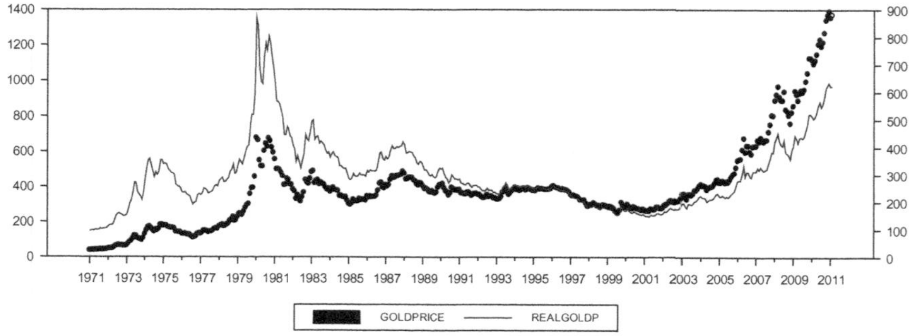

Graph 2. Nominal Gold Price and Real Gold Price 1971–2011. *Sources:* World Gold Council, gold price, London pm fix. StatCan, CPI, table 451–0009.

investment because its price, after adjusting for inflation, gives a low yield and constitutes a rather stable store of value.[20]

Moreover, the quantity of world gold reserves at the IMF which were around 1150 million ounces in 1971 fell to 950 million ounces in 1979 and remained at that level until 1988. Although 'demonetarization' of gold was proclaimed, central banks continued to keep a large reserve of it until 1988 (36%). The level of gold reserves has dropped to 10% over the last 20 years.[21] Central banks who have been net sellers of gold in the past (on average of 400 to 500 tons per year) have now reversed the trend by selling very little in 2009 – becoming net buyers of nearly 100 tons in 2010 (Table 2).[22]

As reported by the World Gold Council, the estimated total gold demand for 2001 was 3729 tons and 10 years later slightly over 4000 tons. However, the change in demand between jewellery and investments as a safe haven is substantial. The proportion of demand for gold as a money commodity changed from 10% in 2001 to 40% in 2011. Note a jump of nearly 100% in gold demand for investments between 2007 and 2011 which was a period of great uncertainty created by the financial crisis. Note also the relative stability of gold demand as an ordinary commodity in the domain of technology (dental and industrial use). The substitution in the gold demand is between jewellery and speculative demand. Both demands constitute hoards, but jewellery is less liquid than gold bars and gold ETFs, therefore, indicating a gold rush.

As pointed out by A. Freeman, 'The great bulk of all the gold ever produced remains in existence and, indeed, the small volume of actual gold consumption, in comparison to the stock of gold, is a singular feature of gold in comparison with other commodities such as oil… In consequence,

Table 2. Gold Demand (Tons).

	Coins, Bars and ETF	Jewellery	Technology	Total
2001	357 (10%)	3009 (81%)	363 (9%)	3729
2005	601 (16%)	2716 (72%)	433 (12%)	3753
2006	676 (20%)	2296 (67%)	462 (13%)	3435
2007	688 (19%)	2414 (68%)	465 (13%)	3571
2008	1181 (31%)	2190 (58%)	439 (11%)	3812
2009	1360 (39%)	1758 (50%)	373 (11%)	3493
2010	1333 (35%)	2060 (54%)	420 (11%)	3812
2011	1641 (40%)	1963 (49%)	463 (11%)	4067

Source: World Gold Council (2011), Gold Demand Trends, table 10. ETF is exchange trade funds or share bullion funds.

what is really going on is a shift to and from hoards, [coins, gold bars] and ornaments or other temporary resting places for gold in which function it has the social use of either display or treasure, that is, an ostentatious hoard'.[23] This form of 'gold rush' continued after the announcement by the Fed in November 2010 of a quantitative easing of 600 billion dollars. The price of gold is now around $1600 US showing that gold remains a safe haven; its price remains important and deserves an explanation.

As said in the 'Introduction' Section, four possible benchmarks have been suggested to ground the value of money: labour power, gold, oil and SDR. The latter has been advocated by China and other countries.

Critique of China's Proposed Reform of the IMS

In March of 2009, the governor of the Central Bank of China, Zhou Xiaochuan, spoke in favour of reforming the International Monetary System. He received the support of many countries including India, Russia, France and Brazil. The main proposition made by Mr. Zhou was to give a larger role to SDRs as the new reserve currency which would be independent from major currency economies. Mr. Zhou said, 'As an international currency, the SDR should be anchored to a stable benchmark and issued according to a clear set of rules.'

The main question is how to define the benchmark? Mr. Zhou favours Keynes' proposition of Bancor which would be based on the value of 30 representative commodities. In Mr. Zhou's view, Bancor would not simply be 'fiat' money as proclaimed by Keynesian and post-Keynesian economists. In my opinion, it is not necessary to have 30 commodities instead of one like gold or oil.[24] The economic acceptability of a *numéraire* depends on the market [25] and not on law or regulation by a superpower or an international institution like the IMF.

The market price of gold in SDRs is necessary for grounding international currency to the real world. The importance of a variable price of a SDR in gold shows the world that a particular commodity backs the value of money in SDR. The management of the supply of SDR and its price will depend on consensus of the international community giving a larger role to the IMF and the willingness of the United States to accept that their currency will be confined exclusively to a national currency. This cannot happen unless the US imperial power is considerably diminished by letting its money be depreciated to a point unacceptable by other countries. A prediction is that the IMF would control the change of the market value of the SDR in the same way that each country controls the exchange rate for its money. For instance, IMF could favour a controlled devaluation of SDR in the same way as it can augment the quantity of SDR as any independent central bank does when it wants to augment the liquidity in the system. It could be for trade and balance adjustment, or to give the necessary liquidity to countries that do not have the creditworthiness to borrow from private markets. *This position is not a return to a gold standard or a gold exchange standard. It is the continuation of the existing state (a variable standard) with a new independent currency*. After a period of transition, international financial transactions could be made in SDR instead of US dollars bringing more stability to financial markets while putting in place a new international monetary system. One must remember that the suppression of the link between gold and the US dollar caused the phenomenal expansion of derivatives whose role was to counterbalance risk generated by uncertainty in the store of value function of international currency. Also the volatility of financial markets cannot be reduced unless there is a major change in the international monetary system. Mr. Zhou seems to share the same viewpoint when he said,

> *The centralized management of part of the global reserve by a trustworthy international institution with a reasonable return to encourage participation will be more effective in deterring speculation and stabilizing financial markets… With its universal membership, its unique mandate of maintaining monetary and financial stability, and as an international 'supervisor' on the macroeconomic policy of its member countries, the IMF, equipped with its expertise, is endowed with a natural advantage to act as the manager of its member countries reserves.* (Zhou Xiaochuan, 2009, p. 4)

NUMÉRAIRE AND VARIABLE STANDARD OF VALUE

Dimensional Analysis

Some economists admit that a significant link can be observed empirically between the price of gold measured in dollars and the value of money of other countries also measured with respect to the dollar (weighted exchange rates). They consider that such an empirical link is tautological or redundant because the dollar is present on both sides of the equation. A dimensional analysis of the variables will help to clarify the dimension of the β coefficient. If a homogenous relation exists between the two sides of the equation, then one would expect $\beta = [1]$ which is a dimensionless or abstract number with both sides of the equation being of the same dimension.

In physics, dimensional analysis is applied to heat and its thermal unit is British Thermal Unit (BTU). Similarly in economics, dimensional analysis is applied to value and its unit of measurement is one unit of money. In economics, there are four fundamental dimensions: $[M]$ for money, $[R]$ for real object, $[T]$ for time and $[1]$ for a number without dimension. All other variables have secondary dimensions derived from fundamental ones. For instance, the dimension of price $[p]=[MR^{-1}]$, that is price is a certain quantity of money $[M]$ per unit of $[R]$. The rules of simple algebra apply to dimensional analysis.[26]

Let $[M]$ be the dimension of the dollar (US).

Let $[G]$ be the dimension of gold.

Let $[A]$ be the dimension of money of other countries.

Let $[MG^{-1}]$ be the dimension of the price of gold in US dollar.

Let $[AM^{-1}]$ be the dimension of the value of the US dollar with respect to the value of money of other countries – that is one unit of dollar equals xA quantity of money of other countries. When the dollar is devalued, it requires less quantity of money of other countries $(x-\Delta x)A$. It is a weighted exchange rate with respect to the dollar.

Let $[AM^{-1}] \sim \beta[MG^{-1}]$ be a proportional relation between the value of the dollar and the price of gold in dollars.

The dimension of β is $[AM^{-1}]\,[MG^{-1}]^{-1}=[(AG)M^{-2}]$.

Therefore, the proportionality relation is not homogenous and β is not a dimensionless number. Another way to look at the proportionality coefficient without M is to specify the inverse of the exchange rate and specify the proportionality relation as $[MA^{-1}] \sim \alpha[MG^{-1}]$.

Therefore, $\alpha=[GA^{-1}]$. The proportionality coefficient is the value of money of other countries measured in gold. The null hypothesis would be $\alpha=0$; that is there is no relation between gold and the value of money. Our maintained hypothesis is $\alpha \neq 0$. The econometric analysis in the fourth part becomes crucial to determine whether or not the estimated proportionality coefficient is significant.

Definition of Walras' and Marx's Numéraire

Many economists and bankers avoid discussing the *numéraire* because they are happy with the Walras' relative price approach and limit their conception of money within a national framework which puts an end to the discussion of international reserve currency. They tend to assume that the central bank is the highest authority and imposes a consensus by declaring domestic currency as legal tender money. This legal tender status is extended to private commercial banks because the central bank acts as the lender of last resort and also the state has the power of taxation which gives credibility to state money. This is an accepted fact, but not an excuse for keeping silent about a flexible exchange rate and the necessity for an international currency that connects with the real world. Quoting Marx on universal money:

> *It is only in the markets of the world that money acquires to the full extent the character of the commodity whose bodily form is also the immediate social incarnation of human labour in the abstract. Its real mode of existence in this sphere adequately corresponds to its ideal concept.* (Marx, 1867, vol. 1, p. 142)

The above quote shows the essential weakness in the concept of money made by post-Keynesians. Their implicit assumption is that the state will always be able to control the labour force and establish the creditworthiness of state money. What many post-Keynesians do not realise is that state money is based on a particular commodity: labour power to be disciplined in the framework of a national economy.[27] The question at the international level is which commodity could be used: the labour force of a superpower or some other commodity? Marx's labour theory of value is at the core of the foundation of money value but he did not consider that the world would dispense with a money commodity. An important point is to show that Marx's foundation of the value of money based on a commodity remains relevant.

The Walras' Numéraire

Most economists believed that the break from the gold dollar standard after 1971 expelled gold as a money commodity from the international monetary system and that the US dollar is the new *numéraire* that does not require 'a bodily form that is the immediate social incarnation of human labour in the abstract' (Marx). They repeat the tautology a dollar is a dollar, which is equivalent to saying that the dollar as a *numéraire* is 1 which will be shown below as a logical error.

Referring to Kindleberger's (1981) article of the N-1 problem, let

$[x_1, x_2, \ldots, x_{n-1}, x_n]$ be a bundle of goods and
$[p_1, p_2, \ldots, p_{n-1}, p_n]$ be their absolute prices.

Assume that x_n is chosen as the general equivalent good (*numéraire*). The $(n-1)$ relative prices are then $[p_1/p_n, p_2/p_n, \ldots, p_{n-1}/p_n]$.

Assume that $p_n = 1$, a usual assumption in a mainstream macroeconomic course.

The relative prices are therefore $[p_1, p_2, \ldots, p_{n-1}]$, and they are now expressed *in money prices*. According to the definition of a price, it is a quantity of money per unit of a particular commodity. In dimensional analysis, let us assume that M is the money and x_n is the gold G. If $p_n = 1$, then $[p_n] = [M/x_n] = 1 \rightarrow [M] = [x_n] = [G]$. Therefore, money M has the same dimension as G because gold is a money commodity chosen as a general equivalent.

Most economists find this an unacceptable statement and they decline to discuss the absolute price system and prefer to stay with a relative price system that avoids committing themselves to choosing a particular commodity. This is very far from Marx's conception of money where absolute values and prices have a key role in the labour theory of value. In a Walrasian equilibrium, prices are determined when there is no excess supply and demand for any commodity. This equilibrium rules out the possibility that money can function as a store of value. Many economists think when they assume $p_n = 1$, they have defined a purely abstract *numéraire* with no real foundation. Then x_n should be an abstract number [1] *which is a contradiction with respect to the real world* to which it belongs by definition.[28]

The Marx's Numéraire

The Marxian formulation starts with exchange values instead of prices, as follows:

> Let $xA \leftrightarrow yB \leftrightarrow \ldots \leftrightarrow wD \leftrightarrow zC$ be equivalence relations between commodities.
> Let [A, B, … D, C] be a bundle of commodities.
> and $[x, y, \ldots w, z]$ be their absolute abstract values.

Assume that C is chosen as the general equivalent commodity (*numéraire*).

The relative forms of values are $[x/z, y/z, \ldots w/z]$. Assume that $z = 1$.

The relative values become $[x, y, \ldots w]$ and are transformed *in money values* because C chosen as the money commodity becomes a standard of prices and represents *the immediate social incarnation of human labour in the abstract*. According to the definition of a money value or price, it is a quantity of money per unit of a particular commodity. Assume that M is money and C belongs to the space of real objects. Hence, $z = [M/C] = 1 \rightarrow [M] = [C]$. Therefore, there is no formal difference between Walras' and Marx's *numéraire* even if Walras' prices are equilibrium prices and Marx's values transposed into market prices are compatible with the existence of money hoarding. The *numéraire* cannot be an abstract number equal to unity (as the standard teaching in a basic economic course). It was demonstrated at the end of Section 'The Walras *Numéraire*' that money is linked to the real world and x_n or C belongs to the world of commodities.

Specification of a Variable Standard of Value

Assume that $z(t)$ is the *variable price* of gold which is equal to a number $\neq 1$. $z(t) = a(t) = [M(t)/G]$ or $M(t) = a(t)G$. Replacing (t) by its dimension $[T^{-1}]$, we have $[M/T] = [a/T]$ $[G]$.

What does this mean? Simply that a certain quantity of money per period $[M/T]$ is equal to a certain quantity $[a/T]$ of G for the same period. It is clear that if the price of G is constant over time, for example, in a discrete time period, the dimension T cancels itself on both sides of the equality and we have $M = aG$; that is M is a certain (fixed) proportion of G during the discrete time period. What is the particular nature of G?

Following Marx's definition of the universal equivalent:

> *The commodity that functions as universal equivalent, is, on the other hand, excluded from the relative value form... The particular commodity, with whose bodily form the equivalent form, is thus socially identified, now becomes the money-commodity, and consequently its social monopoly, to play within the world of commodities the part of a universal equivalent.* (Marx, 1867, vol. 1 pp. 68–69)

Assuming that the commodity chosen as the general equivalent has two use values: one as an *ordinary commodity* with its price related to its cost measured in terms of labour power (congealed and living labour) and the second as an *extraordinary commodity* used as a general equivalent and its value cannot be revealed. To quote Marx on this point:

> *The use-value of the commodity-money becomes two-fold. In addition to its special use-value as a commodity (gold for instance, serving as a commodity serving to stoop teeth, to form the raw material of articles, of luxury, & c.) it acquires a formal use-value, originating in its specific social function.* (Marx, 1867, vol. 1, ch. 2, p. 89)

Therefore, the ordinary use value of gold has a cost price in term of abstract labour (supplied by gold miners) as in any other commodity. The extraordinary use value of gold (as social monopoly) can influence the price of gold far above its cost price, especially when gold is viewed as a safe haven. The extraordinary use value of gold linking to paper money is determined by the gold market ($35 or $1650 an ounce). This is a price whose value (abstract labour) cannot be revealed because it serves as the general or universal equivalent. This is the speculative or market price as a reserve of value and it is this price which links the foundation of money to the real world.

This point of view is in total contradiction with post-Keynesian economists who believe that state money is the only reality. The Chartalist post-Keynesian school[29] following Knapp (1924) and Kaldor (1964) argues that even if central bank money is a debt, there is no obligation to reimburse it. Quoting S. Bell, 'The general acceptability of both state and bank money derives from their usefulness in settling tax and other liabilities to the state. This enables them to circulate widely as means of payment and media of exchange.'[30]

In his writings on the subject, J. Smithin (2009) shares this viewpoint. When applied to the US economy, this concept assumes that the US dollar is the *numéraire* for the entire world and that there is an implicit assumption behind this statement that money is linked to the labour force. However, as it stands, the American labour force is not an obvious measure for the value of the dollar. Keynes was much more explicit about the wage and labour force in the short run. Keynes' assumption of a fixed wage rate in the short term is a basic assumption for grounding money in the real world. Indeed, the commodity behind that assumption is labour power and the stability of money rests upon the discipline of the labour force. Financial markets are in a permanent trade-off with the state and in this lies the foundation of class struggle outside the work place. Certainly, with financialisation at the world level, financiers who evaluate the creditworthiness of indebted states call for a reduction of state expenditures in health, education and social benefits. Financiers, with the help of the state, also advocate raising income taxation for workers but not for the rich and the privatisation of services in the public sector. This is the significance of disciplining the labour force in order to maintain the value of money. A good illustration is the financial pain imposed on the people of Greece in 2011–2012 to remain in the euro zone.

Many Marxists share a similar viewpoint when they argue that the monetary expression of labour time (MELT) is defined by the ratio of value added in money terms to the value created by the labour power. Money is then grounded to the real world by the labour force as a commodity. However, the labour theory of value being the foundation of the Marxist approach assumes that the MELT equation is validated because the denominator is measured in abstract units of labour time. The numerator is monetary value added as the social expression of abstract labour and the problem in transforming abstract values into prices is absent. By taking concrete labour time in the denominator, one has to specify how the nominal wage rate is determined. Is the wage rate fixed as Keynes assumed or is it determined by other prices?[31] Stated in a previous quotation, Marx assumes that it is abstract labour produced by human labour that makes for equality between commodities, and that money is a direct expression of that social labour and *requiring a link to a money commodity*. This is a concept that most contemporaneous Marxists are not ready to accept, because of their flawed understanding of the value of money in the real world. Finally, the labour force assumption as a commodity is usually accepted in a closed economy. *It is not relevant to open economies* unless necessary arbitrages are done through exchange rates with respect to the dominant economy. In the past, US workers accepted supporting this type of repression with stagnant or lower real wage rate – but there are limits to pauperisation. The moment of truth is approaching when the US administration will not be able to attract savings from the rest of the world at a near zero cost. Because of this, one would expect the price of gold to continue to rise.

MODEL AND DATA

Theory Behind the Facts

Established in the first two sections was the necessity for maintaining a *de facto* link between the value of money and a commodity. The hypothesis that there is a link between the price of gold and the value of the US dollar will be verified with empirical analysis in this section and in the last section with econometric tests. The strength of this link and other determinants will be specified to explain the variations in the price of gold. Inflation is certainly a relevant variable because if gold is a hedge against inflation, one would expect a positive relation between the price of gold and inflation. Can monetary policy be another valid explanation for the variation of the price of gold? If so, then one would expect a negative relation between the price of gold and the interest rate. The DJ index can function as an index for fear like the VIX index. Since the latter is not compiled over a long period, the choice is the DJ as a proxy variable and a negative relation is expected for the period (1988–2004) as shown in Graph 5. There are many other variables that can be specified in the gold price equation and in the value of money equation. Since there is a simultaneous two equation model (z and A or E), the same variables will enter the reduced form and the structural form will be identified by imposing a priori restrictions.

Econometric Model

From Section 'Dimensional Analysis', the econometric equation to be tested is $[MA^{-1}] = \alpha[MG^{-1}]$; that is the value of money is a proportion of gold price. This is the measure of the Euro exchange rate. For the value of money measured as weighted index with respect to the dollar, it is the inverse:

$$[MA^{-1}] = \beta[MG^{-1}]$$

What are the determinants of the value of money and gold price when there are so many possible exogenous shocks? In economics, it is the ability and skill of the economist to select the most important determinants and to add a random variable for the others.

Therefore, let $z(t) = \mathrm{f}[X'(t); u(t)]$, where $X(t)$ is a column vector of the most significant determinants of the price of gold and $u(t)$ is a random variable which accounts for all other (stochastic) influences on the price of gold. With the data chosen, the vector of explanatory variables is:

$$X'(t) = (E \text{ or } A,\ J,\ p,\ i)$$

where E or A is the exchange rate of the US dollar with respect to another currency such as the Euro (E) or a broad index of other currencies identified as (A). This feedback of the value of money (exchange rate E or A) on gold price specifies a simultaneous model. The coefficient between these two variables in either equation is the crucial test of the null hypothesis. If it is not significant, the null hypothesis is accepted and the hypothesis of gold as a variable standard of value must be rejected. Other determinants which include the DJ index, the consumer price index and the interest rate are added as a complementary explanation of the variance of gold price. Therefore, the linear regression of the price of gold on these four determinants is:

$$z(t) = \alpha + \beta' X(t) + u(t)$$

where $X(t)$ is a column vector of four components; β' is a line vector of four parameters; $z(t)$, $u(t)$ and α are scalars. The constant and random variables represent all other exogenous variables (wars, revolutions, structural changes, etc.) whose occurrences are impossible to predict or unaccounted for explicitly.

Of course, this specification can become complicated depending on the assumptions made about $u(t)$ and $X(t)$. If for instance $u(t)$ and $X(t)$ are not independent from each other because our model is simultaneous, then the model needs to be estimated with at least two equations. This is possible with cointegration analysis where all variables are assumed stochastic and series are non-stationary. Also it is quite likely that there is a lagged response of the price of gold to the various determinants. In which case, the model could take the form of

$$z(t) = \alpha + \beta'[H(L)X(t)] + u(t)$$

where $H(L)$ is an infinite polynomial in the lag operator L. It can be approximated by a rational function of two finite polynomials $B(L)$ and $C(L)$ of order m and n, respectively. Therefore,

$$z(t) = \alpha + \beta'[B(L)/C(L)]X(t) + u(t) \text{ or}$$

$$C(L)z(t) = \alpha' + \beta'[B(L)X(t)] + v(t).$$

With auto correlated residuals, a privileged specification will be the Hildreth-Lu specification, $(1-\rho L)z(t) = \alpha' + \beta' X(t) + v(t)$ if variables are stationary. If not, an error correction model (ECM) or an estimation based on cointegration would be more appropriate.

The Data

The symbols and data used are monthly series:

z (Gold price), World Gold Council, January 1971–February 2011
$g = z/p$ (real gold price)
J (DJ index), StatCan, table 176-0046, January 1971–February 2011
p (US consumer price index, 1982–1984 = 100), StatCan, table 451-0009, January 1971–February 2011
i (US interest rate), FRB (Fed Reserve Board) H.15, January 1971–February 2011
A (weighted average of exchange rates of strong currencies per US dollar), FRB, G.5/H.10, January 1973–February 2011
E (Exchange rate US$ per Euro), FRB, G.5/H.10, January 1999–February 2011.

Note an inverse correlation between A/US$ and US$/Euro when the latter increases it depreciates the dollar. Therefore, a positive correlation is expected between gold price and the exchange rate E (i.e. US$/Euro). The opposite is expected with the exchange rate A/US$; that is a negative correlation is expected between the gold price and the exchange rate index. 1971 was selected because it was the year the US administration (Nixon) decided that the US dollar would no longer be linked to gold and this was accomplished by terminating the Bretton Woods Agreement. In regression with *A*, series start in 1973 and in regression with *E*, series start in 1999. Note in Graph 2 (page 60) that a sharp increase in the gold price followed from 1971 to 1982 until the Reagan administration decided to raise the interest rate in 1981 to 18% in order to preserve the value of the US dollar.

The data in Graph 3 is in log form and the slope of a curve expresses the rate of growth of a particular variable. Obviously, the series are non-stationary and a first difference would likely transform them to the stationary series. Therefore, a cointegration analysis is presented after the regression analysis. In Graph 3, from 1985 one observes a negative correlation between gold price and the value of the US dollar. The link is strong and particularly obvious: when the value of the US dollar increases and the real value of the gold price decreases.

Because the euro has existed since 1999, it is interesting to concentrate the analysis on this period because it corresponds to a decrease in the value of the US dollar with a positive relationship between the price of gold and the value of the euro observed in Graph 4. Note from the data that the value of Euro in 2010 is less reliable as a reserve currency and does not reflect well the devaluation of the US dollar caused by speculative attacks against the euro.

It is interesting to note in Graph 5 a discontinuous relation between the gold price and the DJ index over the whole period. Before 1988, gold price is moving in a somewhat erratic manner compared to the DJ. An inverse

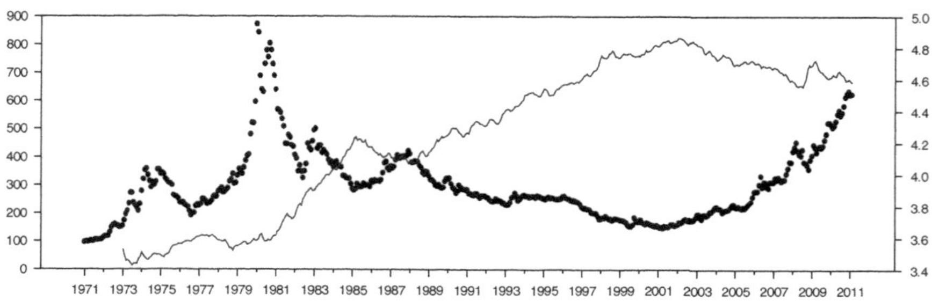

Graph 3. Real Gold Price and the Value of the US$ 1973–2011. *Sources:* BROAD, FRB G.5/H.10, Jan 1973–Feb 2011.

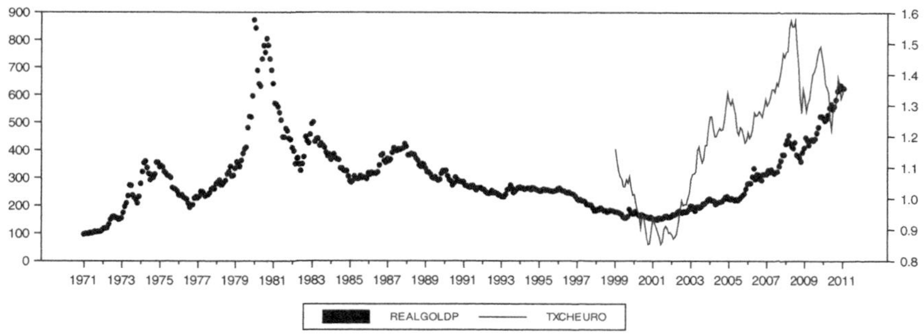

Graph 4. Real Gold Price and Euro 1999–2011. *Source:* Euro, FRB G.5/H.10, Jan 1973–Feb 2011.

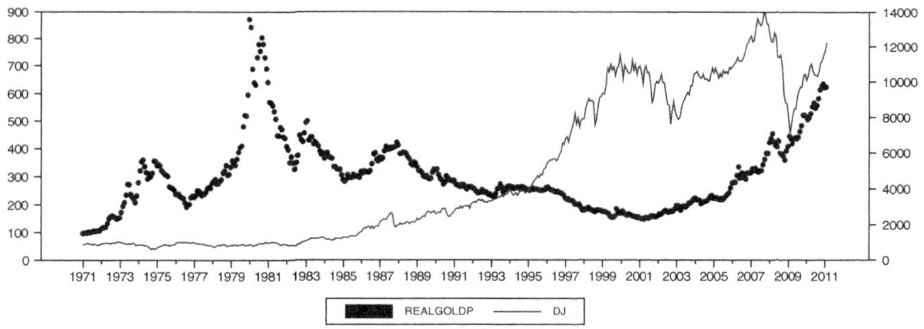

Graph 5. Real Gold Price and Dow-Jones Index 1971–2011. *Source:* DJ, StatCan, table 176-0046, Jan 1971–Feb 2011. Gold price, Graph 2.

relation holds for the period 1988–2003 but for the period 2004–2011 a positive relation is observed. The DJ index is a measure to express the amount of optimism or pessimism and is inversely correlated with fear indexes such as VOX or VIX (Loranger, 2010). When optimism prevailed on the stock market in the period 1988–2003, speculators divested their gold stock. But since 2004, the 'irrational exuberance' of investors has also affected the gold market and, except during the crash of 2007–2009, the gold price is positively correlated with the DJ. Therefore, the sign of the coefficient of this variable in various regressions (Section 'Regression Analysis') will be unstable unless a dummy variable is introduced to cope with this situation.

REGRESSION ANALYSIS

In order to facilitate the presentation of the econometric analysis, detailed estimated equations are reported in the appendix.

Elasticity of Gold Price

Firstly, econometric analysis has been conducted in terms of levels instead of relative change of the variables and not published because the series were non-stationary. Evidently, the Ordinary Least Squares (OLS) estimator cannot be applied unless series are transformed to make them stationary. Each series was tested for unit root by applying the augemented Dickey–Fuller test (ADF) procedure and the result being one unit root for each series[32] (see Table A4). In order to transform non-stationary series into stationary ones, the variables are transformed in log expressed in first differences. Elasticity coefficients are obtained and are independent of the unit of measurement of variables with a prefix *DL* added to each variable. The coefficient will indicate which determinant has the greatest impact on the variation of gold price. To avoid multicollinearity with the price index, real gold price is used instead of nominal gold price.

$$\underset{}{DLg} = \underset{(2.81)}{0.008} + \underset{(5.71)}{0.6662 DLE} - \underset{(-2.89)}{0.1985 DLJ}$$

Nobs = 145 $^{-}R^2 = 0.1925$ DW = 1.87 (Table A1)
Standardising with respect to *DLE*:

$$DLE = -0.012 + 1.51 DLg + 0.299 DLJ$$

Figures in parentheses are *t*-values extracted from Table A1 and note that all coefficients are significant at a level of less than 1% and the DW statistic indicates 0 autocorrelation. Therefore, the test of proportionality between the value of money and the price of gold is significant *and the null hypothesis must be rejected.* The value of money is elastic (1.51) with respect to the price of gold and the latter significantly depreciates the value of the US dollar whose dimension is $[ME^{-1}]$. The negative relation between the DJ index and the gold price is confirmed (−0.1985), but its impact on the value of money is positive because the standardisation is reversed. A similar result is obtained with the value of money measured by a broad index of other monies with respect to the dollar $[AM^{-1}]$. Note that the coefficient of the weighted average is negative. But a positive coefficient could easily be obtained by taking the inverse $[MA^{-1}]$ with the same dimension as the Euro $[ME^{-1}]$, where E is A.

$$\underset{}{DLg} = \underset{(3.11)}{0.007} - \underset{(-8.48)}{1.4359DLA} - \underset{(-2.49)}{0.1230DLJ}$$

Nobs = 457 $\bar{R}^2 = 0.1356$ DW = 1.53 (Table A1).

Again, the hypothesis of 0 autocorrelation is accepted although the explained variance of gold price is smaller with a determination coefficient of 13% only. Even if there is a significant relation between gold price and the value of money, there are many other causes or shocks that can impact the price of gold. Standardising with respect to DLA:

$$DLA = 0.005 - 0.696DLg - 0.009DLJ.$$

Note that it is the gold price coefficient that has the greatest impact on the value of money, since the other two coefficients are near 0. *Therefore, the null hypothesis must be rejected in favour of a significant link between the value of money and the price of gold.* The interaction between gold price and the value of the US dollar in this specification is a simultaneous one. The specification of a dynamic simultaneous model of two equations is required.

Cointegration Analysis

As previously mentioned, tests of unit roots were made for each variable (Table A4) and the hypothesis of 0 unit root is rejected in each case. The specification of an EMC or cointegration model is appropriate for this situation. Moreover, the model is a dynamic model according to the number of lags specified. A two-lag specification seems appropriate in order to let monetary policy fully impact on gold price. It has been established in another study (Capie, Mills, & Wood, 2004) that gold price reacts quickly to other variables. Therefore, the advantage of using this type of model is to separate short-term fluctuations from stable long-run relations.

A cointegration relation is defined as a *stationary linear combination* of variables where some or all are non-stationary.[33] All variables are stochastic and react simultaneously. The number of cointegration relations r (rank) or the number of unit roots (q-r) is determined by a rank test, q being the number of variables in the system. The tested hypothesis is to reject (*q*-*r*) unit roots if the trace of the cointegration matrix is above the critical value at 5% level and accept it when it is below the critical level. At least one cointegration relation has to correspond to the gold price equation or the money value equation. With more than one cointegration relation, there is an identification problem, the solution being to specify a priori constraints or restrictions on some parameters of the cointegration matrix. The model is a dynamic one and lags need to be specified in order to estimate short-run matrices for each lag.[34] By separating short-term effects from long-run relations, the purpose of the model is to estimate a stable relation between the set of chosen variables. Short-run results are not reported and the analysis will concentrate on stable long-run relations among variables.[35]

(a) Estimation with A

Unrestricted 2 cointegration relations

$$\mathrm{LA} = 0.201\mathrm{Lz} + 0.366\mathrm{LJ} - 0.458\mathrm{Lp} + 0.116\mathrm{Li}$$
$$\mathrm{Lz} = -2.610\ \mathrm{LA} + 0.174\mathrm{LJ} + 3.021\mathrm{Lp} - 0.047\mathrm{Li}$$

Nobs = 458 lag = 2 rank = 2 (Table A2)

Note here that long-term variables are in log level instead of first differences. Nominal gold price *z* is used instead of real gold price *g*. The rank test indicates there is at least one cointegration relation and the possibility of two because the calculated trace value (47.578) is very close to its critical value at the 5% level. Two cointegration relations were specified and the unconstrained estimated results appear in Table A2 and are presented above in a more usual form indicating that a cointegration relation is well identified in the gold price equation with the expected sign.

Standardisation of the first cointegration relation with respect to the value of money is a poor choice because of the positive coefficient (0.201). This being opposite to what is seen in Graph 3 where a negative relation is observed. However, the second cointegration identified with the price of gold is in accordance with the previous results: when the value of the US dollar increases, the price of gold decreases. In order to better identify this two equation system, some a priori constraints need to be specified. From Graph 5, a negative relation exists between the price of gold and the DJ index. The elimination of the *LJ* variable in the gold price equation and the *Lp* variable in the money equation will give an exactly identified model with significant Student-*t* values.

Restricted

$$LA = 0.036Lz + 0.281LJ + 0.078Li$$
$$\quad (0.67) \quad (8.91) \quad (2.60)$$

$$Lz = -1.950LA + 2.956Lp - 0.093Li$$
$$\quad (-7.61) \quad (11.10) \quad (-2.16)$$

However, note that the coefficient of the gold price in the value of money equation is not significant; the null hypothesis could be accepted and the interest rate coefficient has the wrong sign. It looks as if the value of the dollar is essentially controlled by the stock market with a positive sign. This equation requires a better identification with more explanatory variables or it should be excluded because there is only one significant cointegration relation corresponding to the second cointegration relation. All coefficients are significant with proper expected signs. Therefore, the null hypothesis is rejected. If the standardisation is made with respect to *1*, the causality is reversed.

$$LA = -0.513Lz + 1.516Lp - 0.048Li.$$

The value of other currencies measured in dollars reacts negatively to the price of gold (it takes fewer dollars to buy a unit of A); it reacts positively to inflation and increases with an austere monetary policy (although this effect is relatively small). It is clear that the null hypothesis is rejected.

(b) Estimation with E:

Unrestricted 1 cointegration relation

$$Lg = 0.603LE + 2.554LJ - 0.300Li$$
$$\quad (1.74) \quad (5.41) \quad (-5.95)$$

or:

$$LE = 1.658Lg - 4.235LJ + 0.498Li$$
$$\quad (5.05) \quad (-4.42) \quad (4.01)$$

Nobs = 146 lag = 2 rank = 2 (Table A3)

From Table A3, the rank test shows that *there is no cointegration relation with this set of data*. This is rather surprising result. Setting aside the rank test, it was decided to specify two lags and one cointegration relation in order to compare with the previous set of results. One of the most interesting outcomes is that there is a positive relation between *LE* and *Lg*. This means that when the dollar depreciates with respect to the euro (it takes more dollars to by one euro), the price of gold increases and when there is an increase in the gold price, the value of the dollar decreases. According to *t* values, the second equation is the best one: euro is a significant function of real gold price. *The null hypothesis is rejected.* The negative relation between the euro and the *DJ* is validated and the impact of the US monetary policy is positive for the euro. A quantitative easing policy decreases the value of the dollar with respect to the euro.

For the econometric tests, the best results are for the proportional variation model and the one cointegration model. The reason being that the series are non-stationary and by taking first differences of log variables, this eliminates non-stationary property from the series although remaining a simultaneous exercise.

An alternative is to use a cointegrated model where series can be non-stationary and form a stationary linear combination. This is the best method because it is a dynamic model with a few lags and gives long-run stable relations between variables. Explanatory variables are treated as stochastic regressors instead of fixed values. However, the existence of two significant cointegration relations does not work with the two sets of data. As shown in Table 3, only one cointegration relation can be clearly identified with significant coefficients and, *in all cases, the null hypothesis is rejected.*

Table 3. Best Estimated Equations.

(a) Proportional variations

Other money A

$DLg = 0.007 - 1.4359\ DLA - 0.1230\ DLJ$ or

$DLA = 0.005 - 0.696\ DLg - 0.009\ DLJ$

Euro R

$DLg = 0.008 + 0.666\ DLE - 0.198\ DLJ$ or

$DLE = -0.012 + .510\ DLg + 0.299\ DLJ$

(b) One cointegration relation

Other money A

$Lz = -1.950\ LA + 2.956\ Lp - 0.093\ Li$ or

$LA = -0.513\ Lz + 1.516\ Lp - 0.048\ Li$

Euro E

$Lg = 0.603\ LE + 2.554\ LJ - 0.300\ Li$ or

$LE = 1.658\ Lg - 4.235\ LJ + 0.498\ Li$

Therefore, gold as a variable standard of value matters in determining the value of money, although it can be influenced by many other shocks.

CONCLUSION

The object of this paper was to show that the value of money cannot be understood without referencing it to its place in the real world and also referencing it as a commodity. The first section was devoted to examining the new form of the US dollar in relationship to financial derivative products and the phenomenal expansion and the size of the derivative market as the basis for the strength of the dollar. Which commodity is best suited to link the value of the dollar to the real world: can oil or gold be the variable standard of value for the dollar? If so, what kind of international monetary reform should be undertaken? In the second section, using dimensional analysis, a formal identification of Walras' *numéraire* proved to be the same as Marx's *numéraire*. This may be contestable because there is a difference between Walras' approach and Marx's approach. While Walras' general equilibrium rules out any excess of money, Marx's money circuit is based on the existence of value reserve and, therefore, on hoarding. In Walras' approach, money is neutral and only relative prices are relevant. In Marx's approach, it is the absolute level of value and prices that is relevant because money needs to be grounded to a commodity chosen as a general equivalent. This viewpoint seems passé for most post-Keynesian and Marxian economists because they believe that state money with a flexible exchange rate is the only relevant hypothesis for money. However, post-Keynesian and Marxian economists ignore that there is a commodity backing the value of their money – the labour power. If this is accepted, it has consequences for the credibility of money: state indebtedness demands that the burden is shifted to the labour force and a new form of class struggle develops outside the work place by the reduction and cutting of social services and the systematic replacement of those services by the private sector.[36]

The US dollar has been disconnected from gold as *de jure* reserve currency since 1971: gold remains a *de facto* variable standard of value for the US dollar. The plausibility of such a hypothesis is based on what has been observed on the exchange rate markets: by moving from a fixed exchange rate system to a variable one. The value of money changed from a fixed gold standard to a variable one. Therefore, the null hypothesis was to show there is no link between the value of money and the price of gold when it acts as a variable standard of value. In the third section, data and an econometric model were used to test the null hypothesis. The results presented in the last section show that with a one equation model, *the null hypothesis is clearly rejected in favour of a significant strong link between the value of the dollar and gold.* However, in a simultaneous model of two equations, the null hypothesis could be accepted according to the (weak) specification formulated. The rank test with the euro data is in accordance with no cointegration relation, the simultaneous model is rejected in favour of a one equation model. Significant links between gold price and other explanatory variables exist, in particular, with respect to interest rate: a tight monetary policy impacts negatively on gold price after a few periods. Finally, the relation between gold price and the DJ is negative: gold price decreases when the DJ increases. The obvious negative relation in the period of 1988–2004 seems to be dominant.

Obviously, additional research using more variables is required. With a single cointegrated equation, the null hypothesis is rejected whether the value of the dollar is measured with respect to the euro or to any other combination of exchange rates. It can be safely concluded that despite the strong opposition by economists from different schools of thought, gold is still relevant for determining the value of money. Labour power cannot be a good substitute for gold because it would imply that a wage rate in a particular country would be chosen and accepted universally.

NOTES

1. In addition to the classical industrial circuit of capital, a monetary or credit circuit is added and there is a possibility that the monetary circuit does not close and remains in disequilibrium with the real circuit. The existence of value reserve now becomes important and we are confronted with three possible cases analogous to Minsky's financial instability hypothesis: hedge, speculative or Ponzi situations.
2. This view was defended by the Stanford School whose proponents were C. Kindelberger, E. Déprés, W. Salant and later by H. Johnson, M. Friedman and many others. One could add that when the international monetary system is under pressure because of the threatened explosion of the euro, speculators convert their gold reserve into dollars in order to have more liquidity to pay off their obligations.
3. R. Zoellick, *Financial Times* (11/08/2010).
4. R. A. Mundel (1997). Underlining has been added. Since last year, central banks are now net buyers of gold. In the late 1990s, gold was widely dismissed by central bankers as a reserve asset, so much so that the Bank of England and the Bank of Canada (to name only these two) sold all their gold reserves.

5. Gill (2011) is one of the rare Marxist economists who maintained that there is a link between labour value, money and gold. Most Marxist economists are happy with the MELT concept (monetary expression of one unit of labour time) to link money with labour. See Section 'Specification of a Variable Standard of Value' for a more complete explanation.

6. In the French edition edited by Marx.

7. See in particular B. Eichengreen (2011). He outlines that the rejection of gold as a universal currency is a very unusual situation over time except for temporary periods of non-convertibility due to wars, catastrophes or other unforeseen black swans.

8. The acronyms are as follows: asset back securities, asset back commercial papers, collateralized debt obligations, credit default swaps, respectively.

9. The market collapse for these products was unforeseen because traders used econometric models that assumed risk randomness. The models did not take into account systemic risk arising from the mimetic behaviour of investors. Moreover, though these models were supposed to sustain an 'originate and distribute' model, they actually resulted in a concentration of risk in certain financial institutions leading to their collapse. Totally ignored was Minsky's hypothesis of financial fragility where risky behaviour (Ponzi finance) increases with the length of the business cycle. See in particular Barbera (2009).

10. The power of leveraging is at the heart of the financial fragility of the banking system with ratios of 40 or 60 to 1 for the most speculative institutions. For instance, one pays $5 to buy a derivative of $200 which gives a ratio of 40. Because derivatives are contingent values, they are not reported in a firm's balance sheet. But accounting rules could change with financial reform at the world level.

11. The weakness of risk or meta-commodity as a variable standard of value is that it is fractioned in many different forms and is changing continuously over time.

12. Bryan and Rafferty (2006). Financial derivatives like ABS and CDO contracts on exchange rates and other types of derivatives are ultimately related to physical assets, even when they are piled over each other to form a new derivative. This is why they are difficult to value and why the German chancellor, in particular, was reluctant to support their expansion.

13. (642−596 = 46/596 = 7.7%).

14. (21.6−15.8 = 5.8/15.8 = 37%).

15. For Bryan and Rafferty, fundamental values are unknowable because they are not fixed but variable equivalence as it is said in the previous quotation.

16. Marxists consider MELT (monetary expression of one unit of labour time) concrete labour as equivalent to abstract labour in that definition and hence abstract labour is no longer an unknowable value. I beg to differ on this point because the quantity of labour power at the world level is an unknown. A more detailed discussion on the topic is found at the end of Section 'Specification of a Variable Standard of Value' on page 69. See also Marx's quotation about universal money as 'the immediate social incarnation of human labour in the abstract' on page 65.

17. Bryan and Rafferty (2006) in a note on page 150 outline that Menger (1892) saw money as a commodity selected by the market, not by the state. 'It is the marketable characteristics of the commodity money ... that sets it apart from other possible money: a process of natural selection by market processes'. Menger

contended that it was these qualities, not state decree, that saw precious metals nominated as money.

18. Marx (1867, *Capital*, book 1, chapter 3, p. 95). Note that Marx is indifferent in his use of price for relative value. To be more precise, the last sentence should be read: 'But money itself has no relative value'.

19. The price of oil doubled after Khomeini's takeover in 1978.

20. Even considering the value of $1500 reached by gold in mid-June 2011, the real value is around $665. This represents an average annual increase of 2.1%. As a reader pointed out, the value of the dollar was kept artificially high from 1980s onward, both in relation to gold and oil. The apparent attractiveness of the dollar kept the value of gold artificially low and caused many central banks to sell it just until the crisis.

21. The proportion was 30% in 1971, 38% in 1978, 36% in 1988, 17% in 1998 and 10% in 2008 (IMF, 2008).

22. WGC (2011) Chart 2 Official sector net gold sales since 2000. As mentioned in 'The Overview' of the annual report (2011), this reversal of the trend is maintained for 2011.

23. Personal correspondence with A. Freeman, June 2011.

24. With one money commodity, one can show the relative value of 30 or more other commodities and reversing the equations of all relative values of commodities, one gets the relative value of the money commodity. The idea of a 'basket of commodities' would confuse the issue. Marx's form II (total or expanded form) is a more coherent concept than a basket of commodities.

25. See Menger' s quotation (1892, note 21, p. 14).

26. A good introduction to dimensional analysis is found in F. J. De Jong (1967).

27. Of course, most progressive economists do not share this viewpoint. But most capitalist countries apply an austerity policy which is based on disciplining the labour force.

28. The real space viewed as a set of real objects cannot contain an abstract number. Another incongruous question is how can x_n be a universal equivalent outside the community of economists if it is an abstract number with no particular reference to the real world? Assuming that a dollar is a dollar represents a tautological statement.

29. The term Chartalist is derived from Latin meaning ticket or token (Knapp, 1924).

30. Bell (2001, p. 161). Note, in passing, the absence of any reference to money as a store of value.

31. See Loranger (2004) where the wage rate is determined simultaneously with prices when the profit rate is invariant in the transformation of values into prices. Other determinations are possible in particular from the dynamic equation $p=(1+r)[Ap_{-1}+\ wl$, where p, r, w are market price, profit rate and wage rate, and A, l are matrices of constant coefficients.

32. If a series has a unit root, it is an indication that it is not stationary.

33. Results reported in Tables A2 and A3 have coefficients with opposite signs compared to those reported in this section. When a linear combination is estimated, all variables are on the left side of the relation and only an error term appears on the right side justifying it as an error correction model.

34. Short-run matrices are the coefficients of first differences variables transformed in log. The size of these matrices is equal to the number of variables in the system.

35. The constant term is specified outside the cointegration matrix and is not reported here as the season dummy variables.

36. This statement is not shared by some progressive economists who think that the capacity of borrowing is not limited within a national framework. This is an illusion because even in a large economy like the US economy, quantitative easing is limited by the capacity of the international market to absorb US securities of all kinds.

ACKNOWLEDGEMENTS

I thank Radhika Desai, Alan Freeman, Victor Kasper Jr. and Paul Zarembka for their invaluable comments and please note this is an original work for which I am fully responsible.

REFERENCES

Bank of International Settlements. (2010a). *Triennial Central Bank survey of foreign exchange and derivative markets*. Activity in 2010 – Final results. Retrieved from http://www.bis.org/publ/rpfxf10t.pdf

Bank of International Settlements. (2010b). *Quarterly Review*, various years.

Barbera, R. J. (2009). *The cost of capitalism*. New York, NY: McGraw Hill.

Bell, S. (2001). The role of the state in the hierarchy of money. *Cambridge Journal of Economics*, *25*(2), 149–163.

Bryan, D., & Rafferty, M. (2006). *Capitalism with derivatives: A political economy of financial derivative, capital and class*. New-York and London: Palgrave MacMillan.

Capie, F., Mills, T. C., & Wood, G. (2004). Gold as a hedge against the US dollar. World Gold Council, Study no 30, September, London.

De Jong, F. J. (1967). *Dimensional analysis for economists*. Amsterdam, The Netherlands: North Holland Pub.

Eichengreen, B. (2011). *Exorbitant privilege*. New York, NY: Oxford University Press.

Gill, L. (2011). *La crise financière et monétaire mondiale*. Montreal: M Editeur.

IMF. (2008). *International Financial Statistics*. Washington, DC: International Reserves.

IMF. (2010). *World Economic Outlook*. Washington, April 2010.

Kaldor, N. (1964). *Essays on economic stability and growth*. London: Duckworth.

Kindleberger, C. P. (1981). *International money: A collection of essays*. London: Allen and Unwin.

Knapp, G. (1924). *The state theory of money*. London: MacMillan.

Loranger, J. G. (1982a). Crise et inflation: un essai sur une théorie qualitative de la monnaie. In: G. Dostaler (Ed.), *La crise économique et sa gestion*, Boréal Express, Montreal. Also in « Les classiques des sciences sociales » J.M. Tremblay ed. Chicoutimi, 2005.

Loranger, J. G. (1982b). Le rapport entre la pseudo-monnaie et la monnaie: de la possibilité à la réalité des crises. *Critiques de l'économie politique*, no 18, Paris, jan.-mars 1982. Also in «Les classiques des sciences sociales» J.M. Tremblay ed. Chicoutimi, 2005.

Loranger, J. G. (1982c). Pseudo-validation du crédit et étalon variable de valeur. *Économie appliquée*, vol. 35, no 3, Paris. Also in «Les classiques des sciences sociales» J.M. Tremblay ed. Chicoutimi, 2005.

Loranger, J. G. (1986). Circuit of capital: A new look at inflation. *Review of Radical Political Economics, 21*(1-2), 97–112.

Loranger, J. G. (1991). Modelling the soft budget constraint: Inflation explained by the circuit of capital. *Metroeconomica, 42*(10), 71–92.

Loranger, J. G. (2004). A profit-rate invariant solution to the Marxian transformation problem. *Capital and Class, 82*, 29.

Loranger, J. G. (2010). *The myth of demonetarization of gold.* Working Paper 2011–03, Dept of Economics, Université de Montréal, Montreal.

Marx, K. (1867). *Capital, Book I, II, III.* New York, NY: International publishers.

Menger, K. (1892). On the origin of money. *Economic Journal, 2*, 239–255.

Minsky, H. P. (1975). *John Maynard Keynes.* New York, NY: Columbia University Press.

Minsky, H. P. (1982). *Can "It" happen again?* New York, NY: M.E. Sharpe.

Mundel, R. A. (1997). The International Monetary System in the 21st century: Could gold make a comeback? Lecture delivered at St. Vincent College, Letrobe, Pennsylvania, 12 March 1997.

Patnaik, P. (2009). *The value of money.* New York, NY: Columbia University Press.

Smithin, J. (2009). *The importance of money and debt/credit relationships in the enterprise economy.* Draft paper, York University, Toronto, April 2009.

Xiaochuan, Zhou. (2009). *Reform of the International Monetary System.* The People's Bank of China, March 2009, Beijing.

World Gold Council. (2011). *Gold Demand Trends*, February 2011.

Zoellick, R. (2010). *Financial Times*, November 8.

APPENDIX: DETAILED REGRESSION RESULTS

Table A1. Regression of Gold Price (Proportional Variables).

Dependent Variable *DLg*					
Monthly data from 1999:02 to 2011:02					
Usable observations	145	Degrees of freedom	142		
Centred R**2	0.203797	R Bar **2	0.192583		
Durbin-Watson Statistic	1.875949				
Variable	Coeff	Std Error	T-Stat	Signif	
1.	Constant	0.008385019	0.002980229	2.81355	0.00559500
2.	DLE	0.666160057	0.116575023	5.71443	0.00000006
3.	DLJ	−0.198513754	0.068575828	−2.89481	0.00439374

Dependent Variable *DLg*					
Monthly data from 1973:02 to 2011:02					
Usable observations	457	Degrees of freedom	454		
Centred R**2	0.139426	R Bar **2	0.135635		
Durbin-Watson Statistic	1.528639				
Variable		Coeff	Std Error	T-Stat	Signif
1.	Constant	0.007078165	0.002276294	3.10951	0.00199185
2.	DLA	−1.435918003	0.169195184	−8.48675	0.00000000
3.	DLJ	−0.123013187	0.049467072	−2.48677	0.01324919

Note: An asterisk after a letter indicates that the variable is at its optimal level.

Table A2. Cointegration Model with A and 2 LAGS.

Sample:	1973:01 to 2011:02 (458 observations)						
Effective sample:	1973:03 to 2011:02 (456 observations)						
Obs. – No. of variables:	445						
System variables:	*Lz LA LJ Lp Li*						
Constant/Trend:	Unrestricted constant						
Lags in VAR:	2						
Rank test							
p-r	r	Eig. Value	Trace	Trace*	Frac95	*p*-Value	*p*-Value*
5	0	0.139	115.675	112.121	69.611	0.000	0.000
4	1	0.049	47.578	32.496	47.707	0.051	0.589
3	2	0.034	24.837	16.498	29.804	0.173	0.684
2	3	0.019	8.873	6.004	15.408	0.384	0.698
1	4	0.000	0.057	0.036	3.841	0.812	0.849
Unrestricted BETA (transposed)							
	Lz	*LA*	*LJ*	*Lp*	*Li*		
Beta(1)	−0.201	1.000	−0.366	0.458	−0.116		
Beta(2)	1.000	2.610	−0.174	−3.021	0.047		
Restricted BETA (transposed)							
	Lz	*LA*	*LJ*	*Lp*	*Li*		
Beta(1)	−0.036	1.000	−0.281	0.000	−0.078		
	(−0.672)	(.NA)	(−8.910)	(.NA)	(−2.604)		
Beta(2)	1.000	1.950	0.000	−2.956	0.093		
	(.NA)	(7.611)	(.NA)	(−11.108)	(2.157)		

*Trace and -*p*-value are calculated values for small sample.

Table A3. Cointegration Model with E and 2 LAGS.

Sample:	1999:01 to 2011:02 (146 observations)						
Effective sample:	1999:03 to 2011:02 (144 observations)						
Obs. – No. of variables:	135						
System variables:	*Lg LE LJ Li*						
Constant/Trend:	Unrestricted constant						
Lags in VAR:	2						
Rank test							
p-r	r	Eig. Value	Trace	Trace*	Frac95	*p*-Value	*p*-Value*
4	0	0.128	29.738	27.730	47.707	0.733	0.824
3	1	0.036	10.017	9.312	29.804	0.976	0.985
2	2	0.023	4.699	3.991	15.408	0.837	0.898
1	3	0.009	1.292	0.998	3.841	0.256	0.318
(a) Unrestricted cointegration relation							
	Lg	*LE*	*LJ*	*Li*			
Beta(1)	1.000	−0.603	−2.554	0.300			
	(.NA)	(−1.742)	(−5.415)	(5.949)			
Beta(2)	−0.322	1.000	−0.221	−0.070			
(b) Restricted cointegration relation							
	Lg	*LE*	*LJ*	*Li*			
Beta(1)	1.000	−2.574		0.234			
	(.NA)	(−7.624)		(4.558)			
Beta(2)	−0.105	1.000	−.0945				
	(−1.221)	(NA)	(−4.850)				

Table A4. Unit Root Test ADF with 6·Lags.

Variables	Calculated T
Gold price (z)	1.796
Euro (E)	−1.121
Exchange rate (A)	−1.456
DJ (J)	−0.115
CPI (p)	−0.139
Txint (i)	−1.529
Critical value 5%	−2.867

Note: All calculated T values are above the critical algebraic value, so the null hypothesis (0 unit root) must be rejected.

GLOBAL WAGE SCALING AND LEFT IDEOLOGY: A CRITIQUE OF CHARLES POST ON THE 'LABOUR ARISTOCRACY'☆

Zak Cope

ABSTRACT

This essay demonstrates that US economist Charles Post's attempted rebuttal of the 'labour aristocracy' thesis is both theoretically and empirically flawed. Defending the proposition that colonialism, capital export imperialism and the formation of oligopolies with global reach have, over the past century and more, worked to sustain the living standards of a privileged upper stratum of the international working class, it rejects Post's assertion that the existence of such cannot be proven. The essay concludes with a working definition of this 'labour aristocracy', setting the concept within the field of global political economy and reclaiming its relevance to the Marxist tradition.

Keywords: Labour aristocracy; imperialism; class consciousness; monopoly; competition; wage differentials

☆Portions of this chapter are drawn from Cope (2012) with permission of the publisher.

Contradictions: Finance, Greed, and Labor Unequally Paid
Research in Political Economy, Volume 28, 89–129

ISSN: 0161-7230/doi:10.1108/S0161-7230(2013)0000028005

Nowadays, given the enormous gap between the living conditions of people in the First World and people in the Third World, a statement such that the problems facing most workers in the former are significantly less daunting than those facing the majority of the world's workers residing in the latter may appear self-evident.[1] That the lack of any revolutionary movement aiming at the abolition of capitalism in the rich countries may have something to do with the affluence of the workers there might, at first blush, seem equally uncontroversial. After all, as English Radical William Cobbett famously challenged in the early nineteenth century, 'I defy you to agitate any fellow with a full stomach'. On the left, however, the idea that the global divide between the rich and poor nations has its reflection in the divide between rich and poor workers is very often anathema.

US economist Charles Post is today the leading left theorist concerned with refuting the Marxist concept of the 'labour aristocracy'.[2] This term has traditionally come to delineate that most well-off section of the workers of the world constituted through what I shall refer to herein as the global stratification of labour, that is, 'the scaling of radically different wages paid for the same labor in countries of the [global] North and the South' (Amin, 2011). More precisely, the labour aristocracy is that section of the global workforce that is afforded its prosperity in large part by the redistribution of surplus value extracted from non-aristocratic labour. The condition for this redistribution is the labour aristocracy's political rapprochement with capital engaged in the super-exploitation of subject labour in the (neo)colonial countries.

Post has challenged the idea that 'super-profits, derived from either imperialist investment in the global South or corporate monopoly, and shared with a segment of the working class, is the source of enduring working-class racism and conservatism in the United States and other industrialised capitalist societies' (Post, 2010, p. 5). The proposition central to Post's rejection of the labour aristocracy thesis is that the 'existence of a privileged layer of workers who share monopoly super-profits with the capitalist class cannot be empirically verified' (Post, 2010, p. 3). For Post, as opposed to those writers whom he criticises – Marx and Engels (1955, p. 132), Zinoviev (1984 [1916]), Lenin (1964, 1970, 1974), and Elbaum and Seltzer (1982, 2004) – 'wage-differentials among workers in the advanced capitalist countries [cannot] be explained either by Britain's dominance of key-branches of global production in the late-nineteenth century, by profits from investments in the global South, or by the degree of industrial concentration' (Post, 2010, p. 4). As we will see, however, not only is Post wide of the mark in his specific criticisms of the aforementioned authors, his narrow concern with wage differentials *inside* the imperialist countries misses the most significant economic and political repercussions of global labour stratification.

The following critique of Post's views on the labour aristocracy will proceed according to the order in which he himself has traced the intellectual evolution of the labour aristocracy thesis.[3] Beginning with a rebuttal of Post's critique of Marx and Engels, we will go on to take issue with Post's dismissal of the classical Marxist understanding of the concept and his repudiation of the role of oligopoly in determining wage differentials.

IN DEFENCE OF ENGELS ON THE LABOUR ARISTOCRACY

Engels famously argued that there is a material basis for metropolitan workers' social chauvinism, that is their patriotic attachment to a (neo-) colonialist government. In 1882, when asked in a letter by German Socialist Karl Kautsky what the English working class thought of colonialism, Engels replied:

> Exactly the same as they think about politics in general, the same as what the bourgeois think. There is no working class party here, there are only Conservatives and Liberal-Radicals, and the workers merrily devour with them the fruits of the British colonial monopoly and of the British monopoly of the world market. (Engels quoted in Lenin, 1969, p. 65)

For Engels, 'opportunism' in the British Labour movement was a result of and is conditioned by the preponderance of two major economic factors, namely, in Lenin's words, 'vast colonial possessions and a monopolist position in world markets' (Lenin, 1969, p. 65). As he wrote to Marx in 1858:

> The British working class is actually becoming more and more bourgeois, so that this most bourgeois of all nations is apparently aiming ultimately at the possession of a bourgeois aristocracy and a bourgeois proletariat as well as a bourgeoisie. Of course, this is to a certain extent justifiable for a nation which is exploiting the whole world. (Marx & Engels, 1955, p. 132)

Denying the existence of a Victorian-era labour aristocracy, Post (2010, p. 7) defines Marx and Engels' position thus:

> Marx and Engels [argued] that British capitalists accrued higher-than-average profits from their 'industrial monopoly' in the world-market of the mid-nineteenth century. These super-profits allowed British capitalists to recognise the skilled workers'

craft-unions and accept their restrictive apprenticeship-practices, which, in turn, enabled the labour-aristocracy to secure a rôle in supervising less-skilled workers, higher-than-average wages, and more-secure employment.

Post rejects this picture of embourgeoisement – detached as it is from Marx and Engels's emphasis on the division of labour established by *colonialism* – by asserting, firstly, that the supervision of unskilled workers by skilled workers was not universal (there being only weak evidence for skilled workers in textiles and mining acting as task masters). Secondly, he claims that 'craft-unions were unable to secure stable, year-round employment for all of their members'. In the face of technological advancement and the parallel deskilling of labour, Post asserts, by the end of the nineteenth century it became increasingly difficult for the craft-based unions to maintain traditional restrictions over the training and supply of labour. Thirdly, Post underlines that the alleged ascendancy of the British labour aristocracy in the decades after 1870 actually coincides with the decline of Britain's domination of the world market and the rise of German and US competition. During this period, he argues, wages fell for the entire British working class. Finally, Post writes, '[the] profits earned through the export of British machinery divided by the number of skilled metal-workers "would not have amounted to the average weekly wage of an engineer in Manchester in 1871"'. Overall, Post argues that the flexibility provided to the capitalist class by its receipt of super-profits cannot provide an explanation for the growth of the labour aristocracy from the mid-to-late nineteenth century. Rather, he suggests that it was the high productivity and skill levels of workers in certain Victorian industries that accounts for their high wages (Post, 2010, p. 18).

We may deal with each of these criticisms in turn. Before doing so, however, an important point to note about Post's critique of Marx and Engels is 'that every contemporary political commentator on the phenomenon of the classic, late nineteenth century labour aristocracy not only recognised its existence, but usually predicated part of their political activity on either fostering it (The Liberal Party, Disraeli [with his "one nation" conservatism – ZC]), organising it (the New Model Trade Unions), or fighting its bankrupt political standpoint (the revolutionaries)' (Clough, 1993). Clough considers in this regard the example of the Reform League, a British lobby set up in 1865 under the primary auspices of the First Working Men's International to agitate for universal male suffrage and a secret ballot. Its central committee was made up of six middle class Liberals and six workers. However, despite the efforts of Marx and others, the workers in the organisation quickly gave in to the Liberals' pressure to qualify the demand for universal male suffrage to those men of a certain 'registered and residential' position. This property qualification quite explicitly excluded the mass of workers engaged in unskilled or casual labour from electoral representation. In fact, the new voting system agreed to by the Reform League was introduced in 1868 by Tory Prime Minister Benjamin Disraeli in the clear understanding that the one in five workers it enfranchised would use their votes 'moderately' (*ibid*). In the general election the same year, the Liberal Party attempted to garner the support of the enfranchised upper stratum of English workers by paying them £10 a head to canvass for the Liberals. In response to the blatant bribery nurturing reformism within England's labour elite, Marx wrote:

> The Trades Unions are an aristocratic minority – the poor workers cannot belong to them: the great mass of workers whom economic development is driving from the countryside into the towns every day has long been outside the trades unions – and the most wretched mass has never belonged; the same goes for the workers born in the East End in London; one in 10 belongs to Trades Unions – peasants, day labourers never belong to these societies... The Trades Unions can do nothing by themselves – they will remain a minority – they have no power over the mass of proletarians. (Marx & Engels, 1996, p. 614)

Moreover, Marx found to his chagrin that the leaders of the English working class were unwilling to lend the necessary political support to the Irish independence struggle being conducted by the Fenian movement of the time or even to the more distant Communards of Paris in 1871. It was the distinctly bourgeois politics of the burgeoning British labour aristocracy that finally convinced Marx (Marx & Engels, 1996a) that the overthrow of British capitalism depended, first and foremost, on the liberation of its colonies, in particular, its Irish one.

> For a long time, I believed that it would be possible to overthrow the Irish regime through English working class ascendancy .... Deeper study has convinced me of the opposite. The English working class will never accomplish anything before it has got rid of Ireland .... The lever must be applied in Ireland.

Not only does Post show complete disregard for the evident realities of British politics in the nineteenth century, but his attempt to define the Victorian labour aristocracy out of existence is similarly quixotic. Post is certainly correct that the position of the labour aristocracy was, and is, precarious and in flux. Indeed, as reflected in hidebound theory, it has been a recurrent weakness of the Marxian position on the labour aristocracy to assume that what Marx, Engels and Lenin sometimes suggested in their fragmentary and century-old analyses were its major characteristics, in particular, its being a thin upper stratum of highly skilled and organised male labour *in any given nation*, must remain unchanged. In fact, application of the Marxist method demonstrates how the evolution of the labour aristocracy is intrinsically bound up with the historical development of the class struggle as waged *internationally*, in particular, with the increasing incorporation of super-exploitation into the circuit of capital.

After the depression of 1873, the restructuring of capitalist production signalled the rise of trusts, cartels, syndicates and industrial oligopolies, first in Germany and the United States and then in 'free trade' England and other capitalist nations (Nabudere, 1979, p. 21). By 1880, Britain's unique position as the 'workshop of the world' was being effectively challenged. Thus, while world industrial production increased seven times between 1860 and 1913, British production increased only three times and French production four times as against Germany's seven times, and the United States' twelve times (Stavrianos, 1981, p. 259). Bolstered by the second industrial revolution, Fordist production techniques and state capitalist intervention in the economy, the core capitalist nations sought to use their unprecedented power for imperial expansion. Amin demonstrates that it was during this period that unequal exchange resulting from a global disparity between the rewards of labour (at equal productivity) began to assume increased importance to the capitalist cycle. Between 1880 and 1930, imperialist capital obtained a higher output in the colonised countries by establishing modern facilities and intensifying the exploitation of low-wage labour power there (Amin, 1976, p. 131).

In its own heartlands, as Post highlights, the expanded mechanisation of capitalist production displaced the traditional autonomy and organisational hegemony of the craft union-based early-to-mid-Victorian labour aristocracy. At this time, labour organisation became much broader and more anti-capitalist than it had been previously. However, Post obscures the extent to which capitalism has historically allowed for divisions within the working class to be reformed and recreated in new ways by those groups within it with the necessary sway to influence its development. As such, far from straightforwardly leading to the 'radical decline' of the traditional organisations of the labour aristocracy, the 'technological transformation of the labour-process' (Post, 2010, p. 16) in the mid-to-late nineteenth century established the basis for *new* forms of skilled labour and narrow craft organisation. Thus, Gray (1981, p. 32) writes:

> Attempts to rationalise production were limited by the strength of skilled labour, market conditions and the absence of managerial experience; the prospectuses of inventors and

> entrepreneurs might promise to eliminate independent and wilful skilled men, what actually happened as machinery was introduced is another matter. To accept areas of craft control over production could also appear a more viable strategy than grandiose schemes of rationalisation, especially with the limited character of managerial technique... Although skill is partly a question of bargaining power and cultural attitudes, there were few if any groups of skilled workers whose position did not involve control of some specialised technique indispensable to their employers – that control was indeed the basis of their bargaining power.

Similarly, Davis (1986, pp. 42–43) shows how, in the United States, a corporate assault on the power of skilled labour beginning at the end of the nineteenth century 'broke the power of craftsmen and diluted their skills' but 'carefully avoided "levelling" them into the ranks of the semiskilled' through according them significant economic benefits and cultivating new social norms.

As the number of organised craft workers acting as piece masters and subcontractors dwindled relative to the increasing size of the workforce, the coalition upon which what Hobsbawm (1951, p. 326) has called 'the Liberal-Radical phase of parliamentarism' also declined. Moreover, the extension of the franchise brought the looming prospect of the popular majority voting against the propertied interest. Thus, there began a concerted effort by the British rulers to kill the working class party with kindness, that is in the words of conservative British constitutionalist Sir Walter Bagehot, to 'willingly concede every claim which they can safely concede in order that they may not have to concede unwillingly some claim which would impair the safety of the country' (Bagehot, 2001 [1867], p. 202). With this imperative to the fore, between 1907 and 1911, the British government introduced a series of welfare reforms (most notably the Liberal government's 1909 Finance Bill, the so-called People's Budget, and the 1911 National Insurance Act) that delivered real benefits to the British working class, benefits decidedly denied the indigenous subjects of Britain's overseas Empire.

The periodic unemployment and short-range mobility of workers in the late nineteenth century, contrary to Post, do not make it impossible to identify a body of relatively privileged workers. For example, whilst painters were a low-paid and casualised trade, 'joiners, bricklayers and masons, despite vulnerability to seasonal unemployment, often appear in the better-paid and more secure section of the working class' (Gray, 1981, p. 23). Clough (1992, p. 19) notes that, on average, unemployment was three times higher for the unskilled than for the skilled worker. Although there were both continuities and discontinuities within the labour aristocracy – based on geography, ideology, gender and ethnicity – there is no doubt that British trade and industry in the mid-to-late nineteenth century was characterised by specific groups of workers having divergent levels of pay, economic security and measures of control in the immediate work situation (Gray, 1981). It was these better-off workers who furnished the support base and leadership of the British trade union movement of the time. In 1885, Engels (1977) wrote:

> [The] great Trade Unions [are] the organisations of those trades in which the labour of grown-up men predominates, or is alone applicable. Here the competition neither of women or children nor of machinery has so far weakened their organised strength. The engineers, the carpenters and joiners, the bricklayers are each of them a power to the extent that as in the case of the bricklayers and bricklayers' labourers, they can even successfully resist the introduction of machinery... They form an aristocracy among the working class; they have succeeded in enforcing for themselves a relatively comfortable position, and they accept it as final. They are the model workingmen of Messrs Leone Levi and Giffen, and they are very nice people nowadays to deal with, for any sensible capitalist in particular and for the whole capitalist class in general.

How was the economic welfare and conservative political conformity of this most 'aristocratic' section of the working class afforded? Quite straightforwardly, the economic and political benefits accruing to the skilled working class of Victorian England were directly attributable to their exceptional position in the international division of labour at the time, that is to British colonial imperialism.

> If we look at the sectors where skilled workers and their organisation were strongest, we find them to be closely connected to Empire: textiles, iron and steel, engineering, and coal. Textiles because of the cheap cotton from Egypt, and a captive market in India; iron and steel because of ship-building and railway exports, engineering because of the imperialist arms industry, and coal because of the demands of Britain's monopoly of world shipping. In a myriad of different ways, the conditions of the labour aristocracy were bound up with the maintenance of British imperialism. And this fact was bound to be reflected in their political standpoint. (Clough, 1993)

Post's apolitical and narrowly national explanation of the aristocratic traits of the leading craft-unions thus ignores their basis in Britain's *global* ascendancy. For it was not simply its skills, its productivity or the forms of its industrial organisations which afforded the upper stratum of British labour its middle class privileges, but its centripetal position in the labour markets and political apparatus established through imperialism.

Post's claim of increasing immiseration for British workers in the last quarter of the nineteenth century is also open to challenge. In fact, during this period, as a corollary to vastly improved transportation, increased primary goods exports and super-exploitative conditions in colonial markets, the wages of Britain's domestic working class improved. Thus, wages measured against prices rose by 26% in the 1870s, 21% in the 1880s, while slowing down to 11% in the 1890s (Clough, 1992, p. 19; Halevy, 1939, p. 133). Certainly, much of these improved circumstances disproportionately benefitted the skilled upper stratum of workers, the labour aristocracy of the time. This subset of the British workforce earned perhaps double that of its unskilled counterpart, a large proportion of which was barely able to feed its families. Indeed, a study by Liberal economic theorist Sir Leo Chiozza-Money in 1905, *Riches and Poverty*, found that out of a British population of 43 million, 33 million lived in poverty and 13 million in destitution (cited in Clough, 1992, p. 20). Yet even within the latter group, there were important gradations of income unconducive to working class unity. Halevy (1939, p. 133) highlights how the benefits of colonialism came not to be restricted only to a small section of British workers:

> [The fall in]... current prices [resulting from British monopoly capital's colonial trade] had enabled a very large body to come into existence among the British proletariat, able to keep up a standard of living almost identical with that of the middle class. The self-respecting workman in the North of England wanted to own his own cottage and garden, in Lancashire his piano. His life was insured. If he shared the common English failing and was a gambler, prone to bet too highly on horses... the rapid growth of savings banks proved that he was nevertheless learning the prudence of the middle class.

The phenomenon of falling prices bringing middle class living standards and, hence, middle class *aspirations* to metropolitan workers was noted as early as 1903 by US sociologist and economist Thorstein Veblen:

> The workers do not seek to displace their managers; they seek to emulate them. They themselves acquiesce in the general judgment that the work they do is somehow less 'dignified' than the work of their masters, and their goal is not to rid themselves of a superior class but to climb up to it. (cf. Heilbroner, 1980, pp. 230–231)

At the dawn of the imperialist era, super-profits generated by imperialism trickled down to the broad urban masses of the advanced countries, stimulating new needs therein, including

> soap, margarine, chocolate, cocoa and rubber tires for bicycles. All of these commodities required large-scale imports from tropical regions, which in turn necessitated local infrastructures of harbours, railways, steamers, trucks, warehouses, machinery and telegraph and postal systems. Such infrastructures required order and security to ensure adequate dividends to shareholders. Hence the clamour for annexation if local conflicts disrupted the flow of trade, or if a neighbouring colonial power threatened to expand. (Stavrianos, 1981, p. 262)

Clearly, as Stavrianos suggests, and given the very public promotion of social-imperialist doctrines and practices, if the economy provided jobs, rising living standards and a strong sense of national identity to the citizens of the colonial powers, these were not likely to passively accept rival countries affecting the flow of super-profits, hence the aforementioned 'clamour' for annexation. The clamour was, of course, amplified to a deafening din by the imperialist politicians and ideological state apparati, then as today (Cope, 2012, p. 105; Diamond, 2006; Mackenzie, 1987; Schneider, 1982).

Post's claim of falling wages for the entire British working class in the last quarter of the nineteenth century is fallacious. Although wages were a diminishing portion of national income, measured in real terms, they *improved* for the British working class, especially for its skilled, unionised members (Stavrianos, 1981, pp. 266–267).

> Whether the real wages of the British working class rose or fell during the early years of the Industrial Revolution in the late 18th and early 19th centuries remains a disputed issue. A definitive answer is difficult because the large-scale urbanisation accompanying industrialisation altered the structure of worker consumption, as, for example, by the introduction of rent for lodging. But there is no question about the steady rise of real wages in the second half of the 19th century. The following figures show that between 1850 and 1913 real wages in Britain and France almost doubled.[4]

It may be argued that the rising purchasing power of wages depicted here merely indicates that British workers were receiving some of the benefits from the increased productivity of *domestic* labour employed in those industries producing workers' consumption goods (Table 1). Rising British wages are in this regard perfectly consistent with an increased domestic rate

Table 1. Rising real wages in Northwestern Europe, 1850–1913 (1913 = 100).

Year	Great Britain	France	Germany	Russia
1850	57	59.5	–	–
1860	64	63	–	–
1870	70	69	51.8	–
1880	81	74.5	59	–
1890	90	89.5	71.8	53.5
1900	100	100	78	49.5

Sources: Stavrianos (1981, pp. 266–267); Sternberg (1951, p. 27); Broadberry and Burhop (2009); Allen (2003, p. 37).

of surplus value or exploitation (this being the ratio between the *necessary* labour time required to produce workers' consumption goods and the *surplus* labour time workers expend beyond that) (see below). Yet it must be understood that greater productivity in industries producing workers' consumption goods may come from two distinct sources. First, it may be the result of their more intensive exploitation, that is of their being paid less absolutely to activate the *same* materialised composition of capital. Second, it may result from their being paid proportionately less to activate a *greater* materialised composition of capital. Scientific and technical improvements lead to cheapened production costs for workers consumption goods and, hence, a decrease in necessary as opposed to surplus labour. Capitalists will introduce new technological advances to the production process if the amount of labour expended on producing labour-saving machinery is less than the amount of labour displaced by its introduction.

Mechanisation, however, involves substituting living (value-creating) labour for dead labour and, hence, constitutes a growing restriction on the rate of surplus value and the rate of profit. As such, capitalists must strive to increase productivity *without* proportionate wage increases. Nonetheless, if British workers were wholly responsible for producing their own consumption goods, it could properly be said that rising British wages in the Victorian era represented returns to British labour according to increased domestic exploitation, possibly as forced upon capitalists by working class militancy. This explanation for rising British wages, however, ignores the extent to which they were, in fact, afforded by an increase in the proportion of workers' consumption goods produced by *colonial* labour.

Between 1870 and 1913, merchandise imports to Britain increased from £279 million to £719 million, and with it the country's trade deficit from £33 million to £82 million (Clough, 1992, p. 18; Michell & Deane, 1962, pp. 828–829, 872–873). As Patnaik notes, the rising consumption of sugar, beverages, rice, cotton and wheat by West Europeans at this time depended heavily on unpaid import surpluses from colonial countries (Patnaik, 1999). Thus, although the outsourcing of the production of workers consumption goods to oppressed nations occurred on a much smaller scale during the last three decades of the nineteenth century than it has during recent times, the rising real wage of British workers at that time is in no small measure attributable to their receipt of colonial *loot*. A primary reason for nineteenth century British wages falling relative to gross domestic product (GDP) but rising in terms of purchasing power is that value was being transferred from colonial societies wherein the (then largely rural) workforce was on the losing side of the international class struggle.

Whilst most left theorists have for a long time fallen into the habit of gauging exploitation on a *national(ist)* basis, commonly examining wages in relation to profits in the rich countries (and thereby 'proving' that the most exploited workers in the world are those of the developed nations), in the context of global imperialism, value creation and distribution must be examined as an *international* process.

As Smith correctly argues, 'GDP, which claims to be a measure of the wealth produced in a nation, is in reality, a measure of the wealth captured by a nation' (Smith, 2010). As such, GDP is expanded by surplus value extracted from workers in low-wage countries and is not a valid measure of 'gross domestic product', since it may rise or decline independently of (domestic) labour's share of it. Commodities produced by low-wage workers in the labour-intensive export industries obtain correspondingly low prices internationally. However, as soon as these goods enter into imperialist-country markets, their prices are multiplied several fold, sometimes by as much as 1000%. As Chossudovsky notes, 'value added' is thus 'artificially created within the services economy of the rich countries without any material production taking place' (Chossudovsky, 2003, p. 80). Jedlicki (2007), meanwhile, observes that 'value added' already incorporates those wage and capital differentials which some Western socialists aim to justify in the name of superior First World 'productivity'. In doing so, 'a demonstration is carried out by using as proof what constitutes, precisely, the object of demonstration'.

Post (2010, p. 24) observes that '[i]n the United States today, real wages for both union and non-union workers have fallen, and are about 11% below their 1973 level, despite strong growth beginning in the mid 1980s'. By measuring wages against GDP figures and reported profits, Post intends to convince his readership that the living standards of the US working class have been declining and that a renewed offensive against capital would entitle them to a greater share of the wealth they ostensibly create. However, there are at least two problems with the idea that US wages have fallen.

Firstly, whilst wages in the United States have indeed fallen since 1973 as a proportionate share of GDP, in real terms the poor in that country were better off in 1999 than they were in 1975. For example, Cox and Alm (1999) show that whereas in 1971 31.8% of *all* US households had air-conditioners, in 1994 49.6% of households *below the poverty line* had air-conditioners. These authors also demonstrate that the United States poor in 1999 had more refrigerators, dishwashers, clothes dryers, microwaves, televisions, college educations and personal computers than they did in 1971. Wages decidedly did *not* shrink, then, relative to the purchasing power necessary to consume these items.

US economists Meyer and Sullivan (2011) have constructed a measure of consumption which challenges mainstream assessments of declining US living standards. They note that most income-based analyses of economic well-being in the United States do not reflect the full range of available household consumption resources such as, for example, food stamps, or lessened marginal tax rates. Second, they demonstrate that official statistics account for inflation using a price index which reflects a cumulative upward trend based on substitution bias, outlet bias, quality bias and new-product bias. Third, official government income measures fail to reflect important components of economic well-being such as consumed wealth, the ownership of durables such as houses and cars or the insurance value of government programs. Thus, a retired couple who own their own home and live off savings, for example, are income-poor but may still be materially well-off. Taking into account the flawed methodologies of official reports on declining US household income, the authors construct a very different picture of US living standards:

> Our results show evidence of considerable improvement in material well-being for both the middle class and the poor [in the US] over the past three decades. Median income and consumption both rose by more than 50 percent in real terms between 1980 and 2009. In addition, the middle 20 percent of the income distribution experienced noticeable improvements in housing characteristics: living units became bigger and much more likely to have air conditioning and other features. The quality of the cars these families own also improved considerably. Similarly, we find strong evidence of improvement in the material well-being of poor families. After incorporating taxes and noncash benefits and adjusting for bias in standard price indices, we show that the tenth percentile of the income distribution grew by 44 percent between 1980 and 2009. Even this measure, however, understates improvements at the bottom. The tenth percentile of the consumption distribution grew by 54 percent during this period. In addition, for those in the bottom income quintile, living units became bigger, and the fraction with any air conditioning doubled. The share of households with amenities such as a dishwasher or clothes dryer also rose noticeably.

Nor, indeed, did US incomes decline relative to the costs of those items necessary to the reproduction of the worker as such (the 'value of labour-power', in Marxist terms). Thus, between 1970 and 1997, the real price of a food basket containing one pound of ground beef, one dozen eggs, three pounds of tomatoes, one dozen oranges, one pound of coffee, one pound of beans, half a gallon of milk, five pounds of sugar, one pound of bacon, one pound of lettuce, one pound of onions and one pound of bread fell so that it took 26% less of the workers' time to buy it (*ibid*, pp. 40–41).

It may be argued that several of these items are almost exclusively produced within the United States and that, therefore, it is the increased productivity of US agriculture that accounts for the relative cheapness of these goods over time. Certainly, tomatoes, oranges, carrots, onions, milk, bread and other foodstuffs are produced in great quantities within US borders. However, it must be understood that US agricultural production is heavily subsidised by the government. Indeed, half of the value of all Organisation for Economic Co-Operation and Development (OECD) agriculture, according to OECD estimates, consists of government subsidies (Patnaik, 2007, p. 44). As she explains:

> Since these are rich industrial countries where the farm sector employs less than 5 percent of full time workers and correspondingly contributes 4 percent or less to GDP, they can easily afford to give budgetary support to the extent of 2–3 percent of GDP, which amounts to half or more of the total value of agricultural output. In India where agriculture employs two thirds of the workers and contributes over a quarter of GDP, a similar order of support would not be possible even if every single rupee of central government revenues went to agriculture alone. (*ibid*, p. 43)

Second, Patnaik (2007, p. 25) notes that as much as 60–70% of Northern food items have tropical or sub-tropical import content. Finally, the developed world's investment in agriculture, including in the fossil fuel, chemical and machine production which facilitates its great productivity, is in part made possible by the economic buoyancy guaranteed by the import of large quantities of surplus value from the underdeveloped world (Cope, 2012). More generally, it is the globalisation of production which plays the major role in cheapening the costs of the reproduction of labour power in the developed countries and, hence, the apparent surfeit of surplus labour performed by production workers therein.

According to the International Monetary Fund, although OECD labour's share of GDP decreased, the globalisation of labour in the last three decades 'as manifested in cheaper imports in advanced economies' has increased the 'size of the pie' to be shared amongst citizens there and thus a net gain in total workers' real compensation (IMF, 2007, p. 179). Smith (2008, pp. 10–11) notes that

> WEO 2007 estimates that between 1980 and 2003, real, terms-of-trade adjusted wages of unskilled workers (defined as those with less than university-level education) in the US increased by 14%, and that around half of this improvement resulted from falling prices of imported consumer goods… [Broda and Romalis (2008)] calculate that 4/5 of the total inflation-lowering effect of cheap imports is accounted for by cheap Chinese imports, these having risen during the decade [1994 to 2004] from 6% to 17% of all US imports, and that "the rise of Chinese trade ... alone can offset around a third of the rise in official inequality we have seen over this period".[5]

In the United Kingdom, declines in the cost of living during the past decade are similarly attributable to trade with China.[6] The important point to note here is that a fall in wages relative to GDP does not by itself account for the purchasing power of said wage, nor, crucially, need it compensate for the transferred surplus value (super-profits) inhering in the average OECD wage.

To return to Post's critique of Marx and Engels, the author goes awry in claiming that the United States and German challenge to Britain's monopolistic position on the world market could only have led to lower standards of living for British workers. It is true that British capital's pre-eminence was profoundly challenged by the rise of monopoly capitalism in Germany and the United States between the 1870s and World War I (WWI). Furthermore, as Hobsbawm notes, the effective end of Britain's industrial monopoly eroded those 'economic devices which created a satisfied "aristocracy of labour" ... automatically (that is, without the deliberate adoption of reformist policies)' (Hobsbawm, 1951, p. 328). However, British capitalism's inherent need to expand remained undiminished. On the contrary, to better compete with its imperialist rivals, Britain escalated its extraction of surplus labour embodied in colonial foods and raw materials but, crucially, never paid for in colonial wages. In doing so, Britain was able to supplement the consumption of its own workforce, still at that time exploited in the main, at the expense of that in the colonised nations. By what means did British colonialism drain surplus from the colonial world?

State-guaranteed colonial investments made through qualified solicitors and bankers (largely self-financed in India where exports exceeded imports by some £4 million per year in the 1850s) had steadily increased throughout the 'classical' era of capitalism so that by 1870 36% of British overseas capital was in the Empire alongside half the annual flow (Barratt Brown, 1974, pp. 133–138). Later, Britain increased its level of foreign investment by an average £660 million every decade between 1870 and the outbreak of WWI (Nabudere, 1979, p. 64). Its net annual foreign investment between 1870 and 1914 was a then unprecedented one-third of its capital accumulation and 15% of the total wealth of its Empire (cf. Edelstein, 1981, pp. 70–72; Hehn, 2002, p. 135). According to Elsenhans, the percentage of total capital exported to the world economy's periphery up to 1914 was as follows: Britain, 37.9%; France, 34.5%; Germany, 31.1% and United States, 54% (Elsenhans, 1983; cf. Feis, 1930, pp. 23, 46, 70; Woodruff, 1975, p. 340). Later, in the highly protectionist interwar period when nearly half of Britain's trade was with its dominions and colonies and one-third of France's exports went to its colonies (Hehn, 2002, p. 145), the imperial powers (not including a Germany stripped of her colonies) could use super-profits to purchase social peace.

Overseas investment greatly facilitated Britain's capital exports. The £600 million invested in overseas railway building between 1907 and 1914, for example, created a captured market for iron, steel and rolling stock. It also worked to cheapen the (transportation) costs of food and raw materials (Clough, 1993, p. 17), thus reducing the costs of British constant *and* variable capital, and buoying profit rates.[7] Moreover, enforced bilateral 'trade' with the colonies financed much of this capital export. The core nations of Europe and North America increased their purchase of raw materials and foodstuffs from the oppressed nations in the decades before WWI, maintaining a constant excess of merchandise imports over exports (Frank, 1979, p. 190). By 1928, Europe had a net export deficit of US$2.9 billion which was offset by the colonial world's merchandise export surplus of US$1.5 billion.

> In [1913] the British government exported merchandises valued at £635 million and had imports totalling £769 million. In addition it imported gold worth £24 million and thus had an import surplus of £158 million in the movement of merchandise and gold. To offset this deficit, the British had items totalling £129 million (from earnings of the merchant marine £94, earnings of traders' commission £25, other earnings £10 million). The British thus would have a deficit of £29 million, except for interest and dividends from their investments abroad, which amounted to £210 million. Addition of this item to other 'invisible' exports reversed the balance of payments in favour of the United Kingdom, giving it a net surplus of £181 million. Theoretically, the British could take this balance in increased imports of merchandise and still have the balance of payments in equilibrium. Actually, they left the whole net balance abroad as new investment. In fact, in 1913, London advanced to colonial and foreign concerns long-term loans for £198 million – almost exactly the amount of the current profits from investments abroad. (Woytinsky & Woytinsky, 1955, p. 199)

Effectively, then, British imperialism's trade deficits with the colonies financed much of its overseas capital investment. British re-investment in foreign and colonial ventures of nearly £200 million in 1913 may thus be compared to its export deficit and import surplus of £158 million in the same year, representing pure profit of which India alone contributed two-fifths (Frank, 1979, pp. 192–193).

These sums may also be compared with the profit required to subvent the labour aristocracy. Let us assume that Britain's 1.5 million unionised workers in 1892, representing 11% of all British workers in trade and industry, constituted the core of the labour aristocracy of the time (with the very partial exception of the miners, unskilled unions were then negligible)

(Clough, 1992, p. 20). Skilled workers in 1900 could expect an average weekly wage of 40s (£104 annually). Since these earned almost double that of unskilled workers, we will take the 'excess' annual wage of the labour aristocracy to amount to £52 annually, a total wage bill for the group of £78 million per annum. At £59.2 million in 1913 (Frank, 1979, pp. 192–193), it is likely that at least three quarters of this total can be accounted for by Britain's trade deficit with India alone. Post errs, then, in examining profits from foreign investments and machinery exports as the sole measure of British parasitism. More crucially, his narrow focus on profit levels is indicative of his glaring indifference to the extraction of *surplus value*, that is, to exploitation *per se*.

According to Marx, during the time they are employed, production workers spend part of their day reproducing the value of the goods necessary to their own reproduction, that is, the cost of their own labour power (or *variable capital*). Marx calls this *necessary labour*. For the rest of the working day, these workers produce value exceeding that of their labour power, what Marx called *surplus value* (the combined value of gross domestic investment, the non-productive or service sector and profits). The *rate of surplus value* (or of exploitation) is the ratio of surplus labour to necessary labour or of surplus value to the value of variable capital. Fundamentally, however, capitalists are not interested in creating surplus value, but in generating *profit*. Profit, as the unpaid labour time of the worker appropriated by the capitalist as measured against total capital invested, must be properly distinguished from surplus value. In bourgeois accounting terms, profit is simply the excess of sales revenue over the cost of producing the goods sold.

Thus, the price of production of a commodity does not directly correspond to its value within a single industry or group of industries (Marx, 1977b, pp. 758–759). Rather, as capital is withdrawn from industries with low rates of profit and invested in those with higher rates, output and supply in the former declines and its prices rise above the actual sums of value and surplus value the industry produces, and conversely. As a result, competing capitals using different magnitudes of value-creating labour ultimately sell commodities at average prices. As a result, surplus value is distributed more or less uniformly across the branches of production. An *average rate of profit* is formed by competing capitals' continuous search for higher rates of profit and the flight of capital to and from those industrial sectors producing commodities in high or low demand. Overall, where one commodity sells for less than its value, there is a corresponding sale of another commodity for more than its value.

This equalisation of profit rates under capitalism ensures that surplus value does not necessarily adhere to the particular industry (or territory, given international restrictions on the mobility of capital and/or labour) in which it was created. Instead, surplus value is transferred *from* those industries (or territories) providing less socially necessary labour *to* those providing more. Thus, even branches of production which may enjoy the same rate of exploitation, that is, the same underpayment of the workforce for the value produced by its labour, will have different rates of profit depending upon the organic composition of capital involved in the production process.[8] Capitals equal in size yield profits equal in size, no matter where the investment is made or how the capital is shared between constant and variable capital (or, indeed, between capitalists and workers).

As Marx (1977a, p. 238) recognised, though purely at the level of divergent international 'productivity' levels, super-profits derived from foreign trade enter into the rate of profit as such:

> Capitals invested in foreign trade can yield a higher rate of profit, because, in the first place, there is competition with commodities produced in other countries with inferior production facilities, so that the more advanced country sells its goods above their value even though cheaper than the competing countries. *In so far as the labour of the more advanced country is here realised as labour of a higher specific weight, the rate of profit rises, because labour which has not been paid as being of a higher quality is sold as such.* The same may obtain in relation to the country, to which commodities are exported and to that from which commodities are imported; namely, the latter may offer more materialised labour in kind than it receives, and yet thereby receive commodities cheaper than it could produce them. Just as a manufacturer who employs a new invention before it becomes generally used, undersells his competitors and yet sells his commodity above its individual value, that is, realises the specifically higher productiveness of the labour he employs as surplus-labour. He thus secures a surplus-profit. As concerns capitals invested in colonies, etc., on the other hand, they may yield higher rates of profit for the simple reason that the rate of profit is higher there due to backward development, and likewise the exploitation of labour, because of the use of slaves, coolies, etc. Why should not these higher rates of profit, realised by capitals invested in certain lines and sent home by them, enter into the equalisation of the general rate of profit and thus tend, *pro tanto*, to raise it, unless it is the monopolies that stand in the way. There is so much less reason for it, since these spheres of investment of capital are subject to the laws of free competition. (my emphasis)

My own definition of super-profits, accounting for global divergences in *the rate of exploitation at equivalent levels of productivity*, is the extra or above average surplus value the metropolitan capitalist countries extort from workers in colonial or neocolonial countries by means of capital export imperialism, debt servitude and unequal exchange (Cope, 2012).

IN DEFENCE OF LENIN ON THE LABOUR ARISTOCRACY

For Lenin, Zinoviev and the Bolsheviks, super-exploitation (the lower than average return to nationally oppressed wage labour, often at levels insufficient for their households to reproduce their labour power) generates super-profits which may be used to supplement the 'wages' of core-nation workers. According to Lenin (1970 [1916]), it is not only capitalists who benefit from imperialism:

> The export of capital, one of the most essential economic bases of imperialism, still more completely isolates the rentiers from production and sets the seal of parasitism *on the whole country* that lives by exploiting the labour of several overseas countries and colonies. (my emphasis)

Super-profits derived from imperialism allow the globally predominant bourgeoisie to pay inflated wages to sections of the proletariat, sections who thus derive a material stake in the preservation of the capitalist system.

> [In] all the civilised, advanced countries the bourgeoisie rob – either by colonial oppression or by financially extracting "gain" from formally independent weak countries – they rob a population many times larger than that of "their own" country. This is the economic factor that enables the imperialist bourgeoisie to obtain super-profits, part of which is used to bribe the top section of the proletariat and convert it into a reformist, opportunist petty bourgeoisie that fears revolution. (Lenin, 1963 [1918], p. 433)

Although not articulated as such by any of the writers Post criticises, there are several pressing reasons why the *haute-bourgeoisie* in command of the heights of the global capitalist economy engages in such 'bribery' (sic), even where it is not forced to by militant trade union struggle within the metropoles. *Economically*, the *embourgeoisement* of First World workers has provided oligopolies – that is those few giant firms dominating key industries – with the secure and thriving consumer markets necessary to capital's expanded reproduction. *Politically*, the stability of pro-imperialist polities with a working class majority is of paramount concern to cautious investors and their representatives in government. *Militarily*, a pliant and/or quiescent workforce furnishes both the national chauvinist personnel required to enforce global hegemony and a secure base from which to launch the subjugation of Third World territories. Finally, *ideologically*, the lifestyles and cultural mores enjoyed by most First World workers signify to the Third World not what benefits imperialism brings, but what capitalist industrial development and parliamentary democracy alone can achieve (Cope, 2012, p. 30).

In receiving a share of super-profits, a sometimes fraught alliance is forged between workers and capitalists in the world's core nations. As long ago as 1919, when global wage scaling was nowhere near so marked as today, the first congress of the Communist International (COMINTERN) adopted a resolution, agreed on by all of the major leaders of the world Communist movement of the time, which read:

> At the expense of the plundered colonial peoples capital corrupted its wage slaves, created a community of interest between the exploited and the exploiters as against the oppressed colonies – the yellow, black, and red colonial people – and chained the European and American working class to the imperialist 'fatherland'. (Degras, 1956, p. 18)

Post (2010, pp. 18–21) challenges this compelling interpretation of the roots of opportunism, reformism and national chauvinism amongst core-nation workers, suggesting that profits earned in the global South by US transnational corporations today are negligible compared to the total wage bill of the US working class.

> Imperialist investment, particularly in the global South, represents a tiny portion of global capitalist investment even today, in the era of globalisation. Foreign direct investment made up only 5% of total world-investment prior to 2000–95% of total capitalist investment took place within the boundaries of each industrialised country. Nearly three-quarters of total foreign direct investment flowed from one industrialised country – one part of the global North – to another. Less than 2% of total world-investment flowed from the global North to the global South. It is not surprising that the global South accounted for only 20% of global manufacturing output, mostly in labour-intensive industries such as clothing, shoes, automobile-parts, and simple electronics. The rapid growth of transnational corporate investment in China in the last decade has changed this picture, but only slightly. Foreign direct investment as a percentage of global gross fixed-capital formation jumped from 2.5% in 1982, to 4.1% in 1990 to 9.7% in 2005. The percentage of foreign direct investment flowing to the global North fell from 82.5% in 1990 to 59.4% in 2005. However, the global South still only accounts for less than 4% of global fixed-capital formation. While China has led the growth of transnational capital-accumulation, the bulk of the capital invested in China remains in labour-intensive manufacturing – the low and medium end of transnational corporate organised global-production chains.
>
> Even accepting [that as much as 50% of repatriated foreign profits of US companies emanate from the global South] profits earned from investment in the global South make up a tiny fraction of the total wages of workers in the global North... Total profits earned by US companies abroad exceeded 4% of total US wages only once before 1995 – in 1979. Foreign profits as a percentage of total US wages rose above 5% only in 1997, 2000 and 2002, and rose slightly over 6% in 2003. If we hold to our estimate that half of total foreign profits are earned from investment in the global South, only 1–2% of total

> US wages for most of the nearly 50 years prior to 1995 – and only 2–3% of total US wages in the 1990s – came from profits earned in Africa, Asia and Latin America. Such proportions are hardly sufficient to explain the 37% wage differential between secretaries in advertising agencies and machinists working on oil pipelines, or the 64% wage differential between janitors in restaurants and bars and automobile workers.

Post is here reiterating the familiar view amongst Western economists, socialist and otherwise, that the super-exploitation of Third World labour is today entirely marginal to capital accumulation on a world scale. Thus, economist Raphael Schaub writes: 'The data reveals that most of the FDI stock is owned by and is invested in developed countries… FDI stock and flows have increasingly been concentrating in the industrialized countries since the 1960s' (Schaub, 2004, pp. 26–27). British socialists Ashman and Callinicos concur that 'the transnational corporations that dominate global capitalism tends to concentrate their investment (and trade) in the advanced economies … Capital continues largely to shun the global South' (Ashman & Callinicos, 2006, p. 125). However, Smith (2007) provides the following reasons as to why this interpretation, based as it is 'on an uncritical regurgitation of deeply misleading headline statistics' is wrong and how 'far from "shunning" the global South, northern capital is embracing it and is becoming ever more dependent on the super-exploitation of southern low-wage labour'.

Firstly, nearly 50% of manufacturing foreign direct investment (FDI) is received by the developing economies (US$82.1 billion between 2003 and 2005 compared with US$83.7 billion to developed countries). Meanwhile, FDI within the developed world is hugely inflated by non-productive 'finance and business' activities (US$185 billion, or more than twice the inward flow of manufacturing in the period cited) (United Nations Conference on Trade and Development [UNCTAD], 2007, p. 227). Moreover, intra-OECD manufacturing (particularly in those Transnational Corporations (TNCs) which have offshored or outsourced much of their production processes to low-wage nations) is heavily dependent upon capital infusions from the Third World. Smith cites the example of the restructuring of Royal Dutch Shell having increased the United Kingdom's inward FDI by US$100 billion even though nearly all of Shell's oil (and, he adds, profit) production takes place in Latin America, Central Asia and the Middle East. Post's citation of the low level of global fixed capital formation that takes place in the global South, moreover, suggests a misunderstanding of the purpose of imperialism, namely, to siphon and extort surplus value from foreign territories (Grossman, 1992). That imperialism is moribund, that is that it holds back the full potential development of the productive forces, has long been noted by its critics. Thus, where oligopolies dominate Third World markets, there is not the same urgent imperative to replace cheap labour with expensive machinery.

Secondly, whilst the United States, Europe and Japan (the 'Triad' powers) invest in each other at roughly equivalent rates, there is no investment flow from the Third World to the developed world to match investment from the latter to the former. Whereas '[r]epatriated profits flow in both directions between the United States, Europe and Japan, between these "Triad" nations and the global South the flow is one-way' (Smith, 2007, p. 15). So much is this the case that profit repatriation from South to North now regularly exceeds new North–South FDI flows. Jalée (1968, p. 76) has earlier described this process of 'decapitalising' the Third World:

> [There] are many well-meaning people, both in the imperialist countries and the Third World, who still have illusions as to the usefulness of private investment in the underdeveloped countries. It is simple to make the following calculation. A foreign private enterprise sets up in a Third World country where it makes a regular, yearly profit of 10% on its investment. If the whole of these profits are transferred abroad, at the end of the tenth year an amount equal to the original investment will have been exported. From the eleventh year onwards, the receiving country will be exporting currency which it has not received; in twenty years it will have exported twice as much, etc. If the rate of profit is 20% instead of 10% the outflow will begin twice as early. If only half the profits are exported the process will be only half as rapid. This example is a somewhat oversimplified hypothesis, but reflects reality. There is no end to the loss [of Third World capital] through such outflows, except [through] nationalisation or socialisation of the enterprises.

Smith also makes the point that much supposed 'South–South' FDI is, in fact, 'North–South' FDI (Smith, 2007). Not only is it the case that United States and United Kingdom TNCs using profits earned in one Third World country to finance investments in another show the FDI as originating in the former (Lipsey, 2006, p. 3), but 10% of Southern FDI originates from the British Virgin Islands, the Cayman Islands and other offshore tax havens and, hence, likely originates from imperialist sources.

Thirdly, FDI flows are purely quantitative and say nothing about the type of economic activity they are connected to. As such, mergers and acquisitions, merely representing a change in ownership, should be distinguished from 'greenfield' FDI in new plant and machinery. Whilst intra-OECD FDI is dominated by mergers and acquisitions activity, between 2000 and 2006, 51% of all Greenfield FDI was North–South (UNCTAD, 2007, p. 206).

Fourthly, and perhaps most significantly for the present purposes, undue fixation on FDI flows as a means of calculating the value of imperialist super-exploitation to the capitalist system and the wealth of the developed nations ensures that obscured from view are the tens of thousands of Third World-owned factories whose hundreds of millions of workers supply inexpensive intermediate inputs and cheap consumer goods to the imperialist countries via the vertical integration of production (Smith, 2007, p. 18). Rather than FDI being the major means of securing this supply, outsourcing and subcontracting by TNCs has become a prevailing mode of monopolistic capital accumulation in recent decades.

Finally, data on FDI stocks and flows are given in dollars converted from national currencies at current exchange rates. However, a dollar invested in a Third World country typically buys much more resources than a dollar invested in the First World. Measuring the value of Southern FDI in Purchasing Power Parity (PPP) dollars, we find that UNCTAD totals must be multiplied by a factor of 2.6 (the weighted average PPP coefficient between the OECD and non-OECD countries). Furthermore, as Harvie and de Angelis highlight, whereas in the United States $20 commands one hour of labour time, *in India the same US$20 is sufficient to put ten people to work each for ten hours* (Harvie & de Angelis, 2004). Thus, between 1997 and 2002, some US$3.4 billion of intra-imperialist FDI flows commanded 190 billion labour hours at just under US$18 per hour. Meanwhile, some US$800 billion of FDI flowing into the Third World commanded 330 billion hours at US$2.4 per hour (an average labour cost ratio of 7.5:1). As such, the 19% of the global total of FDI that went from the North to the South in this period *comprised 63% of total 'labour commanded'* (*ibid*).

Post's acceptance of capitalist accounting figures at face value, that is, without critiquing their real world significance in terms of average socially necessary labour and surplus labour (Cope, 2012), can only lead him to the absurd positions that (a) the world's largest capitals have practically no interest in the Third World and (b) that the most exploited workers in the world (i.e. those whose higher productivity supposedly generates the biggest profits) are also the world's richest. Thus, in an article for the Trotskyist Fourth International, Post writes that 'global wage differentials are the result of the greater capital intensity (organic composition of capital) and higher productivity of labour (rate of surplus value) in the advanced capitalist social formations, not some sharing of "super profits" between capital and labour in the industrialized countries. Put simply, the better paid workers of the "north" are more exploited than the poorly paid workers of the "south"'.[9] Post shows complete disregard for the massive infusions of capital which result from global surplus value transfer and the all-too obvious facts of Northern working consumption goods being the product of super-exploited Third World labour. For Post, the North's purportedly greater 'capital intensity' and its workers higher 'productivity' may as well have dropped from the sky.

OLIGOPOLY AND GLOBAL WAGE DIFFERENTIALS

Post's third and final version of the labour aristocracy thesis is that presented by Elbaum and Seltzer. They argue that the severely limited competition faced by oligopolies and large-scale industrial concerns means that these can secure higher-than-average profits (the authors' singular definition of super-profits) which allow them to afford their unionised workers higher wages and benefits and more secure employment than their counterparts in the 'marginal' industries, in the retail and services sector, in agriculture and amongst the under- and un-employed.

In refuting this thesis, Post cites studies which demonstrate the absence of a strong correlation between industrial concentration and higher-than-average profits and wages. Instead, for Post, the lower wages of female and black and minority ethnic workers can be explained by capitalists' recruiting them into the more labour-intensive industries. The stratification of labour, then, is based on how 'competition and accumulation – not monopoly – continually differentiate in terms of technique, profitability, and wages and working conditions' (Post, 2010, pp. 27–28). As such, profit and wage differentials are rooted in differences in labour productivity. It is not, then, that workers in unionised capital-intensive industries share in their oligopolistic employers' super-profits, but that their higher-than-average wages may be accounted for by the lower unit costs of these industries and effective, militant union organisation.

Tellingly, Post is entirely oblivious to the lower unit costs of non-OECD manufacturing. Smith (2010, p. 215) tabulates data from the World Bank (2006) showing value added versus labour costs between 1995 and 1999 for 64 countries. This table demonstrates that unit labour costs (i.e. the average cost of labour per unit of output) are an average 1.6 times lower for non-OECD manufacturing workers than OECD manufacturing workers. Thus, if an OECD worker is paid $1 for an hour's work and creates $20 worth of output in that hour, a non-OECD worker paid at the same rate would create $32 worth of output in that hour. Obviously, OECD wages are greatly in excess of non-OECD wages, by around 1000%, so one hour of OECD labour appears to generate much more value added than one hour of non-OECD labour. Nonetheless, in purely price-based terms, terms abstracted from the ratio between what Marxists call necessary and surplus labour, non-OECD manufacturing workers are 60% more exploited (more 'productive') than OECD workers.

Post is certainly correct, however, in highlighting as he does how the technical division of labour as organised according to the uneven development of the productive forces is crucial to the issue of labour stratification. The national, 'racial' and gender hierarchies upon which social chauvinism is predicated are de- and reconstructed in the age of globalisation (i.e. globalised imperialism). As Bhattacharyya, Gabriel, and Small (2002, p. 8) write:

> Overall, several global developments have helped to reconfigure old patterns of ethnic relations and create new forms of racial privilege and politics. These include: economic restructuring in the West, including the demise of heavy industries, the rise of the new technologies, and the expansion of old and new service industries; the growth in significance of transnational and multinational operations; the emergence of new global divisions of labour and, finally, the rise of international agencies and global economic blocs, all of which have served to transform 'national' production forms and processes and their corresponding social relations. These relations have been racialised in a number of ways; the role assigned to migrant labour in the new service economy; the shift of production sites from inner city areas, where migrant communities have traditionally resided, to greenfield (high-technology) sites, where they traditionally have not, and finally internal patterns of migration within the Third World and the use of female labour in the production of microchips and the manufacture of designer sportswear.

The facts of racist workers' and labour organisations' *responsibility* for the exclusion of black and minority ethnic workers from particular industries, occupations and countries are largely beyond the scope of the present essay. Suffice it to note that global wage differentials are politically grounded in such a way that the conservative political behaviour of the metropolitan working class must be taken into account.

Just as serious an issue is Post's dismissal of the role of oligopoly, alongside its political, military and cultural supports, in sustaining wage differentials on a *global* scale. By focusing on critiquing the possibility of super-profits derived from the uneven development of (1) *branches of industry*, Post misses the greater significance of super-profits generated via the uneven development of (2) *countries* and (3) *regions* in the world economy (Strauss, 2004). Amin (2000, pp. 4–5) cites five major sources of monopoly super-profits through which the imperialist countries constrain competitive production in the developing world and ensure that value is transferred *sui gratis* from the global South to the North.

- Technological monopolies sustained mainly by state control, military spending in particular. Metropolitan 'defence' systems, as afforded by taxing the affluent Western public, function as a massive fund for research and development in 'private' industry;

- Financial control of worldwide markets ensuring that national savings are subject to international banking interests based largely in the developed countries. The US trade deficit currently swallows fully 80% of all global savings in the form of foreign purchases of US municipal, state and government bonds;
- Monopolistic access to the planet's natural resources. 'Petrodollar warfare', for example, enables the transfer of surplus value from the global South to the global North, as the militarily secured denomination of oil sales in US dollars forces countries to maintain large dollar reserves, creating a consistent demand for dollars and upwards pressure on the dollar's value, *regardless of economic conditions in the United States*;
- Media and communication monopolies provide developed countries with a crucial means by which to manipulate political events. The corporate and government media monopolies, largely based in the metropolitan countries, present a picture of the world perfectly suited to their own anti-social agenda; and
- Monopolies of weapons of mass destruction, particularly by the United States, ensure that Third World states are literally *forced* to comply with imperialist diktat, upon pain of terrible war (Amin, 2000, pp. 4–5).

The dominance of OECD-based monopolies in non-OECD markets entail for the latter: (1) a constant drain on available capital, (2) deteriorating terms of trade and (3) massive surplus value transfer resulting from unequal exchange. To pay for the product of OECD-based oligopolies, non-OECD countries must send abroad a greater amount of socially necessary labour time than they would were their own industries free to develop according to the demand of their own peoples. Developing countries are compelled under capitalism to compete with one another for access to the capital, electronic and military goods monopolised by the OECD. This ensures that each must drive down wages to gain comparative advantage over the other, hence contributing additional surplus value than would result simply from unequal exchange based on divergent materialised compositions of capital.

POST ON LABOUR ARISTOCRATIC MILITANCY

Post (2010) misunderstands the significance of the labour aristocracy thesis when he ascribes to it the notion that bourgeois workers are politically quiescent, in his words, unable to 'play a leading rôle in radical and revolutionary working-class organisations and struggles'. He thus sets up a straw man version of the labour aristocracy thesis which he attempts to then refute by citing examples of the economic struggles of relatively well-paid, skilled and securely employed workers, both in the developed world and elsewhere, against their employers. Indeed, besides the examples cited by Post, it may be noted that the English trade union movement has always been strongest in those trades wherein workers were most independent, most in demand and best paid. The wool combers, for example, were the first group of English workers to organise against the common exploitation of their employers (Mantoux, 1970, p. 78). More generally, there is some sociological truth in the idea that it has been mostly skilled workers and intellectuals who have been members of Communist parties in Europe. That does not, however, change the reality that these have been small in numbers or that the main policy they have pursued has been narrowly economistic and at least tacitly social-imperialist.

Proponents of the labour aristocracy thesis do *not* assert that the interests of the *haute-bourgeoisie* and the labour aristocracy are identical or entirely congruous. There *is* a conflict of interest between rich workers and capitalists and this may at critical moments manifest itself in widespread strikes and social turmoil. In South Africa, for example, where the white working class *per se* constituted a labour aristocracy (Davies, 1973), there was frequent conflict between it and the state over the impact of the job colour-bar system on production costs, output and profits (Phakathi, 2012, p. 283). The labour aristocracy thesis affirms, however, that workers in the major imperialist countries cannot and will not overthrow the capitalist system so long as a system of super-exploitation exists to maintain lagging profit rates and guarantee them high living standards.

Post is distinctly disingenuous, therefore, in disregarding the pro-capitalist–imperialist tendencies of the metropolitan working class in the twentieth century and beyond. As Sassoon (1997) has amply demonstrated, the effective parties of the left in the imperialist countries have functioned as vehicles to enforce the partial regulation and socialisation of capitalism, as opposed to having posed any serious threat to its replacement. Indeed, those parties and organisations that the metropolitan working class has supported throughout the twentieth century and beyond have certainly been no less imperialist or militarist than their 'conservative' counterparts. It is demonstrably absurd to meekly attribute the reformism of the working bourgeoisie to 'false class consciousness', job insecurity ('precarity') or Stalinist or social democratic 'betrayal' as is typical amongst Western Marxists.

Yet whilst independent parties of the working class, distinct from the two or three main imperialist parties, have had practically zero electoral significance for the past century, that situation is changing today. That Western 'workers' are today *fascism's* major constituency has been shown by Oesch in his survey of literature showing an 'increasing proletarianization [sic] of right-wing populist parties' electorate' since the 1990s (Oesch, 2008, p. 350). In particular, studies show that workers have become the core electoral base of the Austrian Freedom Party, the Belgian Flemish Block, the French National Front, the Danish People's Party and the Norwegian Progress Party. At the same time, 'working class' votes for the Swiss People's Party and the Italian Lega Nord are only barely surpassed by those of small-business owners, shopkeepers, artisans and independents. It seems reasonable to suggest, then, that during the 1990s, right-wing populist parties constituted a new type of working-class party. Oesch queries why persons 'strongly exposed to labor market risks and possessing few socioeconomic resources', 'located at the bottom of the occupational hierarchy', might vote for right-wing populist parties and finds the answer in popular cultural protectionism and deep-seated discontent with the functioning of the 'democratic' system, as opposed to 'economic grievances' *per se* (Oesch, 2008). In fact, it is a mistake to postulate a rigid dichotomy between the racist authoritarian nationalism of metropolitan labour and its socioeconomic position. The degree of core-nation workers' exposure to labour market risks and their possession of socioeconomic resources are directly related to their location, not at the bottom of the occupational hierarchy but, at the level of the global economy, right at its top. As such, the political intent to oppress, disenfranchise and exclude 'non-white', non-Christian people from state boundaries is not only based on actual or potential competition over jobs. Rather, it is an expression of 'working class' support for an imperialist system that more and more openly subjects entire nations in order to monopolise their natural resources and capital. That global imperialism has found it necessary to admit persons from neocolonial states across its borders for economic, diplomatic, political and other reasons has consistently met with the disapproval of the metropolitan workforce. This has only intensified as Keynesian social democracy has been replaced with neoliberal economic restructuring and the accompanying growth of the racialised police state. The super-wages of metropolitan labour do not only depend upon militarised borders and job market discrimination but also on the degree to which workers can influence state policy in their own favour. In the absence of trade union vehicles (appropriate to an earlier, social democratic phase of labour organisation),

First World democracy, based as it is upon the oppression of more than three quarters of the world's population, finds its *sine qua non* in racist national chauvinism. As such, it is not uncommon for brazenly national-chauvinist parties to gain support from groups of persons considering themselves politically left-wing. With 20% of its members considering themselves 'left', Jean-Marie Le Pen's fascist Front National, for example, did well in the 1995 French elections with the slogan 'neither right nor left, but French', garnering 30% of the working class vote and 25% of the unemployed vote (Weissmann, 1996). More recently, a 2011 poll found that while 48% of Britons would vote for a far-right anti-immigration party committed to opposing so-called Islamist extremism with 'non-violent' means, 52% agreed with the proposition that 'Muslims create problems in the UK' (Townsend, 2011).

None of the above testifies to the labour aristocracy constituting what Post refers to as 'the *revolutionary and internationalist* wing of the labour-movement' (his emphasis).

WHAT IS THE 'LABOUR ARISTOCRACY'?

Post castigates sections of the left for writing about a 'labour aristocracy' for which 'there is no single, coherent theory'. To clarify my position, I will attempt to outline the fundamentals of such a theory.

The labour aristocracy is that section of the international working class whose privileged position in the lucrative job markets opened up by imperialism secures for it wages approaching or exceeding the *per capita* value created by the working class as a whole. As such, the class interests of the labour aristocracy are bound up with those of the *haute-bourgeoisie* so that if the latter is unable to accumulate super-profits, then the *super-wages* (wages supplemented by super-profits) (Edwards, 1978, p. 20; Emmanuel, 1972, pp. 110–120) of the labour aristocracy must be reduced.

The labour aristocracy provides the major vehicle for bourgeois ideological and political influence within the working class. As highlighted above, for Lenin, these conditions allow for ever-greater sections of the metropolitan working class to be granted super-wages.

As it has developed over the course of the last century, the labour aristocracy was first transformed from being a minority of skilled workers in key imperial industries to a majority of core-nation workers dependent on imperialist state patronage. From WWI to the 1970s, social-democratic politicians and trade union bureaucrats were the reputable middlemen in the social partnership forged between globally ascendant oligopoly capital and metropolitan labour. Even as the Keynesian social contract was systematically dismantled under the ensuing neoliberalism, however, the massive proletarianisation and super-exploitation of Third World labour in the final decades of the last century provided that unprecedented standards of living and the widespread introduction of supervisory and circulatory occupations further insulated metropolitan labour from the intrinsic conflict between capital and labour.[10] Nineteenth century restrictions imposed by labour aristocratic unions on membership for the mass of workers have today been entirely substituted for restrictions on immigration from the Third World which are national in scope and allow the maintenance of profound global wage differentials.

Divergent global rates of exploitation have profound consequences in terms of the amount of wealth workers in different countries consume. Fig. 1 compares total contribution to global production to share of total working class and middle class household consumption for the world's population, ranked in order of income. In the Lorenz curve used to depict global income equality, where the *x*-axis is cumulative population and the *y*-axis is cumulative income, perfect income equality is expressed in a diagonal straight line. The reality of income distribution, however, shows a curve that is more or less flat for the first two-thirds of its trajectory, but rises ever more steeply towards the end. The definition of the 'Gini

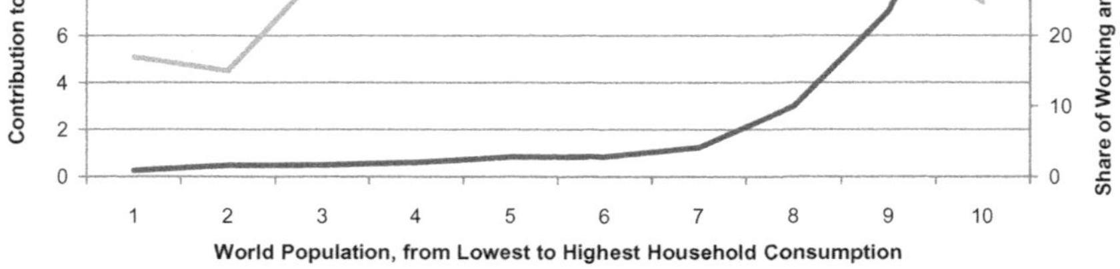

Fig. 1. Global Production versus Global Consumption. *Sources:* CIA World Factbook; ILO LABORSTA Database; Köhler (2005, p. 9); Piketty and Saez (2004, 'Figure 1: The Top Decile Income Share, 1917–2002', p. 48); United Nations.

Inequality Index' is the ratio between the area bounded by the curve and the straight diagonal, and the total area under the straight line. Plotted according to international income distribution, we refer to this as the 'world consumption curve'. Smith has suggested that generating a 'world production curve' by plotting each country's production of social wealth and superimposing this on said consumption curve can illustrate much in regard to global exploitation.[11] In a world without exploitation, the two curves would be identical, that is each person/household would produce what they consume. In fact, however, the global production curve diverges greatly from the consumption curve. In Fig. 1, the area bounded by the two curves to the left of their intersection ought to be the same as the bounded area to their right were the world's workers to consume what they themselves produce. The ratio between this area and the area under either of the two curves (by definition identical, since total production = total consumption) might be called the 'global exploitation index'. The countries closest to the point of intersection are those whose total contribution to global wealth is closest to their total consumption of it. All countries to the right are net exploiters, that is imperialists, and all countries to the left are net exploited.

According to mainstream economic doctrine, since markets equalise the income of workers, capitalists and nations with the value of their product, the production curve must be identical to the consumption curve; any deviation of one from the other being the result of the interruption of market forces. As the neo-classical marginalist economist John Bates Clark put it:

> [Where] natural laws have their way, the share of income that attaches to any productive function is gauged by the actual product of it. In other words, free competition tends to give labour what labour creates, to capital what capital creates, and to entrepreneurs what the coordinating function creates. (Clark quoted in Baran, 2012, p. 29)

As Smith notes, 'Marx pointed out the fundamental error in this view: workers are paid not for what they produce, but for what they consume'.[12] As such, the two curves described and depicted below directly juxtapose neoclassical and Marxist value theory. Moreover, by graphically illustrating the great disjuncture between contribution to global production and share of global consumption, Fig. 1 refutes the views of Post and others on the left who persist in denying the effects of global labour segmentation and stratification on the transformation of the global class structure.

For Post's non-Marxist, marginalist, view of income distribution, global wage differentials are the result of productivity differentials conditioned by differences in the level of the productive forces at different societies' disposal. However, as Marx argued, it is only living labour and not machinery or constant capital which adds value. According to Marx (1977a, p. 53), an hour of average socially necessary labour always yields an equal amount of value independently of variations in physical productivity, hence the tendency for labour-saving technological change to depress the rate of profit. Although increased productivity results in the creation of more use values per unit of time, only the intensified consumption of labour power can generate added (exchange) value. Since wages are not the price for the result of labour but the price for labour power, higher wages are not the consequence of (short-term) productivity gains accruing to capital. Rather, in a capitalist society, the product of machinery belongs to the capitalist, not the worker, just as in a feudal or tributary society part of the product of the soil belongs to the landlord, not the peasant. As Engels (1995, pp. 181–182) wrote:

> Marx demonstrates that machinery merely helps to lower the price of the products, and that it is competition which accentuates that effect; in other words, the gain consists in manufacturing a greater number of products in the same length of time, so that the amount of work involved in each is correspondingly less and the value of each proportionately lower. Mr. Beaulieu forgets to tell us in what respect the wage earner benefits from seeing his productivity increase when the product of that increased productivity does not belong to him, and when his wage is not determined by the productivity of the instrument [i.e. the machine—ZC].

In Fig. 1, the economically active population (EAP) is defined as all persons who furnish the supply of labour for the production of goods and services. As such, the EAP includes hundreds of millions of persons engaged in private, so-called subsistence farming in the Third World. We have favoured Eurocentric assumptions that subsistence farmers contribute nothing to global production (even though most contribute money to capitalist landlords and supply goods for sale on the market), and assumed that only wage labour capable of generating surplus value is considered productive. Total global production is defined as the working hours of full-time equivalent production sector wage employment in all countries.[13] The total production workforce was obtained by multiplying the EAP in each country by the rate of full employment for its corresponding global income quintile (Köhler, 2005, p. 9) and then by multiplying this total by the percentage of each country's workforce in industry and agriculture. The figure thus obtained was then multiplied by 133%, since I define 'underemployment' as being employed for only one-third of the hours of a full-time worker. To calculate capitalists' share of household income expenditure, Piketty and Saez's (2004) measure of the income share of the top echelons of the US income distribution has been used as a global benchmark. Capitalists typically earn more than they can possibly consume, and much of their household consumption is reinvested. Since accumulated wealth is almost entirely in the hands of capitalists, the share of wealth of the top 10% of the population has been subtracted from total household consumption expenditure figures for each country. Doing so allows a more focused comparison of relations between the world's working and middle classes, the major bone of contention between exponents and opponents of the labour aristocracy thesis. Rather than adjusting each country's figure by the ratio of its Gini index to that of the United States (so that for countries with more unequal income distributions like Brazil or Pakistan, a larger portion of its national income would be subtracted), I have assumed a flat rate of 42% for capitalist household income expenditure in all countries.

To suppose that these stark inequalities are purely the result of superior economic efficiency and skill levels on the part of the core capitalist nations, or that they are the reward of a section of the global working class for its exceptional militancy, is to stretch reality to breaking point (Cope, 2012, pp. 221–251).

CONCLUSION

The failure on the part of the left to rigorously examine the structuration of the international class structure by imperialism, as evidenced by the global contradiction between production and consumption highlighted above, has in no small measure added to the serious difficulties facing the socialist movement, both historically and today. Socialist movements in the metropolitan countries have tacitly accepted the global division between imperialist and exploited nations by obfuscating and divaricating from the issue of international surplus value transfer. Working class internationalism and the struggle against racism and colonialism within the imperialist countries are both sacrificed at the altar of narrow appeals to material self-interest on the part of the wealthiest sections of the ineluctably global workforce. Historically, such economism has its corollary in a deeply conservative reformism and chauvinist acceptance of the status quo ante, such that imperialist governments have been and are permitted to carry out virtually any act of aggression and penal repression against foreign countries and minority communities without fear of widespread national opposition.

Metropolitan labour's dependence upon imperialism for its existence as such – that is as labour whose affluence is predicated upon the maintenance of the core-periphery divide – clearly precludes the possibility that its conservatism is based purely on intellectual myopia. However, to paraphrase Noam Chomsky, intellectuals have the responsibility to expose untruth wherever they see it. This is all the more imperative when disclosing that the reality of vested interests can only assist conscious workers and their representatives, those really committed to socialism, to combat working class acquiescence in the creeping fascination of the body politic associated with the ascendancy of the neoliberal police state.

Understanding how the 'labour aristocracy' is formed means understanding imperialism, and conversely. Those socialist organisations which do not understand the embourgeoisement of labour typically play down the significance of imperialism, so that even those ostensibly opposed to imperialism very often miss their target. Thus, some socialist organisations prioritise peace work and opposition to militarism, equating imperialism with the exercise of brute force against one or more sovereign nations. Their foil may be a particular administration, its foreign policy or even the military–industrial complex *tout court*. Alternatively, imperialism might be opposed as benefitting only a handful of ultra-rich bankers and foreign investors (or even, at a stretch, a handful of very well-paid union bureaucrats and highly skilled professionals). In this case, only the richest 1–5% of society is seen as upholding the rule of monopoly capital.

The approach recommended here to readers, by contrast, is to treat imperialism as essentially involving the transfer of surplus value from one country to another and an imperialist country as a net importer of surplus value. This approach allows us to gauge the size and boundaries of the labour aristocracy and, hence, to work out the logistics of mounting really effective opposition to capitalism and its military, legal, financial and political bulwarks.

NOTES

1. The term First World refers to the developed countries of the United States and Canada, Europe (excluding Russia and parts of Eastern Europe), Japan, Israel, Australia and New Zealand. 'Third World' refers to the underdeveloped countries of Asia (excluding Japan and Israel), Africa, 'Latin' America, the Caribbean and Oceania (excluding Australia and New Zealand).

2. The term was originally coined in 1872 by Russian anarchist Mikhail Bakunin, who criticized the idea, which he attributed to Marxists, that organised workers are the most revolutionary social group (Post, 2006a, 2006b, 2010).

3. It is important to note that Post misses much of the important contributions made to the theory of global labour stratification by dependency, unequal exchange

and world systems theorists both inside and outside academia. See, for example, Emmanuel (1976); Amin (1976); Sau (1978); Stavrianos (1981); Edwards (1978); Communist Working Group (1986); Sakai (1989); Cope (2012).

4. *Ibid.* See 'Measuring Worth: Exchange Rates between the United States Dollar and Forty-one Currencies' online: http://www.measuringworth.org/datasets/exchangeglobal/, accessed 1 May, 2010, and http://en.wikipedia.org/wiki/Russian_Ruble, accessed 1 May, 2010). In 1900, the average real wage of Russian agricultural day workers, building, factory and railroad workers – the latter category paid almost twice as much as the previous two – was 251 rubles (Allen, 2003, pp. 38–42) or 49.5% of the average French real wage. Russian wages were very constant throughout the period of Russia's industrial capitalist boom (c.1861–1913) and Russian workers, unlike their British, French and German counterparts, 'did not receive rising incomes in step with the economic growth of the country' (*Ibid*, p. 37). Alongside miserable wages, another factor helping to explain the relatively militant ethos of Russian labour in the pre-war period is its higher socialization. In comparison to German workers, 70% of whom in 1895 were employed in industries employing 50 or less (Bernstein, 1961), nearly 50% of Russian workers worked in industries with over 1000 employees. Fully 83% of the Russian population was engaged in agriculture as compared to 23.8% of Germans in the immediate pre-war period (Kemp, 1985, p. 191).

5. The IMF calculation was made by deflating nominal wages by the rate of inflation as reported by the official consumer price index (CPI).

6. '"Made-in-China" helps make rich countries richer' in People's Daily, China, August 20, 2005.

7. By 1925, the Caribbean, South Africa, Asia and Oceania (furnishing about 73% of colonial produce), produced some 54–60% of all oil seeds, 50% of all textiles, 34–35% of all cereals and other foodstuffs, 100% of rubber, 24–28% of all fertilisers and chemicals, and 17% of all cereals alone (an average increase of 137% of 1913 levels of raw material production) (Krooth, 1980, pp. 84–85).

8. The term 'organic composition of capital' refers to the ratio between variable and constant capital, that is to the amount of value-creating labour power against technology and raw materials utilised in the labour process. A greater ratio between capital outlay and wages may result from the increased materialised composition of capital (i.e. fixed capital costs) or from the diminishing share of wages in total capital outlay. Whereas in the first case, the rate of profit is threatened by a diminution of the living labour involved in production, in the second case it may be buoyed by the diminution of necessary labour costs (rising surplus value). The latter is typically the result of the greater productivity of labour in those industries producing workers' subsistence goods. In the capitalist world system, reduced labour costs have always been associated with the extortion of subordinate peasantries and the (related) super-exploitation of dependent wage labour.

9. Charles Post, 'Ernest Mandel and the Marxian Theory of Bureaucracy', available at: http://www.internationalviewpoint.org/spip.php?article848.

10. Class struggle pivots around the exploited section of the working class' retention or otherwise of the surplus value it creates at the point of production. Since the fundamental class antagonism in capitalism is thus between the producers of surplus value and the capitalists who receive it in the first instance, unproductive

labourers receive what Resnick and Wolff (2006, pp. 206–220) call 'subsumed class income' from the distribution of already appropriated surplus value. As imperialism comes to form the central core of the capitalist system, the physical toil needed to produce surplus value is increasingly the sole preserve of super-exploited Third World labour.

11. The idea for Fig. 1, a graphical comparison between global consumption and global production, was suggested to me by Dr. John Smith in private correspondence. I am indebted to John Smith for the use of the idea herein.

12. Private correspondence from John Smith.

13. For a Marxist view of productive and unproductive labour, see Amin (1976, p. 244); Marx (1968, p. 157); Marx (1977a, pp. 518–519); Resnick and Wolff (2006, pp. 206–220); Shaikh and Tonak (1994, p. 25).

REFERENCES

Albritton, R. (2009). *Let them eat junk: How capitalism creates hunger and obesity*. London: Pluto Press.

Allen, R. C. (2003). *From farm to factory: A reinterpretation of the Soviet Industrial Revolution*. New Jersey: Princeton University Press.

Allen, R. L. (1974). *Reluctant reformers: The impact of racism on American Social Reform Movements*. Washington, DC: Howard University Press.

Amin, S. (1976). *Imperialism and unequal development*. Sussex: The Harvester Press.

Amin, S. (2000). *Capitalism in the age of globalization: The management of contemporary society*. London: Zed Books.

Amin, S. (2011). *The law of worldwide value*. New York: Monthly Review Press.

Anderson, P. (1964). Origins of the present crisis. *New Left Review*, 23, January–February, pp. 26–51.

Ashman, S., & Callinicos, A. (2006). Capital accumulation and the state system. *Historical Materialism*, *14*, 107–131.

Bagehot, W. (2001 [1867]). *The English Constitution*. Cambridge: Cambridge University Press.

Baran, P. (2012). Some theoretical implications. *Monthly Review*, *64*(3), 24–59.

Barratt Brown, M. (1974). *The economics of imperialism*. London: Penguin.

Bernstein, E. (1961). *Evolutionary socialism: A criticism and affirmation*. New York: Schocken.

Bhattacharyya, G., Gabriel, J., & Small, S. (2002). *Race and power: Global racism in the twenty first century*. London: Routledge.

Broadberry, S., & Burhop, C. (2009). 'Real wages and labour productivity in Britain and Germany, 1871–1938: A unified approach to the international comparison of living standards', 'Appendix: Time series of German-British comparative real wages, 1871–1938 UK = 100', Max Planck Institute for Research on Collective Goods, Bonn, p. 25. Retrieved from http://www.coll.mpg.de/pdf_dat/2009_18online.pdf

Brown, M. K., Carnoy, M., Currie, E., Ducter, T., Oppenheimer, D. B., Shultz, M. M., & Wellman, D. (2005). *Whitewashing race: The myth of a color-blind society*. Berkeley, CA: University of California Press.

Chossudovsky, M. (2003). *The globalization of poverty and the new world order*. Montréal: Global Research.

CIA World Factbook. Retrieved from https://www.cia.gov/library/publications/the-world-factbook/fields/2048.html

Clough, R. (1992). *Labour: A party fit for imperialism*. London: Larkin Publications.

Clough, R. (1993). Haunted by the labour aristocracy Part 1: Marx and Engels on the split in the working class. *Fight Racism! Fight Imperialism!*, no. 115, October/November.

Communist Working Group. (1986). *Unequal exchange and the prospects of socialism*. Copenhagen: Manifest.

Cope, Z. (2012). *Divided world divided class: Global political economy and the stratification of labour under capitalism*. Montréal: Kersplebedeb.

Cox, M., & Alm, R. (1999). *Myths of rich and poor: Why we're better off than we think*. New York: Basic Books.

Curtis, M. (2003). *Web of deceit: Britain's real role in the world*. London: Vintage.

Curtis, M. (2004). *Unpeople: Britain's secret human rights abuses*. London: Vintage.

Davies, R. (1973). The white working class in South Africa. *New Left Review*, *I*(82). November–December.

Davis, M. (1986). *Prisoners of the American dream*. London: Verso.

Degras, J. (Ed.). (1956). Platform of the Communist International adopted by the first congress. *The Communist International, 1919–1943: Selected Documents* (Vol. 1, pp. 1919–1922). Oxford: Oxford University Press.

Diamond, M. (2006). *Lesser breeds: Racial attitudes in popular British culture, 1890–1940*. London: Anthem Press.

Dikhanov, Y., & Ward, M. (2001). Evolution of the global distribution of income in 1970–99. Retrieved from www.eclac.cl/povertystatistcs/documentos/dikhanov.pdf

DuBois, W. E. B. (1915). The African roots of the war. *The Atlantic*, May.

Edelstein, M. (1981). Foreign investment and Empire 1860–1914. In R. Floud & D. McCluskey (Eds.), *The Economic History of Britain Since 1700* (pp. 70–98). Cambridge: Cambridge University Press.

Edwards, H. W. (1978). *Labor aristocracy: Mass base of social democracy*. Stockholm: Aurora Press.

Elbaum, M., & Seltzer, R. (1982). The labor aristocracy. Part II: The U.S. Labor Movement since World War II. *Line of March*, *12*, 69–118.

Elbaum, M., & Seltzer, R. (2004). *The labour aristocracy: The material basis for opportunism in the labour movement*. Chippendale, Australia: Resistance Books. Retrieved from http://readingfromtheleft.com/PDF/LabourAristocracy.pdf

Elsenhans, H. (1983). Rising mass incomes as a condition of capitalist growth: Implications for the world economy. *International Organization*, *37*(1), 1–39.

Emmanuel, A. (1972). *Unequal exchange: A study of the imperialism of trade*. London: New Left Books.

Emmanuel, A. (1976). The socialist project in a disintegrated capitalist world. *Socialist Thought and Practice: A Yugoslav Monthly*, *16*(9), 69–87.

Engels, F. (1977 [1892]). *Condition of the working class in England*. Moscow: Progress Publishers.

Engels, F. (1995). Engels to Paul Lafargue. In: *Marx and Engels: Collected Works* (Vol. 47). New York: International Publishers.

Evans, M. (2011). *Algeria: France's undeclared war*. Oxford: Oxford University Press.

Feis, H. (1930). *Europe the world's banker*. New Haven: Yale University Press.

Frank, A. G. (1979). *Dependent accumulation and underdevelopment*. London: Macmillan Press.

Gray, R. (1981). *The aristocracy of labour in nineteenth century Britain: 1850–1914*. London: Macmillan Press.
Grossman, H. (1992). *The law of accumulation and breakdown of the capitalist system: Being also a theory of crises*. London: Pluto Press.
Gupta, P. (1975). *Imperialism and the British Labour Movement, 1914–1964*. London: Macmillan Press.
Halevy, E. (1939). *History of the English people* (Vol. 2). London: Pelican.
Harvie, D., & de Angelis, M. (2004). *Globalisation? No question: Foreign direct investment and labour commanded*. Retrieved from http://www.ntu.ac.uk/research/school_research/nbs/discussion_papers/31295.pdf
Hehn, P. H. (2002). *A low dishonest decade: The great powers, Eastern Europe, and the economic origins of World War II, 1930–1941*. New York: Continuum.
Heilbroner, R. (1980). *The worldly philosophers*. New York: Simon and Schuster.
Hobsbawm, E. (1951). The taming of parliamentary democracy. *The Modern Quarterly*, *6*(4).
Hobsbawm, E. (1964). *Labouring men*. London: Penguin.
Ignatiev, N. (1995). *How the Irish became white*. London: Routledge.
ILO LABORSTA Database. Data for all countries, total labour force. Retrieved from http://laborsta.ilo.org/applv8/data/EAPEP/eapep_E.html
International Monetary Fund IMF. (2007). *World Economic Outlook 2007: Spillovers and cycles in the global economy*. Washington, DC: International Monetary Fund.
Jaffe, H. (1980). *The pyramid of nations*. Milan: Victor.
Jalée, P. (1968). *The pillage of the Third World*. New York, NY: Monthly Review Press.
Jedlicki, C. (2007). Unequal exchange. The Jus Semper Global Alliance: Living wages North and South. Retrieved form http://www.jussemper.org/Resources/Labour%20Resources/Resources/Jedlicki_UnequalExchange.pdf
Kemp, T. (1985). *Industrialisation in nineteenth century Europe*. London: Longman.
Köhler, G. (2005). The global stratification of unemployment and underemployment. 'Underemployment or informal employment, based on LABORSTA "employee" or "paid employment".' Retrieved from http://s3.amazonaws.com/zanran_storage/www.caei.com.ar/ContentPages/394534208.pdf
Krooth, R. (1980). *Arms and empire: Imperial patterns before World War II*. California: Harvest Press.
Lenin, V. I. (1963 [1916]). A caricature of Marxism and imperialist economism. In: *Collected Works* (Vol. 23). Moscow: Progress Publishers.
Lenin, V. I. (1963 [1918]). Letter to the workers of Europe and America. In: *Collected Works* (Vol. 28). Moscow: Progress Publishers.
Lenin, V. I. (1964 [1916]). Imperialism and the split in socialism. In: *Collected Works* (Vol. 23). Moscow: Progress Publishers. Retrieved from http://www.marxists.org/archive/lenin/works/1916/oct/x01.htm
Lenin, V. I. (1969). *British labour and British imperialism: A collection of writings by Lenin on Britain*. London: Lawrence and Wishart.
Lenin, V. I. (1970 [1916]). Imperialism: The highest stage of capitalism. In: *Selected Works* (Vol. 1). Moscow: Progress Publishers. Retrieved from http://www.marxists.org/archive/lenin/works/1916/imp-hsc/pref02.htm
Lenin, V. I. (1974 [1915]). The collapse of the Second International. In: *Collected Works* (Vol. 24). Retrieved from http://www.marxists.org/archive/lenin/works/1915/csi/index.htm

Linder, M. (1985). *European labor aristocracies: Trade unionism, the hierarchy of skill and the stratification of the manual working class before the First World War*. Frankfurt: Campus Verlag.

Lipsey, R. (2006). *Measuring foreign direct investment. The International Association for Research in Income and Wealth*, 29th Conference. Retrieved from http://www.iariw.org/abstracts/2006/lipseya.pdf

MacKenzie, J. M. (1987). *Imperialism and popular culture*. Manchester: Manchester University Press.

Mantoux, P. (1970). *The industrial revolution in the Eighteenth century*. London: Methuen and Co. Ltd.

Marx, K. (1968 [1863]). *Theories of surplus value*. London: Lawrence and Wishart.

Marx, K. (1977a [1867]). *Capital: A critique of political economy* (Vol. I). London: Lawrence and Wishart.

Marx, K. (1977b [1894]). *Capital: A critique of political economy* (Vol. III). London: Lawrence and Wishart.

Marx, K., & Engels, F. (1955). *Marx and Engels: Selected correspondence*. Moscow: Foreign Languages Press.

Marx, K., & Engels, F. (1975). *Marx and Engels: Articles on Britain*. Moscow: Progress Publishers.

Marx, K., & Engels, F. (1996). *Minutes of the London Congress of the International*. In *Marx and Engels Collected Works* (Vol. 22). New York: International Publishers.

Marx, K., & Engels, F. (1996a). *Marx letter to Engels, London, 10 December 1869*. In *Marx and Engels Collected Works* (Vol. 43). New York: International Publishers.

Meyer, B. D., & Sullivan, J. X. (2011). The material well-being of the poor and the middle class since 1980. Paper prepared for the American Enterprise Institute. Retrieved from http://nd.edu/~jsulliv4/well_being_middle_class_poor4.3.pdf

Michell, B., & Deane, P. (Eds.). (1962). *Abstract of British historical statistics*. Cambridge: Cambridge University Press.

Nabudere, D. W. (1979). *Essays on the theory and practice of imperialism*. London: Onyx Press.

Oesch, D. (2008). Explaining workers' support for right-wing populist parties in Western Europe: Evidence from Austria, Belgium, France, Norway, and Switzerland. *International Political Science Review*, *29*(3), 349–373.

Patnaik, U. (1999). *The long transition: Essays on political economy*. Delhi: Tulika.

Patnaik, U. (2007). *The republic of hunger and other essays*. London: Merlin Press.

Perryman, W. (2003). *Unfounded loyalty: An in-depth look into the love affair between blacks and democrats*. New York: Pneuma Life Publishing.

Phakathi, T. S. (2012). Worker agency in colonial, apartheid and post-apartheid gold mining workplace regimes. *Review of African Political Economy*, *39*(132), 279–294.

Piketty, T., & Saez, E. (2004). Income inequality in the United States, 1913–2002. Retrieved from http://elsa.berkeley.edu/~saez/piketty-saezOUP04US.pdf

Post, C. (2006a). The myth of the labor aristocracy, Part 1, Against the current, 123, July–August. Retrieved from http://www.solidarity-us.org/node/128

Post, C. (2006b). The "labor aristocracy" and working-class struggles: Consciousness in flux, Part 2, Against the current, 124, September–October. Retrieved from http://www.solidarity-us.org/node/129

Post, C. (2010). Exploring working-class consciousness: A critique of the theory of the "labour-aristocracy". *Historical Materialism*, *18*, 3–38.

Resnick, S. A., & Wolff, R. D. (2006). *New departures in Marxian theory*. London: Routledge.
Sakai, J. (1989). *Settlers: The mythology of the white proletariat*. Chicago, IL: Morning Star Press.
Sassoon, D. (1997). *One hundred years of socialism: The West European left in the twentieth century*. London: Fontana Press.
Sau, R. (1978). *Unequal exchange, imperialism and underdevelopment: An essay on the political economy of world capitalism*. Calcutta, India: Oxford University Press.
Schaub, R. (2004). *Transnational corporations and economic development in developing countries*. Retrieved from http://www.pikpotsdam.de/members/edenh/theses/masterschaub.pdf
Schneider, W. H. (1982). *An empire for the masses: The French popular image of Africa, 1870–1900*. Connecticut: Greenwood Press.
Shaikh, A., & Tonak, A. E. (1994). *Measuring the wealth of nations: The political economy of national accounts*. Cambridge: Cambridge University Press.
Smith, J. (2007). 'What's new about "New Imperialism"'. Talk given to conference of socialist economists Trans-Pennine Express Working Group. Retrieved from http://www.socialsciences.manchester.ac.uk/disciplines/politics/research/hmrg/activities/documents/Smithimperialism_000.pdf
Smith, J. (2008). *Offshoring, outsourcing and the "Global Labour Arbitrage"*. Paper to IIPPE 2008 – Procida, Italy, 9–11 September.
Smith, J. (2010). Imperialism and the globalisation of production. PhD thesis. Retrieved from http://www.mediafire.com/?5r339mnn4zmubq7
Solomon, N., & Erlich, R. (2003). *Target Iraq: What the news media didn't tell you*. New York, NY: Context Books.
Stavrianos, L. S. (1981). *Global rift: the Third World comes of age*. New York, NY: William Morrow and Company, Inc.
Sternberg, F. (1951). *Capitalism and socialism on trial*. New York, NY: John Day.
Strauss, J. (2004). Monopoly capitalism and the bribery of the labour aristocracy. *Links: International Journal of Socialist Renewal, 26*. Retrieved from http://links.org.au/node/30
Townsend, M. (2011). Searchlight poll finds huge support for far right "if they gave up violence." Level of far-right support could outstrip that in France or Holland, says poll for Searchlight. The Guardian, 26 February. Retrieved from http://www.guardian.co.uk/uk/2011/feb/27/support-poll-support-far-right
United Nations. Household consumption expenditure (including non-profit institutions serving households). Retrieved from http://unsd/unsd/snaama/dnltransfer.asp?fID=6
United Nations. (1999). *Globalisation with a human face: Human Development Report 1999*. New York: Oxford University Press. Retrieved from http://hdr.undp.org/en/reports/global/hdr1999/
United Nations Conference on Trade and Development, UNCTAD. (2007). *World Investment Report 2007*. Geneva: United Nations.
Villar, O., & Cottle, D. (2012). *Cocaine, death squads, and the war on terror: U.S. imperialism and class struggle in Colombia*. New York, NY: Monthly Review Press.
Wade, R. H. (2008). Globalisation, growth, poverty, inequality, resentment, and imperialism. In J. Ravenhill (Ed.), *Global Political Economy*. Oxford University Press.
Weissmann, K. (1996). The epoch of national socialism. *The Journal of Libertarian Studies, 12*(2), 257–294.
Woodruff, W. (1975). *America's impact on the world*. London: Macmillan.

World Bank. (2006). World development indicators 2006, Table 2.6. Retrieved from http://books.google.co.uk/books?id=gE7bCAqKkkUC&pg=PT221&dq=%22+World+Development+Indicators+2006%22&ei=BeNVS_SzMZewyATBuNSnBA&cd=2#v=snippet&q=51%2C510&f=false
World Bank. (2008). *World development indicators*. Washington, DC: World Bank.
Woytinsky, W. S., & Woytinsky, E. S. (1955). *World commerce and governments*. New York, NY: Twentieth Century Fund.
Zinoviev, G. (1984 [1916]). The social roots of opportunism. *New International*, *2*, 99–135.

UNPAID REPRODUCTIVE LABOUR: A MARXIST ANALYSIS

Cecilia Beatriz Escobar Meléndez

ABSTRACT

This article aims to discuss the effects of unpaid reproductive labour on labour productivity and production. We make use of a Marxist approach, recognising in its method and categories the necessary and adequate tools in order to disclose reality. Capitalism is regarded as patriarchal, and patriarchy as a set of social relations that dominate women and women's labour-power for the benefit of men and capital. We argue that unpaid reproductive labour involves both class and gender struggles, which affect in a contradictory manner the capitalist accumulation process. Such assertion is reached by using an analytical instrument (based on linear algebra) developed in order to observe the impact that an insufficient fulfilment of the workers' necessities has on labour productivity and production.

Keywords: Unpaid reproductive labour; labour-power; gender struggle; class struggle; capitalism; patriarchy

Contradictions: Finance, Greed, and Labor Unequally Paid
Research in Political Economy, Volume 28, 131–160

ISSN: 0161-7230/doi:10.1108/S0161-7230(2013)0000028006

INTRODUCTION

Reproductive labour is mostly performed by women[1] and has important effects, albeit generally hidden, on the capitalist accumulation process. In this chapter, we are interested in exploring some of these effects, focusing our attention on one particular kind of reproductive labour, the one that is *unpaid*. Relations of power and power conflicts are involved. Both class struggle (capital vs. labour) and gender struggle (mainly men vs. women) are intrinsic part of the working of capitalist societies and therefore both will be taken into account. As it is explicitly stated in the title of our work, Marxist categories will be used. They are expressions of specific social relations established by individuals on specific material conditions: the capitalist mode of production.

What do we understand by 'reproductive labour'? The process of production is the social production of human life. The different modes of production that have existed through history have produced precisely that, each one with its own specific way of distributing labour among different activities determined by the development of the productive forces. Yet capitalism, in which commodity production has been generalised, is not organised according to the needs of social reproduction, that is consumption, but according to the production of profits and hence the social relations of production are relations of surplus value extraction. The source of this surplus value is the unpaid labour or surplus labour that capitalists squeeze out of workers during the production process. As observed by Marx (1867 [1976], p. 300), the value of labour-power (what the capitalist pays in average for it) and the value which labour-power valorises during the working day (what the capitalist gets in average from it) are two different magnitudes, and this characteristic is what makes labour-power a *sui generis* commodity.[2] Because the labour-power is a capacity of living human beings, in order to produce surplus value it is necessary to reproduce the life of the owners of that peculiar commodity, that is the workers. For that, individuals need not only goods but, among other things, also additional activities to actually consume those goods and thus reproduce their labour-power in a normal quality for present and future. For instance, they need to be healthy, nourished, trained in moral norms of social interaction, etc. This set of activities is the *reproductive labour*, a socio-historical category that in our societies belongs to the capitalist mode of production and that refers specifically to the working class. It is the labour that comprises all the housework and care work, namely the labour performed within the household for the (re)production of the labour-power for capitalist production.[3] It is carried out either by individuals (and/or enterprises) alien to the household as a directly remunerated or paid job, or by the same members of the household (family[4]) without receiving any payment in the form of 'wages' or 'salary'.[5] In the latter, the lack of a direct and explicit sale–purchase relationship makes its contributions to capital accumulation even less visible; this is why we shall focus on this case.

How women ended up as the persons in charge of the reproductive labour is associated with the development of gender relations. Even when the origin of these relations, that are indeed *power* relations, remains obscure and in need of a considerable amount of research, following Marx's materialist conception of history (Marx & Engels, 1845–1846), it is possible to assert that at some point in the development of the productive powers and within the mode of production allowed by them, one particular division of labour between men and women appeared as requirement and result of that mode of production, conferring a different position with respect to the means of production and means of subsistence on each group. It is probable that such division was linked to the sexual division of labour (i.e. maternity), thus imposing different working conditions on men and women. That division, preserved from one exploitative mode of production to the other, is an important explanatory element of the systematic asymmetries of social power between men and women. Engels (1884) proposed a hypothesis about the origins of the family and the gender relations implicated in it. According to him in historical societies, due to the presence of private property and driven by the necessity of inheriting that property to the offspring, men would have imposed sexual (i.e. monogamy) and material constraints on women. If this theory is true, it means that the main control of the means of production and means of subsistence was already in the hands of the men (as a group), so they could enforce those restrictions on the women as a mechanism of maintaining and ensuring property (as individuals). Otherwise, if the women had been in control of the resources, property inheritance would have taken place without the need of monogamy. The question of how men seized that control is still unexplained.

Patriarchy is the term often used to refer to the relationship of domination between men and women. Hartmann (1979) offers a good definition of it. She describes it as

> a set of social relations which has a material base and in which there are hierarchical relations between men and solidarity among them which enable them in turn to dominate women. The material base of patriarchy is men's control over women's labour power. That control is maintained by denying women access to necessary economically productive resources and by restricting women's sexuality. Men exercise their control in

> receiving personal service work from women, in not having to do housework or rear children, in having access to women's bodies for sex, and in feeling powerful and being powerful. (Hartmann, 1979, p. 11)

That material base is what gives rise to the consciousness, values, ideology and so on that support patriarchal relations and that belong to what Marx called the *superstructure* of the mode of production. Patriarchy is then the control of women's labour-power that men exercise thanks to a gendered division of labour accompanied by its correspondent set of social norms that permit them to manage the means of production and means of subsistence as well as the access to them, for that management entails the control of others' conditions of life. These relations respond, here and now, to the capitalist mode of production, to its social relations of production, logic and need of accumulation, that is capitalism is patriarchal, and hence the gender struggle is closely related to the class struggle.[6]

We intend to study what we regard as two contradictory effects of the patriarchal social relations on capital accumulation: on the one hand, we shall explore how the unpaid reproductive labour helps to perpetuate the downward pressure on wages while reducing the negative effects that such pressure has on the quality of the labour-power; and on the other hand, we shall study how a situation arising from the gender power relations may lead to a deterioration of women's labour capacity, negatively affecting the quality of the labour-power. Both cases have direct impact on labour productivity and therefore on capital accumulation. For this, we will make use an analytical instrument (based on linear algebra) developed to make evident the consequences that an insufficient fulfilment of the workers' necessities has on labour productivity and production. Previously, however, we shall make some brief comments on the Marxist issue of the productive and unproductive labour with the intention of placing the reproductive labour in this discussion. This is helpful to understand better the role and position that such labour has in capitalist societies, as well as the role and position that women have as main performers of it. Some concluding remarks are presented in the last section of this paper.

REPRODUCTIVE LABOUR: PRODUCTIVE OR UNPRODUCTIVE LABOUR?

In a rigorous manner, the reproductive labour is neither productive nor unproductive labour. Marxist Political Economy is a socio-historical analysis of how social relations assume specific forms at a certain level of the development of the productive powers; that is the capitalist mode of production is historically determined. This means that the Marxist definition of productive labour is a category of the capitalist mode of production, and it cannot and it should not be applied to any other organisation of production in the way that is applied and understood here; that is it is a category which responds to the social relations proper to this organisation, to its definite social form and to it alone.[7] Hence, given that capitalism is a regime based on the production of surplus value, the productive labour is the one that *directly* produces surplus value for the capitalist, the one involved in the orbit of production establishing direct relations with the productive capital regardless of the commodity that it produces, that is if it is material or not.[8] Whereas, and by opposition, the unproductive labour is the one that is outside the productive orbit but inside the circulation one, namely the labour that participates in the capitalist process of production as a whole but it does not produce surplus value, it realises it, it transforms commodity capital into money capital and vice versa. Put it differently, given the capitalist process of production, the productive labour is the one that is exchanged for (variable) capital, while the unproductive labour is the one that is exchanged for revenue.

There is nothing moral in Marx's category of productive labour, just as there is nothing related to the physical properties of the commodities that it produces. The category is completely abstracted from the content and result of the working activity, from the nature of the necessity that the commodity is meant to satisfy, from the particular use value in which is manifested, from the usefulness of the activity, from how necessary such activity is for the social reproduction process or even for the capitalist reproduction process. The labour is considered solely from the point of view of the social relations of production involved. The productive labour is thus socially and historically determined.

Because what matters is the direct relationship with capital, labour activities out of the capitalist production and circulation but within its socio-economic formation are not taken into account for the definition of the categories in question. They are neither productive labour nor unproductive labour, and this is precisely the case of the reproductive labour. When it is not performed by capitalist enterprises, the reproductive labour does not establish any direct relationship with capital; it neither participates in the production process nor in the circulation process, and hence it cannot be classified as productive or unproductive labour. But there is no moral judgment in such statement; it only means that it is performed out of the direct orbits of production and circulation of capital, inside an apparently private sphere where another kind of social relations, non-directly capitalist ones but relations of domination in the end, are present. Nevertheless, ever since it is performed inside capitalist societies and given that it is an intrinsic part of its patriarchal socio-economic form, in an indirect manner the reproductive labour *does* contribute to the valorisation process, not only through the reproduction of labour-power but also through the indirect production of surplus value for capital. The reproductive labour is then *indirectly productive labour*.[9] This contribution is what we shall discuss next.

UNPAID REPRODUCTIVE LABOUR: EFFECTS ON PRODUCTIVITY AND PRODUCTION

The Coverage of the Concrete Value of Labour-Power[10]

Labour-power, just as any other commodity, has use value and value. Its use value is its utilisation, the working activity as such, 'the living labour it can perform' (Marx, 1867 [1976], p. 300), what the capitalists consume during the labour process, and its value is determined by the socially necessary labour time for its production and reproduction. Since the labour-power is an ability of the living individual, a certain amount of goods and services are required in order to maintain his/her existence in socially normal conditions (the moral–historical element). The socially necessary labour time for the production and reproduction of the labour-power is then the labour time that is required in a given society for the production of those means of subsistence, or put it differently, the socially necessary labour time for the production of a value that is equivalent to the value of those means of subsistence. But the continuous production of surplus value requires the continuous presence of workers in the market and hence 'the sum of means of subsistence necessary for the production of labour-power must [also] include the means necessary for the worker's replacements, i.e. his children' (Marx, 1867 [1976], p. 275).

The way in which the value of any commodity is expressed, its *social form*, is the exchange value, which 'appears first of all as the quantitative relation, the proportion in which use-values of one kind exchange for use-values of another kind' (Marx, 1867 [1976], p. 126). The exchange value of labour-power appears therefore as the *proportion* in which it is exchanged for other commodities, the amount of means of subsistence that the worker receives in exchange for his/her labour capacity during a definite period of time, for example during a working day.

As soon as we talk about the *price-form* of the value of labour-power, such proportion appears as a *wage*, and 'the distinction between the exchange-value of labour-power and the sum of means of subsistence into which this value is converted now appears as the distinction between nominal and real wages' (Marx, 1867 [1976], p. 683). In other words, and assuming that the value of money is constant and equal to 1, the nominal wage is the equivalent of the value of labour-power expressed in money, while the real wage is the means of subsistence placed at the disposal of the worker.[11]

> But although price, being the exponent of the magnitude of a commodity's value, is the exponent of its exchange-ratio with money, it does not follow that the exponent of this exchange-ratio is necessarily the exponent of the magnitude of the commodity's value... With the transformation of the magnitude of value into the price this necessary relation appears as the exchange-ratio between a single commodity and the money commodity which exists outside it. This relation, however, may express both the magnitude of value of the commodity and the greater or lesser quantity of money for which it can be sold under the given circumstances. The possibility, therefore, of a quantitative incongruity between price and magnitude of value, i.e. *the possibility that the price may diverge from the magnitude of value, is inherent in the price-form itself*. (Marx, 1867 [1976], p. 196. Emphasis added.)

This means that at any given moment – and we are interested in looking into this case – it can exist a discrepancy between what the worker needs for the reproduction of his/her labour-power and the wage that he/she receives. After all what lies behind the determination of the price and value of labour-power is the class struggle.

Thus, it will be useful for our purposes to have a characterisation of the price-form of the labour-power that can act as an indicator, as an expression of that situation where exchange value and value actually coincide. It is also convenient, given the analytical instrument that we will use (linear algebra), to define that characterisation in terms of the real wage, that is in terms of the amount of commodities that the worker receives in exchange for his/her labour-power during a specific period of time. So we shall call *concrete value of labour-power* (Montesino, 2007, p. 132) to mean that definite quantity of commodities for which the labour-power is exchanged and which value is exactly equivalent to the value of labour-power. It is measured in *kind*, and the term *concrete* makes explicit this fact.[12]

This characterisation helps us to see more clearly the link between labour productivity and the value of labour-power, a link that the capitalists use in order to get the most from the labour-power they acquire, that is, to maximise the distance between paid labour and the newly added labour. Indeed, for instance (Montesino, 2007, p. 134):

(i) if labour productivity increases while the concrete value of labour-power remains constant, then the value of labour-power, that is the socially necessary labour time for its production, decreases and the rate of surplus value rises;
(ii) if labour productivity increases while the value of labour-power remains constant, or what is the same, while the rate of surplus value is unaltered, then the concrete value of labour-power increases and both workers and capitalists dispose of more commodities for consumption and production;
(iii) if labour productivity increases in a higher proportion than the decrease in the value of labour-power, then the concrete value of labour-power increases but in a smaller proportion than the increase in productivity, meaning that there is a rise in the rate of surplus value as well;[13]
(iv) if labour productivity remains constant, changes in the value of labour-power only modifies the distribution of the new value created, altering in the same direction the concrete value of labour-power while in the opposite direction the rate of surplus value.

Because the real wage actually received by the worker may be or may not be equal to the concrete value of labour-power, we shall look at the capacity of the former to cover the latter; that is we shall talk about the *coverage* of the concrete value of labour-power. If for example the labour-power is exchanged for a quantity of commodities that is smaller than that representing its value, a deterioration of the worker's living conditions will occur and as a result the quality of the labour-power will be undermined along with the labour productivity.[14]

Since we will be working with the concrete value of labour-power, for consistency reasons and in order to be able to perform algebraic operations with them, the rest of the variables considered should also be expressed in kind. Such treatment is not strange to Marx's work. In Chapter 9 of *Capital*, Volume I, Section 2 ('The Representation of the Value of the Product by Corresponding Proportional Parts of the Product', pp. 329–332), Marx, using an example about a factory of yarn, expresses each one of the component parts of the value of the commodity (constant capital, variable capital and surplus value) in their respective equivalent amount of commodities produced during the working day: in lbs of yarn.

Taking the average working day as the socially necessary labour time in order to produce certain amount of commodities within an industry (e.g. a factory of yarn) in average conditions,[15] and assuming that the value of money is constant and equal to 1, such quantity of commodities may be expressed as:

$$C + V + S = \rho, \tag{1}$$

where C is the quantity of commodities corresponding to constant (used-up) capital, V is the quantity of commodities corresponding to variable capital, that is the concrete value of labour-power, S is the quantity of commodities corresponding to surplus value and ρ is the quantity of commodities produced or total product. Expression (1) can also be written as:

$$\rho = C + V + S = V(n + 1 + z), \tag{2}$$

where n is the organic composition of capital (C/V) and z is the rate of surplus value (S/V).[16] If in addition we denote by PrV the real wage that the worker receives and we assume that it is equal to V, that is that 100 per cent of the concrete value of labour-power is covered by the worker's remuneration, then:

$$\rho = C + V + S = V(n + 1 + z) = PrV(n + 1 + z). \tag{3}$$

Let us consider the following example. Using the data provided by Marx in *Capital*, Volume I, Chapter 9, we have that the product of a working day is 20 lb of yarn: 8/10 of which is constant capital, C, while 2/10 is the newly added value, $V+S$. Hence, the proportion of past labour to living labour, $C/(V+S)$, is equal to 4. If the rate of exploitation is 100 per cent, then 1/10 of the product is concrete value of labour-power, V, and 1/10, surplus value, S. Thus, in Fig. 1 the length of the horizontal line represents the amount of lbs of yarn produced during the working day. Then, by Eq. (3): $V = PrV = 2$ lb of yarn, $n = 8$, $z = 1$ and:

$$\rho = V(n + 1 + z) = 2(8 + 1 + 1) = 20 \text{ lbs of yarn.} \tag{4}$$

Assume that due to technological change, labour productivity increases while the concrete value of labour-power and the proportion of past labour

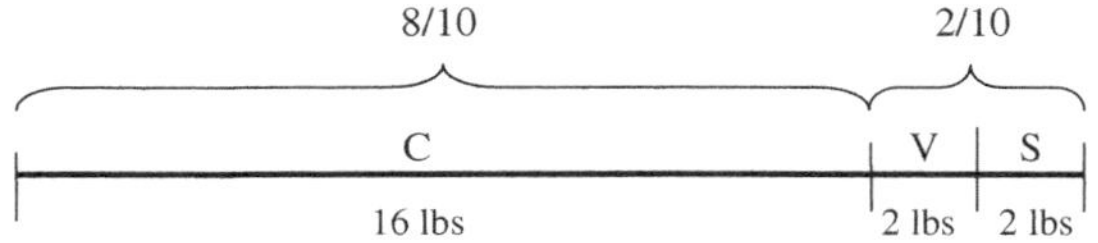

Fig. 1. The Value of the Total Product by Corresponding Proportional Parts of it When $PrV = V$.

to living labour are held constant. What will vary is the relationship between *past* labour to *necessary* labour (i.e. n) as well as the way in which the 20 per cent of the commodities produced by the living labour are distributed between *necessary* and *surplus* labour. If n doubles, $C = 32$ lb of yarn and $V + S = 8$ lb of yarn. The total product will also be doubled, and because the working day has not changed at all, the unit value of the commodities (measured in socially necessary labour time) will be reduced by half. Since $V = 2$ lb of yarn, then $S = 6$ lb of yarn and the new distribution is 5 per cent of the commodities produced correspond to real wages and 15 per cent to surplus value, that is the new rate of exploitation is $z = 3$. In other words, as a result of an increase in the organic composition of capital, which provokes in turn a proportional increase in the total product, past labour and surplus labour have a higher participation in the distribution of the material wealth, while the participation of the paid labour falls.

The increase in labour productivity is an inherent characteristic of the working of the capitalist mode of production inspired by the conflictive interaction of 'many capitals'. Due to capitalist competition, or better said, due to the needs imposed by the logic of capital accumulation (i.e. the valorisation of capital) which are expressed through competition, each individual capital is incited to reduce as much as possible the value of the commodity that it produces. Such reduction is possible by the constant increase of labour productivity. The *main* tool to achieve this goal is the mechanisation of the labour process, the gradual and constant increase of the composition of capital, which implies the replacement of living labour by past labour[17] (see Appendix A).

Note that expression (3) can be seen as the inner product of vector PrV $(= V)$ and vector $(n + 1 + z)$, which consists of the technological component n, the rate of surplus value z and the scalar 1 (this vector is called by Montesino, 2007, the 'socio-technological vector'). The projection of V on the direction of $(n + 1 + z)$ is PrV, that is the real wage that the worker receives, which until now we have supposed identical to V (Fig. 2).

As we know by expression (3), the inner product of PrV $(= V)$ and $(n + 1 + z)$ is equal to the total product, ρ. Hence, the higher is PrV $(= V)$, *ceteris paribus*, the higher will be ρ.

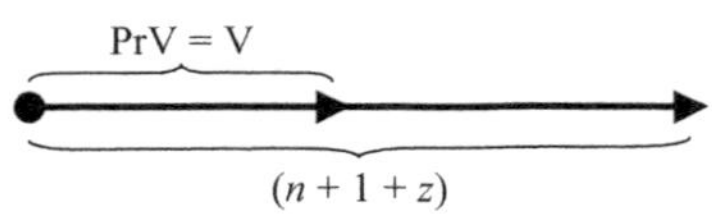

Fig. 2. The Projection of V on the Direction of $(n + 1 + z)$ When $PrV = V$.

Now, assuming for simplicity that n and z are held constant, we will relax the assumption $PrV = V$, allowing for discrepancies between these two magnitudes at one specific moment. As stated above, this is a possibility intrinsic to the price form of the value of the commodities and, in the case of the peculiar commodity labour-power, the determination of its price also entails the capital and labour conflict: V is an objective magnitude, whereas PrV is mostly determined by the capitalist class who has the power to do it and whose motivation is the maximisation of the surplus value. It is realistic therefore to consider that at some point, $PrV < V$.[18] Hence, V will not be in the direction of $(n+1+z)$, implying the existence of an angle $\alpha > 0$ between the two vectors. The level of coverage will be given by:

$$PrV = V\cos(\alpha), \tag{5}$$

where $\cos(\alpha)$ is the proportion of the concrete value of labour-power that is covered by the real wage received, PrV. The greater the angle α, the smaller the percentage of V covered by PrV. Thus:

$$0 \leq \cos(\alpha) \leq 1 \quad \text{if} \quad 90^\circ \geq \alpha \geq 0^\circ. \tag{6}$$

Graphically, it is shown in Fig. 3.

Recalling the data of our example and assuming that we observe an angle $\alpha = 30^\circ$, *ceteris paribus* (i.e. $n = 8$, $z = 1$ and $C/(V+S) = 4$), then the proportion of the concrete value of labour-power covered by the real wage is $\cos(30^\circ) = 0.8660$, that is 13.4 per cent of the concrete value of labour-power cannot be covered by the remuneration that the worker receives, and what he receives instead of 2 lb of yarn is:

$$PrV = V\cos(\alpha) = 2(0.8660) = 1.732051 \text{ lbs of yarn.} \tag{7}$$

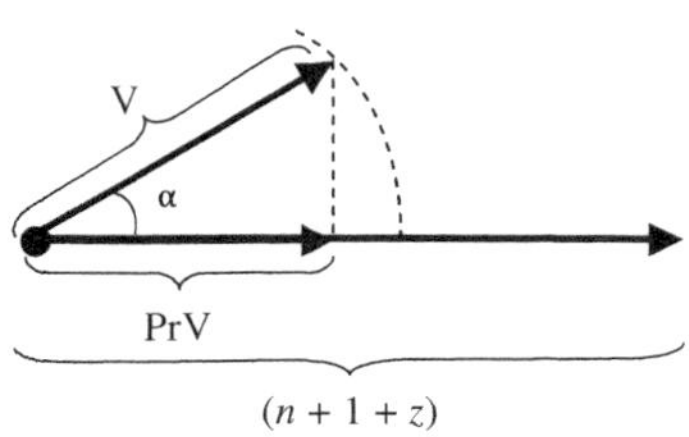

Fig. 3. The Projection of V on $(n+1+z)$ When $PrV < V$.

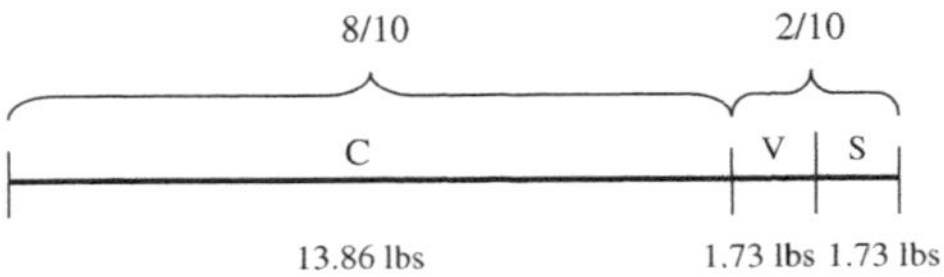

Fig. 4. The Value of the Total Product by Corresponding Proportional Parts of it When $PrV < V$.

The total product is then:

$$\rho = PrV(n + 1 + z) = 1.732051(8 + 1 + 1) = 17.32051 \text{ lbs of yarn,} \qquad (8)$$

which implies $\Delta\rho/\rho \equiv -13.4\% \equiv (PrV - V)/V$. This situation is depicted in Fig. 4.

To sum up, the insufficient coverage of the concrete value of labour-power causes a deterioration of the quality of the labour-power that in turn results in a smaller total product (Fig. 4). Less production means less available material wealth for consumption and accumulation. And, from the standpoint of the individual capital, a reduction in productivity also implies less ability to compete, that is to appropriate surplus value. Finally, the reduced capacity of the worker may also result in a deficient use of technology, negatively affecting n and, ultimately, the development of the productive powers (see Appendix B).

Wage Labour, Unpaid Reproductive Labour and the Coverage of the Concrete Value of Labour-Power

In this section, we intend to study the link between wage labour and unpaid reproductive labour in relation to the normal reproduction of the labour-power. For that, we shall consider the following assumptions:

(a) We understand by 'household' the family as defined in capitalist societies: heterosexual marriage with dependent members (average size household). This is the main (private) entity on which capital relies for the reproduction of the working class, a process that operates *outside* the limits of the immediate spheres of production and circulation of commodities.[19]

(b) Both men and women participate in wage labour as well as in unpaid reproductive labour, although in different proportions: while women spend on average less hours per day performing wage labour and more hours performing unpaid reproductive labour, men do exactly the opposite. This is consistent with the fact that female remuneration is socially regarded as merely 'supplementary'.[20]

(c) The real wage per hour is a given magnitude expressed in kind, and it is the same for men and women.[21]

(d) The time that individuals spend in wage labour is mutually exclusive with the time they spend in unpaid reproductive labour.

(e) Households are time constrained: they dispose of a limited amount of hours per day (i.e. 48 hours, namely 24 hours each, man and woman) for performing all the needed activities for the reproduction of the labour-power. Such hours comprise (1) the total labour time of the household (wage labour and unpaid reproductive labour of man and woman) and (2) the consumption, resting and leisure time, that is the free time or non-labour time available to be distributed between man and woman. None of these two parts can be diminished to zero without jeopardising the reproduction of the labour-power. However, the boundary between one another is flexible; for example, if needed, the household can increase the total labour time at the expense of reducing the total non-labour time.

The total labour time that the household has in a day for the reproduction of the labour-power (LT_H) is given by:

$$LT_H = WL + URL = LT_M + LT_F \tag{9}$$

where WL is the total time spent performing wage labour, URL is the total time spent performing unpaid reproductive labour, LT_M is the labour time that the man engages in wage labour and in unpaid reproductive labour and LT_F is the labour time that the woman engages in wage labour and in unpaid reproductive labour, such that:

$$\begin{array}{lcl} LT_M & = & \lambda WL + (1-\sigma)URL \\ LT_F & = & (1-\lambda)WL + \sigma URL \\ \hline LT_H & = & WL + URL \end{array} \tag{10}$$

where $\lambda, \sigma \in \mathbb{R}$ such that $0 \leq \lambda \leq 1$ and $0 \leq \sigma \leq 1$. According to assumption (b), λ is strictly greater than $(1-\lambda)$, while σ is strictly greater than $(1-\sigma)$. Graphically, in the two-dimensional plane (in a similar fashion with the Edgeworth box) and with a given LT_H, it is shown in Fig. 5.

In Fig. 5, we suppose that $\sigma = 2(1-\sigma)$ and $\lambda = 2(1-\lambda)$; that is women spend the double of the time performing URL than men, whereas they spend only the half of the time spent by men in WL. This assumption is based on the

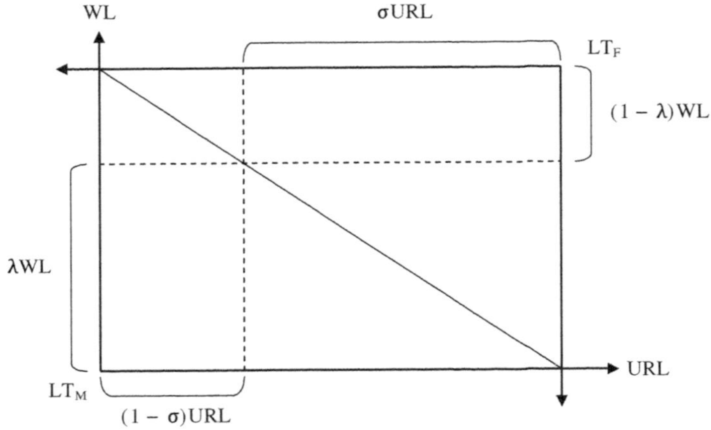

Fig. 5. The Graph of the LT_H by LT_M and LT_F.

information provided by the Department of Economic and Social Affairs of the United Nations (2010, pp. 100–102) (see also footnote no. 1). In particular, for instance:

$$\begin{aligned} LT_M &= \frac{2}{3}WL + \frac{1}{3}URL \\ LT_F &= \frac{1}{3}WL + \frac{2}{3}URL \\ \hline LT &= WL + URL \end{aligned} \tag{11}$$

In order to be consistent with what the statistics report about the 'total work burden' (i.e. the performance of WL and URL) for men and women, which is superior for the latter, we should also assume that the URL participates in a greater proportion than WL in LT_H (in Fig. 5, width is greater than height). For example, if approximately the 60 per cent of LT_H is allocated to URL while the 40 per cent to WL, and if the household disposes of 16 hours per day of non-labour time, then:

$$\begin{aligned} LT_M &= 8 + 6.7 = 14.7 \\ LT_F &= 4 + 13.3 = 17.3 \\ \hline LT_H &= 12 + 20 = 32 \end{aligned} \tag{12}$$

The man has 9.3 hours per day of free time, while the woman has 6.7 hours.

Based on these assumptions, we will study three cases in relation to the reproduction of the labour-power within the household: Case 1, in which the concrete value of labour-power is 100 per cent covered by the real wage received by the household; Case 2, in which it is insufficiently covered; Case 3, in which even when the concrete value of labour-power is completely covered, the distribution of the means of subsistence received by the household creates conflicts between man and woman.

Case 1: $PrV = V$, or the *normal* reproduction of the labour-power

According to assumption (c), the real wage per hour is equal for men and women, then the total remuneration received by the household is:

$$PrV = PrV_M + PrV_F. \tag{13}$$

Given that the man spends longer hours in wage labour than the woman, his remuneration is the main one, a fact that allows him to have the control over the resources received by the household. Man and woman bear capitalist exploitation, but the burden of the unpaid reproductive labour is greater for the woman due to the gender oppression that she has to face as well.[22] In addition we suppose that:

$$PrV = PrV_M + PrV_F = V, \tag{14}$$

that is, as shown in Fig. 6, the means of subsistence that the household receives cover entirely the concrete value of labour-power. Yet, as we know, such means of subsistence require of a process of preparation or transformation in order to be apt for consumption; that is they require the production process that involves the reproductive labour. The greatest part of these tasks is performed by the woman, but their outcome is enjoyed by all the members of the family.[23]

If the unpaid reproductive labour did not exist, if the majority of the activities were performed by individuals outside the household (i.e. by capitalist enterprises – leaving aside the informal economy or non-capitalist forms of production), the cost of production of the labour-power would be greater, and capital would be forced to pay higher wages.[24] Put it differently,

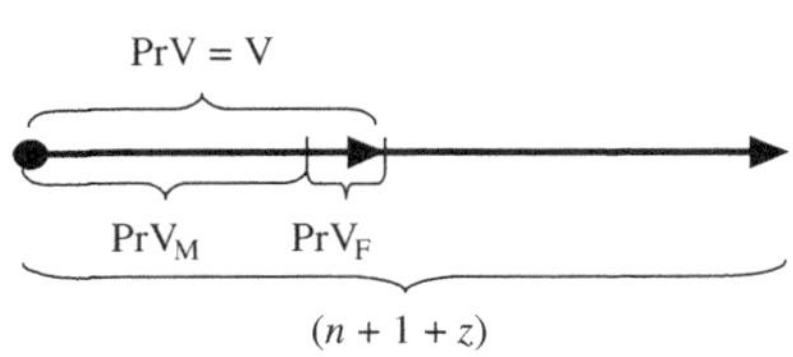

Fig. 6. The Projection of V on $(n+1+z)$ When $PrV = PrV_M PrV_F = V$.

the unpaid reproductive labour is one of the factors that help capital to maintain the downward pressure on wages, helping it in turn to achieve its goal of reducing worker's individual consumption as much as possible. If wages should be superior than what they are in average, if capital, thanks to the family organisation of the reproductive labour, does not have to carry all the cost of the reproduction of the working class, it means that the households are *partially self-reproduced*, even when wages are equivalent to the value of labour-power. This grants flexibility to capital to pay wages below the value of labour-power, increasing thus, although 'artificially' (i.e. without changes in technology or in work organisation), the rate of surplus value. In general, a transference of value from the households to the capitalists, an *indirect* appropriation of surplus value, is present, and this is precisely one of the contributions of the unpaid reproductive labour to the capitalist accumulation.[25]

Case 2: $PrV < V$, or a *class* conflict

Due to the flexibility mentioned above, capital is in a position to pay wages below the value of labour-power at any given moment. For instance, capital can implement through the state an 'austerity measure' (highly famous in many European countries nowadays) enacting a general reduction in wages as a counteracting factor of the economic crisis, such that $PrV = PrV_M + PrV_F < V$. Men and women would see their wages per hour reduced in the same proportion, as shown in Fig. 7.

This situation involves a deep class struggle for the distribution of the commodities produced, as it implies the deterioration of the living conditions of the working class. If a greater number of hours of wage labour is not possible, the reduced means of subsistence received by the household will call for an increase in the time allocated to the unpaid reproductive

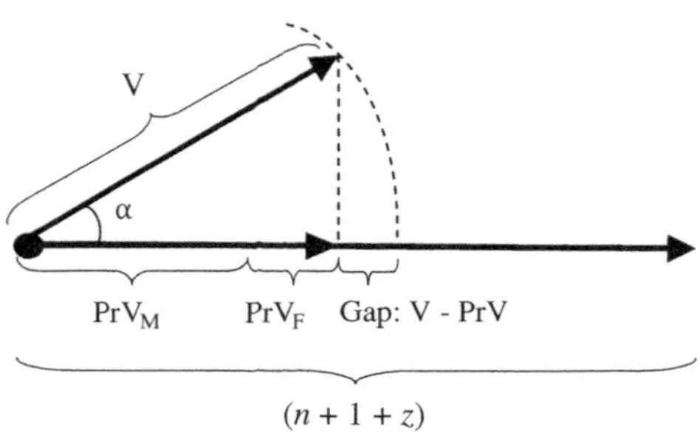

Fig. 7. The Projection of V on $(n+1+a)$ When $PrV = PrV_M + PrV_F < V$.

labour so as to try to cover as much as possible the gap between PrV and V. For example, and returning to the data considered in previous sections, if a reduction of 20 per cent in the real wages takes place, that is if $\alpha = 36.87°$, the means of subsistence received by the household will be $PrV = 1.6$ lb of yarn, of which 1.07 lb are PrV_M, and the remaining 0.53 lb, PrV_F. In order to maintain the labour-power in its normal quality, the household must compensate the 0.4 lb of yarn that are missing, otherwise a deterioration will occur, provoking negative consequences for the workers and the capitalists (recall Appendix B). Fortunately, we know, 'the capitalist may safely leave this to the worker's drives for self-preservation and propagation' (Marx, 1867 [1976], p. 718), and the reduced amount of means of subsistence can be partially or completely covered by more household production, that is by more unpaid reproductive labour. Even if we assume that there is no gender conflict for the distribution of the products, either of the wage labour or of the reproductive labour, the woman is always the one bearing the greatest weight of an increased labour time. Thus, given the situation presented by expression (12) and knowing that the rate of surplus value is 100 per cent, it is possible to obtain the increment in URL that those 0.4 lb of yarn mean to the household: 1.2 hours, such that 0.8 hours correspond to the unpaid reproductive labour performed by the woman, and 0.4 hours to the man's, and therefore:

$$\begin{array}{r} LT_M = 8 + 7.1 = 15.1 \\ \underline{LT_F = 4 + 14.1 = 18.1} \\ LT_H = 12 + 21.2 = 33.2 \end{array} \tag{15}$$

The non-labour time is now 8.9 hours per day for the man and 5.9 hours for the woman.

In brief: (1) the unpaid reproductive labour helps to maintain the quality of the under-remunerated labour-power in a level that is closer to its normal, in other words, it helps to reduce the negative effects of an insufficiently remunerated labour-power and (2) it helps to maintain the situation $PrV < V$, and/or to push it towards it.

Capital disposes of an indirect source of *gratis* labour which is economically invisible and socially diminished, a favourable environment for its perpetuation. Indeed, if $PrV < V$ is not temporary, after some time a new value of labour-power would be established as a result of new arrangements in the market, but above all as a result of new arrangements within the households. The socially necessary labour time for the reproduction of labour-power would be modified, set in a lower level than before, and labour-power would be adapted to the new conditions, thanks to its social and historical element. But this process also has limits, after which the reduction of the worker's individual consumption is transform into a negative aspect for capital.

Case 3: $PrV = V$, accompanied by a *gender* conflict

We suppose that capitalists pay wages equivalent to the value of labour-power like in expression (14) above: $PrV = PrV_M + PrV_F = V$. Within the household, however, there exists an inadequate distribution of the means of subsistence received as wages, such that the family is not able to carry out the normal reproduction of the labour-power. In particular, given that the man possesses the control over the resources received, he is in conditions of withdrawing and keeping for himself part of those means of subsistence (e.g. he can use them for consumption that is not related to the normal reproduction of the labour-power), hindering thus the household production process. An insufficient household production, if not countered, leads to a deterioration of the quality of the labour-power and, consequently, to the decline of the labour productivity and production (recall Appendix B). This situation can be characterised as a gender conflict. As we know, due to the patriarchal relations, men and women hold different social position and social power. The woman has a restricted access to the household's resources (and to productive resources in general), and she does not have enough bargaining power to claim them nor is likely to emerge victorious from a clash against the man. Even so, the greatest responsibility for the 'proper' working of the household falls on her (and as a result, she is also the one to blame if things do not work as they are supposed to).

The outcome of the wage labour of both man and woman works as an input in the household production. As suggested above, the two types of labour show an inverse relation: less hours of unpaid reproductive labour implies higher cost of production of the labour-power and therefore higher wages; and lower wages may be partially or completely compensated by more hours engaged in unpaid reproductive labour, that is by a greater household production. None of them can be zero. A minimum amount of means of subsistence in the form of wages is necessary in order to carry out the household production, and the same holds for the products of the unpaid reproductive labour. In this sense, the man could easily keep for himself an important proportion of his wage, letting the household with a minimum amount while enjoying the products of the unpaid reproductive labour. Naturally, even if he keeps only a small part of his wage, the burden of an increased unpaid reproductive labour is higher for the woman. In terms of our example, if he retains 0.4 lb of yarn (i.e. around 30 per cent of his remuneration) when wages are $PrV = PrV_M + PrV_F = 2$ lb of yarn, then 1.2 hours of additional unpaid reproductive labour would be needed in order to maintain the labour-power in its normal quality, from which 0.8 hours correspond to the woman's unpaid reproductive labour, and 0.4 hours to the man's (see expressions (12) and (15) above).

Note that the *direct* beneficiaries of a situation like this are not the capitalists but men. Actually, such situation could be counterproductive for capital. Even in the questionable event in which the man is willing to compensate his harmful actions towards the normal reproduction of the household by increasing the hours that he spends performing reproductive labour,[26] such increment will always be smaller than the one experienced by the woman, suggesting a gender conflict due to time use and, in general, a situation of conflict between man and woman – since the latter has to sacrifice non-labour time in order to counteract the consequences of the former's behaviour. Beyond certain limit, this circumstance leads to a deterioration in the woman's living conditions and hence to a deterioration in the quality of her labour-power. But the deterioration of the woman's labour capacity has detrimental effects on the provision of unpaid reproductive labour and, given that she is the main provider of it, this implies that the quality of the labour-power of the rest of the members of the family will be damaged as well. The negative effects of an insufficient coverage of the concrete value of the labour-power would not be triggered by wages below the value of labour-power, but by a poorly reproduction of women's labour capacity. This is a clear adverse consequence of the patriarchal social relations on capital accumulation.

CONCLUDING REMARKS

As Marx showed throughout his work, contradiction is at the core of the capitalist mode of production. The logic that eagerly drives capital after profits dictating actions and movements is, beyond some limits, the cause of its loss. Its very historical role, the utmost development of the productive forces, is compromised by its own normal working and by its requirements of self-preservation. Capital moves between several definite and growing boundaries, beyond which crises burst. It is hence innate to this conflictive working that the patriarchal social relations have contradictory effects on capital accumulation. They also, beyond certain limits, transform their contributions into disadvantages for capital. Both positive and negative effects work together in reality, for they are one; that is they belong to the same set of social relations and norms that participate in the process of production and reproduction as a whole.

In the particular form of patriarchal domination that we study, the unequal distribution of tasks by gender within the households, that is the control of women's labour-power within a gender division of labour related to the reproduction of labour-power, we find that whenever there is a conflict between man and woman over the resources of the household, the outcome can be harmful for capital accumulation, because it entails losses of labour productivity. But when no gender conflict appears, when each individual performs his/her role as imposed by the patriarchal and capitalist social relations, there are important contributions for capital accumulation. The presence of the unpaid reproductive labour, and moreover, the organisation of the reproductive labour in 'families', is a mechanism that helps capital to achieve its goal of increasing the rate of surplus value as much as possible. Capital needs an increasingly high labour productivity, along with an increasingly high rate of surplus value, in order to carry on the accumulation process. This implies an intense and constant attack to the living conditions of the working class, an attack that is counteracted by the class struggle but also by the family organisation where the woman is the key element.

An interesting question arises: Is the unpaid reproductive labour necessary for the capitalist accumulation process? Could capitalism work properly without it? Moreover, are the patriarchal social relations needed for the capitalist mode of production? Appearances seem to say that capitalism could not only work without the unpaid reproductive labour, since it has shown some advances towards that direction,[27] but it could even obtain profits by taking over the activities that are now performed in the private sphere of the household. Nevertheless, although important and real, the mentioned advances have been no more than modifications of the family as it was known in previous modes of production, its adaptation to the needs of capital exploitation, not its dissolution but its evolution into an organisation more functional to capital. In other words, the family organisation of the reproductive labour and, in general, the patriarchal social relations are constituent parts of the capitalist mode of production as a whole, of its social relations, morality, ideology, productive process, social interaction and so on. All elements participate and contribute to the working of the capitalist system. Their counterproductive effects are no more than parts of the normal working of a socio-economic organisation that makes room for itself at the time that sets obstacles to its movement.

Capitalism and patriarchy are so intertwined that they are indeed one. Capitalism has subsumed patriarchal social relations to its own logic, it has used them for its benefit, it has developed them and adapted them according to its needs; and patriarchy, being far more old than capitalism, the survivor of several radical and historical economic changes, and being so deeply installed in society, has found its way to continue alive, and with no doubt it is perfectly able to do so even after capitalism's end, but here and now it responds to capital's demands.

There are several economic and social interests, imposed by the logic of capital accumulation, carefully keeping this state of things, this system organised on domination over domination: capital is eager for having free and cheap labour in order to pursue profits, and men are eager for having and controlling women's work and labour-power in order to keep their superior and advantageous position.[28]

It follows that the fight for the dissolution of the patriarchal domination is at the same time the fight for the dissolution of the capitalist relations of exploitation, and in the end, the fight against all forms of subjugation: the construction of a society with *no* social classes. Still, it is highly important to recognise the gender conflict as a *real* conflict, that is to avoid falling into the trap of regarding it as something subsumed or of secondary importance in the struggle against capital, or even worse, as something that will be 'automatically' solved once capitalism is vanquished. On the contrary, given the wide net of *résistance* that patriarchy has shown over the centuries, the battle against it must be stressed and strengthen. After all, no really unified, powerful and effective working class can exist as long as this conflict exists, and – as stated by the League for the Revolutionary Party (1989) – as long as male workers continue identifying themselves with at least one element of bourgeois consciousness: sexism. The gender struggle therefore must be developed within the class struggle and *during* the construction of that society with no social classes, having at all times present that the forms of domination that women face are not mere conceptions that we can throw away by 'changing our mind', that is by getting rid of the *idea* according to which women are inferior to men, but by rising up against the very social organisation of the production of life, against the economic activity on which it lies, against the capitalist relations that have become an unbearable alien power (see Marx & Engels, 1845–1846). Only when such movement is universally organised, along with highly developed productive powers so that no material basis for oppression can exist any longer, is that new and higher forms of social relations will become reality.

NOTES

1. See for instance the statistics presented by the Department of Economic and Social Affairs of the United Nations (2010, pp. 101–102): 'women spend more time than men on domestic work, on average roughly twice as much or more. Many women are also employed, although they tend to spend less time in paid work than men… Nevertheless, the total work burden – considering both paid and unpaid work – is higher for women than men'.

2. Labour-power was transformed into commodity with and for the development of capitalist social relations of production, and along with it the abstract labour as value-creating substance acquired status of empirical reality and theoretical category. See Part II of Marx's *Capital*, Volume I, and Rubin 1928 [1979].

3. The necessary activities for the production and reproduction of the labour-power do not include, naturally, the housework, care-work and so on carried out for the reproduction of the members of the capitalist class. This is another issue that is not interesting for us at the moment. However, it should be noted that in general the household labour is socially considered a menial activity and therefore is rewarded as such. Several frameworks have been proposed in order to explain this matter. See for instance England (2005) for an account of five of those frameworks, all of them related with the fact that this labour is mainly a women's occupation.

4. 'The family as economic unit not only fills the capitalists' fundamental need for the reproduction of labor power, but the family-based division of labor also enables capitalism to keep down the social wage: public services like child care, education and health care. To the degree that workers accept the myth of the family as a private refuge from their jobs and dealings with their bosses, no matter how bad things really get in reality, they are restrained from making demands on the state for social needs. Whatever needs are not met at home become the failure of the individual family, especially the wife, rather than the bosses' (League for the Revolutionary Party, 1989). See also, from a historical perspective, Engels (1884).

5. A combination of the two mentioned types of performing reproductive labour is also observed.

6. 'Racial hierarchies, like gender hierarchies, are aspects of our social organization, of how people are produced and reproduced. They are not fundamentally ideological; they constitute that second aspect of our mode of production, the production and reproduction of people. It might be most accurate then to refer to our societies not as, for example, simply "capitalist", but as "patriarchal capitalist white supremacist"' (Hartmann, 1979, p. 13). '[T]he crucial elements of patriarchy as we *currently* experience them [in capitalism] are: heterosexual marriage (and consequent homophobia), female childrearing and housework, women's economic dependence of men (enforced by arrangements in the labour market), the state, and numerous institutions based on social relations among men – clubs, sports, unions, professions, universities, churches, corporations, and armies… It appears as if each woman is oppressed by her own man alone' (Hartmann, 1979, p. 14. Italics of the author). Yet, such domination is *social*. On the coexistence of patriarchy and the modes of production: 'There appears to be no *necessary* connection between *changes* in the one aspect of production and changes in the other. A society could undergo transition from capitalism to socialism, for example, and remain patriarchal' (Hartmann, 1979,

p. 13. Italics of the author). Something similar is stated by the League for the Revolutionary Party (1989): 'women's oppression is not just a historical legacy; it is specifically molded to serve capitalism. But women have undeniably been oppressed for thousands of years. What is to say that the specific capitalist mode will not be replaced by another system with its own specific internal drive to oppress women?'

7. 'Marx throws out as useless the question of what kind of labor is productive in general, in all historical epochs, independently of the given social relations. Every system of production relations, every economic order, has its concept of productive labor. Marx confined his analysis to the question of which labor is productive from the standpoint of capital, or in the capitalist system of economy' (Rubin, 1928 [1979], p. 316).

8. 'Capitalist production is not merely the production of commodities, it is essentially the production of surplus-value... That laborer alone is productive, who produces surplus-value for the capitalist, and thus works for the self-expansion of capital… the notion of a productive laborer implies not merely a relation between work and useful effect, between laborer and product of labor, but also a specific social relation of production, a relation that has sprung up historically and stamps the laborer as the direct means of creating surplus-value' (Marx quoted by Rubin, 1928 [1979], p. 315).

9. Workers performing reproductive labour in the way stated above belong also to the Industrial Reserve Army and/or to the Relative Surplus-Population, with all the benefits that such organic part of capital runs for it. See Martínez Peinado (1986).

10. This instrument was first proposed by Montesino (2007) in his PhD dissertation.

11. Recall that nominal and real wages may differ due to labour productivity, and even move in opposite directions. For instance it is possible to observe a fall in nominal wages while the mass of workers' means of subsistence that those wages buy increases.

12. We do not suppose that the worker is paid in kind. We simply measure such remuneration, when it is the exact expression of the value of labour-power, in means of subsistence or quantity of commodities.

13. This is in fact, according to Marx, the normal state of things in capitalism: 'the increasing productivity of labour is accompanied by a cheapening of the worker… and it is therefore accompanied by a higher rate of surplus-value, even when real wages are rising. The latter never rise in proportion to the productivity of labour' (Marx, 1867 [1976], p. 753).

14. 'The ultimate or minimum limit of the value of the labour-power is formed by the value of the commodities which have to be supplied every day to the bearer of labour-power, the man, so that he can renew his life-process. That is to say, the limit is formed by the value of the physically indispensable means of subsistence. If the price of labour-power falls to this minimum, it falls below its value, since under such circumstances it can be maintained and developed only in a crippled state, and the value of every commodity is determined by the labour-time required to provide it in its normal quality' (Marx, 1867 [1976], pp. 276–277).

15. We shall not enter in the process of transforming values into prices of production. As it is known, for industries in average conditions values and prices of production are the same.

16. Since C, V and S have the same unit of measure, for example lbs of yarn, that is, their respective value is measured in lbs of yarn, we can divide C lb of yarn by V lb of yarn and obtain n, which is the definition of the organic composition of capital (see Marx, 1867 [1976], p. 762). Similarly, if we divide S lb of yarn by V lb of yarn, we will obtain z, which is the rate of surplus value.

17. The process of competition, as well as the interaction of the two levels of abstraction: capital in general versus many capitals or individual capital, which refers to the contradiction between the private and social character of capitalist production, are at the heart of the Marxist law of the falling rate of profit. Recall that the average or general rate of profit can be expressed as $r = z/(n+1)$. Hence, the constant increase in n, which is the result of the coercive action of the accumulation process expressed in the interaction of 'many capitals', that is competition, when it is not followed (and that is precisely what happens in the end, even if the concrete value of labour-power is held constant!) by a more than proportional increase in z (one of the counteractive factors that confer to the law its character of 'tendency', see Chapter 14 of Volume III of *Capital*), produces a fall in r. See Marx (1857–1861 [1973], specially p. 340) and Mateo Tomé et al. (2012).

18. Marx regarded the reduction in wages below the value of the labour-power as one of the counteractive factors of the tendency of the rate of profit to fall (see Marx, 1894 [1981], Ch. 14). While for Rosa Luxemburg, '[t]he real wage permanently tends to be reduced until the absolute minimum, until the physical vital minimum, this means that there exists a permanent tendency of capital to pay the labour-power *below* its value' (Luxemburg, 1925 [1972], p. 228. The translation is ours. Emphasis of the author), tendency that would be counteracted by the action of the syndicates and the class struggle. There are fundamental differences between exchange of commodities that are *not* labour-power and exchange of commodities that involve labour-power. In the second case, '[t]he two people who face each other on the market place, in the sphere of circulation, are not just a *buyer* and a *seller*, but *capitalist* and *worker* who confront each other as *buyer* and *seller*. Their relationship as *capitalist* and *worker* is the precondition of their relationship as *buyer* and *seller*' (Marx, 1867 [1976], p. 1015. Emphasis of the author). This social relationship, unlike the one of the buyers and sellers of other kind of commodities, derives from the fact that the worker confronts the objective conditions of labour, that is the means of production and the means of subsistence, as something *alien* to him, and this separation is so radical that such conditions 'appear as *independent persons* confronting the worker, for as their owner the capitalist is merely their personification, in opposition to the worker who is the owner of nothing but his labour-power' (Marx, 1867 [1976], p. 1017). Precisely because of this *qualitative* element in the exchange of labour-power for other commodities, this exchange can affect the *quality* of such commodity, and vice versa. Changes in the quality of the labour-power are expressed in a greater or a smaller labour productivity and, if its value remains constant, this modifies the exchange value of labour-power, something that does not happen with the rest of commodities. But if labour-power is exchanged for less than its value, this affects *its* quality because what is on stake is the reproduction of the life of the worker under normal conditions (Montesino, 2007, p. 133). We shall concentrate in this case, leaving aside the problem of the quantitative incongruity between prices and values of the rest of commodities, which implies the problem of

the equalization of the rate of profit in the context of 'many capitals', but no direct *class struggle*. Consequently, we shall continue assuming that the industry in which we are focusing operates in *average* or socially normal conditions.

19. '[T]he maintenance and reproduction of the working class remains a necessary condition for the reproduction of capital. But the capitalist may safely leave this to the worker's drives for self-preservation and propagation. All the capitalist cares for is to reduce the worker's individual consumption to the necessary minimum' (Marx, 1867 [1976], p. 718).

20. According to Philp and Wheatley (2011), presenting data provided by Hakim (2000), at least three-fifths of the female working age population combine employment with family life, although they are not overly committed to their careers, while another one-fifth is indeed centred in their jobs. The remaining one-fifth comprises the female working age population who do not sell their labour-power and are fully engaged with household work. According to the results presented by *The World's Women 2010: Trends and Statistics,* 'In general, women's increased participation in paid employment has not been accompanied by an increase in men's participation in unpaid domestic work (comprised mainly of housework and caring for dependent household members). Time use statistics... show that in all regions, women dedicate much more time to domestic work than men do' (Department of Economic and Social Affairs of United Nations, 2010, p. 99). Recall also footnote no. 1.

21. This is a conservative assumption, since it is a well known fact that men's average wage is higher than women's for the same activity and labour time.

22. In fact, the reproduction of women's life and labour-power is conditioned by or 'earned' through the performance of reproductive labour. As pointed out by Marx (1867 [1976], p. 990), the rule of the capitalist over the worker is provided by the rule of the capitalist over the means of subsistence of the worker. In this way, capital ensures the constant presence of the worker in the labour-market. In a similar manner, the control of the means of subsistence within the household gives to the man the rule over the woman's labour-power and life.

23. We make abstraction of the conflict over the distribution of the products of the domestic work, a problem that may well arise in a situation of power relation.

24. '"The numerical increase of labourers has been great, through the growing substitution of female for male", ... Since certain family functions, such as nursing and suckling children, cannot be entirely suppressed, the mothers who have been confiscated by capital must try substitutes of some sort. Domestic work, such as sewing and mending, must be replaced by the purchase of ready-made articles. Hence the diminished expenditure of labour in the house is accompanied by an increase expenditure of money outside. *The cost of production of the working-class family therefore increases*, and balances its greater income' (Marx, 1867 [1976], p. 518, footnote no. 39. Emphasis added).

25. Because the unpaid reproductive labour is performed outside the capitalist process of production, strictly speaking it is not possible to talk about any relationship of exploitation, even when the term 'unpaid' is used. In theory, the wage that the capitalist pays to the worker includes the necessary means of subsistence for the reproduction of the person performing the reproductive labour, but this is neither a direct remuneration to such person nor a 'job position'. If it were, if a person outside the household were providing the services of cleaning, for example, the wage received

by him/her would be paid by a capitalist enterprise that would charge prices that include a profit, and the amount of money that the household would need for having this task done would be higher. Also because of this, the word 'unpaid' is adequate to describe the reproductive labour performed by the members of the household, since thanks to that household production organized by patriarchal social relations, capital disposes of cheaper labour-power (see also footnote no. 4).

26. Given the environment within the family, it is reasonable to question whether the man would be willing to make such compensation. Indeed, the man could refuse to give up part of his free time, leaving the woman with even more domestic work (recall footnote no. 20).

27. 'However terrible and disgusting the dissolution of the old family ties within the capitalist system may appear, large-scale industry, by assigning an important part in socially organized processes of production, outside the sphere of the domestic economy, to women, young persons and children of both sexes, does nevertheless create a new economic foundation for a higher form of the family and the relations between the sexes' (Marx, 1867 [1976], pp. 620–621).

28. 'Job segregation by sex… is the primary mechanism in capitalist society that maintains the superiority of men over women, because it enforces lower wages for women in the labor market. Low wages keep women dependent on men because they encourage women to marry. Married women must perform domestic chores for their husbands. Men benefit, then, from both higher wages and the domestic division of labor. This domestic division of labor, in turn, acts to weaken women's position in the labor market. Thus, the hierarchical domestic division of labor is perpetuated by the labor market, and vice versa. This process is the present outcome of the continuing interaction of two interlocking systems, capitalism and patriarchy' (Hartmann, 1976, p. 139). '[T]he domination of the struggle by labor-aristocratic leaders convinced many male unionists that their jobs were directly threatened by female employment; they failed to see that capitalism's process of bringing women into new lower paid jobs was an attack on the entire class' (The League for the Revolutionary Party, 1989).

REFERENCES

Department of Economic and Social Affairs of United Nations. (2010). *The world's women 2010. Trends and statistics*. New York: United Nations Publication.

Engels, F. (1884). *The origin of the family, private property and the state*. Retrieved from http://marxists.org/archive/marx/works/1884/origin-family/index.htm

England, P. (2005). Emerging theories of care work. *Annual Review of Sociology*, *31*, 381–389.

Hakim, C. (2000). *Work-Lifestyle Choices in the 21st Century: Preference Theory*. New York: Oxford University Press.

Hartmann, H. (1976). Capitalism, patriarchy, and job segregation by sex. *Signs*, *1*(3), 137–169.

Hartmann, H. (1979). The unhappy marriage of Marxism and feminism: Towards a more progressive union. *Capital & Class*, *3*(2), 1–33.

League for the Revolutionary Party. (1989). Women and family: The ties that bind. *Proletarian Revolution*, No. 34. Retrieved from http://www.marxists.org/history/etol/newspape/socialistvoice/womenPR34.html

Luxemburg, R. (1925 [1972]). *Introduction to political economy*. [Spanish version]. Cordoba: Ediciones Pasado y Presente.

Martínez Peinado, J. (1986). Marxism and demographic dynamics. *Cuadernos de Economía*, *14*, 491–519. [Written in Spanish].

Marx, K. (1857–1861 [1973]). *Grundrisse: Foundations of the critique of political economy*. London: Penguin.

Marx, K. (1867 [1976]). *Capital* (Vol. I). Harmondsworth: Penguin.

Marx, K. (1894 [1981]). *Capital* (Vol. III). London: Penguin.

Marx, K. (1968). *The economic and philosophic manuscripts of 1844*. Madrid, Spain: Alianza Editorial.

Marx, K, & Engels, F. (1845–1846). *The German ideology*. Retrieved from http://marxists.org/archive/marx/works/1845/german-ideology/ch01.htm

Mateo Tomé, J., & Lima Santiago, V. (2012). Methodological aspects in the analysis of technological change. A holistic perspective. *Principios. Estudios de Economía Política*, *20*, 105–126. [Written in Spanish].

Montesino, M. (2007). *Importance of the value of labour-power and of the reproductive rationality for the management of development*. [Written in Spanish]. Unpublished data. National University of Honduras, Honduras.

Philp, B., & Wheatley, D. (2011). Time use, exploitation and the dual-career household: Competing perspectives. *American Journal of Economics and Sociology*, *70*(3), 587–614.

Rosdolsky, R. (1977 [2004]). *The making of Marx's capital*. Mexico: Siglo XXI Editores.

Rubin, I. (1928 [1979]). *Essays on Marx's theory of value*. Mexico: Ediciones Pasado y Presente.

APPENDIX A
THE MECHANISATION PROCESS

Starting from the data provided by Marx in Chapter 9 of *Capital*, Volume I, and keeping constant the concrete value of labour-power ($V = PrV$) as well as the ratio $C/(V + S)$, we explore the effects of increasing n by 1 from one period to another. As productivity increases, the concrete value of labour-power (V) represents a smaller proportion in the total product (ρ), while the opposite occurs with the constant capital (C) and the surplus value (S). The higher organic composition of capital provokes the rate of surplus value to rise (by reducing the socially necessary labour time to produce V, or which is the same, by increasing the quantity of commodities produced during the surplus labour time), and hence the participation of the worker in the distribution of the commodities is a decreasing proportion (relative surplus value), whereas the participation of the capitalist is an increasing one. The capitalist class as a whole disposes of a rising material wealth, while the living conditions of the working class remain unchanged in absolute terms. (The importance of the relative wage in Marxist Economic Theory is not small, its role is in fact more decisive than the role of the real wage as it constitutes the basis of the law of the relative pauperisation of the working class. See for instance Luxemburg, 1925 [1972]) (Fig. A1).

In reality, during the mechanisation process, the concrete value of labour-power can increase (as long as it does not cancel out the increase in productivity, that is as long as the rate of surplus value is rising, which is ultimately the logic of the whole process of mechanisation; see Mateo Tomé & Lima Santiago, 2012), and even though we would observe a fall in

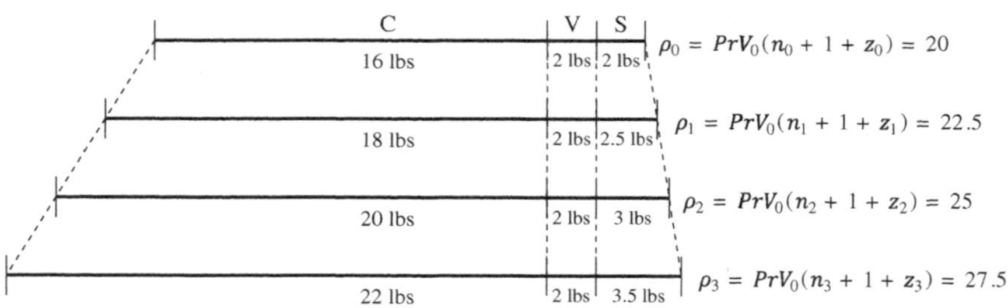

Fig. A1. The Effects of a Rising Composition of Capital on Labour Productivity When $V = PrV$. *Source:* Adapted from Montesino (2007, p. 135).

the relative wage (see Rosdolsky, 1977 [2004], p. 330). According to Rosa Luxemburg, this is the normal movement of capitalist production:

> Capitalist production cannot move one step forward without reducing the participation of the workers in the social product. With each innovation of the technique, with each improve of the machines... it is reduced the participation of the workers in the product and increases the one belonging to the capitalists. (Luxemburg, 1925 [1972], pp. 225–226. The translation is ours.)

Recall that the imperative process of mechanisation is also the source of the Relative Surplus-Population and the Industrial Reserve Army (i.e. unemployment, migration, poverty, etc.), central part of the capitalist law of population. This Army has a dual function for capital: to place at its service exploitable labour-power able to satisfy its changing needs, and to exercise a constant pressure upon the active industrial army (i.e. the workers that are employed) so as to keep the wages at its minimum possible. See Marx 1867 [1976], Rosdolsky (1977 [2004]) and Martínez Peinado (1986).

APPENDIX B
EFFECTS OF AN INSUFFICIENT COVERAGE OF THE CONCRETE VALUE OF LABOUR-POWER ON PRODUCTION

As the coverage of the concrete value of labour-power decreases, that is as the angle α raises from 0 to α_3, *ceteris paribus*, the worker's productivity decreases. This is illustrated by the inner product of $(n+1+z)$ and the projection of V, $PrV = V\cos(\alpha)$, which shows an increasingly smaller length. Both worker and capitalist dispose of less commodities to distribute between them as means of subsistence and means of production and surplus value, respectively. Clearly, the capitalist enjoys the greatest advantage. In Marx's words (Marx, 1968, p. 51): 'Wages are determined through the antagonistic struggle between capitalist and worker. Victory goes necessarily to the capitalist'. Less available commodities implies a decreasing material wealth, and less productivity, a decreasing competitive capacity for the individual capital. The Industrial Reserve Army plays a major role in enabling capitalists to remunerate workers below the value of labour-power. As it is part of capitalism's nature, this action has contradictory effects on the accumulation process. In the short run, it may help to counteract the tendency of the falling rate of profit, but when the deterioration in the quality of the labour-power takes effect, the outcome can be quite the opposite (Fig. A2).

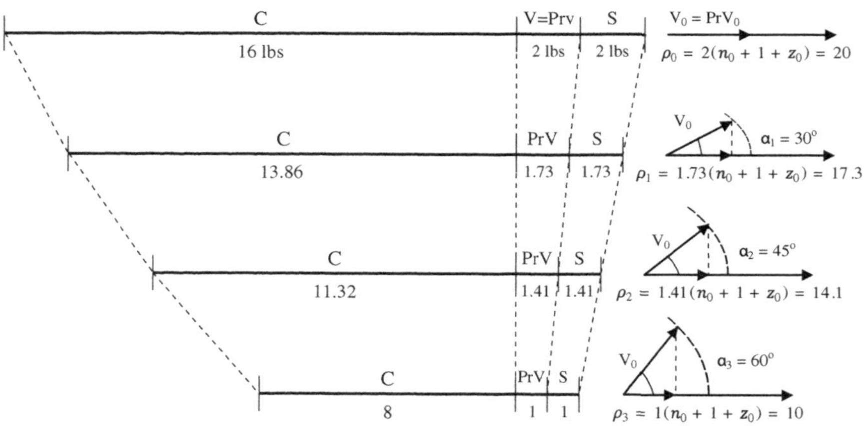

Fig. A2. The Effects of a Rising Angle on Labour Productivity When Everything Else Remains Constant. *Source*: Adapted from Montesino (2007, p. 143).

VALUE THEORY AND FINANCE☆

Tony Norfield

ABSTRACT

This paper offers a framework for understanding the financial system using Marx's theory of value. It examines how to interpret the Marxist concepts of the rate of profit and fictitious capital when analysing the financial sector, showing how accounting terms such as 'return on equity' and 'leverage' can also be understood in this context. The analysis argues that the capitalist system's rate of profit should be conceptualised in a way that includes finance, but that one should not mix up the accumulation of financial assets with the accumulation of advanced capital. While the costs of finance are negative for the system's average rate of profit, the paper concludes by noting how this is not inconsistent with financial operations being very profitable for imperialist powers that can use the financial system to appropriate surplus value from elsewhere *in the global economy.*

Keywords: Finance; rate of profit; return on equity; leverage; imperialism; parasitism

☆This paper has benefited from comments made by anonymous reviewers, from critical remarks on an earlier draft by Ben Fine and from discussions around the topic at the 5–7 July 2012 conference in Paris, France, of the AHE, FAPE and IIPPE. The contents of this paper, faults and all, remain the responsibility of the author.

Contradictions: Finance, Greed, and Labor Unequally Paid
Research in Political Economy, Volume 28, 161–195

ISSN: 0161-7230/doi:10.1108/S0161-7230(2013)0000028007

INTRODUCTION

> But all science would be superfluous if the outward appearance and the essence of things directly coincided. (Marx, 1974c, p. 817)

This paper uses Marx's theory of value to explain the role of the financial sector for the capitalist economy. In the Section 'Value Theory, Finance and the Rate of Profit', this is done by examining how finance is unproductive of value and is a burden on capitalist profitability. Here I discuss the gaps in Marx's analysis in Volume 3 of *Capital* and some shortcomings of Hilferding's *Finance Capital* in this regard. I present an alternative account of how to derive a rate of profit for the capitalist system as a whole, one that includes the financial sector. The subsection entitled 'Financial Capital and the Rate of Profit' develops this argument by analysing the special position of banks in the credit system and the creation of various kinds of 'fictitious' assets. These assets have been important in the latest 'financial' form of the crisis, but they have to be seen as having a special role in relation to capital investment and overall profit rate calculations.

The Section 'Implications of the Profit Formula: Borrowing, Equity and Leverage' draws out the implications of the general rate of profit formula for the different functional forms of capital – industrial, commercial and financial – and shows that the system rate of profit appears to them in different ways. These are examined by discussing a common metric for major capitalist corporations: the 'return on equity'. While the return on equity for industrial and commercial companies is shown, in general, to be positively correlated with system profitability, this is not necessarily the case for the financial sector. Financial companies, especially banks, can employ high 'leverage' to boost potential returns, and the privileged position of banks puts them in a favourable position to borrow funds to expand their business operations well beyond the limits of their own capital advances. The Section 'Value, Finance and Imperialism' briefly discusses another important implication of this paper's approach to finance. If one takes account of the fact that the global capitalist system is dominated by a small group of powerful countries, then the burden of finance on the system as a whole can appear in a very different way for them. The expansion of the financial sector can be very profitable for a major power if it can appropriate value from *other* countries.

VALUE THEORY, FINANCE AND THE RATE OF PROFIT

Marx's theory of value explains the origin of capitalist profit and how the dynamic of capital accumulation takes particular forms, resulting in a tendency of the rate of profit to fall. This tendency is what Marx termed 'just *an expression peculiar to the capitalist mode of production* of the progressive development of the social productivity of labour' (Marx, 1974c, p. 213).[1] In this section, I will explain how to include the capitalist financial system in a value-theoretic framework by examining of the rate of profit. This is not because I plan to estimate figures for the rate of profit today; the point is to discuss the relationships between profitability and value production. The results highlight the dynamic of the financial system, giving a foundation for the later analysis. I begin with the standard formula for the rate of profit on productive capital and then discuss how this should be modified to include other functional elements of capital. But first it is necessary to outline briefly some elements of Marx's theory of value.

Value theory applies solely to capitalism, the historically specific form of social organisation in which the products of human labour are commodities and in which labourers work for the profit of the capitalists, the owners of the means of production. The value of commodities is a function of the socially necessary labour–time that went into their production, both directly in terms of the new expenditure of 'living' labour by the workers and indirectly as a result of the value transferred to the product by the means of production. The profit of the capitalist employers depends on the amount of surplus value produced by the workers, which in turn results from the time that they work after reproducing the value of their own labour power.

This leads to the definition of *productive labour* in Marxist theory, which refers to the labour that produces value and surplus value for capitalism. Marx's analysis in *Capital* is focused on the dynamic of this process, and Volumes 1 and 2 deal almost exclusively with industrial capital because this 'is the only mode of existence of capital in which not only the appropriation of surplus value, or surplus product, but simultaneously its creation is a function of capital'. Industrial capital is, then, the most general and most important form of capital, and the one that is considered to employ *productive* workers (Marx, 1974b, p. 57). Not all productive labourers are directly employed by industrial capital, however. One such group of productive workers is involved in the transport and packaging of commodities, since this function also adds to their use-value.[2] Another group includes producers of use-values that are *not* material commodities who nevertheless work for a capitalist company, for example, in private hospitals and education.[3] In the following sections, however, I will use the shorthand of 'industrial' capital to refer to employment in and the operations of productive capitalists.

Many workers employed by capitalist companies do not produce value and surplus value. These are the ones operating in what Marx calls the 'sphere of circulation'. One area of this is the selling or buying of commodities, including the accounting processes, as in the case of those working for commercial capital. Another important area covers the workers in the more specifically *financial* sphere, providing loan capital so that others may do the producing, or performing other services in the exchange of titles to the ownership (and use) of money and other assets. This includes banks, pension funds, asset managers and other financial companies. However necessary these functions may be for the operation of the capitalist market system, and whatever profits the labourers in these occupations may bring to their capitalist employer, via mark ups, fees or interest payments, workers in the sphere of circulation do not produce new value (hence, no surplus value) for the system as a whole. Neither are the costs of these operations transferred to the values of commodities. Their work is not part of the production by capital of use-values as commodities. Their work *may* have the effect of leading to a greater output of value and surplus value in the capitalist system, but the higher values are the result of the productive sector's output.

Another group of workers is not employed by private capital at all, but is nevertheless important to consider briefly: public sector workers in local and central government. They have become increasingly important in the post-1945 period, along with the expansion of state expenditures and taxation. This is a big topic to analyse in its own right, and it falls outside of the focus of our inquiry into the role of finance. However, it is worth making some brief points on this subject.

Public expenditure is largely financed through taxation, so it is a drain on the total surplus value produced in the private capitalist sector, even though some of the expenditures may also benefit sections of private capital. There is a real basis in the logic of capital accumulation for the attacks on 'bureaucracy' and on publicly provided services. Hence, another qualifying factor when assessing the profitability of the capitalist system would be to allow for unproductive state spending that is a drain on the total surplus value produced. However, this factor is excluded from the analysis that follows, since I wish to focus on the analysis of *private capitalist operations* that are unproductive.

Nevertheless, the state as an economic actor is not entirely excluded from my analysis. In particular, the foundations of capitalist finance depend upon the state to establish the basis of the monetary system in which it operates – from laws relating to property rights and commercial dealings to the legitimacy of the currency and the role of a central bank to provide institutional backup for the private banking system. Interstate relationships and the inequalities of state power in the global capitalist system are also important for understanding the role of finance for imperialism.

Qualifications to the Simple Rate of Profit Formula

In Marx's analysis, the rate of profit, *r*, is expressed as the total surplus value produced, divided by the advance of both constant and variable capital, or:

$$r = \frac{S}{C + V} \tag{1}$$

This simple formula is the one commonly used to represent the rate of profit on total social capital. However, it leaves out of account two important qualifying factors, aside from the issue of state expenditure and taxation noted above. The first concerns the period of turnover of the capital advanced, also allowing for what Marx terms 'fixed' and 'circulating' capital (Marx, 1974b, Part 2). In what follows, I discuss an *annual* rate of profit. The second, and the more important qualification in my view, relates to the advance *by capitalists* of funds that do *not* produce value and surplus value. This is unproductive employment of economic resources *within* the private capitalist sector. Such funds need to be allowed for, not only as extra items in the denominator of the rate profit formula as extra capital advanced. They will also deduct from the numerator because the expenses incurred cannot be recovered from the value added to the social product.

Advances of capital that do not produce value and surplus value fall into two categories: commercial capital and financial capital, as noted above. The standard rate of profit formula can be amended to allow for these. Yet this is rarely done in the literature, even though the majority of Marxist commentators would agree that commercial and financial activities are unproductive of value and a drain on the productive sector of the capitalist economy. Shaikh, for example, uses a number of profitability calculations, all of which ignore the capital advances of the financial sector (Shaikh, 2011, p. 58). This is acceptable for his focus on *non*-financial corporate profitability. However, his discussion is of profit trends in the (US) system as a whole, and there is no indication that the financial sector has any role to play in the overall calculation apart from through the impact of interest rate payments taken from non-financial sector profits. Below, I work through the way in which the rate of profit formula for the total capitalist system must be amended. In order to focus on what is important for my argument, I will summarise only the key features of what should be done, leaving the more detailed working out to the appendix section. I also exclude the question of ground rent and landed property as having no direct bearing on the relationships that are being investigated here.

Productive and Commercial Capital and the Rate of Profit

The first scholar to produce an amendment to the rate of profit formula to include commercial capital was Fine (1975, pp. 62–64).[4] His derivation uses Marx's analysis that the commercial capitalists can be considered as buying commodities from the productive capitalists below value and selling them at value, while achieving the same average rate of profit as the productive capitalists. In this activity, the commercial capitalists have to advance cash or other means of payment, and they also need to advance capital to pay for buildings, equipment, the wages of commercial workers and so on. Marx assumes an equal rate of profit between the two types of capital because, in practice, they often overlap and it is considered relatively easy for a producer to move (at least partially) into commerce, or *vice versa*, if the respective rates of profit are significantly different and attractive enough to induce such a change.[5] Here I will show how to derive the formula for the rate of profit including commercial capital in a different way.

First consider the value of the output of productive capital in one year, and assume this to be equal to $C+V+S$, in the usual notation. Then, because the commercial capitalists do not add any value to the product (if we exclude transport and necessary packaging, etc.), all of their costs in the year, from commercial wages to the depreciation of fixed capital – call these X – must be a deduction from the total surplus value, S. Hence, the system's total profit available for distribution or further investment is $S-X$. Furthermore, if the commercial capitalists must advance a total capital of Y, including their money capital advances for purchases, their total fixed capital and commercial wages, then the total capital advances over which the system profit must be measured are $C+V+Y$, not simply the $C+V$ of the productive capitalists.[6]

Hence, the system rate of profit, including both the productive and the commercial capitalists, is:

$$r = \frac{S - X}{C + V + Y} \tag{2}$$

The clear implication is that the rate of profit is lower than implied by the simple calculation of Eq. (1). However, one should note that most analysts working on the estimates of the rate of profit normally use a category from national income accounts that groups together 'industrial and commercial' or 'non-financial' companies when measuring profitability and advances of fixed capital. In this regard, such estimates would broadly correspond with Eq. (2). However, there are still important differences between the formula and empirical estimates. For example, circulating capital and the commercial capitalists' advance of money capital are normally excluded because of the difficulty of getting adequate data for proxy estimates. Kliman (2012) discusses some of these problems of using national accounts data for value-based estimates of profitability, in addition to other important data-related questions not covered here.

Financial Capital and the Rate of Profit

The previous methodology can be extended to incorporate financial capital into the calculation of the system rate of profit. Financial capital operates outside the sphere of the production and circulation of commodities; instead it principally has only a money dealing or credit relationship with those companies. Hence, one question is whether capitalists in the financial sector should be included in the *equalisation process*, but I leave consideration of this point to the Section 'Implications of the Profit Formula: Borrowing, Equity and Leverage'. My analysis argues that financial capital should be included in the *calculation* of the capitalist system's general rate of profit, but only if financial capital is treated in a particular way. In turn, this also changes how we should understand the rate of profit accruing to industrial and commercial capitalists and to financial capitalists.

Before continuing, it is useful to outline briefly Marx's treatment of the financial sector. In Volume 3 of *Capital*, Marx analyses the split of merchant capital, or trading capital, into commercial capital and money-dealing capital (Marx, 1974c, Chapters 16 and 19). The commercial capitalists are the ones buying and selling commodities from the industrialists, and have already been considered in the previous section. The money dealers, by contrast, manage advances of the means of payment, make international payments and so forth. This latter function evolves and, as Marx puts it, 'the management of interest bearing capital, or money capital, develops alongside this money dealing as a special function of the money dealers. Borrowing and lending money becomes their particular business' (Marx, 1974c, p. 402).[7]

Thus, the merchant capital money dealers become 'the general managers of money capital' and form banks. The banks derive their funds from industrial and commercial capitalists, from deposits of money capitalists and from the idle money of all classes (Marx, 1974c, pp. 402–403).[8] Some of the banks' functions remain as forms of money dealing, for example, discounting bills of exchange and foreign exchange transactions, in which case they are still formally under a 'merchant capital' heading, and would earn the average rate of profit on advanced capital in Marx's analysis. Banks also account for the bulk of transactions in financial securities and derivatives, which are forms of money dealing. However, an important function grows with the development of banking operations: the advance of interest bearing capital, both via loans to industrialists and other capitalists, and through the creation of various titles of ownership that attract interest. As Marx noted, in a comment all too relevant for today:

> With the development of the credit system, great concentrated money markets are created, such as London, which are at the same time the main seats of trade in this paper. The bankers place huge quantities of the public's money capital at the disposal of this unsavoury crowd of dealers, and thus this brood of gamblers multiplies. (Marx, 1974c, pp. 511–512)

Marx further notes how the credit system and the stock exchange act both as a spur to capital accumulation and how it develops into a 'colossal form of gambling and swindling', as the gap grows between the ownership and control of capital (Marx, 1974c, p. 441). The credit system is also a mechanism for the centralisation of capital, whereby companies merge or are taken over, via the transactions in shares on the stock exchange.

In this paper, I will discuss the financial sector mainly by examining banks. These are the institutions that have the broadest and most important financial operations, including managing the issue of equities or bonds for industrial and commercial companies. Banks act as intermediaries, drawing in pools of spare liquidity in the economy, especially corporate funds arising from the circuit of capital, to use for loans to industrial and commercial companies. However, the credit operations of banks are far wider than this 'pooling' function would suggest (see the Section 'Financial Capital and the Rate of Profit', which also examines how to conceptualise the accumulation of financial assets). I do not separately consider banks' financial dealings with households, though household deposits will form part of the total funds they can lend to companies. Neither do I specifically consider the operations of insurance companies, pension funds and other financial asset managers. However, these latter are included in the analysis to the extent that they also draw upon social money resources to lend to companies by purchasing their bond and equity issues.[9] While this will omit a number of dimensions of financial activity today, it will include those financial dealings that have the most direct bearing on the process of capital accumulation.

In order to show how financial capital can be included in our calculations of system profitability, it is necessary to define additional variables for this sector. I will limit this to the minimum here; the appendix treats this issue in more detail.

Let Z be the annual costs of financial companies, including depreciation and wage costs. As in the case of commercial companies, these costs are not recovered by additions to the total value of annual output. Instead, the costs will be a deduction from the sum of total surplus value produced, reducing the numerator of the system rate of profit. If W is the total capital advanced by financial capitalists, for their fixed capital, bank equity capital and wages and so on, then this term must also be included in the denominator of the rate of profit for the capitalist system. One final variable needs to be introduced at this stage to reflect the role of the financial sector, particularly the banks, in providing funds to industrial and commercial capitalists for investment. Let D_2 be the *borrowed investment funds* that are used for constant and variable capital and for commercial capital investment. This results in a *general formula for the rate of profit of the total system*, including the productive capitalists, the commercial capitalists and the financial capitalists:

$$r = \frac{S - X - Z}{C_1 + V_1 + Y_1 + W + D_2} \tag{3}$$

In Eq. (3), the terms C, V and Y now have a suffix of '1' to indicate that these investment funds are advanced by the capitalists *in these sectors*, while the D_2 term represents *externally financed* investment from the financial system, via debt or equity issues or bank loans. While the costs of the borrowed funds may have an impact on capital accumulation, and will have an impact on the distribution of profit between different groups of capitalists, the overall system rate of profit can be expressed independently of the rate of interest or other costs of borrowing investment capital.

Eq. (3) is a static representation of the system rate of profit, in the sense that it does not include the influence commercial capital may have of reducing turnover time for productive capitalists, and hence potentially increasing the mass of surplus value produced per year. Neither does it allow for the impact of borrowed funds on the accumulation of capital and the production of surplus value. However, it remains the case that it is only the productive sector that creates value and surplus value, and the equation highlights the important point that the unproductive capitalist functions do not even transfer value to commodities: all their costs are a direct burden on the rate of profit.

Marx and Hilferding on Financial Capital and the Rate of Profit

There is little direct guidance from Marx on how to conceptualise the impact of financial capital on the rate of profit. In Volume 3 of *Capital*, there is an ample discussion of how the rate of interest is determined; that interest is a deduction from surplus value and that gross profit is split into interest and profit of enterprise (Marx, 1974c, Chapter 23). However, this only relates to the distribution of a given total of surplus value. There is no discussion of how the total surplus value is reduced in order to meet the unproductive costs of finance. Neither is it clear what kind of deduction should be made. These omissions no doubt arise from the fact that only Volume 1 of *Capital* was fully completed by Marx. For both Volumes 2 and 3, Engels had a struggle trying to piece together into a coherent presentation the notes that Marx had left.[10] In this section, I review the main points relevant for this paper and Hilferding's development of that analysis.

Marx's comments on bank capital are contained in Chapters 29 to 32 of Volume 3. He says that bank capital consists of a bank's cash plus its holdings of securities of various kinds. This sum of capital can also be divided in a different way, between the banker's invested capital and his deposits (Marx, 1974c, p. 463). However, Marx does not analyse these again, except in the context of his discussion of 'fictitious capital' (see the Section 'Financial Capital and the Rate of Profit').

Nowhere in Volume 3 of *Capital* does Marx consider how, or whether, these sums of capital enter into the formation of the average rate of profit for the whole system. His analysis also sets aside the fact that banks have fixed assets – buildings, equipment and so on – and personnel and other costs that need to be funded. For Marx in Volume 3, banks are essentially considered only as bearers of cash to lend (or to invest in securities) as interest-bearing capital. The issue of the average rate of profit including banks or finance is not dealt with.

Marx was, of course, well aware of the fact that banking operations are very different from those of industrial capital, and not just because banks operate in the 'sphere of circulation', something also true for commercial and money-dealing capital. This may have been a reason to leave the banks out of the calculation of the capitalist system's rate of profit and to look at banks, or financial capital, in a different way. After all, Marx's key argument was that the production of value and surplus value provides the fundamental dynamic for the system as a whole. However, as will be shown in the Sections 'Implications of the Profit Formula: Borrowing, Equity and Leverage' and 'Value, Finance and Imperialism', closer attention to the relationship between the financial and other capitalists when considering profitability can provide some useful insights into the dynamic of finance today.

Hilferding develops Marx's analysis of the operations of the banking system, and extends Marx's analysis of finance, joint-stock companies, the stock exchange, dividends and fictitious capital (Hilferding, 1981, Chapter 7). This is valuable progress, but Hilferding makes less of an advance in dealing with banking capital and profitability, the focus of the analysis here.

'Bank capital', he argues, 'including both the bank's own capital and deposited capital, is nothing but loan capital and as such it is, in reality, only the money form of productive capital' (Hilferding, 1981, p. 173). However, a bank's own capital is not necessarily loan capital. What is deposited in banks is not necessarily the money form of productive capital, and it may not become productive capital when lent out. A bank takes deposits of various kinds from all classes, and its own capital usually comes from equity issues and the capital of the bank's founders. Hilferding's claim follows from his observation of German banks that invested their own capital in industrial enterprises (p. 175). This is an important basis for his definition of 'finance capital', one that stresses 'capital at the disposition of the banks which is used by the industrialists' (p. 225). Many critics have noted that this was (and is) far from being true universally; in particular, contrasting with the much looser connections between banks and industry in the United States, and especially in the United Kingdom (e.g. Ingham, 1984, pp. 33–35). Yet this is not the main problem with his analysis for the current discussion.

Hilferding notes that for capital, 'banking is a sphere of investment like any other, and it will only flow into this sphere if it can find the same opportunities for realising profit as in industry or commerce; otherwise it will be withdrawn' (Hilferding, 1981, p. 172). This is part of his analysis of bank profit. While he says that bank revenue is not profit – because it derives from the gap between lending and borrowing rates of interest – the 'total revenue, calculated on the basis of the bank's own capital, must equal the average rate of profit' (p. 180). In common with Marx, he does not analyse the impact of banking capital and bank operations on the rate of profit itself. Instead, he takes the average rate of profit (of industrial and commercial capital) and implies that banking capital earns this rate. However, as the Section 'Financial Capital and the Rate of Profit' has shown, banking capital and operating costs have to be allowed for as factors that *reduce* the average rate of profit. Hilferding's presentation does not show how this can be calculated, although he would presumably have agreed that there should be a reduction, since it is a clear consequence of Marx's theory of value.

As discussed earlier, my view is that the operations of banking or financial capital impact the overall system rate of profit in two ways. Firstly, by representing an unproductive cost that has to be met out of the total surplus value produced, and also because there is an extra advance of capital over which the (net) surplus value is measured. Secondly, banks also provide funds for other capitalists to invest with, funds that are part of total advanced capital and which may increase the mass of surplus value produced. In this context, the operations of finance are integrated with the production of value, despite having a very different relationship to it. Yet it is also important to consider the mode of operation of banks that falls *outside* of their direct relationships with industrial and commercial companies. That issue is covered next.

FICTITIOUS CAPITAL AND THE ACCUMULATION OF FINANCIAL ASSETS

The first discussion of 'fictitious capital' by Marx does not occur in Chapter 25 of Volume 3 of *Capital* entitled 'Credit and fictitious capital'. Instead, it is covered in later chapters, and especially Chapter 29, entitled 'Component parts of bank capital'. Essentially, fictitious capital is a sum of value represented by a financial security whose price is determined by the capitalisation of future (expected) income (Marx, 1974c, p. 467).[11] As such, even though the security may also represent a claim to ownership of the assets of a company, as with an equity, its value does not represent real capital. In the case of government securities, there is no representation of capital at all. The value of a government bond only represents the net present value of future coupon and principal repayments, based on the financing of these payments from future tax receipts.

In general, the price of such securities goes up as the interest rate goes down, and *vice versa*. For an equity that will have a dividend payment of $1000 in one year's time, if the prevailing rate of interest were 5%, then the price of that equity security would be calculated as $20,000. This is the sum of money capital that could bring a $1000 payment at the 5% rate of interest. A rise in the rate of interest to 10% would cut the price to $10,000; a fall to 2.5% would raise the price to $40,000. This makes the value of securities appear to be divorced from the rate of profit in the capitalist system, and from any relationship to the production of value and surplus value, a feature that is underlined by the far less visible nature of the average rate of profit compared to the market rate of interest.

Furthermore, as the form of fictitious capital developed from the 19th century, with the growth of joint-stock companies, so did a trading market in the assets of companies. Capitalist investors in general view company assets as financial assets with prospective returns – an expansion of value – rather than as assets of companies that are producing *use-values* of particular kinds. This accentuates the inherent tendency of capitalist production to have value expansion as its sole aim. It also implies that, for an increasingly large share of invested capital, the returns will be considered as returns on money-capital advanced, as a form of interest payment (including dividends), rather than as a return on capital directly invested in a particular sphere of production.[12]

In the case of equities as a form of fictitious capital, Hilferding analyses how there is a split between the original owners/founders of a company and the shareholders who have bought into the company through buying the issued equity, or later buying the equity in the secondary market. The original owners benefit from equity issues through what he calls a promoters' profit. This is based on 'the conversion of profit-bearing capital into interest- (or dividend-) bearing capital', where the rate of profit is higher than the rate of interest (Hilferding, 1981, Chapter 7). Assuming the rate of profit is 10% and the rate of interest is 5%, then shares in the company will be worth more than the company's invested capital. The new equity owners merely earn the (lower) rate of interest on their shareholding, while the funds flowing in from the equity issuance can be used by the original owners, either as personal wealth and income (if they sell some shares) or to expand their operations.

In addition, the original owners usually keep 50% or more of the company's total equity and have control over the whole company, though they have increased their economic power through gaining access to a larger value of capital, something that they can extend through majority ownership of other stock exchange companies. Even if they *own* less than 50% of the company, they may issue shares with fewer voting rights so that they retain *control* over all decisions. A recent example is the 2012 Facebook IPO, where Mark Zuckerberg is reported to own only 18% of Facebook's equity but has 57% of voting shares (Surowiecki, 2012). In this way, the credit system, in the shape of the stock market, not only transforms company assets into tradable securities that are a form of money-capital for the purchasers, it also boosts the control of a small group of capitalists over the economy, assisted by their use of 'other people's money'.

There has been a dramatic growth of fictitious capital in recent decades, as shown in the expanding volumes of government bonds, corporate bonds and equities traded on financial markets. However, one area of the growth of fictitious assets that has received little attention in the Marxist literature is the one that helps explain the special role of the banking system: the creation of deposits.

Marx's discussion of banking and credit recognises the fictitious nature of some bank assets, for example in his comments on how banks could issue notes not backed by capital they actually possessed (Marx, 1974c, pp. 541–542). However, these are incomplete observations, and the impression is given elsewhere that banks play the role merely of gathering up surplus funds in the system and lending *these* funds out (Marx, 1974a, p. 587). A similar impression is given in Hilferding's work on banks and finance. While he covers fictitious capital in detail, he does not discuss the deposit creation of banks. Yet, this process of deposit creation – and bank lending – is critical for the expansion of financial assets.

Banks can create new deposits from an original deposit, based on the reserve ratios they need to maintain. If the reserve ratio is 10%, then the deposit of $10,000 at a bank could potentially lead to the creation of an extra $90,000 of new deposits.[13] Whether it actually does so depends on the demand for loans, the interest rates charged and other things besides; it is far from an automatic process. However, for our purposes, the important point is that the extra deposits created are fictitious. They are extra liabilities as bank deposits, also extra assets as interest-bearing loans to bank customers, but they are multiples of the value of the original deposit and are created by a bank's credit operations. Importantly, this credit creation process is supported and promoted by the central bank – the state backed institution that oversees the operations of and provides liquidity to the private banking system. Credit creation does not only depend upon deposits of money arising from the circuits of industrial and commercial capital.

The accumulation of bank financial assets via deposit creation *may* be loans to industrial and commercial companies for their investment purposes, in which case they should be included in the calculations of the system rate of profit conducted earlier (see the D_2 variable in Eq. (3) in the Section 'Financial Capital and the Rate of Profit'). However, the accumulation of financial assets may have nothing whatever to do with such investment. Instead, the funds created could be used to buy existing securities or to make other forms of financial investment.[14] In this case, it would be wrong to include these financial assets as part of the invested capital. Such assets merely represent an *accumulation of financial titles*. Although these may still have claims on revenue in the form of interest or dividend payments, they do not represent any new investment in industry or commerce, or even any new investment in the financial sector's own business operations. The assets are forms of what Marx termed interest-bearing capital; they are not a capital investment.

Another form of accumulating financial assets occurs where financial companies issue *new* financial securities, but the funds raised are *not* used for extra capital investment in their operations (e.g. for their equity capital). In this case, they are used for the purpose of advancing *further loan capital*, or even to buy other financial securities. Hence, neither should these assets be considered as a capital investment. The new assets, bought with the received funds, are financial assets attracting a financial return, usually related to a form of interest payment.

One striking example of this is the explosion of the issuance of a particular kind of security, collateralised debt obligations (CDOs) by banks from the late 1980s. These were largely based on the payments received by the banks from holders of mortgages they had already granted. The advantage of CDOs for banks was that this was a mechanism to boost their earnings and profit potential. They could sell the mortgage-backed securities to investors, receive cash and have fresh capital with which to fund a new round of mortgage business. The interesting thing about CDOs is that although they were used as a means of expanding the volume of financial assets belonging to banks, they were issued as securities that were claims on the banks' *existing assets*. Essentially, this was how banks shortened their own period of circulation, boosting their profitability by not having to wait until the mortgages were fully repaid. From an estimated $68 bn in 2000, global CDO *issuance* increased nearly eightfold to a peak of $521 bn in 2006 (SIFMA, 2012). Alongside this, profits reported by the US financial sector, the source of most CDO issues, more than doubled over the same period – before the collapse that occurred shortly afterward as mortgage defaults soared.

Other financial securities newly created and issued by banks include a variety of derivatives used for hedging and speculative purposes, for example interest rate swaps and options on interest rates and currency values. These may appear on a bank's balance sheet as an asset or liability, and they are also financial products from which they earn dealing margins and other fees. As such, they are part of a bank's business dealings. But they are *not* capital invested in a bank's operations, except perhaps through requiring that a portion of capital be set aside to cover risks taken on via these instruments. Again, it is inappropriate to consider these securities as part of the invested capital of a bank. The process of bank creation of derivatives results in huge volumes of assets *and* liabilities for banks: in many cases with the transactions offsetting each other in terms of a particular bank's risk exposure.

Similar points may be made regarding derivatives traded on financial exchanges. In this case, traders on the exchange, who may work for banks, originate the new derivative contract and the profitability of the exchange is a function of the volume of dealing in such securities. The volume of dealing will be related to the value of contracts outstanding, often measured by the sum of the face values of each derivative. But this does not reflect any extra capital 'invested' and it should not be considered as such. It simply reflects the scale of transactions in derivatives!

In summary, my argument is to exclude financial assets from the calculation of the capitalist system's rate of profit, except to the extent that the value of these assets reflects investments in the operations of industrial, commercial and financial companies. In those cases, the assets may be considered as capital advanced, whether or not the funding goes to productive or unproductive (commercial or financial) enterprises. Otherwise, the large volume of assets recorded by financial companies will simply reflect a (potentially huge) sum of value that is based on loans made, or financial securities and derivatives purchased. The only common element between the former invested assets and the latter assets is that they will in general – except for derivatives – accrue interest or dividend payments.

IMPLICATIONS OF THE PROFIT FORMULA: BORROWING, EQUITY AND LEVERAGE

The Section 'Financial Capital and the Rate of Profit' concluded with an equation that represented the rate of profit for the capitalist system as a whole, allowing both for the unproductive costs of commerce and finance and for the lending of capital to industrial and commercial companies. This differed from Marx's presentation of the issue, where he determined an average rate of profit for the industrial and commercial (mercantile) capitalists and only then considered banks or financial companies from the point of view of them lending money capital and receiving a share of the total surplus value in the form of interest (Marx, 1974c, Chapter 21).

Here I will take the analysis a step further and examine some important relationships using the previous formulae. I will show that once the issue of *borrowed* capital is taken into account, as Marx does in his determination of 'profit of enterprise', then the question of capitalist profitability also has to be examined in a different context.

One important point is that while financial capital is included in my general rate of profit formula, this does not necessarily mean that banks earn the same 'average' rate of profit as the industrial and commercial companies. This was an assumption made by Hilferding, but it does not follow from the analysis here, and neither was it an assumption of Marx's. Marx assumed that there was an equalisation between industrial and commercial profit rates, but he made no comment on the relative profitability of banks compared to the other sectors. I will show that the profitability of banks has a very different form compared to that for industrial and commercial companies, and that there is no systematic mechanism by which the profitability of the latter companies can converge with that for the banks.

Profit of Enterprise, Interest and Surplus Value

Marx divided the total surplus value into 'profit of enterprise' and interest. However, in this analysis, he gives the impression that the only deduction to be made from the total surplus value accruing to the industrial and commercial capitalists is the *interest* paid to 'the owner and lender of money capital' (Marx, 1974c, Chapter 23, p. 371). As already shown, however, the total surplus value available for distribution is *much lower than this*, since it must cover the costs of both commercial capital and financial capital. This implies that the correct formula for the profit of enterprise should be:

$$S - X - Z - D_2 i_A \tag{4}$$

where the final term is the total interest paid on the funds that industrial and commercial companies borrow from the banks, D_2, given an average interest rate of i_A. If the former companies also lent funds to the banks, then they would also receive a portion of the total deposit interest paid by banks, but that would not be profit of enterprise, strictly speaking.

As shown in the Section 'Fictitious Capital and the Accumulation of Financial Assets', banks are able to create *fictitious deposits* in addition to the 'original' deposits arising from the circuit of industrial and commercial capital or from other sources. Not all of these deposits will be lent to industrial and commercial capitalists, and some of the total bank deposits will also be lent to capitalists who invest in financial assets of various kinds. These factors have an important effect on how profitability appears for industrial and commercial capitalists versus the financial capitalists, an effect best explained by examining a common measure of profitability used by all large, publicly quoted capitalist companies: the *return on equity*.

Marxist analysis has traditionally focused on Marx's conception of the rate of profit, almost exclusively in the very simplified form of $S/(C+V)$, but it is not often that capitalist companies pay much attention to this kind of measure. Some companies will report a figure for 'return on capital employed', which broadly represents the same concepts, but the overwhelming focus of large capitalist companies quoted on the stock market is the return on equity. This measures the net profit of the company compared to the value of its equity capital (measured according to the value of the equity when issued, plus retained earnings), and so is a good indicator of the return to the owners of the company of the money capital that they have invested in it. I will use this measure in the following analysis and show how the system rate of profit is linked directly to this calculation for industrial and commercial companies. However, there is a far more tenuous link between the system rate of profit and the profitability of banks.

Return on Equity: Industrial and Commercial Versus Financial Capitalists

The owners of capitalist companies, whether industrial, commercial or financial, must usually advance some of their own capital to begin operations, or to continue to operate. However, they will normally also borrow investment funds from the financial system. When this occurs, while they are concerned about the returns they get on the *total* advance of capital, they are more particularly focused on *the return on the investors' ownership stake*, or the return on equity.

The return on equity for the industrial and commercial capitalists ($\mathrm{RoE_{ICC}}$) is their profit of enterprise (leaving aside any deposit interest received from banks), divided by their own advance of capital, or:

$$\mathrm{RoE_{ICC}} = \frac{S - X - Z - D_2 i_A}{C_1 + V_1 + Y_1} \tag{5}$$

This return on equity formula indicates how profitability can be boosted from the point of view of equity investors without them necessarily providing any more funds for investment. If they use borrowed funds, then, depending on the interest costs, the numerator may increase while the denominator – their own invested capital – stays the same. Within limits, this means that it is possible for the RoE to rise even if the rate of profit on total investment falls. Nevertheless, there will be a general, positive correlation between the system rate of profit, r, and the return on equity for industrial and commercial capitalists. This can be seen by rearranging Eq. (3) to make the total capital advanced the subject. The result is:

$$C_1 + V_1 + Y_1 + W + D_2 = \frac{S - X - Z}{r}$$

After switching the W and D_2 terms to the right hand side, substituting the result for the denominator in Eq. (5) and multiplying the right hand side fraction by r, the result is:

$$\text{RoE}_{\text{ICC}} = \frac{r(S - X - Z - D_2 i_A)}{S - X - Z - r(W + D_2)}$$

This shows that the return on equity for industrial and commercial companies will *tend to decline* as r falls, since the numerator falls *and* the denominator rises. Of course, if the rate of interest fell, then there could be a rise in the return on equity despite a fall in r, but the fall of (borrowing) interest rates has a limit above zero, since it is the source of revenue for the banks. The broadly positive correlation will tend to hold.

By contrast, the return on equity for the banks has a far less clear relationship to the system rate of profit. This sector of capital's RoE is its net interest income, after deducting other costs (assumed to be equal to Z), divided by the total advance of capital, W. Making the simplification that the total loans equal total deposits, D, the net interest income is the total interest received, Di_A, minus the interest rate paid on total deposits, i_D, times the total deposits. This gives the following expression for the return on equity for the banks:

$$\text{RoE}_{\text{Banks}} = \frac{D(i_A - i_D) - Z}{W} \qquad (6)$$

In this case, the trend in the system rate of profit, r, has a less direct impact on the RoE for banks. If there is a trend of falling profitability, then the RoE_{ICC} will fall, as previously indicated. This will reduce these companies' ability to meet interest payments on borrowed funds, so there is likely to be downward pressure on i_A (considered as a percentage return on assets, not simply as an interest rate) through a lower demand for investment funds and also due to potential loan losses. That will probably feed into a lower figure for RoE_{Banks} eventually. Nevertheless, there are some important degrees of freedom on this measure that could make the banks still look profitable, despite lower returns elsewhere.

Firstly, it is evidently the gap between borrowing and investing (or lending) rates that is critical for the banks. Secondly, the banks are able to expand their deposits and loans via credit creation (depending on bank reserve ratios, together with bank credit risk and capital measures). Hence, the volume of interest earnings, and thus the return on equity for banks, can move quite differently from the return on equity for other capitalist companies.

The upshot is that the ability to expand borrowing and assets is a key driver of profitability for the banking system. This creates a different dynamic for the return on equity for financial companies compared to that for industrial and commercial companies. There is clearly no direct relationship between the two calculations of return on equity and they are liable to be different. But it is worth considering briefly whether the pressure of competition might tend to equalise these RoE (or other) measures of profitability.

If we assume that there is a tendency for the rate of profit recorded by industrial capitalists to converge with that for commercial capitalists, due to the potential migration of capital from one functional area of investment to another,[15] does it follow that there is a similar tendency for the profitability of financial capitalists to converge with the others? Is there a tendency for the rate of profit (however measured) to be the same for all types of capitalist?

As the previous discussion showed, profit calculations are very different for banks and financial companies compared to the other sections of capital (interestingly, it is also standard procedure for government statistics to separate financial from non-financial companies in national accounts). This is principally because the banks can create their own assets, but other financial companies are also in the business of attracting funds for (financial) investment and they all operate with assets and liabilities that are different forms of *interest bearing capital*.

There have been few empirical studies of differences in profitability between financial and other companies, and whether these persist over time.[16] One might doubt that such differences could persist, since, through the stock market, capital can presumably flow just as easily between financial companies and industrial and commercial companies as between the latter two groups. However, the difference between companies involved in the production and merchandising of commodities as compared to those whose relationship to commodity production is a credit relationship, or merely a title of ownership relationship (with a return based on interest), suggests that an empirical result would merely measure the accidental coincidence, or otherwise, of profitability between the different sectors. It would not change the fact that they operate in very different ways.

More importantly, the linkages of banks with the rest of the economic system means that the state operates, via the central bank, a licensing policy that restricts the number of new banks that can be set up and, at least in principle if not in practice, will oversee the scale of their operations. In the recent crisis, the state has also been heavily involved in managing mergers and takeovers of banking institutions. There have been remarkably few new banks established in the United States and the United Kingdom in recent decades, despite their apparently excess profitability. The hurdles to starting up a new bank are high. Not simply, in the United Kingdom parlance, being considered a 'fit and proper person' by the authorities to run the operation, when such angels are thin on the ground. Upstart financial capitalists must also have sufficient capital to offset a potential run on the bank. The end result is that the banks are the monopolists of the credit system – with highly privileged access both to the potential deposit funds available from which they can create credit and, just as importantly, access to the central bank's own credit operations that provide them with liquidity. For economically powerful imperialist countries, their banks are in a commensurately powerful position to use leverage and to expand the scale of their operations, as we shall see next.

Rates of Return and Leverage

As one might expect given the previous discussion, industrial and commercial companies borrow far less as a proportion of the equity held by the company's owners than do banks and other financial companies. The ratio of borrowing to shareholders' equity, a common definition of leverage, is much higher for banks, based on their special position in the credit system. The ratio of borrowed funds to equity will change according to economic conditions, with borrowing growing rapidly when times look good and growing less, or even falling, when times are bad. Nevertheless, at *all* times banks borrow far more than do other capitalist companies when compared to the size of their capital or equity base.

As an indication of the divergence, it is considered normal in major capitalist countries for banks to have a leverage ratio of around 20 – in other words, when borrowing is 20 times the size of equity (Haldane, 2011). Industrial and commercial companies, by contrast, are looked upon questioningly by the stock market if their borrowing ratios are high. For the aggregate of US manufacturing companies, debt holdings were *less* than the value of equity in each year from 2001 to 2010. Hence, their leverage was *less than 1*. This was also true for the aggregate measures of mining and wholesale trading companies (US Census Bureau, 2012, Table 794). Another divergence with the banks is that even when the companies borrow funds, they are very likely to use these funds for investment in their *own* productive and commercial operations. The banks borrow funds to lend to *others*, or to invest elsewhere, since that is the economic function they perform.

Higher leverage means higher risk, since the interest on the borrowing must still be paid even if the investment turns out badly. But if investment returns are good, a low cost of borrowed funds relative to the investment returns will magnify the return on equity. This may increase the volatility of returns, and standard portfolio investment theory makes an adjustment for this, deflating the higher returns by the higher volatility when calculating an 'information ratio' on investment performance.

Data on the leverage of banks reveal an important dimension of what happened in the run up to the 2007–2008 crisis. From the 1990s, bank profitability had been coming under pressure from narrowing interest rate margins, which had tended to fall in line with the trend of lower money market interest rates. For US banks, net interest margins fell from around 4.0–4.5% in the 1990s to below 3.5% by 2006 (Federal Reserve, 2009, p. A76). This encouraged banks to step up their credit operations in order to compensate with a higher volume of assets. The result was much higher bank leverage. At the same time, the banks also boosted the volume of their trading in foreign exchange, securities and derivatives, something that was assisted by their 'financial innovation' and the boom in financial markets.[17] These moves increased both bank interest income *and* their trading income from spreads and commissions.

In the early 2000s, a stable rate of economic growth in major capitalist countries gave the basis on which higher leverage did not seem so risky. Ahead of the crisis, leverage ratios for some major institutions hit levels in excess of 100 in the United States and higher than 80 in Europe, four or five times 'normal' levels (see Fig. 1). Once the credit-fuelled bubble burst, however, this gave a particular 'financial' form to the crisis that broke in 2007–2008. The percentage loss incurred on a huge asset base did not have to be high to wipe out the equity capital of many institutions, leading to state-supervised mergers and bailouts.

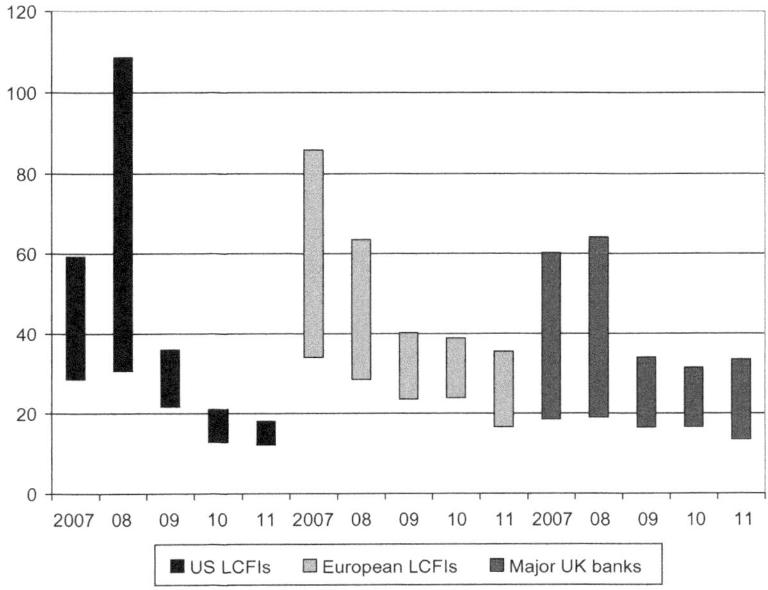

Fig. 1. Leverage Ratios of Major International Banks, 2007–2011 (Total Assets Divided by Bank Capital. High-Low Range in Each Year). *Source:* Adapted from Bank of England (2012, Chart 1.19, p. 14). *Notes:* LCFI stands for 'Large Complex Financial Institution'. UK banks are not included in the European LCFI columns. In 2007 and 2008, the weighted average numbers for leverage ratios were about two-thirds down the relevant bars.

There has been ample coverage in the literature of the origins and evolution of the latest crisis, and I will not add to that here. The only issue I want to highlight in concluding this section is how the financial system can develop a destructive dynamic in the search for extra profit. This can be looked upon as a simple consequence of the way in which banks can expand their assets by credit creation, given that they are at the centre of this process. From the perspective of the money dealing aspects of bank operations, they also have a clear incentive to boost the volume of financial *transactions*. In my view, the momentum and the destructive potential develop as a function of problems with declining returns on capital investment, especially in an environment of low interest rates. It was this that prompted the extra leverage and the explosion of derivatives markets (Norfield, 2012a). However, if one goes beyond the previous analysis of how finance relates to value production in the capitalist system as a whole to its mode of operation for powerful imperialist countries vis-à-vis others, then this highlights new dimensions of the value relationships. I will now turn to this question.

VALUE, FINANCE AND IMPERIALISM

The previous analysis of finance has been at the level of the capitalist system as a whole. This was necessary to clarify the nature of finance and the forms that it takes as compared to the industrial and commercial forms of capital. Although the financial sector is unproductive of value, like commerce, it has a different dynamic. One would expect that there would be limits on the growth of finance, given its unproductive nature and the burden it places on system profitability. These limits are difficult to determine, since they depend on the particular conditions of capital accumulation. However, one important point follows very directly from this analysis if it is extended to allow for the relationships between different countries in the global capitalist system. While the rate of profit overall is burdened by the costs of finance (and commerce), this is less of an issue for a particular country if *revenues from other countries* can offset these costs. In particular, a country's financial sector can expand dramatically if that system can *appropriate surplus value produced elsewhere* in the global capitalist system. In this final section of the paper, I will outline briefly some of the implications when one takes account of the unequal status of different countries.

It is not open to every country to establish a major international banking and financial operation! The field is dominated by the United States and the United Kingdom, which have the largest international financial markets (Norfield, 2012b, 2011b). The privileged financial position of these powers in the world economy is illustrated by two facts. Firstly, they are the only two countries in the world that have large *negative* net international asset positions, but nevertheless earn a net *surplus* on their investment income. This is a result of each getting relatively cheap foreign financing for their profitable foreign direct investment holdings. In the US case, it is mainly via the role of the dollar and foreign central bank purchases of US government securities that help push yields lower (Norfield, 2011b; Warnock & Warnock, 2005). In the UK case, it is mainly via relatively low interest bank borrowing (Norfield, 2011a). Secondly, their domestic financial markets are sources of important trading revenues. The United States and the United Kingdom are the two countries with the largest net international earnings in the world from financial services (WTO, 2012). Such earnings in 2011 covered more than a third of the United Kingdom's big deficit in merchandise trade, and amounted to 2.5% of UK GDP. Finance, from international banking to foreign exchange, financial securities and derivatives trading, is a key prop for the wealth and influence of these imperialist powers, derived from their ability to appropriate surplus value produced in other countries.

It may seem to be poorly timed to talk about the advantageous power of finance for these countries in the wake of the biggest financial crisis capitalism has ever seen! However, their financial privileges can put them in a stronger position than many other countries, even when there is a crisis that engulfs them too. This is especially true for the United States, which has seen its net foreign investment income more than double between 2007 and 2011, to $235 bn. Aside from the direct economic benefits, the United States is also able to use the dominant position of the US dollar in global finance – it is on one side of 85% of all foreign exchange deals! – to impose effective financial sanctions on countries it does not like, for example Iran. In the case of the United Kingdom, the importance of the financial sector is seen in the UK government's persistently strong defence of 'the City' from any attempts to curb financial trading by the European Union authorities.

A full analysis of the question of imperialism and finance was not the aim of this paper. These points are raised only to bring out how the economic advantages for the major powers that have specialised in finance do not depend on financial crises – though such crises can indeed offer other opportunities for gain. The process of surplus value appropriation via finance is, for them, part of a regular daily mechanism, the *normal* operation of the imperialist financial markets that they have played such a strong role in setting up.[18]

CONCLUSIONS

The objective of this paper has been to set out a framework for analysing the role of finance using Marx's theory of value. It was shown that the costs of non-productive forms of capital have to be deducted from the mass of surplus value produced in order to get a more accurate picture of the amount remaining for division between the different groups of capitalists. These non-productive costs also have to be allowed for in the mass of capital advanced, in order to measure the rate of profit for the system as a whole.

The paper also stressed the ability of financial capital (in this case, the banks) to create fictitious assets. But it was argued that these assets should not be included in calculations of how much capital had been invested by industrial, commercial or financial capitalists in their business operations *unless these assets were actually invested in this way*. Otherwise this would confuse the accumulation of credit-money, other forms of interest bearing capital, derivatives and so on with the accumulation of capital.

This paper also showed that the overall system rate of profit manifests itself in very different ways for industrial and commercial capitalists versus financial capitalists. In the former case, there is a direct relationship between the system rate of profit and other measures of profitability used by these corporations, for example the return on equity. In the latter case, the relationship between the system rate of profit and the profitability of banks or financial companies was far less direct. This is principally due to their ability to expand their assets via the credit system, and hence to increase their leverage to levels dramatically higher than for other types of capitalist company.

In conclusion, I would not wish to counter-pose the different functional forms of capital. This is not simply because there are many examples where capitalist companies have operations that cross the lines between productive capital, commercial capital and finance. The key point is that they all have the objective of *value expansion*, no matter that the immediate source of their profits may be very different. However, it is important to distinguish these different functional forms in order to clarify their relationship to the production of surplus value. This analysis also showed that the way in which they register returns on capital helps to explain the particular dynamic of the financial system. A large financial sector is a burden on the capitalist system as a whole. However, it is not necessarily a burden for a particular country, and can even be a benefit, if *other* countries bear the unproductive costs. The operation of the global financial system is part of the mechanism by which major imperialist powers – especially the United States and the United Kingdom – sustain their privileges in and appropriate value from the global economy.

NOTES

1. Elsewhere, Marx states that it is 'in every respect the most important law of modern political economy, and the most essential for understanding the most difficult relations' (Marx, 1973, p. 748).

2. This is also true for those storage costs that do not arise out of the difficulty of realisation. See Marx (1974b, Chapter 6, Sections 2.2 and 2.3, pp. 151–153).

3. See Marx's comments on the 'teaching factory' (Marx, 1974a, Chapter 16, p. 477) and other comments on services production (Marx, 1969, Addenda 12, Section H, pp. 410–411).

4. Fine (1985–1986) develops the argument further and covers the theory of interest, but his formulae do not represent the rate of profit including financial capital.

5. Vertical integration helps industrial companies manage commercial costs internally. Retailers, by contrast, do not often get involved directly in production. In recent decades, the hold of large, imperialist retailers over producers (e.g. Wal-Mart and China) has increased with 'globalisation'. But this is a feature of the imperialist world economy rather than one that, in these cases, indicates an equalisation of profit rates between retailers and producers.

6. Here and below, I assume for simplicity that fixed and circulating capital turns over in one year. The issue of turnover and other factors are considered in more detail in the appendix.

7. Fine (1985–1986) covers the distinction between money dealing capital and interest bearing capital in detail.

8. Michie's discussion of the history and development of the City of London (Michie, 1992) implicitly endorses Marx's analysis of the transition from commerce to credit and capital, although he makes no reference to Marx's analysis in this book.

9. Asset managers will only be investing new funds in companies when they purchase *new* equity and bond issues. UK data show that at the end of 2010, UK individuals held only 11.5% of UK shareholdings, down from 47.4% in 1963, with the rest being held by foreign investors and institutions of various kinds. See the UK Office for National Statistics data (ONS, 2012).

10. See Engels's preface in Volume 3 of *Capital*, noting that in his editing the 'greatest difficulty was presented by Part 5', which is the section that covers the division of profit into interest and profit of enterprise and interest bearing capital (Marx, 1974c, p. 4).

11. This, Marx's definition, differs from Harvey's: 'If this credit money is loaned out as capital, then it becomes *fictitious capital*' (Harvey, 2006, p. 267). A bank loan to a company only becomes fictitious capital if that loan is securitised; if not, it is just a loan on the bank's books. Harvey may be thinking of fictitious deposit creation of credit money (see below), but then the fictitious nature of the deposit does not depend on whether the funds are used as capital.

12. With some two-thirds of UK listed shares owned by institutional funds, these funds often put pressure on major companies to deliver a steady stream of dividend payments, thus making their equity investment operate effectively as interest-bearing capital.

13. The 10% reserve ratio is the one most commonly used in examples, for simplicity rather than accuracy. In this case, £900 of the original £1000 is lent out first, which, when deposited in another bank, allows the second bank to advance another £810 in new loans, and so on in a geometrical progression. Reserve requirements are not the only limit on a bank extending credit, and in crises such as today the demand for loans may be well below what is implied by such requirements.

14. For example, where banks provide finance for 'private equity' funds or hedge funds that then buy equities, bonds or other financial securities.

15. For example, the often cited example of Ford Motor Credit is a case where Ford, a manufacturing company, expanded into financing the purchases of the company's products. GE Capital is also chiefly in this *money-dealing* capital area defined by Marx, rather than operating as a bank. Commercial capital rarely moves directly into production, but it may develop supply-chain links.

16. Using a different measure of profitability, Duménil and Lévy (2004, p. 98) show there were flows of capital between the non-financial and financial sectors of the US economy, attracted by the profitability gap, although these did not close the gap. The 'private equity' phenomenon of recent years might be seen as an example of financial capitalists moving into other spheres. However, it is based on leveraged buy-outs, financed with relatively cheap bank funds and dependent on advantageous tax laws. It represents an example of predatory and parasitic capitalism rather than one of financial capitalists wishing to become 'productive' or even commercial.

17. See Crotty (2007) for an interesting analysis of bank returns and financial innovation. However, in my view he pays too little attention to the broader issue of bank leverage, given that he focuses mainly on the implied leverage from derivatives.

18. See Eric Helleiner's valuable account of the history of the US–UK government role in establishing the post-1945 global financial system, although in my opinion he greatly underestimates the value of contemporary global financial operations for British imperialism (Helleiner, 1996).

19. This presentation follows Engels' approach in Marx (1974c, Chapter 4, pp. 72–73).

20. Money creation is specifically a banking operation. Non-bank financial companies cannot create deposits. See Hall (1992) for an interesting analysis of the deposit creating process, and a critique of the Marxist literature at the time for ignoring it. Dos Santos (2011) does include this element in his useful discussion of the credit system and accumulation.

21. Here I ignore the so-called treasury shares, for simplicity.

22. This assumes that banks only make a return on lending, and excludes the fees and charges they impose on their customers, and any net earnings they derive from financial trading. The latter items could be included, but would unnecessarily complicate the argument here.

REFERENCES

Bank of England. (2012). *Financial Stability Report*. Bank of England, June 2012.

Crotty, J. (2007). If financial market competition is so intense, why are financial firm profits so high? *Political Economy Research Institute Working Paper Series*, 134. Retrieved from http://www.peri.umass.edu/fijligileadmin/pdf/working_papers/working_papers_101-150/WP134.pdf

Dos Santos, P. L. (2011). *Notes towards a new political-economy approach to contemporary credit relations*. Research on Money and Finance Discussion Paper 35, Autumn 2011. Retrieved from http://www.researchonmoneyandfinance.org/

Duménil, G., & Lévy, D. (2004). The real and financial components of profitability (United States, 1952–2000). *Review of Radical Political Economics*, *36*, 82–110.

Federal Reserve. (2009). Profits and balance sheet developments at US Commercial Banks in 2008. *Federal Reserve Bulletin*, *95*(2), A57–A97.

Fine, B. (1975). *Marx's capital*. London: Macmillan Press.

Fine, B. (1985-1986). Banking capital and the theory of interest. *Science & Society*, *49*(4), 387–413.

Haldane, A. G. (2011). 'Risk Off', Speech given on 18 August 2011, Bank of England. Retrieved from http://www.bankofengland.co.uk/publications/Documents/speeches/2011/speech513.pdf

Hall, M. (1992). On the creation of money and the accumulation of bank-capital. *Capital & Class*, *48*, Autumn 1992.

Harvey, D. (2006). *The limits to capital*. London: Verso Books.

Helleiner, E. (1996). *States and the re-emergence of global finance: From Bretton Woods to the 1990s*. New York, NY: Cornell University Press.

Hilferding, R. (1981 [1910]). *Finance capital: A study in the latest phase of capitalist development*. London: Routledge.

Ingham, G. (1984). *Capitalism divided? City and industry in British social development*. London: Palgrave Macmillan.

Kliman, A. (2012). *The failure of capitalist production: Underlying causes of the Great Recession*. London: Pluto Press.

Marx, K. (1969). *Theories of surplus value: Part One*. London: Lawrence & Wishart.

Marx, K. (1973). *Grundrisse: Foundations of the critique of political economy (Rough Draft)* (Martin Nicolaus, Trans.). England: Penguin.

Marx, K. (1974a). *Capital* (Vol. 1). London: Lawrence & Wishart.

Marx, K. (1974b). *Capital* (Vol. 2). London: Lawrence & Wishart.

Marx, K. (1974c). *Capital* (Vol. 3). London: Lawrence & Wishart.

Michie, R. C. (1992). *The City of London: Continuity and change, 1850–1990*. Great Britain: Macmillan Academic and Professional.

Norfield, T. (2011a). The economics of British Imperialism, 22 May 2011. Retrieved from http://economicsofimperialism.blogspot.co.uk/2011/05/economics-of-british-imperialism.html

Norfield, T. (2011b). Dimensions of dollar imperialism, 5 October 2011. Retrieved from http://economicsofimperialism.blogspot.co.uk/2011/10/dimensions-of-dollar-imperialism.html

Norfield, T. (2012a). Derivatives and capitalist markets: The speculative heart of capital. *Historical Materialism*, *20*(1), 103–132.

Norfield, T. (2012b). The City of London: Parasite of the world economy, 3 October 2012. Retrieved from http://economicsofimperialism.blogspot.co.uk/2012/10/the-city-of-london-parasite-of-world.html

ONS. (2012). Ownership of UK Quoted Shares, 2010. Retrieved from http://www.ons.gov.uk/ons/rel/pnfc1/share-ownership—share-register-survey-report/2010/stb-share-ownership-2010.html

Shaikh, A. (2011). The first Great Depression of the 21st Century. *Socialist Register*, 2011.

SIFMA. (2012). See the excel sheet on global CDO issuance and outstanding, updated 4 April 2012. Retrieved from http://www.sifma.org/research/statistics.aspx

Surowiecki, J. (2012). Unequal shares. *The New Yorker*, 28 May 2012.

US Census Bureau. (2012). *The 2012 statistical abstract*. Retrieved from http://www.census.gov/compendia/statab/cats/business_enterprise/profits.html

Warnock, F. E., & Warnock, V. C. (2005). International capital flows and US interest rates. Board of Governors of the Federal Reserve System, *International Finance Discussion Papers*, Number 840, September 2005.

WTO. (2012). World Trade Organization. Retrieved from http://stat.wto.org/StatisticalProgram/WSDBViewData.aspx?Language=E

APPENDIX : DETAILED CALCULATIONS FOR THE SYSTEM RATE OF PROFIT

These notes discuss a more detailed method for calculating the overall rate of profit for the capitalist system than is outlined in Section 'Value Theory, Finance and the Rate of Profit' of the main text. Here I allow for the period of turnover of productive capital and other features that distinguish the different functional sections of capital (industrial, commercial and financial).

Start by considering the value of the annual output of the *productive* ('industrial') capitalist. This is the sum of the transferred value of depreciated fixed constant capital, the transferred value of all the constant circulating capital used up and the new value created by the labour power employed in one year. Let FC be the total value of the fixed capital advanced, with β the annual proportion of the capital that depreciates in value through being used up. Let CC be the value of circulating constant capital that is advanced for the next period of production, and let n be the number of turnovers of circulating capital in the year. Let V be the value of variable capital advanced to pay wages, but note that this is only the value for *one* period of turnover, and let S be the total surplus value produced in one turnover period. Then the total value of the product in one year is:[19]

$$\beta\text{FC} + n\text{CC} + nV + nS \tag{A.1}$$

Now consider the commercial capitalists. Any costs these incur must be recovered from the total value in Eq. (A.1), and essentially will be a deduction from the total surplus value. This is because the total of their wages bill and other circulating costs represent an outlay for which there is no additional value added or transferred to the product. The same is true for the depreciation of their fixed capital. Let L be the total circulating capital costs advanced by commercial capital in a year, and K their advance of fixed capital. For simplicity, assume that the annual rate of depreciation of commercial fixed capital is also β. In addition to these costs, the commercial capitalist must also advance money to buy the commodities that are sold by the productive capitalists. However, while the advance of money capital B does not add or transfer any new value, neither is it used up in the process. It returns to the commercial capitalist on the resale of the commodities. The total profit of the system allowing for the costs of commercial capital is then equal to:

$$nS - L - \beta K \tag{A.2}$$

The total capital advanced by industrial *and* commercial capital is $FC+CC+V+B+L+K$, and expression (A.2) can be divided by this sum of capital advanced to give an amended formula for the rate of profit:

$$r = \frac{nS - L - \beta K}{FC + CC + V + B + L + K} \tag{A.3}$$

If commercial capital has a faster turnaround of buying/selling that shortens the $M-C$ or the $C'-M'$ phases in the standard Marxist notation of $M-C \ldots P \ldots C'-M'$, then there is a reduction of the advanced B, K or L compared to the total surplus value produced. Alternatively, one could see this as an increase in the value of n, the number of turnovers of industrial capital per year, leading to a higher mass of surplus value per year. In this way, commercial capital appears as less of a drain on the surplus value produced and the system rate of profit (per annum) will rise. A smaller negative thus appears to be a productive *increase* of value, although commercial capital creates no new value.

Now consider the banks, or financial capitalists. Let D be the value of their deposits and other borrowings. These deposits include not only the surplus cash resources of industrial and commercial companies, but also the *banking sector's own creation of money* through its recycling of deposits.[20] These extra, created deposits should nevertheless still be included in D, since they are deposits in the banking system, deposits that add to the banks' liabilities.

Let E be the value of bank equity capital, or 'shareholders' equity'. This is equal to the original subscription of equity when the bank (or other financial company) started operations, plus any further share issues, plus retained earnings.[21] This equity capital value does not vary with the bank's share price in the market, but it will be diminished by any losses borne.

The value of D plus E is used to fund the bank's total assets, which I will designate as A. In standard accounting terminology, the bank's total assets equal its liabilities plus its equity capital, so:

$$A = D + E \tag{A.4}$$

Assume that, of the bank's total assets, a value equivalent to E covers the bank's fixed and circulating capital costs (buildings, technology, infrastructure and salary costs) and its core reserve capital. This is a reasonable simplification, and it leaves a value equivalent to D to be lent out. The lending, to create assets, can be to industrial and commercial companies, or to other financial companies (including buying any financial assets in the secondary market). This value D can then be divided into D_1, where it is lent 'internally' to other financial companies, and D_2, where it is lent 'externally' to industrial and commercial companies.

If the average interest rate paid on deposits is i_D, and the average return on bank investment assets is i_A, the bank's net interest income can be written as:

$$Ai_A - Di_D, \tag{A.5}$$

or, alternatively, $D(i_A - i_D)$ if i_A is considered as the return on bank loans.[22]

The sum D_2 represents the funds for investment that industrial and commercial companies have borrowed from banks. These funds are for their extra investments in constant capital, variable capital, plus a proportion of commercial money capital advanced and a proportion of the fixed and circulating costs of commercial capital. For the total constant fixed capital, FC, this can be broken down into FC_1, advanced by the industrial capitalist directly, and FC_2, portion borrowed from the bank. Hence

$$FC = FC_1 + FC_2 \tag{A.6}$$

similarly,

$$CC = CC_1 + CC_2$$

$$V = V_1 + V_2$$

and likewise for the commercial capitalist,

$$B = B_1 + B_2$$

$$K = K_1 + K_2$$

$$L = L_1 + L_2$$

Since, by assumption, all the borrowed funds equal one portion of the total deposits of banks, then:

$$D_2 = FC_2 + CC_2 + V_2 + B_2 + K_2 + L_2 \tag{A.7}$$

Now recall that for the commercial capitalists and the financial sector, the depreciation costs of fixed capital and their personnel and other circulating costs are *not* transferred to the values of commodities. They *must be recovered from the total surplus value produced in society*. If we assume that the depreciation of the fixed assets of financial capitalists in one year is equal to γE, and that the total circulating costs in a year (including wages paid) amount to M, then the total profit remaining for distribution to the *three* sectors is now:

$$nS - L - \beta K - M - \gamma E \tag{A.8}$$

The total capital advanced by all three sectors can be given as the sum of that belonging to the industrial and commercial capitalists, the funds they have borrowed from the financial sector plus the financial sector's own equity (which, for simplicity, here we assume also covers their circulating costs M). Hence, the rate of profit on total social capital can now be written as:

$$r = \frac{nS - L - \beta K - M - \gamma E}{\mathrm{FC}_1 + \mathrm{CC}_1 + V_1 + B_1 + K_1 + L_1 + D_2 + E} \tag{A.9}$$

This formula shows how the capitalist system's general rate of profit is impacted not only by commercial but also by financial capital. (See the main text for the reasons why I exclude purely financial assets from the calculation.)

The total surplus value available for distribution among all capitalists is as noted in Eq. (A.8) above. This implies that the formula for the 'profit of enterprise' is:

$$nS - L - \beta K - M - \gamma E - D_2 i_A \tag{A.10}$$

where the final term is the interest paid on the funds that industrial and commercial companies borrow from the banks, D_2. If the former also lent funds to the banks, then they would also receive a portion of the total deposit interest of Di_D, but that would not be profit of enterprise, strictly speaking. If that portion were represented by α, then the total returns of industrial and commercial companies would be:

$$nS - L - \beta K - M - \gamma E - D_2 i_A + \alpha D i_D \tag{A.11}$$

As shown in the Section 'Fictitious Capital and the Accumulation of Financial Assets', banks are able to create *fictitious deposits* in addition to the 'original' deposits arising from the circuit of industrial and commercial capital or from other sources. This has an important effect on how profitability appears for industrial and commercial capitalists versus the financial capitalists, an effect best explained by examining the *return on equity*, as discussed in the subsection "Return on Equity: Industrial and Commercial versus Financial Capital."

Using the variables already defined, the return on equity for industrial and commercial companies can be expressed as:

$$\mathrm{RoE}_{\mathrm{ICC}} = \frac{nS - L - \beta K - M - \gamma E - D_2 i_A + \alpha D i_D}{\mathrm{FC}_1 + \mathrm{CC}_1 + V_1 + B_1 + K_1 + L_1} \tag{A.12}$$

As for Eq. (5) in the main text, this return on equity expression can be shown to have a direct relationship with the system rate of profit Eq. (A.9) above.

The return on equity for the banks can be expressed as:

$$\mathrm{RoE}_{\mathrm{Banks}} = \frac{D(i_A - i_D) - M - \gamma E}{E} \tag{A.13}$$

As in the main text, this equation highlights the importance of both the interest rate margin and the banks' ability to expand their assets through the creation of deposits. This expression, and that for industrial and commercial companies, could easily be further amended to allow for the banks' net financial dealing revenues, another means whereby banks can attempt to raise their returns.

OF FAT CATS AND FAT TAILS: FROM THE FINANCIAL CRISIS TO THE 'NEW' PROBABILISTIC MARXISM

Julian Wells

ABSTRACT

Popular understandings of the financial crisis tend to focus on the rents extracted by elite personnel in the financial sector. Professional discussions, however, have addressed the faulty assumptions underlying theory and practice – in particular, the assumption that returns to financial assets follow the Gaussian distribution, in the face of much empirical evidence that these have power law distributions with far higher kurtosis. It turns out that the power law tails of returns to financial assets are also a feature of the distribution of company rates of profit, a discovery that stems from proposals to 'dissolve' the traditional transformation problem by abandoning the condition of a uniform rate of profit and instead considering its distribution.

Marx himself was aware of the importance of considering the distributional properties of economic variables, based on his reading of Quetelet. In fact, heavy-tailed distributions characterise a wide range of

Contradictions: Finance, Greed, and Labor Unequally Paid
Research in Political Economy, Volume 28, 197–228

ISSN: 0161-7230/doi:10.1108/S0161-7230(2013)0000028008

variables in capitalist economies, the best-known probably being the Paretian tail component in distributions of income and wealth. Nor is this simply an empirical fact – such distributions emerge readily from a range of agent-based simulations.

Capitalist economies are, in a particular technical sense, complex self-organising systems perpetually on the brink of crisis. This modern understanding is prefigured in Marx's discussion of how the compulsive character of social relations emerges from the atomistic exercise of human free will in commercial society. The developing literature of probabilistic Marxism successfully applies these insights to the wider fields of econophysics and complexity, demonstrating the continuing relevance of Marx's thought.

Keywords: Quetelet; Farjoun and Machover; econophysics; financial crisis complexity; agent-based modelling

OF FAT CATS AND FAT TAILS

> [T]he rate of profit ... seeks the 'ideal' mean position, i.e. a mean position which does not exist in reality. In other words, it tends to shape itself around this ideal as a norm. (Karl Marx, 1981, p. 273).

> [M]ost of our theories ... are deficient because they don't take account of the shapes of the distributions. (Kenneth Arrow)[1]

This review paper aims to show how consideration of the financial crisis, and of responses to it, points to the potential of probabilistic Marxism in the revitalisation of political economy.

To do so, we first move (fairly rapidly) from popular understandings of the crisis to the discourse of professional economists and the significance of (neglect of) the 'fat tails' in the distributions of financial data in blinding so many to the very possibility of crisis. The second section demonstrates that fat-tailed distributions also characterise company profit rates, and thus establishes an empirical link between the probabilistic *dis*solution of the transformation problem in Marxist political economy and wider work on the financial crisis. The third section argues that this is not a re-interpretation, but a *revival* of Marx's own approach.

Our fourth section reviews the wider context of this discourse of fat tails, and some possible implications that it has for the understanding of the capitalist economy, given that the ubiquity of fat tails in the distributions of many economic variables is a signature of a system that is – in a very particular sense – complex and inherently crisis prone.

Having established Marx himself as a pioneer of probabilistic and complexity thinking, in the fifth section we outline some key contributions to the developing literature of probabilistic Marxism. The final section reviews and summarises the material presented.

Popular Understandings of the Crisis

Bob Diamond was the chief executive of Barclays Bank until 3 July 2012, when he was forced to resign in the wake of revelations that Barclays had participated in rigging a key financial indicator, the London Interbank Offered Rate, or Libor. Previously, his activity at the bank in 2010 had been rewarded with a bonus of £6.5 million, on top of his £250,000 salary. This is what one popular UK daily paper had to say on the subject:

> Greed is alive and well within Barclays post the great panic. The bankers still live in their own micro-climate and feel free to pay themselves what they like, despite the hardship

> they have inflicted on the rest of us. … it is pay pornography which puts Barclays top brass at odds with all other stakeholders, including ordinary employees in branches from South Africa to Aberdeen, shareholders and long suffering customers, like the unfortunates who were wrongly sold 'conservative' investments which turned out to be the opposite. (Alex Brummer, *Daily Mail*, 20 March 2011)

Indeed, a search of the *Daily Mail* website (www.dailymail.co.uk) for the words 'fat cat bankers' (19 March 2011) brought up 80 hits, covering a period ranging from 3 March 2006 to 15 March 2011, and thus spanning the run-up to the current financial crisis and its unfolding. The *Daily Mail* is not a left-wing newspaper. Its political history includes publication of the forged 'Zinoviev letter' that brought down Britain's first Labour government in 1924, and a 1934 headline proclaiming 'Hurrah for the Blackshirts!'. (In fairness, one must note its vigorous campaign to bring to justice the racist murderers of the London student Stephen Lawrence, killed in 1993.)

Moreover, its comments on Diamond's bonus appeared in its 'Money' section, presumably of most interest to those of its predominantly petty bourgeois readership who have significant financial assets to manage. Thus, the notion of 'fat cat' bankers resonates even with those whose default position is support for business and a market economy. This is unsurprising, given that in the autumn of 2008 governments had to step in to provide trade credit for the productive sectors of the economy, such was the bankers' mistrust of each other's credit worthiness. The state thus found itself not merely guaranteeing the operation of the market economy, but potentially controlling the direction of its activity.

In effect, capitalism had to be suspended for a few months in the interests of capital – a situation that led the *Financial Times* to demand that 'Bankers must start lending – or else', as a headline of 21 November 2008 put it. The ensuing editorial pointed out:

> [B]anks … are vital utilities – a modern economy cannot function without credit. If bankers do not start lending of their own accord, governments will force them to.

The financial crisis has thus fixed two notions in the lay mind. First, the understanding that elite personnel in the financial sector have been able to appropriate great personal wealth through activities whose public utility is debatable even when they do not go wrong. Second, that they have, with very little pause, been able to resume pocketing it even after their activities brought the system to the brink of disaster.

But while top bankers may indeed be inordinately greedy, this will hardly do as an explanation. The limitations of this understanding are readily seen when it is noted that the two stories that book-end the sequence of 'fat cat' references found in our *Daily Mail* search are both in fact directed at creating resentment of the *public* sector. The first is headlined 'Revealed: Public sector 'fat cats' who earn more than £150,000 per year', while the second is 'Value for money at last: 20,000 state sector fat cats facing pay cuts of up to a fifth'. One has to read some way into the first of these to find the admission that '[o]nly the bankers and businessmen of the City beat top paid civil servants when it comes to pay rises'. Thus, one prejudice is turned against another to neutralise any radical impulse.

To the question of why exceptionally greedy people might flock into this sector, the obvious answer is that it provides exceptional opportunities – but then one has to explain not only why this should be, but why things go disastrously wrong with such regularity. Here, there is an interesting disparity of popular perception on opposite sides of the Atlantic. In the United States, the bankers' fundamental error is widely perceived to be sub-prime lending – bad loans whose badness was then covered up by financial engineering until exposed in the 2008 crisis.[2] But in the United Kingdom, there is no similar discussion: the crisis is seen as having been caused by an over-large financial sector engaged in over-complicated deals which weren't properly understood by those who devised them.

Detailed analysis of these differences of popular perception belongs to another article, but they most probably depend on further differences in political culture. In the United States, the Occupy movement can blame abusive lenders exploiting the poor, while Tea Party members can point to big government's misguided attempts to promote home ownership to the same underclass. However, both positions emphasise bankers' lending decisions. In the United Kingdom, on the other hand, the absence of any significant local problem of bad lending allows free play for the popular perception of City gents as out-of-touch, feather-bedded public school toffs[3] – notwithstanding that Margaret Thatcher's 1987 'Big Bang' reforms not only were explicitly designed to break up cosy old-school-tie cartels but in fact achieved just that.

(These different perceptions reflect objective differences: consider the case of Northern Rock, a former building society that in September 2007 achieved the dubious distinction of being the first UK bank in 150 years to suffer a bank run. The bank's problem was not bad lending but bad borrowing. Its mortgages were sound enough, but 75 per cent of its funding came from borrowing on short-term money markets (Aldrick, 2007). When this source of funding began to dry up as a result of events in the United States, the bank had to ask for liquidity support from the Bank of England, prompting retail savers to queue outside branches to retrieve their deposits. Eventually, Northern Rock had to be nationalised (on 22 February 2008), becoming the only significant mortgage-related casualty in the United Kingdom).

Professional Understandings of the Crisis

One response of professional economists – here understood to mean not only academic researchers but also policy makers and analysts – is that the problem is insufficient or inappropriate regulation, as illustrated by the *Financial Times* editorial quoted above. But even if this is accepted, one must still ask for an explanation of why crises nonetheless break out despite the efforts, best or otherwise, of the regulators. The speculators' delusion that 'this time is different' is mirrored, and inverted, in the regulatory delusion that '*next* time will be the *same*'. Without a proper understanding of the fundamental reasons for instability, regulators are in the position of armies superbly equipped to fight the last war, not the next.

An obvious answer is that the system is inherently crisis prone. The rest of this chapter is devoted to showing how probabilistic considerations relate to this view, and thus the power of the developing current of probabilistic Marxism.

Yes, it really is 'rocket science' (and it is just as dangerous)

The hypertrophy of the financial sector in recent decades received its theoretical underpinning from the efficient markets hypothesis (EMH) usually attributed to Eugene Fama, whose PhD is credited with (re-) introducing the idea that stock prices follow a random walk (*re*introducing, because he in effect reinvented early twentieth century work by Bachelier). The practical underpinning of the sector's innovative practices has been the Black–Scholes formula for calculating the price of options (which really is rocket science, because it depends on Ito's Lemma, a result used in control systems for missiles). For this, Myron Scholes and Robert Merton received the Nobel Memorial Prize in Economics in 1997 – fortunately for all concerned with its award, *before* the crisis precipitated in the following year by the failure of the vehicle they set up to exploit their work, Long-Term Capital Management (LTCM).

The significance of the EMH, were it true, is that profitable trading systems would be impossible. If it seems odd that committed believers in the hypothesis should nonetheless set up a trading firm, the point is that its partisans do not think that the EMH is *strictly* true – merely that markets will not deviate from the efficient price by very much for very long. Nonetheless, small deviations are expected. Even if the profit on trading a $1.00 asset is only $0.01, one can still gain $10,000 if one bets $1 million. LTCM raised $1.25 *billion* and was hugely leveraged as well, which in time-honoured fashion accelerated its fall when the crash came.[4]

As we know, financial growth and innovation was, for various reasons, not discouraged by this debacle, despite the dangers that it had made manifest – Merrill Lynch observed that mathematical risk models 'may provide a greater sense of security than warranted; therefore, reliance on these models should be limited' (Lowenstein, 2000, p. 235). The practical reason was, no doubt, the fact that plenty of money was still to be made. But here we are concerned with *theoretical* discourse. While the ultimate reason that the lessons of LTCM did not receive critical attention from the professional mainstream is the ideological commitments served by the EMH, we do not explore this further; we merely document the fact that the best non-Marxist economists were aware of both the facts and the way in which they rendered the EMH problematic.

Fatness: it is the tails that matter, not the cats

The core assumption of the technology devolving from the EMH and Black–Scholes is that the prices at which financial instruments trade follow a random walk in which the price changes (the returns to the asset) have a Gaussian distribution with a small standard deviation.[5] The problem with this is that it is contrary to facts about asset returns that have been known for a long time. As far back as 1963, Benôit Mandelbrot found returns with Lévy stable distributions (henceforth referred to simply as stable distributions) having theoretically infinite variance. He found, for example, that cotton prices followed a stable distribution with parameter *alpha* equal to 1.7, rather than 2 as in a Gaussian distribution.

At this point, some readers may feel in need of a technical briefing to demystify the jargon. We assume familiarity with the 'bell curve', made notorious by the book of that name by Herrnstein and Murray (1994), arguing that differences in intelligence are largely accounted for by genetic factors, not environment. This curve is simply one way of graphically representing the so-called normal distribution imported from astronomy to social science by the Belgian polymath Lambert Adolphe Jacques Quetelet. It is called the normal distribution because for many decades scientists followed Quetelet in discerning it in the variation of many social and biological quantities, from the incidence of suicides to biomedical data (he proposed the modern body mass index relating height to weight).

The bell curve represents what is called the probability density function (pdf) of the normal distribution (which from now on we will refer to as the Gaussian distribution[6] to emphasise the fact that in reality this distribution is far from being normally encountered in economic data, as we will discuss in more detail below). A way of picturing the pdf is to set up a chart with the variable of interest along the horizontal axis, and plot the relative frequency of each value of the variable on the vertical axis; the resulting diagram is a curve describing the variation of the quantity one is interested in. Fig. 1 shows the pdf of the standard Gaussian distribution, with average value zero and standard deviation of one.

Note that the description above is decidedly loose; to understand the precise significance of the diagram, consider the area *under* the curve and *between* the x-axis values -3 and $+3$ as a proportion of the whole area under the curve. Clearly, this proportion is extremely large, and at a glance may appear to be the whole. But this is not so. Although the pdf curve apparently hugs the x-axis beyond these points, bear in mind also that the curve extends to infinity in both directions. Thus, the area under these tails is about 0.03 per cent of the total, which means that although really extreme values of the variable are very, very unlikely they are not ruled out altogether.

(For comparison, note that 95 per cent of the total probability lies within two standard deviations of the mean, a fact which many practical statistical tests appeal to, while 68 per cent is within one standard deviation.

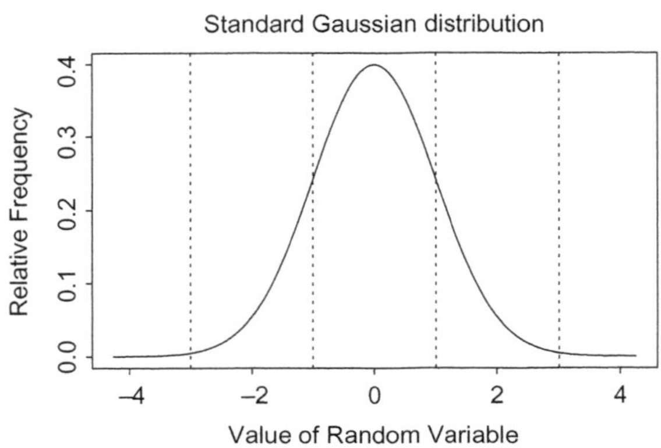

Fig. 1. Probability Density Function of the Standard Gaussian Distribution with Mean of Zero and Standard Deviation of One; 99.7 Per Cent of the Total Probability Lies within Three Standard Deviations Either Side of the Mean (Indicated by Outer Pair of Vertical Dashed Lines).

In Fig. 1, the one and three standard deviation limits are indicated by vertical dashed lines.)

The curve is symmetrical about the peak at the zero point of the horizontal axis (the mode, or 'most common' value) and thus the mean (the arithmetical average) is also zero. The standard deviation is a measure of the variance, or 'spread-out-ness', of the data. Non-standard Gaussian distributions are ones with standard deviations greater or less than unity, or with means other than zero (some possibilities are compared to the standard version in Fig. 2), but they all have the *same shape*, in the sense that their pdfs are all described by the same mathematical function linking the mean and standard deviation.

There are many other families of distributions, but the historical, empirical and mathematical importance of the Gaussian distribution is such that any discussion of the amount of probability contained in their tails is by tradition qualified in relation to the Gaussian. Distributions in which extreme values are more common than with the Gaussian are commonly described as heavy-tailed (or fat-tailed) or, in more formal language, to have 'excess kurtosis'.

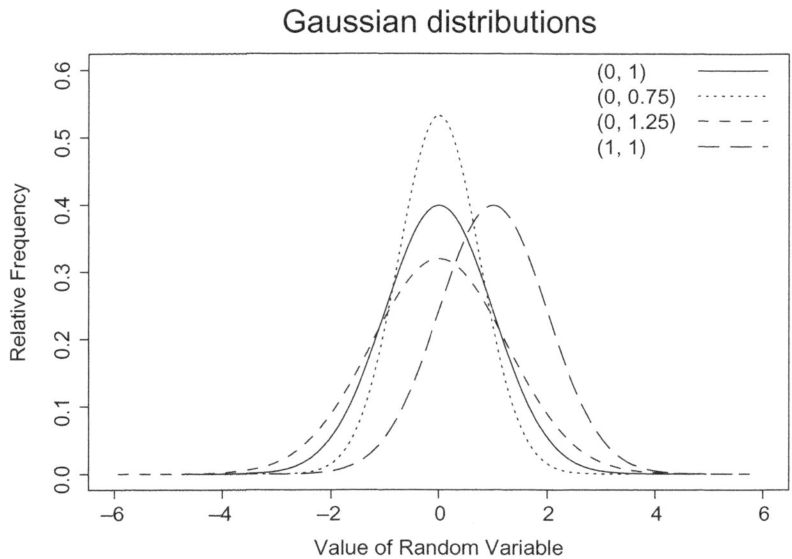

Fig. 2. Non-Standard Gaussian pdfs (Broken Curves) Compared to the Standard Gaussian (Solid Curve).

The pdfs of some alternative distributions are shown in Fig. 3; since all the distributions with which we will be dealing from now on are skewed (more probability on one side of the central mass than on the other), and are also bounded, in that they only cover part of the real number line, we do not illustrate the negative arm of the horizontal axis.

Despite fairly radical differences in the main mass of the probability (think of each curve and the horizontal axis as opposite edges of a long sheet of metal of uniform thickness), the tails of the distributions appear almost indistinguishable. However, they are not identical, and in fact one of the distributions shown, the Pareto distribution, exhibits tail behaviour that is radically different in kind to that of the others (which are in fact close relatives of each other, as members of the exponential family of distributions).

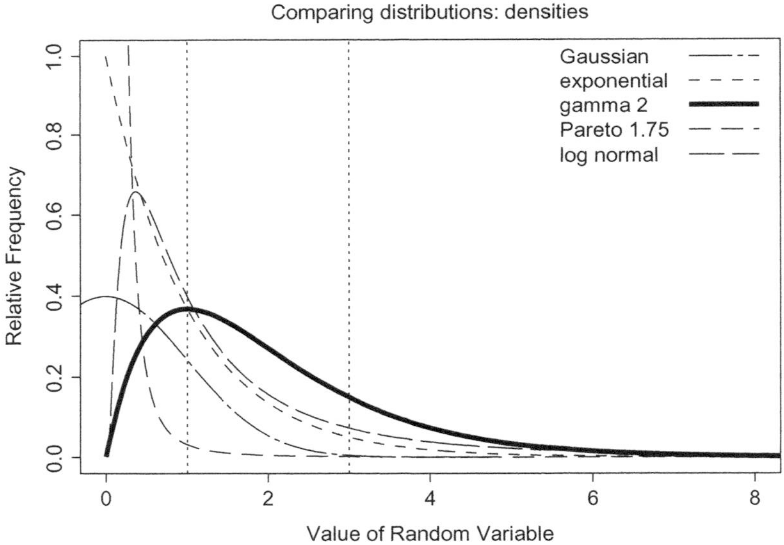

Fig. 3. Gaussian and Non-Gaussian Distributions Compared: Probability Density Functions. Fig. 3 compares (a) the standard Gaussian, (b) the standard exponential, (c) a gamma distribution with shape = 2 and scale = 1, (d) a Pareto distribution with location = 10^{-2} and scale = 1.75 and (g) the standard lognormal distribution. For each distribution, we plot a random sample with $n = 10^5$. The gamma distribution is emphasised for reasons to be discussed below.

But the tails of the standard Gaussian and the Pareto are indistinguishable in Fig. 3, where they apparently merge at three standard deviations from the origin. To see their difference requires a different way of picturing the distributions which focuses attention on the extreme values, known as a Zipf plot[7]. This is drawn as follows. Arrange a set of numbers having a given distribution in order of their values; plot the *logarithm* of the values on the horizontal axis and the *logarithm* of each number's rank on the vertical axis. Fig. 4 displays the Zipf plots of simulated data having the distributions whose pdfs were shown in Fig. 3. Note that the ordering is from large to small, so the highest value observation has rank one and hence is plotted at zero on the vertical axis.

Fig. 4 shows several important things. First, the profiles of the distributions are indeed different, and in the case of the Pareto, clearly different in kind (its theoretical counterpart is straight at all points, whereas the tails of the others are everywhere curved). To see the tail differences, we have to look very far indeed into the tails. Second, we noted above that in the density plot of Fig. 3, the tails of the standard Gaussian and the Pareto appear to merge at around three standard deviations from the origin. Here,

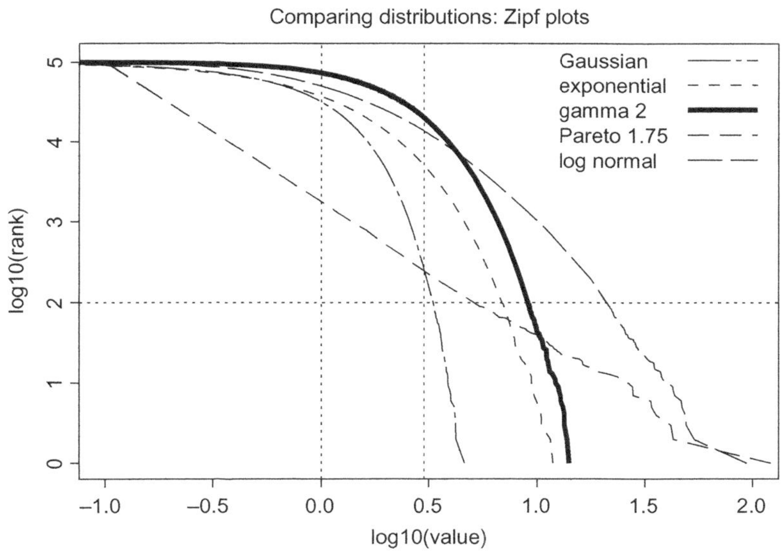

Fig. 4. Gaussian and Non-Gaussian Distributions Compared; Zipf Plots of Sample Data. The x-Range Is Chosen for Comparability with Subsequent Figures.

however, it is clear that so far from merging at this point they in fact cross. Third, at the point where they cross, there are only a few hundred observations further out in the tail (those close to or below the horizontal dotted line). Given that the figure plots 100,000 observations sampled from each of the distributions, these extremes of the tails contain just a few tenths of a per cent of the total data.

Note that the curved tails of the Gaussian and their relatives in the exponential family might appear to be approaching a maximum value along the horizontal axis, but this asymptotic appearance is an illusion. In fact, they extend to infinity, but approach it at an ever slower rate, in contrast to the straight tail of the Pareto. This straight tail is a property that the Pareto shares with other members of the power law family, and with the stable distributions which, as we noted in the previous section, were identified by Mandelbrot as characterising the returns to financial assets. Straight-line tail plots are self-similar in all regions and at all scales. The empirical price-change distributions discovered by Mandelbrot are thus examples of the fractal geometry that he also pioneered.

The practical importance of power law distributions is that their tails contain much more of the total probability than do the Gaussian distributions assumed by conventional EMH. Events so far from the main mass of the distribution that they would not be expected to occur within the life of the universe itself – were they to obey a Gaussian law – can instead be expected to occur quite often. It has been calculated (by H. Eugene Stanley, who we will encounter below) that if stocks followed a Gaussian random walk, then the probability of 1987's Black Monday crash taking place in any hundred-year period was 10^{148} (Beinhocker, 2007, p. 180). The current age of the universe in milliseconds is only 4.32×10^{20}.

In this connection, it should be noted that Fama cannot be entirely blamed for practitioners' obliviousness to power law tails. He was a student of Mandelbrot at the University of Chicago; his PhD noted the existence of fat tails in the returns to the Dow Jones Industrial average (Lowenstein, 2000, p. 71) and he published (Fama, 1968) a technical paper on stable distributions. (Scholes, on the other hand, has less excuse for overlooking them, given that he was Fama's student.) It is perhaps a sign of the influence of events on scholarship that while Fama's widely cited 1970 survey article on EMH drew attention to these facts, he made no mention of them at all in a twentieth anniversary survey of EMH work (published in 1991, hence during the first wave of post-war financial liberalisation).

The need for distributionally correct models of phenomena, especially in respect of extreme behaviour, is well understood in engineering and the physical sciences. The hydrology literature is a case in point. However, it might fairly be categorised as a minority sport in economics, although interest in it is not confined to the usual suspects among the heterodox. Indeed no less a figure than Kenneth Arrow has asserted that it is and should be a promising area for future development. He points to the fact that many economic variables turn out to have fat tails – not merely price changes, but sizes of firms and cities, and wealth and income.

> [T]his reflects an underlying heterogeneity in the population .... The fat tails mean that a relatively small number of events, or people or something, have a big influence. And I think most of our theories of price changes, of changes in investment in response to different conditions are deficient because they don't take account of the shapes of the distributions. (Dubra, 2005, pp. 11–12)

We return to Arrow's point about the relationship between fat tails and the influence of small numbers of observations in a later section. In the meantime, we point out that the fat-tailed empirical distributions of a number of economic variables come about because they appear to be mixtures of distributions, with the main mass of the data being governed by an exponential law and the tail by a power law.

THE RATE OF PROFIT AND ITS DISTRIBUTION

It might be thought that there would be little connection between the returns to speculation in financial assets and the returns to capital invested in productive activity (by 'productive' we here mean the everyday notion of physical production of goods and services in general, rather than the more specialised notion of productive activity found in Marx). Surprisingly, this turns out to be wrong; there is such a connection, and it lies in the kind of statistical facts we have discussed above. Company rates of profit turn out to have power law tails of exactly the same kind as do returns to ownership of financial assets.

Dissolving the Transformation Problem

The transformation problem in Marx's value theory is the supposed need to show that a set of equations can exist which will describe a system of transformations from values to prices that is common to both inputs and outputs, and which yields equal profit rates. As is well known, no such set of equations is possible – a result which, it is claimed, discredits Marx's theory because he 'forgot to transform the inputs'. But this is to demand a solution that either imposes static equilibrium on a dynamic capitalist economy or defies the facts of nature, because in general prices and values at the end of the production period will differ from those at its start, and capitalists cannot go back in time to purchase fresh inputs at the old prices. This temporal single system (TSS) interpretation of Marx refutes the claims of logical inconsistency in Marx's theory, and thus rehabilitates conclusions drawn from it – in particular, those relating to the fall in the rate of profit (Freeman & Carchedi, 1996; Freeman, Kliman, & Wells, 2004; Kliman, 2007).

An alternative approach to vindicating Marx is proposed by Farjoun and Machover in their book *Laws of Chaos* (1983). (But it is one that is entirely compatible with TSS.[8]) They point out that profit rates *do not* equalise in fact, no matter how powerful competition may be in imposing a *tendency* for them to do so. The reason is that the competitive process creates an equally powerful tendency to the dispersion of profit rates, namely technical innovation in search of higher profits. They point out that market economies consist of interactions among a large number of uncoordinated agents and that, this being so, the methods of classical statistical mechanics are applicable.

This 'dissolution' of the transformation problem is performed by following what might be called a binocular approach: to gain perspective by examining two different economic spaces (the firm space of labour values and the market space of prices) and show that they each contain analogous variables which can be taken to be identical in value with high probability. As part of their project, Farjoun and Machover draw a heuristic analogy between the company rate of profit and the energy of a particle in an ideal gas, leading to the conjecture that the rate of profit (once weighted by the size of the firm) should follow a gamma distribution.[9]

Testing Farjoun and Machover

The originality of Farjoun and Machover's work is demonstrated by the fact that to our knowledge there is effectively no previous literature on the functional form of profit rate distributions.[10] The sole exception is a brief discussion in Gibrat's *Les Inegalités Economiques* (1931), a work best known for the conjecture that firm size, measured by the number of employees, should follow a log-normal distribution (Gibrat's Law, also known as the 'law of proportionate effect'). What is much less well known is that this example is just one of many, one of which involves company profit rates. The book as a whole is an illustration of the alleged ubiquity of log-normal distributions in economics, particularly in respect of income and wealth, and indeed, the work is an extended polemic against Pareto and his eponymous distribution. As we shall see, there is a small but active community of scholars whose work has been profoundly influenced by Farjoun and Machover's work. Nonetheless, it appears that so far there has been only one extended attempt to test their hypothesis, namely Wells (2007).[11]

Data

Wells used accounting data for UK companies for the years 1991–1995 to test these rival hypotheses for 17 profit rate definitions found in the Marxist literature on the rate of profit, together with four standard accounting ratios.[12] The tests were carried out for both company-level data and data weighted by the capital measure relevant to each profit rate definition ('capital level' data, in Wells's terminology).

Exploratory analysis of the data showed not only that the company-level profit rates have extremely large ranges but also that the ranges are inversely related to the size of the company. Smaller companies are more likely to be family businesses, vehicles for solo professional contractors and the like, rather than genuine capitalist enterprises (in the sense of Bryer, 2000, namely those that account for and target the *rate* of profit, rather than the volume of the surplus). Thus, weighting the data by company size was hoped to provide a non-arbitrary way of reducing the influence of extreme values. Furthermore, such weighting is essential to testing Farjoun and Machover's hypothesis of a gamma distribution.

Tests

The methods used were in principle capable of identifying other possible distributional laws. Randomly sized random samples from the data were used to estimate *L*-moments of the data for each year and hence plot clouds of points in *L*-skewness/*L*-kurtosis space.[13] Standard distribution families such as the gamma, the Pareto and the extreme value have loci in this space which are well approximated by polynomial functions. Hence, if the cloud plots are aligned along one or other locus, one can select an appropriate model. Since the clouds were of annual data, given a plausible model it would be possible to calculate the relevant parameters for each year, and use these as alternative indicators of the state of the business cycle.

Results

The *L*-moment stage of the tests gave mixed results. For all profit rate definitions save one, the clouds of points failed to convincingly cluster near any one of the distribution loci. The partial exception was the rate defined by Farjoun and Machover in their work (referred to as Gillman4 in Wells (2007), because of its congruence with the 'fourth test' in Gillman (1956). However, although the cloud of annual points lay within the region containing members of the *four*-parameter generalised gamma distribution, it was not oriented along the locus of the ordinary three-parameter gamma. Rather, the cloud's major axis lay north–south in *L*-skewness/*L*-kurtosis space.

Further investigation using Zipf plots of the annual data for the various measures revealed the following:

- For all measures, and for both firm-level and capital-level (size-weighted) data, the differences between years were driven by the right tails of the distribution.
- For nearly all measures, those tails clearly had the straight-line shape that is the signature of power law distributions.
- The sole possible exception was Gillman4, where only in the very extreme ends of the tails can power law behaviour be tentatively identified (Wells, 2007, p. 162).

Implications

Power law tails are common to the distributions of a wide variety of profit rate measures, and at the capital level appear to be present even for the profit rate which instantiates Farjoun and Machover's concept and which may follow the predicted gamma law, once the tails are discounted.[14] Furthermore, some of the accounting measures of the rate of return exhibited the 'cross-over' tail behaviour characteristic of certain stable distributions.[15]

Fig. 5 compares the size-weighted data for several years for Gillman4, with emphasis on the tails. As can be seen, the tail observations falling below the horizontal dotted line show the straight-line pattern characteristic of power law tails. This size-weighted data is derived by merging all the samples used to estimate the *L*-statistics, and thus in principle is a sample from the total number of individual units of capital (i.e. units of £1 sterling) advanced in production in the economy as a whole. Since the data is of

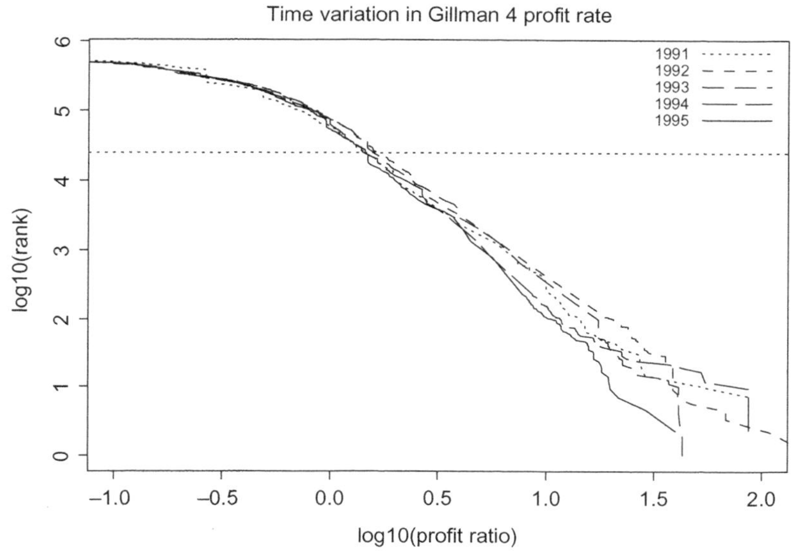

Fig. 5. Zipf Plot of Annual Variation in Weighted Gillman 4 Measures.

returns to individual units of capital, it is thus directly comparable to rates of return on financial assets.

The fact that their distributions have similar characteristics – fat tails – to rates of return to investment in purely financial assets is remarkable, given the association of fat tails with financial instability.

Two important points should be noted; first, the data are computed as profit *ratios*: thus, a return corresponding to zero on the chart actually represents a percentage rate of return of 100, while the very largest observations are of profit rates of the order of 10,000 per cent. These are clearly very extreme tails. Second, the merged samples used to construct Fig. 5 contain between 250,000 and 500,00 observations, depending on the year; the significance of the horizontal dotted line is that it is drawn at the level of the 25,000th largest observation. The power law tails thus account for between one per cent and a half of one per cent of the total capital. Thus, they must represent the returns of mainly small enterprises. What is unclear is whether the enormous rates of return measured here are returns to innovation and entrepreneurship, or result from accounting devices in what are not genuinely capitalist enterprises.[16]

Further discussion is beyond the scope of this chapter, but the significant point is the empirical parallelism between the returns to productive investment and to financial speculation, and thus the connections between company profitability, the transformation problem in Marxist political economy, and wider issues of financial and economic stability.

MARX'S PROBABILISM

The results on company profits just discussed, however much they are addressed to problems in Marxist economics, might seem to be a long way from Marx himself, particularly when they stem from the rejection of a point widely regarded as the cornerstone of Marx's analysis, namely the equalisation of profit rates.[17] But there is good reason to think that Marx himself had a firmly statistical approach, and in particular was clearly familiar with the importance of probability distributions.

Probability Density Functions

In his volume III discussion of profit rate equalisation, Marx says:

> Between those spheres that approximate more or less to the social average, there is again a tendency to equalization, which seeks the 'ideal' mean position, i.e. a mean position which does not exist in reality. In other words, it tends to shape itself around this ideal as a norm. (Marx, 1981, p. 273)

Our claim is that here Marx clearly has in mind a probability density function, something that there is reason to believe he had informally from his reading of Quetelet (see below). Further, when Marx comes to discuss intra-industry variations in productivity, and hence the individual values of commodities, he considers how differences in distribution – symmetric or not, light- or heavy-tailed – affect the relation of the mean to the whole (1981, pp. 283–284).

> Let us now assume that great quantities of these commodities are produced in something like these same normal conditions, so that this value is also the individual value for the individual commodities making up this mass. If only a relatively small proportion are produced in worse conditions, and another portion in better conditions, so that the individual value of the one part is greater than the mean value of the great bulk of the commodities, and that of the other part lower than this mean, then these two extremes

> will cancel one another out so that the average value of the commodities at the extremes is the same as the value of the mass of average commodities ...

[the distribution is symmetric with light tails]

> ... and the market value is determined by the value of the commodities produced under average conditions. The value of the overall mass of commodities is equal to the actual sum of values of all individual commodities taken together, both those produced in average conditions, and those produced in better or worse ones.

[Marx defines the total probability mass]

> In this case ...

[that of the symmetric distribution described above]

> ... the market value or social value of the mass of commodities – the necessary labour-time they contain – is determined by the value of the great middling mass.

[that is, the distribution has sufficiently light tails that the mean is defined]

> Now assume on the contrary that the total quantity of the commodities in question brought to market remains the same, but the value of those produced under better conditions is not balanced out by the value of those produced under better conditions, so that the part of the total produced under worse conditions forms a relatively significant quantity, both vis-a-vis the average mass and vis-a-vis the opposite extreme.

[in other words a skewed distribution with one heavy tail containing the commodities produced under worse conditions]

> In this case it is the mass produced under the worse conditions that governs the market, or social, value.

[by shifting the mean away from the mode; the opposite case is also mentioned]

It might be objected that to read the foregoing as an account of statistical distributions is to propose Marx as having – at best – a misty prophetic vision of probability density functions somehow hovering behind his purely literary discussion, and so to impose on him our own latter-day statistical concerns.

But documented evidence of Marx's reading suggests that his vision was neither misty nor prophetic, but extremely concrete and based on thorough engagement with Quetelet. Marx himself cites Quetelet in only a few places, but these references include work from as early as 1829, while Alcouffe and Wells (2009) have provided arguments to suggest that Marx followed Quetelet's work right through to 1869, when the second edition of the latter's classic *A Treatise on the Development of Man and his Faculties* was published. More specifically, it is known that Marx made excerpts from two of Quetelet's works, the *Treatise* (from the English translation published in 1842) and his subsequent *Du système social et des lois qui le règissent* (1848).[18]

Both these works include charts depicting probability densities (though Quetelet does not use that term): in the *Treatise*, these are plates 2 ('viability' of individuals) and 4 (propensity to crime, literary ability, physical strength), and in *Du Système*, they are on pages 80 (marriage) and 93 (theoretical curve for crime). The marriage chart is reproduced in Fig. 6; although there is no vertical scale in the original, examination of the associated data table (Quetelet, 1848, p. 318) shows that he has here silently smoothed the data.[19]

Given the empirical results reported above, and also Marx's discussion of the distribution of individual values of commodities, it is certainly interesting that the curves here are markedly asymmetrical. In case this appears inconsistent with Quetelet's preoccupation with the (symmetrical) Gaussian distribution, it should be pointed out that for him it is the *individual* propensity to marry at *any given age* that is so distributed, not the overall propensity of the population at any age.

Further discussion must await publication of the actual notebooks, but Marx clearly had at least the *opportunity* to see these. Note also that it was Quetelet who introduced the distinction between the 'real' means of astronomy and the 'ideal' means of social statistics, which include the 'average

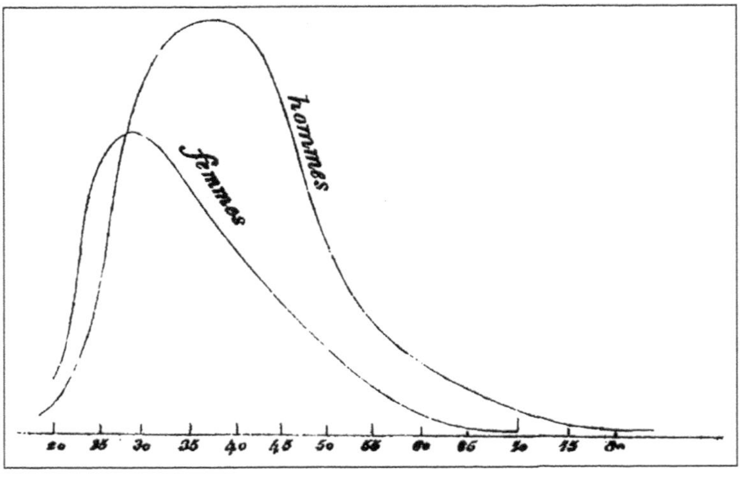

Fig. 6. Pioneering pdf Diagram from Quetelet (1848, p. 80).

man', a term he also coined. As we have seen, Marx describes the average rate of profit as an 'ideal' mean in *Capital* volume III, the manuscript of which he was working on around the time that he was reading Quetelet's (1848) work.

At the very least, Marx's conceptualisation of values and profit rates as probability densities is a hypothesis awaiting disproof. Granted this, his attitude to the assumption of a uniform rate of profit as a condition of the transformation problem (and thus the importance of the alleged problem) becomes a matter for debate in just the way suggested by Farjoun and Machover and their followers. The 'ideal' mean 'does not exist in reality', according to Marx. Not only this, but his concern with whether or not the mass of the extreme values is sufficiently light to allow 'the value of the great middling mass' to determine the social value becomes of great interest, for if it does not then in modern language we have a distribution with an undefined mean, and hence with a fat tail or tails. This, as we noted above, is a distinguishing feature of the stable family of distributions, identified a century later by Mandelbrot as a model for cotton prices, and a key exhibit in the critique of orthodox economics and its role in the financial crisis.

FROM FAT TAILS TO TALES OF COMPLEXITY

Economics and Physics

Farjoun and Machover motivate their probabilistic response to the transformation problem by reference to the apparently disorderly, uncoordinated and random interactions of isolated individuals that characterise a market economy, an insight they credit to Rosa Luxemburg (for details, see Farjoun & Machover, 1983, pp. 8, 60, 79–80, 141).

As we saw, this led them to an analogy with the statistics of ideal gases. This field was pioneered in the nineteenth century by James Clerk Maxwell – who, it is relevant to point out, was inspired to do so by reading an account of Quetelet's *Treatise* in the *Edinburgh Review*.[20]

Maxwell showed that very simple assumptions about the atomic nature of gases and the interaction of the hypothetical atoms[21] at the micro level led deductively to the already known empirical macro laws linking the volume, temperature and pressure of gases. It was thus perhaps inevitable that it would occur to some with knowledge of both physics and economics to wonder if the insights of statistical mechanics might be applied to economies composed of individual agents uncoordinated by any plan. The resulting field of so-called econophysics has become an interesting territory occupied at one end by economists with relatively mainstream backgrounds and by Marxists at the other.

Priority of innovation clearly belongs to the latter, in the persons of Farjoun and Machover, whose work we discussed above. However, the present nomenclature was coined by the group associated with H. Eugene Stanley. We concentrate on Stanley because of the special importance of his work to the question of the distribution of asset returns, although there are also centres of activity in India (the first econophysics gathering was at Kolkata in 1995), Germany, Italy and Romania, among others.

Part of the reason why the early findings of power law returns were dismissed was that if this type of distribution truly obtains, then the same law of returns should be found over any time scale – in other words that the data for very short period returns should be as fat tailed as those for returns over many days. Early work suggested that although power law tails were found for short-period returns, as one extended the time horizon the distributions appeared to become Gaussian. This was the reason Fama gave, after due consideration of the power law alternative, for assuming Gaussian returns in his 1976 textbook, *Foundations of Finance* (Fama, 1976, p. 21–38). However, Stanley's team was able to sample millions of transactions and show that power law tails existed over three orders of magnitude, from five minutes to 16 days. Among other works, they examined 30 million daily records covering 6000 US stocks between 1962 and 1996 (Plerou, Gopikrishnan, Amaral, Meyer, & Stanley, 1999).

Work in the econophysics tradition has been influential in establishing as stylised fact the existence of power law tails in the distributions of many economic variables. Among other contributions, one may mention Amaral et al. (1997) on the growth of firms; Ausloos, Miskiewicz, and Sanglier (2004) on length and frequency of booms and recessions; Axtell (2001) on firm size; Cook and Ormerod (2003) on rates of firm demise and Dragulescu and Yakovenko (2003) on income and wealth. Surveys of the field include Markose (2005) (introducing a collection of articles in the *Economic Journal*), Scafetta and West (2007) and Yakovenko (2008). Much of this work is explicitly motivated by opposition to such neoclassical shibboleths as market efficiency and representative agents, sometimes forcefully expressed (e.g. see McCauley, 2004). However, some of it appears to suffer from 'boy and hammer' syndrome (everything looks like a nail); an internal critique of econophysics is provided by Gallegatti, Keen, Lux, and Ormerod (2005), to which McCauley (2006) is a response.

Complexity

In a previous section, we noted Mandelbrot's finding that returns to financial assets had the power law type tails associated with stable distributions. It turns out that power law tails (i.e. ones with straight lines in their Zipf plot) play an important role in the new field of complexity, developed in particular by scholars associated with the Santa Fe Institute, which has sought to foster collaboration between economists and physical scientists (see Markose, 2005, for an introduction). Complexity, in this context, means the study of how systems of uncoordinated agents may nonetheless spontaneously develop order, in the sense that regularities emerge that cannot be analytically derived from the rules governing the interactions. Order is thus said to be an 'emergent property' of such systems, while the regularities of interest are captured by considering the distributions of relevant variables.

Modern desktop computers are sufficiently powerful that it is straightforward to repeatedly simulate sufficiently large systems (i.e. ones with enough agents) for enough periods to find whatever regularities emerge from a given model. An agent-based model (ABM) greatly relevant to Marxist political economy will be considered in some detail below.

The significance of power law tails – which, to recall, are those of distributions with excess kurtosis – is that they are associated with complex systems which achieve 'self-organizing criticality' (SOC). These are systems which will quickly reorganise into a new order when challenged by a sudden change in internal or external parameters (see Beinhocker, 2007, p. 156 ff, p. 328). The concept of SOC and its association with power law distributions was first introduced by Bak, Tang, and Wiesenfeld (1987, 1988) in the context of so-called sandpile models, where addition of a few grains at a time proceeds smoothly for a while before triggering an avalanche. This is the significance of Arrow's remark, quoted above, associating fat tails with systems in which relatively few of the elements are influential in changes. Complex systems, in the sense discussed here, are crisis prone.

Marx on Chance and Necessity, and the Emergence of Economic Laws

That Marx considered capitalism to be prone to crisis is a statement few would bother to contest. What we claim in this section is that he also conceived of capitalism as a complex system in the sense discussed above, in other words one with law-like structural relationships that are emergent properties of its own functioning. Further, we claim that this conception was linked to a probabilistic approach underlying the more technical statistical thinking we have already described.

We could illustrate the probabilistic foundations of Marx's thought by reference to many of his works, as discussed in Wells (2006, 2007) and Alcouffe and Wells (2009), accounts that also discuss both Quetelet's influence on Marx and the lack of serious attention that has been paid to this. (At a late stage in the preparation of this paper, Alain Alcouffe brought to our attention the work of Michel Vadée (1992); from a first reading, it is clear that Vadée has preceded us in both closely reading Marx in relation to Quetelet, and in stressing the importance of Marx's doctoral dissertation (Marx, 1975) in understanding the deep-rooted character of his probabilism. However, it seems that Vadée does not consider the more technical aspects of statistics that we find in Marx.)

Here, we confine ourselves to the evidence from the *Grundrisse*; there are at least six places in the work where Marx considers the uncertainties of a capitalist economy, and the need for probabilistic and statistical concepts to theorise it (for further details, see Alcouffe & Wells, 2009), but we will notice only the following quotation, which shows that Marx regarded his conception of social laws as an emergent property of unfree societies in general as being sharply illuminated by its generalisation under capitalism:

> ... as much as the individual moments of this movement arise from the conscious will and particular purposes of individuals, so much does the totality of the process appear as an objective interrelation, which arises spontaneously from nature ... *Their own collisions with one another produce an* **alien** *social power standing above them, produce their mutual interaction as a process and power independent of them.* Circulation ... is also the first form in which the social relation appears as something independent of the individuals ... extending to the whole of the social movement itself. (Marx, 1973, pp. 196–197; emphasis added: 'alien' is Marx's emphasis)

Under capitalism, the social laws possessing the apparent force of laws of nature are the 'laws' of economics, as discussed in this excerpt from Chapter 51 of *Capital*, Vol. III:

> Since ... everyone seeks to sell his commodity as dearly as possible (*apparently ... guided* in the regulation of production itself *solely by his own free will*), the inner law enforces itself only through their competition, their mutual pressure upon each other, whereby the deviations are mutually cancelled. *Only as an inner law, vis-a-vis the individual agents, as a blind law of Nature, does the law of value exert its influence here* and maintain the social equilibrium of production amidst its accidental fluctuations. (Marx, 1959, p. 880, emphases added)

In short, although individuals in a society founded on competitive markets are truly free agents and not victims of blind fate, they *appear* to be governed by natural law. But as Marx stresses, these social and economic laws are *not* 'natural' but – in modern language – emergent properties of complex systems. In Marx's language, his concern was the inner connection of chance and necessity.

PROBABILISTIC MARXISM

It is clear that Farjoun and Machover have priority of innovation in the marriage of statistical mechanics with economics that has come to be known as econophysics, even if a greater mass of work in this vein has been produced outside Marxist circles than within them. There is, however, a parallel with non-Marxist scholarship in that Farjoun and Machover's following is in the main not found in economics but in disciplines such as computer science (Paul Cockshott, Greg Michaelson and Ian Wright) and geography (Trevor Barnes, Jurgen Essletzbichler, David Rigby, Eric Sheppard and Michael Webber).

(A partial exception to the foregoing should be noted, in the person of Duncan Foley; however, although he is an external professor at the Santa Fe Institute, his econophysics work is not directly linked to his undoubtedly significant Marxist scholarship.)

A conference on Probabilistic Political Economy was held at Kingston University London in 2008 to celebrate the 25th anniversary of *Laws of Chaos*.[22] Space considerations preclude a detailed survey either of the conference, or of previous work in this tradition. Other works that the interested reader should consult are Cockshott and Cottrell (1994, 1998); Cockshott, Cottrell, and Michaelson (1995); Julius (2005); Puty (n.d.); Sheppard and Barnes (1986, 1990); Webber (1987); Webber and Rigby (1986, 1996). Instead, we mention what is perhaps the most significant contribution to appear since the 2008 conference, *Classical Econophysics* (Cockshott, Cottrell, Michaelson, Wright, & Yakovenko, 2009).

Classical Econophysics

The first book-length contribution in this field is not, strictly, a Marxist work (though several of its authors have published in such journals as *Capital and Class*); rather, its title is, the authors tell us, chosen to suggest the combination of classical political economy and econophysics, and they develop the concerns of Smith and Ricardo (and Babbage) as well as of Marx.

Those concerns are (page 2) work and the physical production of goods, value and prices, and the class distribution of revenue. Thus, the six chapters of their first section ('Work, information and value') alternate discussions of labour and technology in general with discussion of information theory and information technology, and culminate in outlining their responses to Hayek's computational critique of a planned economy, as well as to the contention that there is no coherent solution to Marx's transformation problem. As the authors point out, much of the material has previously appeared, in one form or another, in other places. But it is helpful to see it combined in the way that it is; linking econophysics and information theory is not as unlikely as might seem at first glance, since the concept of entropy arises in both contexts.

Here, we draw attention to just one element of the work, thus re-worked by Cockshott and his co-authors, namely Wright's work on the social architecture of capitalism (SAC). We single this out because it draws attention to all the elements we want to draw attention to in this chapter: on the one hand that econophysics, complexity theory and ABM achieve their full development when informed by Marx's value theory, and on the other that these paradigms bring to fruition an essential part of Marx's thought.

The Social Architecture of Capitalism

Wright's SAC is an example of the ABM discussed above; it convincingly demonstrates economic inequality to be an emergent property of an exchange economy in which labour power is a commodity.[23] He builds a computer simulation of an economy in which identical agents engage in random exchange. The only built-in structure is that the agents may belong to one of three possible classes – employers, workers or the unemployed. The initial assignment is random, and they can change status during the simulation. At the start, each agent is endowed with an equal share of a fixed quantity of money.

Remarkably, the economy that emerges is quite the opposite of one in which 'just anything' can happen, in the following precise sense: after a relatively short time, it settles down with distributions of (analogues of) income, wealth, firm size and other variables that have a remarkable qualitative similarity to widely accepted stylised facts about the real world (such as the Pareto distribution of income among the wealthy). The model is admittedly highly simplified (e.g. there is no fixed capital, and hence no distinct industries) and thus its precise interpretation is uncertain; arguably, it represents simple commodity production. However, that what emerges from so simplified a model is nonetheless so similar, in qualitative terms, to actually existing capitalist economies suggests that it is indeed capturing something fundamental about them.

CONCLUSION

We began by considering both lay and professional thinking about the financial crisis of 2008. Once one moves away from the symptoms – greedy bankers and reckless behaviour – consideration of theoretical understandings leads from the empirical justification of the assumptions underlying the orthodox understanding of financial markets to the theoretical perspectives of econophysics and complexity.

Much of the literature in this tradition comes from workers entirely innocent of any knowledge of Marx, but the approach that was subsequently dubbed 'econophysics' was first proposed by Farjoun and Machover as part of a response to the 1970s debate on the transformation problem in Marxist economics.

On the one hand, work by their followers has achieved two things. First, attempts to verify their core hypothesis about company profit rates in production have revealed an empirical link between these and the statistics of speculative returns to financial assets. Second, ABM informed by Marxist categories has demonstrated how many features of exchange economies can be understood as emergent properties conditioned by the class facts of capitalist society – thus linking this school to complexity thinking in general.

On the other hand, quotation from the *Grundrisse* established the claim that Marx is a precursor of modern complexity thinking; we also showed that in Volume III of *Capital*, he made informal use of powerful statistical ideas in his critique of political economy, an achievement based on a close reading of the pioneering work in social statistics of his contemporary, Quetelet. Taken together, these facts illustrate not only the continued relevance of Marx's conceptual categories but their power when applied in the manner that Marx himself envisaged.

NOTES

1. Interview with Juan Dubra (2005).

2. I am indebted to an anonymous reviewer for drawing this disparity of perception to my attention.

3. 'Merchant banker' is Cockney rhyming slang for 'wanker', a term whose secondary meaning in British English is 'ineffectual dilettante'. See http://www.cockneyrhymingslang.co.uk/slang/merchant_banker, a site which is part of the British Library web archive (http://www.webarchive.org.uk/ukwa/).

4. LTCM also acted as a kind of reverse Ponzi scheme – to increase their own leverage the principals forced many investors to cash out just before the firm got into trouble.

5. We ignore the wider and in many ways even more fundamental problem of assuming that markets necessarily have equilibrating tendencies, let alone that any such outcomes are efficient, in the relevant sense.

6. 'Gaussian' because it was first described by the German mathematician Carl Friedrich Gauss.

7. Named for George Zipf, who invented it as part of his investigations into the frequency of words in natural languages (Zipf, 1932).

8. Personal communication from Alan Freeman.

9. Based on this probabilistic conception of Marxist economics, Farjoun and Machover's book goes on to make many other intriguing claims which we have no space to consider here.

10. There is some *subsequent* literature, notably Wright's (2005) proposal, in the work discussed later, and Alfarano, Mishael, Irle, and Kauschke (2008), who suggest a Subbotin distribution.

11. Other work influenced by this has either tested the distribution across *industries*, rather than firms, or has considered empirical densities rather than any functional form that these might have (e.g. see Zachariah, 2006).

12. Different reporting requirements for different sizes of firms, and the differing variables involved in the various profit rate measures, mean that the number of observations for the different measures ranged from 40,000 to 70,000.

13. *L*-moments are alternatives to the usual Pearsonian product moments, and are so-named because they are linear combinations of the data. Their superior ability to distinguish between the tails of otherwise similar distributional models has gained them an audience among hydrologists, who have a strong professional interest in the frequency of extreme events (the '100-year flood'); see Hosking and Wallis (1997) for details.

14. To go further depends on methods for non-arbitrarily locating the boundary between the exponential and power law regimes in the data.

15. For a stable distribution with parameter *alpha*, there is an initial power decay with exponent *alpha* >2 before the true tail with exponent *alpha*. The effect is most noticeable for large *alpha* (Borak, Hardle, & Weron, 2005, Figure 1.1, p. 3).

16. For details of their derivation and use, see Wells (2007, pp. 104–107, 153).

17. Strictly speaking, Marx spoke of the equalisation of *industry* profit rates, which in principle is compatible with non-equalisation of *company* profit rates. But Wells (2007) shows that empirical tests which purport to demonstrate industry-level

equalization, such as those popularised by Glick (1985), are very sensitive to debatable assumptions about the appropriate level of aggregation.

18. The notes on the *Treatise* are in Heft XVI, of 1851, while those on the 1848 work are in a notebook, London 1865/1866, according to the editors of the MEGA (Marx & Engels, 2004, p. 1297). I am indebted to John Stachel for information about Marx's London notebook, and for the reference to the MEGA.

19. Presumably informally, but the results are consistent with those produced using Tukey's '3RS3R' smoother as implemented by the smooth() function in R 2.12.1.

20. The review, anonymous at the time, was in fact by the astronomer John Herschel (1850). Statistical thinking thus found its way from astronomy to physics *via* the social sciences.

21. The atomic nature of matter was at that time a widely accepted hypothesis, but it was only finally demonstrated conclusively by the French physicist Jean Perrin in the wake of Einstein's work on Brownian motion.

22. The conference website is http://staffnet.kingston.ac.uk/~ku32530/PPE/programme.html. See http://staffnet.kingston.ac.uk/~ku32530/PPE/PPEindex.html for links to the text of *Laws of Chaos*.

23. Besides the discussion in Cockshott et al. (2009), readers should consult the original paper, published in *Physica A* (Wright, 2005).

REFERENCES

Alcouffe, A., & Wells, J. (2009). Marx, maths and MEGA II. Conference of the European Society for the History of Economic Thought, Thessaloniki.

Aldrick, P. (2007). Weakened Northern Rock may face bid. *Daily Telegraph*. Retrieved from http://www.telegraph.co.uk/finance/markets/2815503/Weakened-Northern-Rock-may-face-bid.html. Accessed 31 October 2012.

Alfarano, S., Milaković, M., Irle, A., & Kauschke, J. (2012). A statistical equilibrium model of competitive firms. *Journal of Economic Dynamics and Control*, *36*(1), 136–149.

Amaral, L. A. N., Buldyrev, S. V., Havlin, S., Leschhorn, H., Maass, F., & Salinger, M. A. (1997). Scaling behavior in economics: I. Empirical results for company growth. *Journal de Physique I France*, *7*, 621–633.

Ausloos, M., Miskiewicz, J., & Sanglier, M. (2004). The duration of recession and prosperity: Does their distribution follow a power or an exponential law? Physica A: Statistical Mechanics and its Applications, *339*(3), 548–558.

Axtell, R. L. (2001). Zipf distribution of U.S. firm sizes. *Science*, *293*, 1818–1820.

Bak, P., Tang, C., & Wiesenfeld, K. (1987). Self-organized criticality: An explanation of the 1/f noise. *Physical Review Letters*, *59*(4), 381–384.

Bak, P., Tang, C., & Wiesenfeld, K. (1988). Self-organized criticality. *Physical Review A*, *38*(1), 364–374.

Beinhocker, E. D. (2007). *The origin of wealth: Evolution, complexity, and the radical remaking of economics*. London: Random House.

Borak, S., Hardle, W., & Weron, R. (2005). Stable distributions. SFB 649 Discussion Paper 2005–008, Humboldt-Universitat zu Berlin.

Bryer, R. A. (2000). The history of accounting and the transition to capitalism in England. Part One: Theory. *Accounting, Organizations and Society, 25*, 131–162.

Cockshott, P., & Cottrell, A. (1994). Value price transformation as a real process. Conference on 'Karl Marx's third volume of Capital: 1894–1994, University of Bergamo.

Cockshott, P., & Cottrell, A. (1998). Does Marx need to transform? In: R. Bellofiore (Ed.), *Marxian economics: A reappraisal* (Vol. 2, pp. 70–85). London: Macmillan.

Cockshott, P., Cottrell, A., & Michaelson, G. (1995). Testing Marx: Some new results from UK data. *Capital and Class, 55*, 103–129.

Cockshott, W. P., Cottrell, A. F., Michaelson, G. J., Wright, I. P., & Yakovenko, V. M. (2009). *Classical econophysics*. London: Routledge.

Cook, W., & Ormerod, P. (2003). Power law distribution of the frequency of demises of U.S. firms. Physica A: Statistical Mechanics and its Applications, *324*, 207–212.

Dragulescu, A., & Yakovenko, V.M. (2003). Statistical mechanics of money, income and wealth: A short survey. In: Modeling of complex systems: Seventh Granada Lectures: AIP Conference Proceedings, New York, pp. 180–183.

Dubra, J. (2005). Interview with Kenneth Arrow. MPRA Paper No. 967, March 2005. Retrieved from http://mpra.ub.uni-muenchen.de/967/ (Posted 29 November 2006, 19:09).

Fama, E. (1968). Some properties of symmetric stable distributions. *Journal of the American Statistical Association, 63*, 323, 817–836.

Fama, E. (1970). Efficient capital markets: A review of theory and empirical work. *Journal of Finance, 25*(May), 383–417.

Fama, E. (1991). Efficient markets: II. *Journal of Finance, 46*(December), 1575–1617.

Fama, E. F. (1976). *Foundations of finance: Portfolio decisions and securities prices*. New York, NY: Basic Books.

Farjoun, E., & Machover, M. (1983). *Laws of chaos: A probabilistic approach to political economy*. London: Verso.

Freeman, A., & Carchedi, C. (Eds.). (1996). *Marx and non-equilibrium economics*. Cheltenham: Edward Elgar.

Freeman, A., Kliman, A., & Wells, J. (Eds.). (2004). *The new value controversy and the foundations of economics*. Cheltenham: Edward Elgar.

Gallegatti, M., Keen, S., Lux, T., & Ormerod, P. (2005). Worrying trends in econophysics. Paper prepared for the Physica A proceedings of the World Econophysics Colloquium, Canberra, November 2005.

Gibrat, R. P. L. (1931). *Les inégalités économiques*. Paris: Sirey.

Gillman, J. M. (1956). *The falling rate of profit: Marx's law and its significance to twentieth-century capitalism*. London: Dennis Dobson.

Glick, M. (1985). *Competition vs. monopoly; profit rate dispersion in U.S. manufacturing industries*. PhD dissertation, New School for Social Research, New York, NY.

Herrnstein, C. A., & Murray, R. J. (1994). *The bell curve: Intelligence and class structure in American life*. New York: Free Press.

Herschel, J. (1850). Quetelet on probabilities. *Edinburgh Review, 92*, 1–57.

Hosking, J. R. M., & Wallis, J. R. (1997). *Regional frequency analysis: An approach based on L-moments*. Cambridge: Cambridge University Press.

Julius, A. J. (2005). *Stable great ratios and stationary dispersion of profit rates in unbalanced growth*. New York, NY: New School for Social Research.

Kliman, A. (2007). *Reclaiming Marx's* 'Capital'*: A refutation of the myth of inconsistency*. New York, NY: Lexington Books.

Lowenstein, R. (2000). *When genius failed: The rise and fall of Long-Term Capital Management.* New York, NY: Random House.
Mandelbrot, B. (1963). The variation of certain speculative prices. *The Journal of Business*, University of Chicago Press, 36(October), 394–419.
Markose, S. M. (2005). Computability and evolutionary complexity: markets as complex adaptive systems. *The Economic Journal, 115*, F159–F192.
Marx, K. (1959). *Capital* (Vol. III). London: Lawrence and Wishart.
Marx, K. (1973). *Grundrisse*. Harmondsworth: Penguin Books.
Marx, K. (1975). Difference between the Democritean and Epicurean philosophy of nature. In: Marx-Engels collected works (Vol. 1). London: Lawrence and Wishart.
Marx, K. (1981). *Capital* (Vol. III). Harmondsworth: Penguin Books.
Marx, K., & Engels, F. (2004). Gesamtausgabe (MEGA), Zweite Abteiling, 'Das kapital' und Vorarbeiten, vol. 15, Das kapital Kiritik der politischen Ökonomie, Dritter banm hamburg 1894, Apparat, Berlin: Akademie Verlag.
McCauley, J. (2004). *Dynamics of markets: Econophysics and finance*. Cambridge: Cambridge University Press.
McCauley, J. (2006). Response to "Worrying Trends in Econophysics". Retrieved from http://arxiv.org/pdf/physics/0606002
Plerou, V., Gopikrishnan, P., Amaral, L. A. N., Meyer, M., & Stanley, H. E. (1999). Scaling of the distribution of price fluctuations of individual companies. *Physical Review, E60*, 6519–6529.
Puty, C. C. B. (n.d.). *A simulation model of the general rate of profit with capital accumulation.* Universidade Federal do Pará, Belém, Brasil. Retrieved from www.ucm.es/info/ec/jec10/ponencias/909puty.pdf
Quetelet, L. A. J. (1842 [1969]). *A treatise on man and the development of his faculties.* Gainesville, FL: Scholars' Facsimiles and Reprints.
Quetelet, L. A. J. (1848). *Du système social et des lois qui le régissent*. Paris: Guillamin.
Scafetta, N., & West, B. J. (2007). Probability distributions in conservative energy exchange models of multiple interacting agents. *Journal of Physics: Condensed Matter, 19*, 1–18.
Sheppard, E., & Barnes, T. J. (1986). Instabilities in the geography of capitalist production: Collective vs. individual profit maximization. *Annals of the Association of American Geographers, 76*, 493–507.
Sheppard, E., & Barnes, T. J. (1990). *The capitalist space economy: Geographical analysis after 'Ricardo, Marx and Sraffa*. London: Unwin Hyman.
Vadée, M. (1992). Marx penseur du possible. Paris: Méridiens-Klincksieck.
Webber, M. (1987). Rates of profit and interregional flows of capital. *Annals of the Association of American Geographers, 77*, 1.
Webber, M. J., & Rigby, D. L. (1986). The rate of profit in Canadian manufacturing industry, 1950-1981. *Review of Radical Political Economics, 18*(1/2), 33–55.
Webber, M. J. & Rigby, D. L. (1996). The Golden Age illusion: Rethinking postwar capitalism. New York, NY: Guilford Press.
Wells, J. (2006). The dogs that didn't bark. LSE seminar paper. Retrieved from http://staffnet.kingston.ac.uk/~ku32530/dogs.pdf
Wells, J. (2007). The rate of profit as a random variable. Unpublished PhD dissertation, The Open University: Milton Keynes.
Wright, I. (2005). The social architecture of capitalism. *Physica A: Statistical Mechanics and its Applications, 346*(3–4), 589–620.

Yakovenko, V. M. (2008). Econophysics, statistical mechanics approach to. In B. Meyers (Ed.), *Encyclopedia of complexity and system science*. Springer.
Zachariah, D. (2006). Labour value and equalisation of profit rate: A multi-country study. *Indian Development Review*, *4*(1), 1–21.
Zipf, G. (1932). *Selective studies and the principle of relative frequency in language*. Cambridge, MA: Harvard University Press.

DOES INVESTMENT CALL THE TUNE? EMPIRICAL EVIDENCE AND ENDOGENOUS THEORIES OF THE BUSINESS CYCLE

José A. Tapia Granados

ABSTRACT

Theories of the business cycle can be classified into two main groups, exogenous *and* endogenous, *according to the way they explain economic fluctuations – either as responses of the economy to factors that are external (exogenous shocks) or as upturns and downturns of the economic system internally generated (by endogenous factors). In endogenous theories, investment is generally a key variable to explain the dynamic status of the economy. This essay examines the role of investment in endogenous theories. Two contrasting views on how changes in investment and profitability push the economy towards expansion or contraction are represented by the insights of Kalecki, Keynes, Matthews and Minsky versus those of Marx and Mitchell. Hyman Minsky claimed that investment 'calls the tune' to indicate that investment is the only variable not determined by other variables, so that future profits, investment and the dynamic status of the economy are determined by current investment*

Contradictions: Finance, Greed, and Labor Unequally Paid
Research in Political Economy, Volume 28, 229–259

ISSN: 0161-7230/doi:10.1108/S0161-7230(2013)0000028009

and investment in the near past. However, this hypothesis does not appear to be supported by available empirical data for 251 quarters of the US economy. Statistical evidence rather supports the hypothesis of causality in the direction of profits determining investment and, in this way, leading the economy towards boom or bust.

Keywords: Business cycle theories; investment and profits; Keynesian economics; Marxian theory

INTRODUCTION

Modern economists often discuss 'the business cycle', though some American economists avoid this term and prefer to refer to 'economic fluctuations', while British authors generally favour 'trade cycle'. Indeed, a plethora of terms have been used in economic jargon to refer to this bipolar phenomenon: boom-and-bust cycle, expansion and contraction, upturn and downturn, mania and panic, and prosperity and depression have been among the terms used since the 18th century. Terms such as revulsion in trade, commercial distress, stagnation, slump, recession or crisis were also used in the past to describe the phase of declining business activity of the 'cycle'.

The so-called Great Recession has stimulated interest in business-cycle theory, in which a major issue is whether there exists a key variable, or variables, that exerts a major influence on the economy and serves as the major determinant of its dynamic condition of expansion or contraction. Many business-cycle theories claim to answer that question, though the answer is often buried in jargon or mathematical equations. This chapter reviews some general aspects on how causes of business cycles have been conceptualised in economic thought, and the views of major theorists of the business cycle are examined, focusing on the role of investment and profits. Empirical evidence is presented and statistical procedures – descriptive statistics, lag regressions and Granger causality tests – are used to test how empirical data fit with some proposed theories.

SOME GENERAL ASPECTS OF BUSINESS-CYCLE THEORIES

The earliest conjectures on the business cycle and depressions were probably the underconsumption theories proposed at the turn of the 18th century by Lord Lauderdale, Thomas R. Malthus and Simonde de Sismondi. These authors attributed downturns in business activity to economic circumstances, that is to endogenous factors (Mitchell, 1927, Ch. 1). 'General gluts' would occur because purchasing power available in society is not sufficient to buy the output produced, low wages would not allow labour 'to buy its own product'. These underconsumption theories were, however, rejected by Jean Baptiste Say, David Ricardo and most economists of the 19th century, who accepted the idea that sufficient demand is always available to purchase the produced supply. Later baptised as Say's law, this would be the supposed theoretical reason precluding the possibility of 'general gluts'.

Haberler's opinion was that underconsumption theories have a scientific standard quite lower than other theories of the business cycle (Haberler, 1960). Schumpeter (1954, p. 740) suggested the same thing, asserting that underconsumption theory, 'as Marx well knew, is beneath discussion since it involves neglect of the elementary fact that inadequacy (...) of the wage income to buy the whole product at cost-covering prices would not prevent hitchless production in response to the demand of non-wage earners either for "luxury" goods or for investment'. Of course, Karl Marx also rejected Say's law, though his reasons for it were quite different from those of Malthus, Sismondi or Rodbertus.

Leaving underconsumption aside, with the weapon of Say's law at hand, the nascent discipline of economics was quite aloof to the possibility of general gluts of markets and thus paid little attention to commercial crises and business-cycle issues. Indeed, apart from Marx and Jevons, economists were scarcely interested in this field (Morgan, 1990, p. 15) and a major contribution such as *Les Crises commerciales et leur retour periodique en France, en Angleterre, et aux Etats-Unis* came from a non-economist, Clément Juglar, in 1862.

The years between 1870 and the start of World War I saw major developments in economics, where the 'cycle' displaced 'crises' from economists' minds and crises theories were displaced by business-cycle theories (Besomi, 2005; Schumpeter, 1954, p. 1123). It was also the time when three exogenous theories that attribute business cycles to astronomical or biological influences were proposed. In papers published by W. S. Jevons between 1875 and 1882 and in two books authored by H. L. Moore in 1914 and 1923, the fluctuations of the economy were attributed to weather, determined in turn by astronomical phenomena – sun spots in Jevons's view, the planet Venus in Moore's (Morgan, 1990, pp. 18–33). In 1920, the geographer Ellsworth Huntington proposed autonomous changes in the rate of death as the factor stimulating or depressing business. When mortality rises, it causes sadness and a drop in spending, which leads to a slowdown of the economy; conversely, a decrease in mortality would cause increasing spending and prosperity. These views, today scarcely considered or even known, are typical examples of exogenous business-cycle theories in which the oscillations between prosperity and depression are attributed to phenomena external to the economy itself.

In the late 1920s, exogenous theories of the business cycle found an unexpected source of inspiration in the work of the Russian statistician Evgeny Slutzky, who showed that applying a linear operator to a series of random numbers could generate apparent cycles. Following Slutzky's idea, Ragnar Frisch (1933) was the first in proposing that the fluctuations of the level of activity in modern industrial economies may be due to the effects of erratic, uncorrelated shocks upon an otherwise interrelated system (Adelman, 1960). Frisch proposed the separation of the impulse problem (the discontinuous shocks providing oscillating energy to the system) and the propagation mechanism (the inner workings of the system, leading it towards equilibrium). In the 1950s, Irma Adelman and Frank L. Adelman showed that applying perturbations to the endogenous variables of the propagation mechanism as well as applying random shocks to 'energise' the system enabled the Klein-Goldberger econometric model of the US economy to show oscillations resembling the empirically observed business cycles. In the words of Ira Adelman (1960), she and her husband had not 'proved that business cycles are stochastic in origin', though they had presented evidence creating 'a strong presumption in favour of this hypothesis' which would be 'especially significant in view of the absence (to date) of a completely satisfactory endogenous theory of business cycles'.

The view that business cycles are exogenously determined by random shocks strongly influenced economics in the 1960s and 1970s. Indeed, disputes between Keynesian and monetarist authors during the period of decline of Keynesian economics can be seen as arguments about which parts of the propagation mechanism are either actually working, or the most important for the dynamics of the economy. These disputes were later superseded by rational expectations and assumptions about the inter-temporal substitution of leisure for labour.

We arrive to the views of late 20th century macroeconomists supporting the real-business-cycle (RBC) theory who conceptualise business cycles as the consequence of a self-equilibrating economy responding to random events affecting aggregate supply. They often mention, in the tradition of Schumpeter and Hayek, technological innovations or 'shocks' as causes of economic fluctuations. Other exogenous factors such as demographic changes, political influences or variations in relative prices have also been proposed. This type of 'supply shocks' is often referred to without specifying its nature, though for instance James Hamilton (1988, 1994) proposed changes in oil prices as a key determinant of recessions.

Nowadays, however, economists supporting a theory of business cycles determined by exogenous factors – Austrians, monetarists, RBC theorists – are probably a minority compared to economists who view the fluctuations of the market economy as mainly determined by endogenous factors – Samuelsonians, Keynesians, new-Keynesians, post-Keynesians, institutionalists and socialist economists.[1] At any rate, as Thomas E. Hall put it 20 years ago, it is important to keep in mind the distinction between endogenous and exogenous theories, 'because they imply a very different behavior for an economy'. Those supporting exogenous factors as causes of the business cycle tend 'to view economies as being inherently stable but shocked by outside forces' while endogenous theorists 'generally consider economies as being inherently unstable and subject to self-generating cycles. This distinction in macroeconomics is very old and exists today between the monetarists (primarily exogenous) and Keynesians (primarily endogenous)' (Hall, 1990, p. 10).

Wages are a key variable explaining recessions for many economists. However, authors agreeing with this claim adhere to quite different schools of thought and have proposed diverse, indeed opposite mechanisms to explain why changes in wages would cause economic downturns. Both too high and too low wages have been viewed as causes of recession.

In the view of Arthur Pigou (1927) presented recently, for example, by Lee Ohaniann (2008), a qualified representative of the RBC school, it is too high wages that cause too high costs for business, with the consequent decay in economic activity leading to a downturn. Consequently, in this view, a decrease in wages would increase supply and would also have a stimulating effect on economic activity. A different perspective is offered by those who from a variety of theoretical positions support the so-called profit-squeeze hypothesis (Boddy & Crotty, 1975; Boldrin & Horvath, 1995; Bhaduri & Marglin, 1990) in which high wages lead to recession through the demand side. The pathway would be here from high wages to low profits, and from low profits to falling investment and the lack of effective demand with unsold goods that characterises recessions. Some authors who support the profit-squeeze hypothesis also seem to hold underconsumptionist views, since they deemphasise the role of investment in business cycles by claiming that, with a 'relatively weak response of investment to profitability (...), consumption necessarily assumes the dominant role in effective demand'

(Bhaduri & Marglin, 1990). In a purely underconsumptionist view, too low wages generating too low purchasing power for consumer goods reduce aggregate demand and cause recession, so that an increase in wages during a slump would tend to stimulate recovery.

INVESTMENT LEADS (I): KALECKI AND KEYNES

It is a common view today that Michał Kalecki independently discovered many elements of what later would be called Keynesian theory. Many would even agree that Kalecki's construct is superior to that of Keynes in crucial aspects. At any rate, as we will see, for both Keynes and Kalecki, and for the whole Keynesian school, investment is the key variable explaining macroeconomic dynamics, and leading the cycle.

In the early years of the Great Depression, Kalecki published several articles in *Przegląd Socjalistyczny,* an independent Polish 'Socialist Review'. Signing as Henryk Braun, Kalecki (1990, pp. 37–53) commented on different aspects of the world financial crisis.[2] In one of the articles, he referred to Keynes as 'a representative of British imperialism' and 'possibly the leading bourgeois economist' (Kalecki, 1990, pp. 45–47). In 'Is a capitalist' overcoming of the crisis possible?' (1932), Kalecki argued that during a crisis investment shrinks and

> it is precisely here that one should seek the starting-point of processes that will bring an upswing of the business cycle. Owing to the fact that during a crisis investment activity is at a lower level than that required for simple reproduction (maintenance) of the existing capital equipment, thus equipment is also gradually depleted. Unused and outdated machines are sold for scrap and new ones are not purchased to replace them. Besides, a considerable number of machines–and equipment in general–still kept in factories has not been reconditioned nor maintained properly, and may have become obsolete as well (due to technological progress), and is therefore only partially usable. On the other hand, since in a certain phase of the crisis the output of consumer goods generally starts declining more slowly than the rate of this contraction of capital equipment, there is a real need to employ the existing equipment more fully, which in turn requires investment. There is then a better chance of intensifying investment activity, which is the basic foundation for overcoming the crisis (…). In the final analysis (…) of those components of the mechanism of the capitalist economy which could form a foundation for overcoming the crisis, the contraction of capital equipment caused by the decline of investments (and also by the running down of stocks) should be put in first place (…) Finally, we should mention yet another possibility, namely a certain form of inflation consisting of individual states, or groups of states, starting up major public-investment schemes, such as construction of canals or roads, and financing them with government

> loans floated on the financial market, or with special government credits drawn on their banks of issue. This kind of operation could temporarily increase employment, though on the other hand it would retard automatic, 'natural' adjustment processes which might lead to overcoming the crisis. (Kalecki, 1990, pp. 51–53).

These views reveal that Kalecki had already developed a highly elaborated theory of the business cycle in 1932. Kalecki's theoretical scheme was further developed in a booklet titled *Próba teorii koniunktury,* 'Essay on the business cycle theory', that was published by the ISBCP in 1933, the same year that Kalecki presented his views on the business cycle in a congress of the Econometric Society. In 1935, abbreviated translations of his booklet were published in *Econometrica* and *Revue d'économie politique*. In 1936, Kalecki was planning to write a general exposition of his macroeconomic ideas in a book, until he read Keynes's *General Theory*. It was the book Kalecki was planning to write, and he felt deeply disappointed for having been beaten to it by Keynes (Shackle, 1967, p. 127).

In chapter 22 of *The General Theory,* Keynes considered the business cycle

> as being occasioned by a cyclical change in the marginal efficiency of capital, though complicated, and often aggravated by associated changes in the other significant short-period variables of the economic system. (Keynes, 1936, p. 313)

For Keynes, the marginal efficiency of capital is the *expected* rate of return of capital. In terms of 19th century political economy, it is the expected rate of profit, and for Keynes it depends 'not only on the existing abundance or scarcity of capital-goods and the current cost of production of capital-goods, but also on current expectations as to the future yield of capital-goods' (p. 315).

Considering the view that the crisis, 'the substitution of a downward for an upward movement tendency that often takes place suddenly and violently', may be due to too high levels of the rate of interest, Keynes claimed that 'a more typical, and often the predominant, explanation of the crisis is, not primarily a rise in the rate of interest, but a sudden collapse in the marginal efficiency of capital'. But why the marginal efficiency of capital – the expected profitability – would fall suddenly after it had been steadily rising or at least remaining stable during the boom? What Keynes says is that as long as the boom

> was continuing, much of the new investment showed a not unsatisfactory current yield. The disillusion comes because doubts suddenly arise concerning the reliability of the prospective yield, perhaps because the current yield shows signs of falling off (...) Once doubt begins it spreads rapidly. (p. 317)

Keynes suggests that the fall in expectations about profitability may be perhaps caused by the declining current yield. He does not seem to put much faith in that explanation, however, because during the crisis

> it is not so easy to revive the marginal efficiency of capital, determined, as it is, by the uncontrollable and disobedient psychology of the business world. It is the return of confidence, to speak in ordinary language, which is so insusceptible to control in an economy of individualistic capitalism. This is the aspect of the slump which bankers and business men have been right in emphasising, and which the economists who have put their faith in a "purely monetary" remedy have underestimated. (p. 317)

From the dependence of the trade cycle on the psychology of investors, Keynes concluded that in conditions 'of *laissez-faire* the avoidance of wide fluctuations in employment may, therefore, prove impossible without a far-reaching change in the psychology of investment markets such as there is no reason to expect' (p. 320).

One year after *The General Theory* appeared, Keynes clarified in the *Quarterly Journal of Economics* some of the issues that had been raised by the book. For Keynes, his theory could be summed up 'by saying that, given the psychology of the public, *the level of output and employment as a whole depends on the amount of investment*' [my italics, JATG]. Keynes was explaining his theory this way 'not because this is the only factor on which aggregate output depends, but because it is usual in a complex system to regard as the *causa causans* that factor which is most prone to sudden and wide fluctuation' (Keynes, 1937).

Kalecki reviewed *The General Theory* in the Polish journal *Ekonomista* in 1936, praising it as 'a turning point in the history of economics'. For Kalecki, the book had two main components, one discussing the mechanisms determining a short-period equilibrium once the level of investment was given and the other dealing with the determination of the level of investment. Keynes, Kalecki said, had reasonably succeeded in the former, but had failed in the latter. Kalecki agreed that

> investment is the factor which decides the short-period equilibrium, and hence, at a certain moment, the size of employment and of social income. In fact the volume of investment will decide the amount of the labour force which will be absorbed by the existing production apparatus. (Kalecki, 1990, p. 228)

Kalecki saw serious deficiencies in Keynes's belief that the level of investment would be determined by the equalisation of expected profitability and the rate of interest. This would not lead to equilibrium, but to a continuous process in which higher investment led to a never-ending process of higher expected profitability which in turn raises investment:

> Keynes's concept (...) meets a serious difficulty along this path also. In fact, the growth of investment in no way results in a process leading the system toward equilibrium. Thus it is difficult to consider Keynes's solution of the investment problem to be satisfactory. The reason for this failure lies in an approach which is basically static to a matter which is by its nature dynamic. Keynes takes as given the state of the expectations of returns, and from this he derives a certain definite level of investment, overlooking the effects that investment will in turn have on expectations. It is here that one can glimpse the road one must follow in order to build a realistic theory of investment. Its starting-point should be the solution of the problem of investment decisions, of *ex ante* investment. Let us suppose there to be, at a given moment, a certain state of expectations as to future incomes, a given price level of investment goods, and, finally, a given rate of interest. How great then will be the investment that entrepreneurs intend to undertake in a unit of time? Let us suppose that this problem has been solved (despite the fact that it seems impossible to do this without introducing some special assumptions on the psychology of entrepreneurs or on money market imperfections). A further development of the theory of investment could be as follows. The investment decisions corresponding to the initial state will not generally be equal to the actual volume of investment. Therefore, in the next period the volume of investment will generally be different and the short-period equilibrium will change together with it. Hence we should now deal with a state of expectations that in general will be different from that of the initial period, different prices of investment goods, and a different rate of interest. From these a new level of investment decisions will result–and so on (...) Keynes did not explain precisely what causes changes in investment, but, on the other hand, he has fully examined the close link between these changes and global employment, production, and income movements. (Kalecki, 1990, pp. 230–232)

Keynes likely never knew about this review, which was only translated into English in the 1980s. But in the late 1930s, Kalecki went to England and forged an awkward intellectual relationship with Keynes, eventually gaining his respect.

According to Steindl (1991, p. 597), Kalecki published three versions of his theory of the business cycle, corresponding roughly to his 1933 booklet, his 1954 *Theory of Economic Dynamics* and his late works. Though the relation between profitability and investment is explained in slightly different terms in each version of the theory, it remained substantially unchanged in its main aspects. In his 1933 booklet, Kalecki presented profitability as the variable 'that stimulates the desire to invest. This is entirely consistent with reality, since the incentive to invest is expected profitability, which is estimated on the basis of the profitability of existing plants' (Kalecki, 1990, p. 68). However, investment or consumption of some capitalists creates profit for others and, as a class, capitalists 'gain exactly as much as they invest or consume' so that capitalists 'determine their own profits by the extent of their investment and personal consumption (Kalecki, 1990, p. 79). In *Theory of Economic Dynamics* (1954), Kalecki wrote that capitalists 'can decide to consume and invest more in a given period than in the preceding period, but they cannot decide to earn more. It is, therefore, their investment and consumption decisions which determine profits, and not vice versa' (Kalecki, 1991, p. 240). Profits 'in a given period are the direct outcome of capitalist consumption and investment in that period' (Kalecki, 1991, p. 244). More formally, profits at a time t are a linear function of investment at time t and previous times $t-\lambda$; profits 'will thus be a function both of current investment and of investment in the near past; or roughly speaking, profits follow investment with a time lag' (Kalecki, 1991, p. 247). In turn, 'investment at a given time is determined by the level and rate of change in the level of investment at some earlier time' (Kalecki, 1991, p. 292). The final version of the Kaleckian theory of the business cycle would be the one presented in his publications of the late 1960s. In '*The Marxian equations of reproduction and modern economics*' (1968), Kalecki again presented investment and capitalist consumption as the independent variables that determine the levels of national income and profits (Kalecki, 1991, p. 461). In the introduction to *Selected Essays on the Dynamics of the Capitalist Economy, 1933–70,* published posthumously in 1971, Kalecki explained that the theory of economic demand that he had formulated in the 1930s had remained unchanged; however 'there is a continuous search for new solutions in the theory of investment decisions'. But he included in the book his theory of profits of 1954, restating his view that it is 'investment and consumption decisions which determine profits, and not vice versa' (Kalecki, 1971, p. 79).

According to Asimakopulos (1977, p. 329), Kalecki 'emphasized a double-sided relation between investment and profits'. It is true that in a number of places Kalecki argues that investment depends on profits, or that profitability stimulates investment. He argues for instance that the rate of investment decisions is influenced by the increase in profits per unit of time, so that rising profits 'from the beginning to the end of the period considered renders attractive certain projects which were previously considered unprofitable, and thus permits an extension of the boundaries of investment plans in the course of the period' (Kalecki, 1991, p. 282). For Asimakopulos (1977, p. 339), Kalecki poses current investment as predetermined by past decisions, and through its effects on sales and profits contributing to determine expected profitability. In turn, this expected rate of profit influences, along with other factors, the investment decisions made in this period for implementation in future time periods. Even in this presentation, however, investment is the *causa causans*, while profits are just an intermediate link in the causal chain. Considering the major works in which Kalecki presented his macroeconomic theory, it is difficult to disagree with the way Targetti and Kinda-Hass (1982, p. 254) put it: 'the level of profits at a certain date is entirely and solely determined by past decisions to invest'. Even allowing for subtleties, in Kalecki the determination is from investment to profits, and in the relation there is little room, if any, for reverse causation.

INVESTMENT LEADS (II): THE KEYNESIAN SCHOOL

Since *The General Theory* presented a theory of comparative statics, though containing key elements to develop a dynamic theory (Robinson, 1979), it was left for economists following Keynes's tradition to develop such a theory, that is a Keynesian theory of the business cycle. Leaving aside Kalecki, *The Trade Cycle* by Robin C. O. Matthews, published in England in 1959 and republished in the United States as *The Business Cycle*, it can arguably be considered one of the first systematic examinations of business-cycle theory from an explicitly Keynesian point of view.[3] Judging by the authors cited and the ideas discussed, it seemed that Matthews was open-minded towards recent ideas of Paul Samuelson, J. R. Hicks, Milton Friedman and others that were making powerful inroads in economics in the 1950s. The general perspective of the book, however, is plainly Keynesian. Matthews repeatedly also cited Michal Kalecki's *Theory of Economic Dynamics*, at that time the most recent presentation of Kalecki's macro-dynamic ideas.

Mathews opened his book with a discussion of the variables that may produce an imbalance between aggregate demand and aggregate supply. When briefly mentioning Slutsky's views on recessions being the consequence of the economy responding to random shocks of a diverse character, Matthews commented that statistical data indicate

> that economic fluctuations are not due *solely* to random factors, and it is also clear both from an *a priori* reasoning and from our more detailed knowledge of history that certain forces do operate which are in principle capable of causing fluctuations of a systematic character. (p. 202, italics in the original)

According to Matthews:

> The doctrine that consumption expenditure depends principally on the level of national income is one of the foundations of Keynesian economics. It is because of this doctrine that the other main component of national income, investment, is regarded as the prime mover in fluctuations in national income, the role of consumption being a passive one. (p. 113)

To discuss the basic determinants of investment must therefore be a key aspect of the theory of the business cycle. In this respect, the major consideration

> affecting the inducement to do investment is profitability. Investment will be done if the expected profits represent an adequate return on the sum spent. The physical relation between output and capital is important only in so far as it influences the expected rate of return on investment. (p. 34)

In other words,

> the basic postulate is that the amount of investment done is a function of the expected rate of return. If conditions are such as to promise a high rate of return, much investment will be done, and conversely. There will be a certain critical level of expected returns at which zero net investment is done. (p. 36)

Matthews meticulously considered the relation of investment with competition, technical progress, *animal spirits,* finance, inventories and home construction. His conclusion was that

> the chief reason for the waves of high and low investment that are the essence of the cycle is the existence of a cumulative effect by which if investment in any period is high relative to its long-run trend value, it encourages investment in the next period to stay high or to rise further, up to a point, while if investment is low it likewise discourages investment in the next period. (p. 82)

This means that with appropriate investment the economy would grow without interruption, and slumps would be avoided:

> If entrepreneurs can only screw themselves up to do enough investment, it will eventually justify itself, since the income generated will absorb the excess capacity. (p. 178)

A comparison of the theories of the business cycle in Matthews's *Trade Cycle* and in Hyman Minsky's *Stabilizing an Unstable Economy,* written and published three decades later, reveals many common views but also some major differences in emphasis and even in conception. Both Matthews and Minsky were self-professed Keynesians, but Minsky's view of economic fluctuations emphasised the financial factors creating economic disturbances and leading to financial crises and recessions, while Matthews was quite adamant that business cycles are phenomena mostly related to the real economy, in which their causes need to be examined. For Matthews, it was an outdated view

> that the causes of fluctuations lay wholly or largely in the sphere of money and finance. The trend of opinion has now swung in the opposite direction. Most modern theoretical treatments of the cycle are based on an analysis of real forces, and it is implicitly

> assumed that secondary importance, at most, attaches to any effects that may be brought about by changes in the cost and availability of finance. (Matthews, 1959, p. 128)

After a detailed discussion of factors leading to speculation and bubbles in different markets, Matthews had concluded that *financial* crises generally occur after the downturn in the real economy has already started, so that the financial crisis may aggravate the downturn but does not cause it. The contrast is patent with the main thrust of *Stabilizing an Unstable Economy*, where Minsky emphasises the role of financial factors and criticises the neoclassical synthesis for its inability to recognise that 'the instability so evident in our economy is due to the behavior of financial markets, asset prices, and profit flows' (Minsky, 2008, p. 156).

According to Minsky, a basic aspect of modern capitalism is that past financing of investment leaves a legacy of payment commitments, and for these commitments to be fulfilled the income of indebted investors must be sufficient. The price system must therefore

> generate cash flows (...) which simultaneously free resources for investment, lead to high enough prices for capital assets so that investment is induced, and validate business debts. For a capitalist system to function well, *prices must carry profits*. (p. 158, Minsky's italics)

The determinants of profits is thus a key issue, and Minsky (p. 184, italics in the original) concludes that

> Investment and government spending call the tune for our economy because they are not determined by how the economy is now working. They are determined either from outside by policy (government spending) or by today's views about the future (private investment).

Causality, then, 'runs from investment and government spending to taxes and profits' and in recessions

> Big Government, with all its inefficiencies, stabilizes income and profits. It decreases the downside risks inherent in a capital-intensive economy that has a multitude of heavily indebted firms. (p. 186)

Investment is therefore the basic determinant of the dynamic status of the economy. To look for economic factors causing investment to rise or fall is beside the point, since the present level of investment determines the present level of income and the future level of profits and investment. In the colourful words of Minsky, Government spending and investment 'call the tune'. Only the psychological sphere of expectations remains as the source of investment fluctuations. Given adequate investment, profits will rise and the economy will grow.

It is investment, then, which in the view of Kalecki, Keynes and the Keynesians 'calls the tune' by determining profits and thus leading the business cycle.[4]

PROFITS LEAD: MARX AND MITCHELL

Karl Marx and Wesley Mitchell are infrequently cited in modern discussions on macroeconomic issues, perhaps because compared with predominant neoclassical or Keynesian views they provide quite a different perspective on the ways our economy works. Marx and Mitchell share with the Keynesian school the view that investment, or capital accumulation in Marx's terminology, is a key variable in economic dynamics.[5] However, neither Marx nor Mitchell attributes to investment the major causal role in business cycles, because they see investment as depending itself on profitability.

Marx's analysis of the business cycle has been considered an unwritten chapter and 'no coherent picture of it has emerged, or is likely to emerge, that would command the approval of all Marxologists' (Schumpeter, 1954, p. 747). Though this is still probably true, some elements of that analysis are not controversial. What Marx called the industrial cycle – in which periods of capital accumulation alternate with crises – is mostly discussed in manuscripts that were posthumously published. In one of them, Marx wrote for instance that the rate at which the capital is valorised, that is the rate of profit, 'is the spur to capitalist production (in the same way as the valorization of capital is its sole purpose)', so that a decline in this rate 'slows down the formation of new, independent capitals and thus appears as a threat to the development of the capitalist production process; it promotes overproduction, speculation and crises' (Marx, 1981, pp. 348–349). In his notebooks published as *Theories of Surplus Value*, Marx asserted that accumulation is determined 'by the ratio of surplus-value to the total capital outlay, that is, by the rate of profit, and even more by the total amount of profit' (Marx, 1968, p. 542).

Explicit insights on business-cycle theory are also given in the only volume of *Capital* that Marx published himself in 1867 (Marx, 1977). There, in the chapter on 'the general law of capitalist accumulation', Marx stated that the characteristic evolution of modern economies is typically a decennial cycle in which periods of average activity are followed by production at high pressure, crisis and finally stagnation. Periods of capital accumulation (i.e. economic expansions with high levels of investment) are characterised by an increased demand for labour power. During the cycle, there is a constant formation, absorption and reformation of a mass of unemployed workers – the 'industrial reserve army'. This mass of unemployed workers

> during the periods of stagnation and average prosperity, weighs down the active army of workers; during the periods of over-production and feverish activity, it puts a curb on their pretensions. (p. 792)

Periods of capital accumulation are the most favourable for workers in terms of income, because a larger part of the surplus product of industry, which is

> increasing and is continually transformed into additional capital, comes back to them in the shape of means of payment, so that they can extend the circle of their enjoyments, make additions to their consumption fund of clothes, furniture, etc., and lay by a small reserve fund of money. (p. 796)

The tightness of the labour market during periods of capital accumulation (i.e. upturns) will likely produce a rise in wages, and then two things can happen:

> Either the price of labour keeps on rising, because its rise does not interfere with the progress of accumulation (...) Or, the other alternative, accumulation slackens as a result of the rise in the price of labour, because the stimulus of gain is blunted. The rate of accumulation lessens; but this means that the primary cause of that lessening itself vanishes (...) The mechanism of the process of capitalist production removes the very obstacles that it temporarily creates. (p. 770)

In this passage, investment is portrayed as a function of profitability when reference is made to accumulation slackening 'because the stimulus of gain is blunted'. On the other hand, a profit-squeeze mechanism is also suggested, since Marx admits that rising wages might cut profits and in this way induce a fall in the rate of investment that triggers a downturn. Though this is offered as a possibility, Marx seems to reject the implied causal pathway as an important one, because he asserts later in the same paragraph that

> To put it mathematically: the rate of accumulation is the independent, not the dependent, variable; the rate of wages, the dependent, not the independent, variable.

Profit is for Marx the monetary translation of unpaid labour supplied by the working class to the owners of capital. When profit

> accumulated by the capitalist class increases so rapidly that its transformation into capital requires an extraordinary addition of paid labour, then wages rise, and, all other circumstances remaining equal

profit diminishes. But as soon as this diminution reaches the point at which profit that nourishes capital

> is no longer supplied in normal quantity, a reaction sets in: a smaller part of revenue is capitalized, accumulation slows down, and the rising movement of wages comes up against an obstacle. The rise of wages therefore is confined within limits that not only leave intact the foundations of the capitalist system, but also secure its reproduction on an increasing scale. (p. 771)

Marx emphasised the idea that accumulation depends on profitability. He did so, for instance, by quoting the opinion of the English trade unionist Thomas Dunning, who had written that capital

> eschews no profit, or very small profit, just as Nature was formerly said to abhor a vacuum. With adequate profit, capital is very bold. A certain 10% will ensure its employment anywhere; 20% certain will produce eagerness; 50%, positive audacity; 100% will make it ready to trample on all human laws; 300%, and there is not a crime at which it will scruple, nor a risk it will not run, even to the chance of its owner being hanged. If turbulence and strife will bring a profit, it will freely encourage both. (p. 926)

Wesley Mitchell is quite a different case. If Marx rejected what he called bourgeois political economy from his first intellectual contributions and was paid in kind with a plain rejection from academic economists, Mitchell was throughout his long intellectual life a highly respected member of the economic profession. He taught economics in prestigious universities, served for decades as a leading member of the National Bureau of Economic Research and was president of the American Economic Association. However, in the 1950s, his views on the business cycle were considered atheoretical, and soon after his death his work disappeared into oblivion.[6]

Despite the view that Wesley Mitchell's contributions lacked theory, the reality is that Mitchell had presented quite elaborate views on the causes of expansions and recessions (i.e. a theory of the business cycle) as early as 1913 in his voluminous *Business Cycles* (Mitchell, 1913). Part III of *Business Cycles* was republished in 1941 as *Business Cycles and Their Causes*. In his posthumous and unfinished *What Happens during Business Cycles,* Mitchell briefly restated his views on the causes of the business cycle, which had changed very little since his 1913 book. He still viewed the cycle as a continuous endogenous development, with recession processes leading to expansion, and expansion processes leading into recession. Investment had a key role in the transitions from expansion to recession and vice versa. Though capital goods, Mitchell noted, 'form less than 18% of the gross national product, their output is subject to such violent alternations (...) that this minor segment of the economy contributes 44% of the total cyclical fluctuation in output, and nearly half of the cyclical declines' (Mitchell, 1951, p. 153).

For Mitchell, profits had a major role in economics in general and in business cycles in particular. This was probably the result of both his empirical studies of business and economic life and his acquaintance with Thorstein Veblen, one of the proponents, according to Mitchell himself, of the theory that profit is the key variable explaining economic fluctuations (Mitchell, 1927, pp. 42–44). The Veblenian influence seems clear in Mitchell's view of what he called 'the money economy', the organisation of the modern industrial society in which the bulk of economic activity takes place through the activities of institutions – enterprises – that perform with the purpose of producing money profit. Mitchell said that where the money economy predominates, that is where economic activity takes the form of making and spending money incomes,

> natural resources are not developed, mechanical equipment is not provided, industrial skill is not exercised, unless conditions are such as to promise a money profit to those who direct production. (Mitchell, 1913, pp. 21–22)

In one of his late contributions, Mitchell insisted in the centrality of money profits for understanding business cycles:

> Since the quest for money profits by business enterprises is the controlling factor among the economic activities of men who live in a money economy, the whole discussion [of expansions and recessions] must center about the prospects of profits. On occasion, indeed, this central interest is eclipsed by a yet more vital issue–the avoidance of bankruptcy. But to make profits and to avoid bankruptcy are merely two sides of a single issue–one side concerns the well being of business enterprises under ordinary circumstances, the other side concerns the life or death of the same enterprises under circumstances of acute strain. (Mitchell, 1941, Preface)

In Mitchell's endogenous view of the business cycle during the phase of prosperity, the very conditions 'which make business profitable gradually evolve conditions which threaten a reduction in profits' (Mitchell, 1913, p. 502). Though economic downturns often start with a financial crisis in which banks, insurance companies and other financial firms go bankrupt, these financial phenomena are preceded by processes that encroach profits in the real economy, at least in a score of major enterprises or industrial sectors. The various stresses rising costs and putting caps on revenue, and thus limiting profits

> become more severe the longer prosperity lasts and the more intense it becomes, and since a set-back suffered by any industry necessarily aggravates the stress among others by reducing the market for their products, *a reduction in the rate of profits* (my italics,

JATG) must infallibly occur (...) if an average rate of profits could be computed for a whole country, it would not be surprising to find it reaching its climax just before the crisis breaks out. But this result would not mean that there had been no serious encroachment upon profits. On the contrary, it would mean that the critical point is reached and a crisis is precipitated as soon as a decline of present or prospective profits has occurred in a few leading branches of business and *before that decline has become general.* (Mitchell's italics, p. 503)

But the key variable in downturns is investment, led itself by profitability. Rejecting underconsumptionist explanations that view insufficient demand for consumption goods as the trigger of downturns, Mitchell explained that in the late phases of prosperity

the impossibility of defending profits against the encroachments of costs is experienced earlier by enterprises which handle raw materials and producers goods (...) The technical journals usually report that the factories and wholesale houses are restricting their orders some weeks, if not months, before they report that retail sales are flagging. (p. 502)

The decline in profitability in some parts of the economy creates financial strain and reduced sales in other industries, all of which in turn would reduce the incentive to maintain or increase inventories. Investment in wages, raw materials and new machines or production facilities also falls, which eventually reduces the level of business activity, since business failures and reduction of business activity cut both wages and investment, the two basic sources of demand. This vicious cycle would then operate for months or years, sending the economy into a minor or major recession or depression. Eventually, the 'very conditions of business depression beget a revival of activity', favourable conditions for investment are newly created and the economy starts expanding again (Mitchell, 1913, p. 452). This is so because immediately after a depression

within large groups of enterprises or industries, the rate [of profit] rises promptly with the tide of prosperity (...) Indeed it is certain in particular cases and probable on the average that profits begin to pick up before the period of depression is over. (p. 469)

This will increase the volume of investment since in such a situation of business revival

the prospect of good profits leads not only to greater activity among the old enterprises, but also to extensions of their size and to the creation of new enterprises. This expansion of business undertakings is the more important because for a time at least it impacts new energy to the very causes which produced it." (p. 471)

For both Marx and Mitchell, rising (or falling) profitability is the key determinant other hand, via investment, of prosperity (or depression).

EMPIRICAL EVIDENCE

Any cursory examination of economic statistics shows that the main element of aggregate demand fluctuating upward during expansions and downward during recessions is investment, while consumption varies little between expansion and recession (Mitchell, 1951; Sherman & Kolk, 1997). Indeed, as Richard Goodwin once explained, the early efforts in econometric research on the business cycle were the pair of monographs written by Tinbergen in 1939 for the League of Nations. On the basis of general agreement among economists, Tinbergen selected investment as the crucial cycle variable to be explained (Goodwin, 1964).

For Keynes, Kalecki, Mathews, Minsky, Marx and Mitchell, investment and profits are the key variables explaining the dynamics of the capitalist economy. However, in terms of causation from the Keynesian–Kaleckian perspective, investment is the key variable that determines profits, while for Marx and Mitchell, the direction of causality is the opposite, with profits determining investment. Does the empirical evidence support either of these views more than the other?

Rates of Growth of Income Flows

The mean flows of income components during phases of the business cycle, and in the vicinity of its turning points (Table 1), give us insight on how major economic variables change during macroeconomic fluctuations and illustrate the role that these variables may have in the generation of the cycle. NIPA data corresponding to 251 quarters of the US economy show, for instance, that capital income, that is profits – either before or after taxes – is much more volatile than labour income, as represented by wages and salaries – either with or without supplements. During expansions, profits increased on average 1.9% per quarter, while wages and salaries rose 1.1% and 1.0%, respectively, with and without supplements; fixed investment grew 1.3% per quarter. In recessions, all these flows reverse into negative growth, with profits falling 3.9% per quarter before taxes and 3.1% after taxes, private investment falling 1.3% and wages and salaries without supplements falling 0.4% per quarter.[7]

More interesting, however, is to examine the evolution of income flows in the vicinity of turning points. Corporate profits stop growing, stagnate and then start falling a few quarters before the recession. Profits before taxes on average grow 1.7% in the sixth quarter before the start of the recession, but

Table 1. Mean Quarterly Rates of Growth (%) of Profits, Investment, and Wages and Salaries during the Recessions and Expansions of 251 Quarters of the US Economy (1947:I to 2009:III).

Sample (Quarters)	Profits		Private Fixed Investment	Wages and Salaries		Sample Size (Quarters)
	Before taxes	After taxes			(with supplements)	
All	0.7	0.9	0.7	0.7	0.8	251
Expansion	1.9	1.9	1.3	1.0	1.1	201
Recession	−3.9	−3.1	−1.3	−0.4	−0.2	50
Recession −8	0.4	3.0	0.6	0.7	0.8	9
Recession −7	4.3	4.4	2.2	1.8	1.8	10
Recession −6	1.7	2.5	0.7	1.1	1.1	10
Recession −5	−0.4	−0.1	0.2	1.0	1.0	10
Recession −4	−0.8	−0.9	0.8	1.0	1.0	10
Recession −3	−0.4	−0.4	0.6	1.1	1.1	11
Recession −2	0.2	0.2	0.9	1.0	1.1	11
Recession −1	−1.9	−0.8	−0.2	0.7	0.8	11
Trough	−2.5	−0.7	−0.8	−0.8	−0.6	11
Trough +1	9.3	10.9	3.7	0.7	0.8	11
Trough +2	7.1	6.3	2.5	1.3	1.4	10
Trough +3	4.9	4.7	2.2	1.2	1.2	10

Notes: Recessions defined as including both the peak quarter and the trough quarter in the NBER chronology, and all quarters between a peak and the next trough. 'Recession −8' means the sample including the expansion quarters preceding recession by 8 quarters; 'Trough +2' means the sample including the second quarters after the end of the recession, etc. All rates of growth (natural log differences) computed with variables adjusted for inflation by transforming nominal figures from NIPA data (www.bea.gov/national) into 2005 dollars.

then drop 0.4% in the next quarter and basically continue decreasing slowly until they plummet in the quarter immediately previous to the recession and during the recession itself (in which, on average, profits before taxes drop almost 4% per quarter). It seems as if the drop of profits about a year before the recession erupts sends a signal for managers and entrepreneurs to cut investment, because the drop in the rate of growth of profits before taxes (from 4.3% to 1.7% and then −0.4%) from the seventh to the fifth quarter before the recession is coupled with a substantial decrease in the rate of growth of investment (from 2.2% to 0.7% and then 0.2% in the same quarters). It may perhaps be that this decrease in investment avoids further losses to some extent, because in the second quarter before the recession, profits stop falling and grow again at 0.2%. However, this is just a temporary step on the brake, because profits before taxes drop almost 2% the quarter immediately previous to open recession and almost 4% per quarter in each of the quarters of the recession.

On average, private fixed investment continues growing in this pre-recession period, however, and only one quarter before the peak investment starts falling. Wages and salaries continue growing even during the quarter immediately preceding the recession, and they only start declining during the recession itself.

Once the recession ends, the recovery of profits is quick, with a quarterly increase between 9% and 11% – considering profits before or after taxes – in the quarter immediately following the recession. In that same quarter, however, wages grow at a very small rate, quite below 1%, while investment grows quite intensely at a rate of 3.7%.

These figures do not seem to support the idea that causality runs from investment to profits, since on average profits reverse their growth and start falling several quarters before investment does. This is also applicable to recent recessions. For instance, preceding the recession that started in the fall of 2007, investment peaked in a kind of plateau that lasted from the second quarter of 2006 until the third quarter of 2007. However, profits had peaked in the first quarter of 2006 and then had steadily dropped in the rest of the year (Fig. 1). In the long expansion of the 1990s, profits started

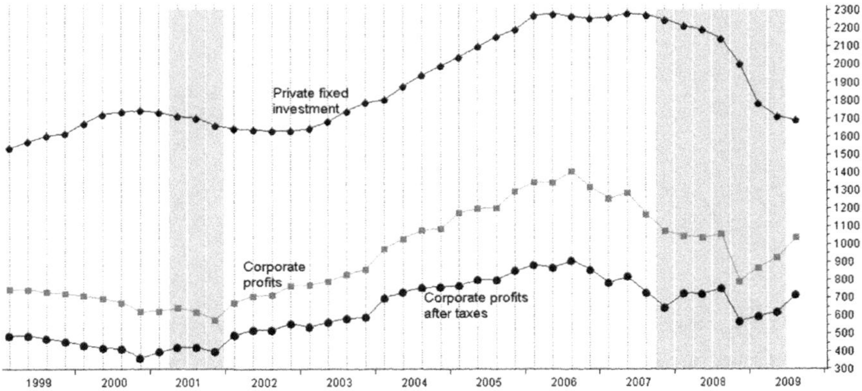

Fig. 1. Corporate Profits and Investment, Quarterly Data Since 1999 to the Great Recession. Dark Areas Are Recessions According to the NBER Chronology. Data from the Bureau of Economic Analysis (NIPA Tables 5.1 and 5.3.5), in Billions of Dollars, Seasonally Adjusted at an Annual Rate (SAAR).

declining long before investment did (profits peaked in 1997:III while investment did in 2000:IV), and the same seems to have occurred in the expansions of the early 1970s and late 1970s (Fig. 2). In all these cases, profits peak several quarters before the recession, while investment peaks almost immediately before the recession. Then the investment trough after the recession is lagged with respect to the profit trough (Fig. 2). These facts do not seem compatible with causation going from investment to profits. If the recovery of profits after a slump were dependent on a recovery of investment, some lag would exist for investment spending to be translated into increased profits for firms selling either (a) capital goods to other firms or (b) consumer goods to wage workers hired as the result of new investment (if, as it seems to be, rising private fixed investment correlates with an increase in hiring). But the graphs do not suggest that lag and as we will see the regression analysis do not provide any evidence of such a lag in the data. The observable lag is from changes in profitability to changes in investment.

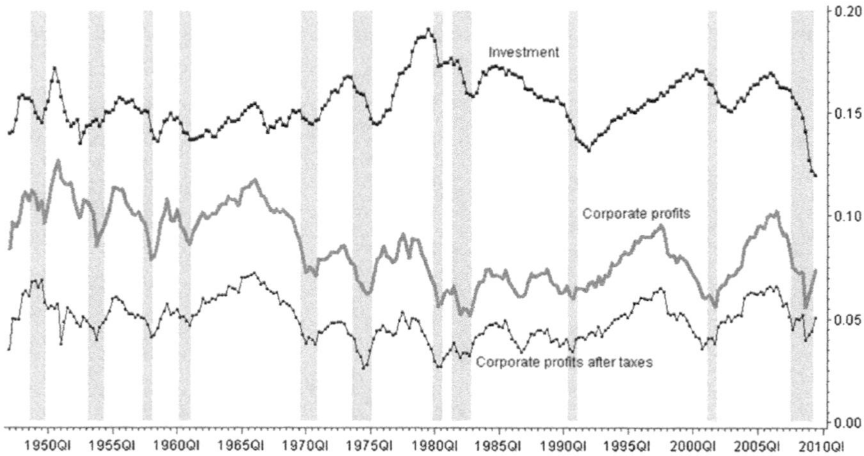

Fig. 2. Corporate Profits (before and after Taxes) and Fixed Investment as a Share of Gross Domestic Income, Quarterly Data Since 1947 to the Great Recession. Computed with NIPA Data (U.S. Bureau of Economic Analysis, www.bea.gov) and the Business Cycle Chronology of the National Bureau of Economic Research, Assuming a Recession Lasts from the Peak Quarter to the Trough Quarter, and Both Quarters Are Included in It.

Regression Analysis

Another way to explore this issue is to test how changes in investment predict changes in profits, and vice versa. We can explore these relations by regressing the rates of growth of a variable on present and lagged values of the rate of growth of the other variable.[8]

Regression models show that the change in profits, particularly profits before taxes (Table 2, panel I), predicts to a significant extent the change in investment, while the change in investment does not predict the change in profits (Table 2, panel III). Considering the model that minimises the Akaike information criterion (AIC), profits *before taxes* during the present quarter and the five former quarters have a very significant and positive effect on investment, with 44% of the variation in investment explained by the variation in profits (Table 2, panel I, model F).[9] Profits *after taxes* during the present quarter and previous quarters also have a noticeable effect on investment, but the effect is much weaker and, compared with profits before taxes, the proportion of change in investment explained is considerably reduced, from 44% to 32% (for model G, the one minimising AIC in panel II, Table 2).

On the contrary, lag regressions do not provide evidence of past investment predicting present profits (Table 2, panel III). The effect at lag zero is very strong and positive, but lagged effects of investment on profits are not significant and even have 'the wrong sign'. If past investments were determining present profits, we would expect significant and positive lag effects of investment on profits. However, the observed lag effects are negative, and not statistically significant.

Granger Causality Tests

Results of Granger causality tests are quite sensitive to the procedure used to transform the series into stationary ones and to the number of lags included in the test regression (Hamilton, 1994). When many lags are included bidirectional, Granger causality is often found, with past profits helping to predict investment and past investment helping to predict profits. However, the hypothesis that profits before or after taxes do not help to predict investment (Table 3, panels A and C) is rejected at very high levels of significance ($p<0.01$, with $p<0.001$ in many cases) in all lag specifications, while the hypothesis that investment does not help to predict profits often fails to be rejected at the 5% significance level. p-Values

Table 2. Results of Regressions to Model Private Fixed Investment as a Function of Corporate Profits or Vice Versa.

Lag	A	B	C	D	E	F	G
Panel I – Private fixed investment regressed on corporate profits							
0	0.77***	0.67***	0.67***	0.66***	0.68***	**0.70*****	0.70***
1		0.65***	0.60***	0.61***	0.59***	**0.61*****	0.62***
2			0.32***	0.29***	0.29***	**0.26****	0.27**
3				0.18*	0.15	**0.16**†	0.15†
4					0.15	**0.10**	0.10
5						**0.26****	0.25**
6							0.06
R^2	0.22	0.37	0.40	0.42	0.42	0.44	0.44
Panel II – Private fixed investment regressed on profits after taxes							
0	0.43***	0.35***	0.35***	0.34***	0.36***	0.37***	**0.37*****
1		0.49***	0.45***	0.46***	0.44***	0.47***	**0.48*****
2			0.24**	0.22**	0.23**	0.21*	**0.23****
3				0.14	0.12	0.13	**0.11**
4					0.12	0.10	**0.12**
5						0.18*	**0.15***
6							**0.20****
R^2	0.10	0.23	0.26	0.27	0.28	0.29	0.32
Panel III – Corporate profits regressed on private fixed investment							
0	0.28***	0.35***	0.36***	**0.35*****	0.35***	0.35***	0.35***
1		–0.13**	–0.09*	**–0.08**	–0.08	–0.08	–0.08
2			–0.10**	**–0.04**	–0.03	–0.03	–0.03
3				**–0.13****	–0.11*	–0.11	–0.11
4					–0.05	–0.04	–0.04
5						–0.02	–0.02
6							–0.01
R^2	0.22	0.25	0.27	0.31	0.31	0.31	0.31

Notes: The explanatory variable is included in the regression at lag 0 only in specification A, at lags 0 and 1 in specification B, and so on and so forth; until specification G in which the covariate is included in the regression at lags 0, 1, 2, ... until 6. Variables are quarterly rates of change computed from inflation-adjusted SAAR data for private fixed investment and corporate profits before and after taxes. Parameter estimates highlighted in boldface correspond to the specification that minimises AIC in the panel. Specifications including up to 20 lags were tested (in specifications with more than six lags, no significant coefficients were found beyond a few that are to be expected by chance).

$^{\dagger}p<0.1$; $^{*}p<0.05$; $^{**}p<0.01$; $^{***}p<0.001$.

Table 3. Granger Causality Tests for Profits and Private Fixed Investment.

Null Hypothesis	Lags	Rate of Change	First Differences
A Profits before taxes do not help to predict investment	15	<0.001	<0.001
	12	<0.001	<0.001
	10	<0.001	<0.001
	7	0.001	<0.001
	5	<0.001	<0.001
	4	0.001	<0.001
	3	<0.001	<0.001
	2	<0.001	<0.001
	1	<0.001	<0.001
B Investment does not help to predict profits before taxes	15	0.011	0.012
	12	0.125	0.058
	10	0.011	0.044
	7	0.014	0.009
	5	0.047	0.004
	4	0.017	0.004
	3	0.001	0.005
	2	0.169	0.170
	1	0.310	0.678
C Profits after taxes do not help to predict investment	15	<0.001	<0.001
	12	0.001	<0.001
	10	<0.001	<0.001
	7	0.001	<0.001
	5	0.001	<0.001
	4	0.005	<0.001
	3	0.002	<0.001
	2	0.001	<0.001
	1	<0.001	<0.001
D Investment does not help to predict profits after taxes	15	0.005	0.019
	12	0.150	0.049
	10	0.064	0.018
	7	0.079	0.014
	5	0.097	0.041
	4	0.082	0.059
	3	0.008	0.027
	2	0.068	0.061
	1	0.851	0.811

Notes: Each panel indicates the null hypothesis, the number of lags included in the test and the p-value (testing series either in rate of change or in first differences). The series of profits and fixed private investment figures were SAAR and inflation-adjusted quarterly data from 1947:II to 2009:III.

obtained with the asymptotic test of Granger causality (not shown) are quite similar. Overall, causality from profits to investment is strongly supported by Granger tests at all lags, while that is not the case for causality from investment to profits.

DISCUSSION AND CONCLUSIONS

From the point of view of statistical theory, a hypothesis test starts with null and alternative hypotheses of scientific interest, and looks for whether there is evidence to reject the default null hypothesis in favour of the alternative. Statistically significant effects that are actually spurious can be chance findings, since in 5% of the tests we will find estimates that are statistically significant at the 95% level of confidence in spite that the null hypothesis is correct (i.e. the effect is zero). Spurious statistical significance can also be found if methodological issues make the evidence against the null stronger than it actually. That can be the case when multiple hypotheses are tested at the same time. A *p*-value that is correct when computed for an individual test is 'devalued' when it is computed for each one of multiple tests; formally, that is the case of *p*-values in Table 2. *p*-Values are suspiciously small specially when the researcher computes multiple tests with a collection of different variables and then chooses those relationships that have shown statistical significance. Terms such as pre-testing bias or, more informally, data snooping, fishing expedition or data mining have been used for that practice. The reader shall judge to what extent the *p*-values in Table 2 are subjected to that kind of bias. At any rate, the regressions there can be considered as descriptive – nothing more and nothing less. Our claim is that the results of those regressions together with (a) the rates of growth of profits and investment (Table 2) during different phases of the business cycle, (b) the results of Granger causality tests (Table 3) and (c) theoretical reasons strongly support a causal effect of profits on investment. We found, however, little evidence in favour of causality in the other direction.

While Marx and Mitchell viewed profitability as the key variable determining the dynamic condition of the economy, with the level of profits primarily determined internally by the workings of the system, authors following the Keynesian–Kaleckian tradition view investment as depending on profits, but since profits depend themselves on previous investment, it is investment that ultimately rules the course of the economy. As Matthews noted, with entrepreneurs screwing themselves up to do enough investment, profits would eventually rise. This is as if entrepreneurs and owners of money in general were able to pull themselves up by their bootstraps. In a sense, supply would create its own demand, and Say's law, tossed out the door, comes back in through the window. Furthermore, in the Keynesian–Kaleckian perspective, a fluctuating economy occurs in which entrepreneurs' changing rates of investment set the future path for the economy. Investment and government spending are in this perspective the only two variables that set the future path of the economy. Were it not for human psychology determining investment, and ruling political forces determining Government spending, there would be no recessions. Then, should not we consider the Keynesian–Kaleckian perspective as an exogenous theory of the cycle?

On the other hand, in the Marx and Mitchell perspective, profits determine investment, and investment determines expansions and recessions, and we have a system in which profits are the major variable that determines its dynamics. To state that we have a profit-led economy (Barbosa-Filho & Taylor, 2006; Mohun & Veneziani, 2008; Rada & Taylor, 2006) probably amounts to something similar. The existence of significant hoards of money during economic crisis has been recently highlighted (Dash & Schwartz, 2011; Wilson, 2009) and it seems then that the conversion of these hoards of money into revenue-producing (and job-producing) investment is a key element for getting the economy out of a slump. But for this to occur, the rise in profitability is a key issue. The destruction of existing capital (by bankruptcies and liquidations) that reduces competition and allows for purchases of capital goods at liquidation prices, coupled with the fall in wages, contribute to create renewed opportunities for the investment of liquid money required for recovery. But those owning banks or big enterprises do not want to hear about destruction of financial capital as a key element to overcoming the crisis, and those earning their income as wages prefer to believe the story that rising wages will create more demand and will lead the economy towards recovery.

These are, however, theoretical and political implications that can be put aside. What for scientific purposes must not be put aside is the statistical evidence that raises serious doubts about the hypothesis that investment is 'the key variable', that investment, as Minsky puts it, calls the tune.

The results of the present investigation should not be particularly surprising, since the role of profitability as the major determinant of investment has been found previously by others (Bhaskar & Glyn, 1995; Blanchard, Rhee, & Summers, 1993). One of the key findings of Tinbergen's early econometric studies on the business cycle was precisely that profits are the major determinant of investment (Tinbergen, 1939). But in an episode that highlights the always present anti-empirical bent of economics,

Tinbergen's pioneering investigations received heavy criticism from none other than Lord Keynes and the nascent figure of the anti-Keynesian field, Milton Friedman (Morgan, 1990). Even a major econometrician and theorist of the business cycle, Richard Goodwin, attempted to downplay the importance of Tinbergen's conclusion asserting that 'if we reverse the direction of causality and say that investment determines profits through the multiplier and income, we rob one of Tinbergen's chief results of much of its significance'. Goodwin argued that 'in the cycle most things go up and down together, and hence the danger of spurious correlation is very great' (Goodwin, 1964, p. 433). While this indeed is true, it is possible to extend the analysis further. Though profits, investment, wages, output and other variables swing up and down 'together in expansions and recessions, observed lags and statistical analysis show that the two potential directions of causation between investment and profits are not equally likely. The hypothesis that profits determine investment is much more consistent with the empirical evidence. If investment 'calls the tune', then that tune is an echo of a previous melody.

NOTES

1. For a modern survey of theories of the business cycle, see Knoop (2004). The encyclopaedia edited by Glasner and Cooley (1997) is a wealth of information.
2. Kalecki had no academic degree, since he had never finished his engineering studies. He had been earning his living as an economic journalist and working as an analyst for the Polish Institute for the Study of Business Cycles and Prices (ISBCP). This probably explains why he published in the Socialist Review under a pseudonym.
3. *Business Cycles and National Income* (Hansen, 1964), first published in 1959, could also lay claim to that distinction.
4. That major differences exist among authors pertaining to this tradition is exemplified by a comment of the editor of Kalecki's *Collected Works*, Jerzy Osiatynski, who says that in Kalecki's *Theory of Economic Dynamics* 'the long-run development of the capitalist economy, and even its passage to the phase of the business upswing, *was only possible under the influence of exogenous factors*' (my emphasis, JATG; Kalecki, 1991, p. 551). This sharply contrasts with assertions by Minsky, who claiming to follow Kalecki's views on economic dynamics argued, however, that cycles and crises 'are not the result of shocks to the system or of policy errors, they are endogenous' (Minsky, 1991).
5. For Marx, capital accumulation takes place when money profits are spent in purchasing capital goods (constant capital in Marxian parlance) or paying wages (variable capital) to expand production. In that respect, the Marxian concept of capital accumulation is wider than the concept of 'investment' in national accounts and mainstream economics, which usually refers to purchase of capital goods.

6. It was Tjalling Koopman who first presented that criticism in his review (Koopmans, 1947) of *Measuring Business Cycles* (Burns & Mitchell, 1946). The accusation was echoed by Robert A. Gordon (1961). From Keynesian quarters, Alvin Hansen (1949) asserted that 'the driving forces back of the cycle movement, Mitchell was never able to disclose'. The view of a Marxist economist was also that Mitchell described the 'ups and downs [of the economy] using little theory' (Devine, 1986).

7. Kalecki pointed out that salaries in national income accounts include both salaries of government officials – which are paid from tax revenues – and salaries of top-level executives – which are rather akin to profits (Kalecki, 1991, p. 237, fn. 17). For the sake of simplicity, it is assumed here that NIPA 'wages and salaries' correspond to labour income. Indeed the referred salaries probably tend to increase in nominal terms during expansions more than wages, while in recessions they probably tend to decrease less than wages.

8. Both investment and profits have trends, and the augment Dickey-Fuller (ADF) test indicates that they have unit roots. However, they are stationary when transformed into rates of growth. Tests of cointegration do not indicate cointegration of investment and profits in levels.

9. The model is $\dot{I}_t = \alpha + \sum_{k=0}^{5}\beta_k \cdot \dot{p}_{t-k}\varepsilon_t$, where the superimposed dot indicates the rate of growth of the variable, I is investment, p is profits before taxes, ε is the error term and the sub-index t refers to time in quarters.

ACKNOWLEDGEMENTS

This text has benefitted from comments and observations by Elena Gouskova, Paul Mattick, Rolando Astarita, Anwar Shaikh, Duncan Foley, Ed Ionides, Wallace Genser, Paul Zarembka and anonymous reviewers. The usual disclaimers apply. The author can be contacted at jatapia@umich.edu.

REFERENCES

Adelman, I. (1960). Business cycles – Endogenous or stochastic? *Economic Journal*, *70*, 783–796.

Asimakopulos, A. (1977). Profits and investment: A Kaleckian approach. In G. C. Harcourt (Ed.), *The microeconomic foundations of macroeconomics: Proceedings of a conference held by the IEA* (pp. 328–372). Macmillan, London.

Barbosa-Filho, N. H., & Taylor, L. (2006). Distributive and demand cycles in the US economy: A structuralist Goodwin model. *Metroeconomica*, *57*(3), 389.

Besomi, D. (2005). *Clément Juglar and the transition from crises theory to business cycle theories.* Paper prepared for a conference on the occasion of the centenary of the death of Clément Juglar, Paris, 2 December 2005. Retrieved from www.unil.ch/webdav/site/cwp/users/neyguesi/public/D._Besomi_

Bhaduri, A., & Marglin, S. (1990). Unemployment and the real wages: The economic basis for contesting political ideologies. *Cambridge Journal of Economics*, *14*, 375–393.

Bhaskar, V., & Glyn, A. (1995). Expectations and investment: An econometric defense of animal spirits. In G. A. Epstein & H. Gintis (Eds.), *Macroeconomic policy after the conservative era: Studies in investment, saving and finance* (pp. 197–223). Cambridge University Press.

Blanchard, O., Rhee, C., & Summers, L. (1993). The stock market, profit, and investment. *Quarterly Journal of Economics*, *108*, 115–136.

Boddy, R., & Crotty, J. (1975). Class conflict and macro-policy: The political business cycle. *Review of Radical Political Economics*, *7*, 1–19.

Boldrin, M., & Horvath, M. (1995). Labor contracts and business cycles. *Journal of Political Economy*, *103*, 972–1004.

Burns, A. F., & Mitchell, W. C. (1946). *Measuring business cycles*. New York, NY: National Bureau of Economic Research.

Dash, E., & Schwartz, N.D. (2011). Banks flooded with cash they can't profitably use. *New York Times*, October 24 (Business, p. 1).

Devine, J. N. (1986). Empirical studies in Marxian crisis theory: Introduction. *Review of Radical Political Economics*, *18*, 1–12.

Frisch, R. (1933). *Propagation problems and impulse problems in dynamic economics*. Oslo: Universitetets Økonomische Institutt.

Glasner, D., & Cooley, T. F. (Eds.). (1997). *Business cycles and depressions: An encyclopedia*. New York, NY: Garland.

Goodwin, R. M. (1964). Econometrics in business-cycle analysis. In A. H. Hansen (Ed.), Business cycles and national income (2nd ed., pp. 417–468). London: George Allen and Unwin.

Gordon, R. A. (1961). *Business fluctuations* (2nd ed.). New York, NY: Harper.

Haberler, G. (1960). *Prosperity and depression: A theoretical analysis of cyclical movements* (4th ed.). Cambridge: Harvard University Press.

Hall, T. E. (1990). *Business cycles: The nature and causes of economic fluctuations*. New York, NY: Praeger.

Hamilton, J. D. (1988). A neoclassical model of unemployment and the business cycle. *Journal of Political Economy*, *96*, 593.

Hamilton, J. D. (1994). *Time series analysis*. Princeton, NJ: Princeton University Press.

Hansen, A. H. (1949). Wesley Mitchell, social scientist and social counselor. *Review of Economics and Statistics*, *31*, 245.

Hansen, A. H. (1964). *Business cycles and national income* (2nd ed.). London: George Allen and Unwin.

Huntington, E. (1920). *World-power and evolution*. New Haven, CT: Yale University Press.

Kalecki, M. (1971). *Selected essays on the dynamics of the capitalist economy 1933–1970*. Cambridge: Cambridge University Press.

Kalecki, M. (1990). In *Collected works of Michal Kalecki. Volume I: Business cycles and full employment* (Jerzy Osiatinsky, Ed.; C. A. Kisiels, Trans.). Oxford: Clarendon Press.

Kalecki, M. (1991). *Collected works of Michal Kalecki. Volume II: Capitalism: Economic dynamics* (Jerzy Osiatinsky, Ed.; C. A. Kisiels, Trans.). Oxford: Clarendon Press.

Keynes, J. M. (1936). *The general theory of employment, interest, and money*. London: Macmillan.

Keynes, J. M. (1937). The general theory of employment. *Quarterly Journal of Economics*, *51*(2), 209–223.

Knoop, T. A. (2004). *Recessions and depressions: Understanding business cycles*. Westport, CT: Praeger.
Koopmans, T. C. (1947). Measurement without theory. *Review of Economic Statistics, 29*, 161–172.
Marx, K. (1968). *Theories of surplus-value (Volume IV of Capital) [1863]*. Moscow: Progress Publishers.
Marx, K. (1977). *Capital – A critique of political economy [1867]* (Vol. I; B. Fowkes, Trans.). New York, NY: Vintage Books.
Marx, K. (1981). *Capital – A critique of political economy [1894]* (Vol. III; F. Engels, Ed.; D. Fernbach, Trans.). New York, NY: Vintage Books.
Matthews, R. C. O. (1959). *The business cycle*. Chicago, IL: University of Chicago Press.
Minsky, H. P. (1991). The financial instability hypothesis: A clarification. In M. Feldstein (Ed.), *The risk of economic crisis* (pp. 158–166). Chicago, IL: University of Chicago Press.
Minsky, H. P. (2008). *Stabilizing an unstable economy [1986]*. New York, NY: McGraw-Hill.
Mitchell, W. C. (1913). *Business cycles*. Berkeley, CA: University of California Press.
Mitchell, W. C. (1927). *Business cycles: The problem and its setting*. New York, NY: National Bureau of Economic Research.
Mitchell, W. C. (1941). *Business cycles and their causes: A new edition of Mitchell's business cycles, Part III*. Berkeley, CA: University of California Press.
Mitchell, W. C. (1951). *What happens during business cycles: A progress report*. New York, NY: National Bureau of Economic Research.
Mohun, S., & Veneziani, R. (2008). Goodwin cycles and the U.S. economy, 1948–2004. In P. Flaschel & M. Landesmann (Eds.), *Mathematical economics and the dynamics of capitalism: Godwin's legacy continued* (pp. 107–130). New York, NY: Routledge.
Morgan, M. S. (1990). *The history of econometric ideas*. Cambridge: Cambridge University Press.
Ohanian, L. E. (2008). Back to the future with Keynes. *Federal Reserve Bank of Minneapolis Quarterly Review*, *32*, 10–16.
Pigou, A. C. (1927). Wage policy and unemployment. *Economic Journal*, *37*, 355.
Rada, C., & Taylor, L. (2006). Empty sources of growth accounting, and empirical replacements à la Kaldor with some beef. *Structural Change & Economic Dynamics*, *17*, 487–500.
Robinson, J. (1979). *The generalisation of the general theory, and other essays*. London: Macmillan.
Schumpeter, J. A. (1954). *History of economic analysis*. London: Allen & Unwin.
Shackle, G. L. S. (1967). *The years of high theory: Invention and tradition in economic thought 1926–1939*. Cambridge: Cambridge University Press.
Sherman, H. J., & Kolk, D. X. (1997). *Business cycles and forecasting*. New York, NY: Addison-Wesley.
Steindl, J. (1991). Some comments on the three versions of Kalecki's theory of the trade cycle. In J. Osiatinsky, (Ed.), *Collected works of Michal Kalecki. Volume II: Capitalism: Economic dynamics* (pp. 597–604). Oxford: Clarendon Press.
Targetti, F., & Kinda-Hass, B. (1982). Kalecki's review of Keynes's general theory. *Australian Economic Papers*, *21*(38), 244–260.
Tinbergen, J. (1939). *Statistical testing of business-cycle theories: Volume II – Business cycles in the United States of America 1919–1932*. Geneva: League of Nations.
Wilson, M. (2009). Sales of safes boom as the economy falters: Looking for security in a cube of steel. *New York Times*, March 6.

PRODUCT INNOVATION AND CAPITAL ACCUMULATION: AN ATTEMPT TO INTRODUCE NEO-SCHUMPETERIAN INSIGHTS INTO MARXIAN ECONOMICS

Jie Meng

ABSTRACT

This article tries to introduce product innovation into Marxist theory of capital accumulation. Although in Grundrisse *Marx has already foreseen the importance of product innovation in overcoming the limits to capital originated from the production of relative surplus value, mainstream Marxist theories of capital accumulation have up till now made few endeavours to envisage this problem. It is argued in this chapter that to introduce product innovation into Marxist theory of accumulation depends on a reconstruction of the fundamental contradictions in capital accumulation, that is the contradiction between production of surplus value and realisation of surplus value, combined with the contradiction between exchange value and use value as the driving force in its development. The production of relative surplus value based on process innovation and consequent productivity enhancement, given any specific*

Contradictions: Finance, Greed, and Labor Unequally Paid
Research in Political Economy, Volume 28, 261–285

ISSN: 0161-7230/doi:10.1108/S0161-7230(2013)0000028010

use value, will lead to overproduction, that is the intensification of those fundamental contradictions in accumulation, which nevertheless could be mitigated by introducing product innovation. In evaluating critically the contribution by Mandel in his long waves theory, we further argue, following the lead of neo-Schumpeterians, that there is a possibility for radical product innovations to be at least semi-endogenously induced in capital accumulation, and thus paving the way for a long boom of capitalism.

Keywords: Product innovation; the fundamental contradiction of capital accumulation; process innovation; the falling rate of profit; neo-Schumpeterian economics

JEL Classification: A10; B24; B51; E11

The neo-Schumpeterian theories of technological innovation and long waves assume that radical product innovations are the most important driving force that facilitates economic growth in the long run. This article tries to introduce neo-Schumpeterian insight into Marxist theory of capital accumulation with a revised explanation of the fundamental contradictions in capital accumulation. The text consists of the following different sections: in the first section, there is a retrospect of relevant theories on product innovation: neo-Schumpeterian theories of innovation and long waves with a Marxist origin, and then the view of Marx himself on product innovation in *Grundrisse*. In the second section, it is expounded that to introduce product innovation[1] into Marxist theory of accumulation depends on a reconstruction of the fundamental contradictions in capital accumulation, that is the contradiction between production of surplus value and realisation of surplus value, combined with the contradiction between exchange value and use value as the driving force in its development. The production of relative surplus value based on process innovation and consequent productivity enhancement, given any specific use value, will lead to overproduction, that is the intensification of those fundamental contradictions in accumulation, which nevertheless could be mitigated by introducing product innovation. It is argued that, up till now, most of the existing Marxist theories have *de facto* hampered serious and formal analysis of the problems with product innovation and accumulation. In the third section, through critically evaluating the contribution by Mandel in his long waves theory, we further argue, following the lead of neo-Schumpeterians, there is a possibility for radical product innovations to be at least semi-endogenously induced in capital accumulation, and thus paving the way for a long boom of capitalism. The final section concludes this article by comparing three types of attitude among Marxist economists towards product innovation.

RELEVANT THEORIES ON PRODUCT INNOVATION AND CAPITAL ACCUMULATION: A RETROSPECT

Neo-Schumpeterian Theories and its Marxist Origin

In 1912, van Geldren, a Marxist from the Netherlands, got his article published in a socialist journal of his country, which was entitled 'Springtide: Reflections on Industrial Development and Price Movements' (van Geldren, 1996). This article, rather than the work by Russian economist Kondratieff of more than 10 years later, is now considered as the real origin of 'long waves theory' in neo-Schumpeterian literature. With abundant statistical data cited, van Geldren confirmed that, between 1850–1873 and 1896–1911, there appeared, respectively, long-term expansion of capital accumulation in the major capitalist countries of Western Europe and North America, which he named as the 'springtide' of capital accumulation. In his theoretical explanation of the formation of 'springtide', van Geldren emphasised the role of radical product innovations and subsequent growth of newly established sectors. As he pointed out, some rapidly growing new sectors contributed to bring about long-run expansion in economy. For the period between 1850 and 1873, the leading sector was the construction of railway, and the side-effect of which was the expansion of metal, steel and coal industries. As far as the upturn period after 1896 was concerned, it was electricity and automobile industries which played the role of leading sectors, facilitating the production of metal, insulated materials and coal.

The pioneering work of van Geldren has ever since remained unknown due to language barrier. In *Late Capitalism*, Mandel for the first time gave a systematic introduction of van Geldren's view. As late as 1996, 'Springtide' was finally available in English with the publication of *Long Wave Theory* edited by Christopher Freeman. As regarding 'long wave' having been named by Schumpeter after Kondratieff, Freeman argued that, if Schumpeter has ever gotten to know van Geldren, the 'Kondratieff long wave' might well be named as 'van Geldren long wave'.[2]

Schumpeter is usually considered the first great academic economist who highlighted that innovations are crucial for capitalism to survive. Although totally unfamiliar with van Geldren's article, Schumpeter himself formulated assumptions as follows: innovations are the most important driving force facilitating economic growth; innovations are not evenly distributed in historical time, but emerge in clusters; significant innovations such as steam-engine, railway, electricity, automobile, contributed to generate expansive long waves of capital accumulation. Nevertheless, the conception of innovations as used by Schumpeter is too broad in content, embracing not only technological innovation (product innovation and process innovation) but also organisational innovation, the opening up of new markets and so forth. In his analytical practice, Schumpeter did emphasise the role of product innovations, which remains conceptually ambiguous to some extent.

The work of G. Mensch, *Stalemate in Technology* (1979), was not directly devoted to long-wave theory, but was regarded as one of three masterpieces in the rehabilitation of long waves theory in 1970s (both of the other two were Marxist works, i.e. Mandel, 1975, and Aglietta, 1976, respectively). Mensch advances Schumpeter's theory in two points: first, he makes a clear-cut conceptual distinction between 'basic innovation' (i.e. radical product innovations which result in establishment of new sectors) and process innovation; the former type of innovation is treated as the most important factor in facilitating economic growth, and economic slump ensues due to scarcity of 'basic innovations'. Second, Mensch tries to confirm in empirical research the Schumpeterian innovations-in-cluster hypothesis. As he claims, during some specific periods of time in the history of capitalism, that is in 1830s, 1880s and 1930s, when are just the periods of depressions, basic innovations turn out to emerge in clusters. Based on these new findings, Mensch puts forward a hypothesis that depression is conducive to induce basic innovations, and which appear in clusters.

Van Duijn, a successor of Mensch, has summarised the theoretical contribution of neo-Schumpeterian school in a methodologically clear-cut way. He differentiates two kinds of variables in economy: on the one hand, product innovation, innovative life cycles and the related investment in infrastructure are posited as the autonomous variables; on the other hand, those variables such as growth of money supply, the distribution of income over profit and labour, etc. are treated as dependent variables, whose fluctuation should be explained through the change of autonomous variables (van Duijn, 1983, p. 129).

The hypothesis as formulated by van Duijn expresses the final theoretical achievement that the neo-Schumpeterian school reached.[3] Nevertheless, since neo-Schumpeterian approach of innovation and long waves is mainly a positive theory, it suffers from the fact that the above-mentioned causation between product innovation and other economic phenomena still needs to be justified in a general theoretical framework of capitalism. This awkwardness could not be evaded by resort to Schumpeter himself. As post-Keynesianist H. P. Minsky argued, 'While Schumpeter may be the source of great insights into the capitalist process, he did not leave a useful theoretical framework for the analysis of capitalism'. Late in his lifetime, Schumpeter actually switched to general equilibrium theory, thus abandoning his idea about innovation in *Theory of Economic Development*. Minsky suggests that 'further progress in understanding capitalism may very well depend upon integrating Schumpeter's insights with regard to the dynamics of a capitalist process and the role of innovative entrepreneurs into an analytical framework that in its essential properties is Keynesian' (Minsky, 1986). By contrast, we are trying to integrate Schumpeterian insights with a reconstructed Marxian approach.

Grundrisse *on the Production of Relative Surplus Value and Product Innovation*

Although neo-Schumpeterian theory of long waves and product innovation can be traced back to a socialist van Geldren, he still fails to exert any influence on the main currents of Marxism of the time. A whole generation of Marxists at the beginning of 20th century obsessed themselves with the controversy of 'breakdown' of capitalism, rather than springtide of capital accumulation. In 1916, Lenin in his *Theory of Imperialism* gave capitalism a final judge that it is 'parasitic and decaying'. Thus, it seemed revisionist-like for van Geldren to imagine at the time 'springtide' of capital accumulation brought about simply by innovations.

Although there is no relevant analysis in *Capital* devoted to product innovation, it is in *Grundrisse* that Marx indeed points to the importance of product innovation for capital accumulation in relation to the contradictions inherent in production of relative surplus value. A thorough citation from *Grundrisse* is needed here.

Beginning with discussion of the production of absolute surplus value, Marx says that:

> The creation by capital of absolute surplus value...is conditional upon an expansion, specifically a constant expansion, of the sphere of circulation. The *surplus value* created at one point requires the creation of surplus value at *another* point, for which it may be

> exchanged. ... A precondition of production based on capital is therefore *the production of a constantly widening sphere of circulation* ...while circulation appeared at first as a constant magnitude, it here appears as a moving magnitude, being expanded by production itself. ... The tendency to create the *world market* is directly given in the concept itself. Every limit appears as a barrier to be overcome.
>
> On the other hand, the production of *relative surplus value*, i.e. production of surplus value based on the increase and development of the productive forces, requires the production of new consumption; requires that the consuming circle within circulation expands as did the productive circle previously. Firstly quantitative expansion of existing consumption; secondly: creation of new needs by propagating existing ones in a wide circle; *thirdly*, production of *new* needs and discovery and creation of new use values. In other words, so that the surplus labour gained does not remain a merely quantitative surplus, but rather constantly increase the circle of qualitative differences within labour (hence of surplus labour), makes it more diverse, more internally differentiated. For example, if, through a doubling of productive force, a capital of 50 and the necessary labour corresponding to it become free, then, for the capital and labour which have been set free, a new, qualitatively different branch of production must be created, which brings forth a new need. The value of the old industry is preserved by the creation of the fund for a new one in which the relation of capital and labour posits itself in a *new* form.
>
> This creation of new branches of production, i.e. of qualitatively new surplus time, is not merely the division of labour, but is rather the creation, separate from a given production, of labour with a new use value; the development of a constantly expanding and more comprehensive system of different kinds of labour, different kinds of production, to which a constantly expanding and constantly enriched system of needs corresponds. (Marx, 1993, pp. 407–409).

Here arises 'the great civilizing influence of capital', since the production of capital requires 'exploration of all of nature', 'the exploration of the earth in all directions, to discover new things of use as well as new useful qualities of the old', 'the development, hence, of the natural sciences to their highest point; likewise the discovery, creation and satisfaction of new needs arising from society itself; the cultivation of all the qualities of the social human beings, ...'. (Marx, 1993, p. 409)[4]

Although Marx never uses the concept of product innovation or even innovation *per se*, his words such as 'production of new needs' (as differentiated from creation of new needs by propagating existing ones), 'discovery and creation of new use-values', 'creation of new branches of production' all point to the same meaning of product innovation or basic innovation as adopted by neo-Schumpeterians. Nevertheless, even as he talks about the need to create a 'qualitatively different branch of production' under the circumstance of overaccumulation, Marx confines his analysis in the main to the significance of product innovation for capital accumulation. In contrast, neo-Schumpeterians attempt as well to explain how product innovations are initiated in historically specific context of capital accumulation.

Marx's genius idea in *Grundrisse*, long before capitalism exhibiting its potential in product innovation and subsequent transforming of social division of labour, foresees astonishingly the real development of capitalism. However, it might be no exaggeration to claim that the above-cited analysis in *Grundrisse* remains almost unknown up till now. Rosdolsky's *The Making of Marx's Capital* has been enjoying international reputation as the most important contribution to the research of *Grundrisse* at least in English speaking world, in which the text on product innovation is unfortunately not mentioned at all.

An interesting question, nonetheless, arises here – why Marx fails to write down all these ideas in *Capital*? Is it because *Capital* remains unfinished manuscript? Or rather, were these ideas introduced in *Capital*, would the cutting edge of critique to capitalism be inevitably weakened? No matter what the reasons might be, the genius of thought in *Grundrisse* seems to shaken the very basis of the theory as given in *Capital* of capital accumulation. All three volumes of *Capital de facto* assume away product innovation, basing the analysis upon an improper premise that the development of productive forces, or technical innovation, embodies only in process innovation and consequent enhancement in labour productivity, which are reflected in the rise of organic composition of capital. It can be argued thus, in *Capital*, Marx only leaves us a partial analysis of development in productive forces and capital accumulation.

TOWARDS A MARXIST FRAMEWORK IN WHICH PRODUCT INNOVATION COULD BE CONCEPTUALISED

Critical Analysis of Contemporary Marxist Theories of Capital Accumulation by Reference to the Fundamental Contradictions in Capital Accumulation

In this section, we would like to argue that product innovation can be conceptualised in the light of fundamental contradiction of capital accumulation, which is defined by Marx as the contradiction between production of surplus value and realisation of surplus value. In recent decades, however, some most influential Marxist theories on contemporary capital accumulation deviate from any plausible explanations based upon the fundamental contradiction of capital accumulation, thus hampering serious and formal analysis of product innovation. The first example is the orthodox theory of falling rate of profit, towards which we shall give more comment shortly after. The second is usually labelled as profit-squeeze theory, which reduces the fundamental contradiction in capital accumulation to class conflicts either in distribution of national income or in labour markets. The outbreak of these conflicts is assumed as a result of autonomous militancy of wage workers.

Compared to the profit-squeeze or class-conflict theory, the orthodox theory of falling rate of profit seems to be relatively superior, because it attributes fundamental contradiction in capital accumulation to the antagonism between productive forces and relations of production; that is, productivity enhancement and subsequent rise in the organic composition of capital leads to a decline of profit rate, which in turn chokes off capital accumulation. Nevertheless, the orthodox theory of falling rate of profit is still flawed by two methodologically unrealistic assumptions, in our view. First, it assumes that, even in the long run, there is no change of use values produced by capital, no change of the leading sectors that are the engine of economic growth, no change of social division of labour. This assumption is explicitly made in Volume 3 of *Capital*, where Marx discusses the law of the falling rate of profit. As he puts, 'We entirely leave aside here the fact that the same amount of value represents a progressively rising mass of use-values and satisfactions, with the progress of capitalist production and with the corresponding development of the productivity of social labour and multiplication of branches of production and hence products' (Marx, 1991, p. 325).[5]

Interestingly, in one page of *Capital*, Volume 3, which is not easy to draw attention of readers, Marx mentions in passing an opinion from British classical economist Richard Jones, who realises that 'the increasing diversity of branches of production' can be seen as one of the factors offsetting the declining of profit rate. Marx cites his view in discussing the law of profit rate to fall, but fails to list it as one of the counteracting factors of this law.[6]

Second, the orthodox theory of profit rate to fall is flawed by the fact that it is solely based upon change in the conditions of production of surplus value, losing sight of the contradiction between production and circulation, between production of surplus value and its realisation. As a result, at least in the existing version of *Capital*, Volume 3, edited by Engels, there appears a emptiness in the logic: Marx never accounts for what the logical relation is between the tendency of profit rate to fall and the contradiction between production of surplus value and its realisation, the latter being discussed by

Marx in Chapter 15 of Volume 3 just after the tendency of profit rate to fall has been elaborated. We could only guess according to the title of Chapter 15 ('Development of the Law's Internal Contradictions' – which is chosen by Engels) that the contradiction between production of surplus value and its realisation is logically subordinated to the general law of profit rate to fall, which implies that a declining of profit rate is the very condition for the contradiction in accumulation to be intensified. However, such kind of interpretation seems to violate the logic of the whole three volumes of *Capital* which is characterised as the unity of production and circulation. For Marx, the contradiction between production and circulation, and between production of surplus value and its realisation, is considered the fundamental one dominating capitalist mode of production, and through which any explanation of causation for the operation of laws of capital accumulation can be imagined.[7]

The second methodological assumptions are not only held by orthodox theory of profit rate to fall, but accepted by its critics following the impact of Okishio theorem. Two Japanese scholars have ever made an attempt to integrate product innovation into Okishio's model, but their contribution is limited, since, in our eyes, the contradiction between production of surplus value and realisation of surplus value is still missing (Nakatani & Hagiwara, 1997). They simply argue in their model that if a line of production switches from the production of an old product to a new product with higher rate of profit, the general rate of profit will rise. They fail to explain why the rate of profit in the former existing line of production is lower than the new one, only accepting it as a given fact. As a result, the role of product innovation in enhancing profit rate through an enlargement in the system of social division of labour, or in the existing system of exchange values, is still obscure in their model.

J. M. Gillman, following the lead of Rosa Luxemburg, makes the above second point methodologically clear.[8] He even devises a completely different explanation of profit rate to fall in the perspective of the contradiction between production and realisation, instead of Marx's original theory. Nevertheless, his explanation suffers from his adherence to underconsumptionism. Gillman inherits the blindness of Luxemburg, excluding possible endogenous expansion of markets occasioned by radical product innovations. As Marx contends in *Grundrisse*, product innovations and the subsequent diversification of new branches can bring about an enlargement in the system of social division of labour, or in the existing system of exchange values, providing new sources of equivalent values, through which the limits to capital accumulation can be overcome periodically.

A Reconstruction of the Fundamental Contradictions of Capital Accumulation

Even if we recognise that the fundamental contradictions in accumulation do enjoy methodological priority in explaining laws of motion of capitalist mode of production, there could be dispute about how to interpret the driving forces of the contradiction. Some Marxists ever try to interpret it in the light of underconsumptionism. A famous paragraph from Volume 3 of *Capital* does provide the possibility of different readings, including the underconsumptionist one:

> The conditions for immediate exploitation and for the realization of that exploitation are not identical. Not only are they separate in time and space, they are also separate in theory. The former is restricted only by the society's productive forces, the latter by *the proportionality between different branches of production* and *by the society's power of consumption*. And this is determined neither by the absolute power of production and by the absolute power of consumption but rather by the consumption within a given framework of antagonistic conditions of distribution, which reduce the consumption of vast majority of society to a minimum level, only capable of varying within more or less narrow limits. It is further restricted by *the drive for accumulation*, the drive to expand capital and produce surplus-value on a larger scale. (Marx, 1991, pp. 352–352. Italic added.)

It is thus not strange at all to interpret the fundamental contradiction of accumulation to the benefit of underconsumptionism, since, as Marx mentions, the realisation of surplus value is constrained 'by the society's power of consumption'. What's more, we can even read in *Capital*, Volume 3: 'the ultimate reason for all real crises always remains the poverty and restricted consumption of the masses'. In recent years, however, with the publication of Marx's original manuscript of *Capital,* Volume 3, researchers have an opportunity to find that, in editing Marx's manuscript, Engels makes a lot of modifications. The above-cited famous sentence is originally inside a bracket. Engels omits the bracket, integrating it into the text. As a result, the meaning of this sentence is changed and is possible to be quoted as the proof of underconsumptionism.[9]

As against the underconsumptionist reading, an alternative interpretation for the fundamental contradictions in accumulation can be argued in terms of two points. In the paragraph cited above, Marx virtually lists three factors that are the determinants of realisation of surplus value, that is 'the proportionality between different branches of production', 'the society's power of consumption' and 'the drive for accumulation'. The last factor, that is the drive for accumulation, can be regarded as the most crucial one among all three in determining the realisation of surplus value. As pointed out by Marx, the realisation of surplus value 'is further restricted by the drive for accumulation'. Both the proportionality and the power of mass consumption are conditioned by real accumulation by capitalists, since in capitalism it is the drive for accumulation that determines economic activities of other agents.

The fact that the realisation of surplus value is in the last analysis dependent upon real accumulation of capitalists can be summarised in a new equation developed from Marx's scheme of extended reproduction (see Okishio, 1961).

$$\alpha S_1^t + \alpha S_2^t = S_{1C}^{t+1} + S_{2C}^{t+1} + S_{1V}^{t+1} + S_{2V}^{t+1}$$

The left hand side of the equation is the intended accumulation of capitalists of two sectors which produce consumption goods and investment goods, respectively. α denotes the rate of intended accumulation, $S_i(i=1,2)$, the surplus value. The right hand side, that is the items of demand, is attributed to the real accumulation of capitalists from the two sectors of social production. The superscripts t and $t+1$ denote the differences between production and realisation in time and in conception.

This new equation implies that how much of surplus value can be realised depends upon the magnitude of real accumulation of capitalists in the two sectors. In contrast, in *Capital* Volume 1, it is the realised surplus value that constitutes the very precondition and source of further accumulation. The first causation, that is that the realisation of surplus value is determined by real accumulation, is implied in Marx's reproduction scheme, and summed up in Kalecki's famous thesis that profit is determined by investment. On the other hand, most contemporary Marxists seem to accept the second relation of causation. For them, it is the level of realised profit rate that determines the rate of accumulation. In our eyes, what is needed here is a more dialectical synthesis of these two different relations of causation, and which will be further discussed later.

For Kalecki (1971), whatever determines investment is treated as the most crucial problem in political economy. Nonetheless, he himself fails to figure out a satisfying theory on the determinants of investment. The problem thus remains as to how to understand the driving forces and the constraints of investment in the perspective of fundamental contradictions in capital accumulation. Here, thus, arises the second point of view we would like to argue for, and which is completely missing in Kalecki's type of analytical framework – the contradiction between value and use value can be seen as driving force in the development of the contradiction between production of surplus value and realisation of surplus value.

According to Marx, the contradiction between production of surplus value and realisation of surplus value tends to be intensified in the production of relative surplus value. Marx lays it bare in *Grundrisse* as well as in *Capital*.

First of all, Marx argues that the growth of relative surplus value tends to decline with the enhancement of labour productivity. For the simplicity of investigation, Marx assumes that what is produced is necessity goods for wage workers, and that constant capital equals to 0. In his elaboration, there exists an implicit assumption that production of surplus value takes place on the basis of given use value. Let r be the ratio of necessary labour time to a working day, and $r = T_N/T$.[10] If labour productivity increases, the necessary labour time for a worker to reproduce his value of labour power, as well as the ratio r, will decline in proportion. For example, if the ratio $r = (1/2)$, and productivity, now grows by 2 times, the ratio will decline to $(1/2 \times 2) = (1/4)$. Supposing the multiplier of productivity growth is m, then the ratio will be $r = T_N/Tm$. The growth of relative surplus value thus can be measured by $T_N-(T_N/m)$. It is obvious that the larger the multiplier (m), the more growth for relative surplus value. Nevertheless, as Marx observes, along with the enhancement in labour productivity, that is with the change in the multiplier m, the increase of relative surplus value tends to decline. This can be seen from $T_N-(T_N/m)$, in which the later item T_N/m tends to be 0, along with the infinite growth of productivity, that is infinite growth of m. Therefore, although the multiplier m is the indicator of productivity enhancement, it is not necessarily the indicator for the growth of relative surplus value, since the growth of surplus value is declining along with productivity enhancement. The tendency for the increase of relative surplus value to decline implies that, given production of any specific use values, process innovation and consequent productivity growth will be confronted by a limit in the long run in increasing surplus value. As Marx sums up, 'The surplus value of capital rises, but in an ever diminishing ratio to the development of productivity. Thus the more developed capital already is, the more surplus labour it has already created, the more tremendously must it develop productivity if it is to valorise itself, i.e. to add surplus value even in a small proportion… . The self-valorisation of capital becomes more difficult to the extent to which it is already valorised. The increase in productivity could become a matter of indifference to capital; its valorisation itself could cease to matter, because its proportions have become minimal; and it would have ceased to be capital' (Marx, 1986, pp. 265–266).[11]

However, the tendency for the rise of surplus value to decline as described above will take place well before the above-mentioned limit is reached. In the very beginning of *Capital*, Marx proposes that with the growth of labour productivity, the unit value of any given commodity will decrease, while the magnitude of use value will increase in the same rate as productivity grows. In volume 3 of *Capital*, Marx proceeds to develop this view in relation to the discussion of the tendency of profit rate to fall. In his view, not only the unit value of commodity but unit profit as well as profit rate may decline along with productivity enhancement. The contradiction between value and its material bearer use value thus tends to be intensified in the production of relative surplus value: the more commodities are produced, the more valorisation becomes dependent upon the realisation of use values.[12] Taking into account the fact that the demand for any given type of use value tends to be saturated in the long run, use value, as one factor of commodity, turns out to be the constraint rather than the bearer of valorisation.

In the history of economic thought, it is French classical economist Quesnay who had first disclosed the significance of this contradiction. As the founder of Physiocracy, Quesnay believes that value is produced by land rather than human labour. For the sake of refuting the labour theory of value, he argues by reduction to absurdity in his debate with the advocates of labour theory of value. Supposing that labour theory of value is right, Quesnay argues, a conclusion can be drawn immediately that the unit value of any given commodity as well as unit profit tend to decline in inverse proportion to labour productivity growth. Nevertheless, in his view, this conclusion is contradictory with the very definition of capitalist production itself, which is characterised with the pursuit of profit. Capitalist mode of production simply cannot survive a sustaining decline of unit value as well as unit profit of commodity. On the other hand, provided that capitalist mode of production would succeed in reproducing itself in reality, labour theory of value has to be refuted (Quesnay, 1962, pp. 203–230). This argument can be termed as the *Dilemma of Quesnay*.

Quesnay for the first time realises that deflation, or a sustaining decline of unit value, can deal a fatal blow to capitalist mode of production. Considering that Quesnay lives in a pre-capitalist world, his view equals to declaring, for the advocates of labour theory of value, a sentence to death of capitalism before it comes into full-fledged existence.

Marx deals with the Dilemma of Quesnay in his elaboration of the law of falling rate of profit rate. For Marx, the Dilemma can be solved in the following way. The fall in unit value of commodity and consequent decline in unit profit is accompanied and counteracted by an increase in the mass of profit. In *Capital* Volume 3, the possible coexistence of the fall of profit rate and the growth of mass of profit is claimed to be another expression of the law of falling rate of profit (Marx, 1991, Ch. 13). Marx's solution, nevertheless, hinges upon whether the demand to any specific commodities could go up hand in hand with labour productivity. Marx seems to take it for granted. That equals to saying, for Marx, the contradiction between production of surplus value and realisation of surplus value can be assumed away in discussing the tendency for profit rate to fall. By arguing in this way, the law of the falling rate of profit is actually separated from the fundamental contradictions of accumulation.

The Dilemma of Quesnay is accordingly not satisfactorily solved in *Capital*. In our view, only by introducing product innovation, or in Marx's words, by taking into account production of new needs, discovery and creation of new use values, creation of new branches of production, the Dilemma of Quesnay, a theoretically premature expression of the fundamental contradictions in capital accumulation, can be to some extent overcome.

A Tentative Interpretation of the Dynamics of Profit Rate in the New Framework in Relation to Product Innovation

We would now like to delineate some basic features of a new theoretical framework, in which product innovation is considered as the main factor in shaping the fundamental contradictions of capital accumulation.

First of all, we need to formulate a new hypothesis as for the relationship between the fundamental contradictions of capital accumulation and the dynamics of profit rates. It is helpful in our view to start from the fact that the contradiction between production of surplus value and realisation of surplus value develops to varied extents in different capitalist branches. The inter-sectoral competition and equalisation of profit rates play the role of eliminating inter-sectoral differences in the development of these fundamental contradictions, synchronising life cycles of these sectors, through which the fundamental contradictions of capital accumulation are socialised across economy, and finally bringing about a decline of equalised profit rate.

It is crucial to note that the empirically given life cycles of specific products or sectors can be conceptualised in relation to the development of the fundamental contradictions of capital accumulation in different sectors or even across the economy. The time spans of these life cycles are determined, first, by the extent of development of these fundamental contradictions in respective sectors; second, by the extent to which the development of these contradictions are socialised across economy. It is in the latter sense that the neo-Schumpeterian idea about a life cycle of technological revolution (Perez, 2002) can be conceptualised in a framework of Marxist accumulation theory. Any change or extension of these different types of life cycles can be considered to be effected by product innovations due to their significance in mitigating those contradictions in accumulation. Unfortunately, the relationship between different types of life cycles and fundamental contradictions in capital accumulation, as well as the role of product innovations in prolonging time span of life cycles, are almost missing in Marxism-inspired empiric analysis of contemporary capital accumulation.

The life cycle of specific products and/or sectors can be identified into the following successive phases, in the perspective of the profit rates to be equalised and to fall: (1) The phase of introduction and rapid growth, during which new products firstly introduced meet the huge social demand, production is enlarged rapidly, surplus profits exist throughout the industry. (2) The phase of maturation, during which large amount of capital is induced into the innovative industry in pursuit of surplus profit. As a result, profit rates of different industries tend to be equalised due to the inter-sectoral competition among capitals, and the life cycles of different industries synchronised. Process innovation characterised with saving of labour tends to be adopted as the more important means of competition. (3) The phase of decay. Since the contradictions in accumulation are more and more socialised and synchronised in different sectors, the intra-sectoral competition weighs more than the inter-sectoral one. Price competition – based on process innovation – as well as product differentiation become the main competitive weapons, the equalised profit rate declines.[13]

Mensch proposes that, according to the empiric explanation of life cycles, any slowdown in the growth of individual sector is due to an exhaustion of possibilities for technological progress. However, it remains to be explained how the decline of investment opportunities spreads from individual sectors to the whole economy. For Mensch, there indeed exists a tendency towards synchronisation of life cycles in different sectors, the reasons of which are claimed to be found in the 'complementary relationships between goods "that simply belong together" in a modernized way of life', for example the relationship between cars and highway construction machinery (Mensch, 1979, p. 18). Nevertheless, without the role of inter-sector competition, it is difficult for the technologically complementary relationship itself to produce a synchronisation of life cycles in the majority of sectors. In later research,

Mensch et al. emphasise that product life cycle is the unity of two kinds of dynamics: '(a) the intrinsic dynamics describing the "natural metamorphosis" of a product over its technological maturation process and evolution of its market share; and (b) the interaction dynamics describing how the product's life cycle is influenced by its technological and market interaction with the manifold of competing commodities at different stages of maturity. Hence we distinguish between intra-industrial (branch specific) and inter-industrial (cross-sectional) interaction dynamics between product life cycles'. For Mensch et al., thanks to the second dynamics, the first dynamics in most branches have to change natural trajectories and finally synchronise with each other (Mensch, Weidlich, & Haag, 1987, p. 375). Although such an analysis hints as to the effect of inter-industrial competition upon product life cycles, it still fails to make an analysis of life cycle in reference to the fundamental contradictions in accumulation as well as the law of profit rates to be equalised and to fall.

About the Relation between Product Innovation and Process Innovation

A problem remains though as regarding the relation between product innovation and process innovation. It can be argued that in the ongoing elaboration, we have dismissed the role of process innovation in capital accumulation while emphasising the importance of product innovation (Gao, 2004). This critique can be further demonstrated as follows. First of all, the difference between product innovation and process innovation is only of relative character. In most cases, process innovations are simultaneously product innovations embodied in equipments, new materials and new forms of energy. Only purely new consumption goods can be considered as product innovation in the strict sense. There are still some innovations which are both innovation of capital goods and that of consumption goods. Second, radical product innovations which could generate long upturn of economic growth are usually those radical innovations of capital goods which result in radical process innovations. Third, innovations of consumption goods cannot take place independently without the help of process innovation, since innovations of important consumption goods not only need huge amount of R&D investment but also process innovations to enhance productivity after its first appearance in market place. In sum, it may well be argued that in the foregoing analysis, we only offer a theory of purely consumption goods innovation, rather than a general theory of product innovation.

An answer to the above critique can be attempted here. There is indeed a debate on the differentiation between product innovation and process innovation even in neo-Schumpeterian literature (Kleinknecht, 1987, p. 68). What we accept here is the differentiation in the tradition of Mensch, van Duijn and Coombs–Kleinknecht, according to which product innovation and process innovation can be distinguished either empirically or in terms of their different significance for capital accumulation. What is crucial is not to blur the difference of these two types of innovations, but how to define their relationship. It can be argued that product innovation could only develop on the basis of process innovation and productivity enhancement. It is radical process innovation that transforms any new consumption goods from luxuries to necessities which can be consumed by the mass. And it is also radical process innovation and consequent productivity growth that make either steel or electronic chips to be cheap enough so that they can be used as genetic inputs in all industries, inspiring subsequent product innovations.[14]

On the other hand, capitalist production is after all production based on specific use values. In capital accumulation, process innovation and productivity growth take place on the basis of given use values and given sectors. If we assume, as Marx has done in *Capital*, that use value as material bearer of exchange value always stay unchanged, process innovation and consequent productivity enhancement will then tend to deepen the contradictions between use value and exchange value, and that between production of surplus value and realisation of surplus value. As a result, capital accumulation will be plunged into overproduction in double senses. First of all, it is more and more difficult for process innovation and productivity enhancement to increase surplus value, due to the reasons Marx has expounded. Second, the more advance in productivity, the more valorisation will become dependent upon sale of use values in an already saturated market. Under the pressure of overproduction, there will be a shift in the mode of competition correspondingly. Price competition, based upon process innovation and productivity enhancement, will not serve as the sole means of competition. Product innovations will be more likely chosen as an effective weapon in competition. Thus, as Schumpeter puts in a frequently cited paragraph: 'In capitalist reality as distinguished from its textbook picture, it is not [price] competition which counts but the competition from the new commodity, the new technology, the new source of supply, the new type of organization (the largest scale unit of control, for instance) – competition which commands a decisive cost or quality advantage and which strikes not at the margin of the profits and outputs of the existing firms but at their foundations and their very lives' (Schumpeter, 1976, pp. 84–85). Accordingly, as regards to the relation between these two types of innovation, it is better to treat them in a more dialectic way, that is to treat the very combination of both types as the manifestation of technical progress in accumulation, rather than either thinking about process innovation as more theoretically fundamental, downplaying the significance of product innovation for capital accumulation or partially emphasising the role of product innovation, paying no attention to its combination with process innovation.

A CRITIQUE OF MANDEL IN RELATION TO PRODUCT INNOVATION AND CAPITAL ACCUMULATION

Neo-Schumpeterian economics not only emphasises the importance of radical product innovations, combined with other types of innovation, in stimulating robust economic growth in the long run, but holds that radical innovations are endogenously generated. A recent example is C. Perez, as she argues, there are always potential innovations outside of existing trajectory of techno-economic paradigm, which will be the objects of huge amount of investment once the capability of existing techno-economic paradigm in sustaining a development surge is exhausted (Perez, 2002).

Marxists such as Baran and Sweezy admit that some big technical revolutions (such as the construction of railway and production of automobile) can bring about long booms in capitalist history. Nevertheless, in their eyes, these big revolutions are too few or far between, thus appearing to be insufficient to change the basic tendency of monopoly capitalism towards stagnation. In their analysis, technical revolutions are considered purely exogenous factors, which actually become an excuse for them to evade an analysis of what are the mechanisms for radical innovations to take place, and how they will influence the whole economy (Baran & Sweezy, 1968).

In comparison, Ernest Mandel offers a more comprehensive theory on technical revolutions and capital accumulation. For him, Marxist theory of capital accumulation can be reduced to a theory of dynamics of profit rates. How radical innovations take place and diffuse to the whole economy is connected with an explanation about the movement of profit rates. In his view, radical innovations and concurrent investment presuppose improvement in the general conditions of capital accumulation, which implies, as he puts, that 'there must be simultaneously a sharp rise in the rate of profit and a significant enlargement of the market', otherwise capitalists will not invest in radical innovations. Furthermore, according to him, the dual conditions cannot be guaranteed to take place simultaneously by the laws of motion of capitalist mode of production. In his words, 'normally, the capitalist way of securing the first condition conflicts with the capitalist way of securing the second'. This is called by Mandel, 'a basic contradiction of the capitalist growth process' (Mandel, 1995, p. 113).[15] Only with the help of so-called exogenous system shocks, such as revolutions and wars, these two preconditions could be met at the same time.[16]

The problem with Mandel is that the elaboration of 'basic contradiction of the capitalist growth process' is not very convincing. A sharp rise in the rate of surplus value is considered by Mandel as the prerequisite for profit rate to go up substantially. And the rise in the rate of surplus value tends to weaken the purchasing power of workers, and choke off a rapid expansion of the market of consumption goods. This is how he argues for 'the basic contradiction of capitalist growth process'.

Mandel's demonstration is based on the assumption that capitalists' expectation of profit, which determines investment decision, is the function of realised profit in the past. Thus, during the period of depression when profit rate is relatively lower, it is difficult for capitalist firms to invest on large scale in radical innovations. That is to say, whether or not individual capitalist firms will choose product innovations as competitive strategy is completely determined by the existing level of general profit rate. This assumption in Mandel brings us back to the controversial problem about the causation between profit rate and investment. As we mentioned before, the causation between profit rate and investment is complicated and cannot be understood in a linear way. Even at the purely aggregate or macro level, we can see from above discussion that there exists a possibility for investment to be determinant of profit rate. Neo-Schumpeterians, such as Mensch, Kleinknecht and others, explore at the levels beneath the aggregate, that is at the micro and meso level, in order to argue that even in the situation of depression when it is characterised with lower profit rate, individual capitalist firms or sectors may take the risk in investing radical product innovations since other strategies of competition are losing effectiveness. Under such circumstances, the expectation of profit for individual capitalist firms is rather a function of the relation between their innovative capacity and future profitability. That is to say, the rate of profit is to a large extent posited by the activities of individual innovative firms.

Accordingly, it is quite unsuitable for Mandel to claim that without a change in general rate of profit, individual capitalist firms will absolutely have no intention in investment of radical innovations. To attribute accumulation only as the function of general profit rate, as Mandel and many others have done, cannot avoid the accusation of fetishising the conception of profit rate.

Interestingly enough, although juxtaposing a radical expansion of market for consumption goods and a sharp rise in profit rate as two necessary conditions for protracted economic growth, Mandel admits at the same time that the Golden Age of capitalism in the wake of World War II takes place just after the world markets have dramatically contracted due to the rise of Soviet bloc and P. R. China. Thus, quite ironically, in explaining the onset of postwar boom, Mandel in his book on long waves only resorts to one condition he posits for the beginning of a long boom of capitalism, that is a rise in profit rate, which is further attributed to a sharp increase in the rate of surplus value during 1930–1940s, thanks to the historical defeat of workers in class struggle (Mandel, 1995, p. 18).

But things are more complicated. In our view, Mandel actually hesitates between two stories about the origin of the Golden Age of capitalism. The first and formal story is his asymmetrical theory of long waves as applied to the postwar boom. The other could be detected in his master piece *Late Capitalism*, in which he sometimes argues that the second necessary condition for the postwar long boom to be generated, that is a radical enlargement of markets, is met by huge investment of two departments of social production in new technologies, and which brings about the endogenous expansion of markets, or in his words 'a cumulative growth in all branches of industry' (Mandel, 1975, pp. 168–169, p. 178). This is, anyway, not an explanation far away from that of neo-Schumpeterians. A theoretical contradiction thus stands out in his work. According to his first story, a radical expansion of markets should take place before huge amount of investment in new technologies. But in the second story, an endogenous expansion of markets comes as the result of huge amount of investment in new technological revolution. Mandel never tries to reconcile this contradiction (Meng, 2012).

CONCLUDING REMARKS

It is rather curious that the problems with product innovation and Marxist theory of accumulation have for decades drawn so little attention. Although there has appeared significant achievement by Mandel in his long waves theory, mainstream Marxian analysis seems to be either indifferent to or fearful of conceptualising product innovation into Marxian theory of accumulation.

In our view, there are roughly three types of attitude towards product innovation among Marxian economists. The first is represented by Baran and Sweezy, who recognise, on the one hand, the role of radical product innovations (railway, automobile, etc.) in generating a long boom, but, on the other hand, downplaying them as pure exogenous factor. In so doing, radical product innovations are *de facto* dismissed by them as object of theoretical investigation in Marxian theory of accumulation.

The second is represented by Mandel. He is the only Marxist theorist who ever tried to incorporate radical product innovations into Marxist theory of accumulation in recent decades. Nevertheless, in his formal theory, such an endeavour is flawed by the fact that he declines to recognise the possibility that a long boom could be generated to some extent endogenously (or semi-endogenously) by investment in radical product innovations and subsequent cumulative growth of all branches of industry. He only embraces this possibility in his lengthy book implicitly. The contradiction inherent in his theory can be considered as resulting from the conflict in him between his political commitment and economic logic. As a Trotstkyist, Mandel is reluctant to abandon the judgment that capitalism has entered its period of historical demise since 1914. Hence, to recognise the possibility of any endogenously or even semi-endogenously generated long boom is conflicting with his belief and has to be refused in advance.

The third type of attitude that has hampered Marxists from introducing product innovation into Marxist theory lies in the unnecessary worry that, were product innovations introduced, Marxist emphasis on class relation and class struggle would be weakened. In Marx, the conflict between labour and capital is regarded as one of the driving forces which facilitate capitalist firms to invest in new technologies in order to reduce the power of labour in production process. Authors such as Harry Braverman even argue that all technological progresses are shaped by class relation. But the class-conflict explanation of the sources of innovations is not necessarily contradictory with another explanation which emphasises the role of competition in inducing innovations. These two explanations can be combined with each other. Innovations driven by class conflicts are mainly of labour-saving character, which aim to increase labour productivity. Radical product innovation is pursued mainly because there is a limit for productivity-enhancing innovations to increase relative surplus value as Marx has already mentioned. To pursue radical product innovation, or establishing qualitatively new kinds of labour in any existing system of division of labour, indeed broadens the sphere of control by capital, weakening the power of workers. But this is just the way through which capitals seek to counteract all the tendencies towards stagnation or breakdown of valorisation. In this sense, to argue that introducing product innovation means diminishing the importance of class relation amounts to an escape from obligation of understanding the reality of capitalist development.

NOTES

1. By product innovation, we mean either production of completely new product or radical improvement of product, following the suit of neo-Schumpeterians.
2. See Freeman (1996). cf. 'introduction'. Compared with van Geldren, Kondratieff is flawed by a lack of theoretical explanation of long waves.
3. Although debating with Mensch on some technical points, C. Freeman and his collaborators actually share the fundamental views with Mensch, that is recognising the prime role of basic innovation or radical product innovation in driving long-term economic growth. See Freeman, Clarke, and Soete (1982). Also cf. Perez (2002).
4. In these sentences, Marx seems to hint that, except for the ecological limits, there are no absolute barriers to capital accumulation.
5. Although many Marxists as well as non-Marxists, such as Sweezy and Joan Robinson, respectively, ever criticise Marx's theory of falling rate of profit since the mid of last century, few attention has been given to the dimension related to the problems of product innovation.
6. For Marx's citation of Jones, see Marx (1991, p. 375).
7. Mandel is usually considered one of the most crucial representatives of orthodox theory of profit rate to fall. He sometimes emphasises the significance of the fundamental contradiction of capital accumulation, as he once puts, 'the inner contradictions of capitalism (which are the roots of any slow-down or breakdown in expanded reproduction, in capitalist growth) must be found in the sphere of production as well as in the sphere of circulation. Reproduction, as Marx so clearly stated in Volume 2 of *Capital*, is the unity of the process of production and the process of circulation' Mandel (1995, pp. 117, 60). Nevertheless, as will be seen further below, this methodologically important insight actually plays no role in his concrete analysis.
8. Cf. Gillman (1957, esp. p. 86). As for his underconsumptionist dimension, see, e.g. p. 108 and p. 111. A similar critique of the orthodox theory of profit rate to fall in the light of the contradiction between production of surplus value and realisation of surplus value can be found as well in Michael Lebowitz (1976). P. Zarembka (2003) also makes it clear, in his critique towards Lenin's economic theory, that it is crucial to analyse capitalist development in the light of the structural contradiction between production and realisation.

9. Cf. M. Heinrich (1996–1997, pp. 452–466). Marx's words, see *Capital*, Volume 3 (Marx, 1991, p. 615). See also Zarembka (2003) on this problem.

10. Here we transform numerical examples by Marx to algebra. See Marx (1986, pp. 259–266).

11. The translation of the paragraph cited here is superior to that from the Penguin version of *Grundrisse*, in which 'self-valorisation of capital' is misleadingly translated as 'self-realization of capital'.

12. Assume for simplicity constant capital in production is zero, the unit value of any given commodity can be denoted as $\lambda = v + s = v(1 + e)$. Thus, we have $v = \lambda/(1 + e)$. Here, v denotes variable capital in the unit commodity, s denotes unit surplus value or unit profit, e denotes the rate of surplus value. By definition $s = ve$, we have $s = \lambda \times e/1 + e$. If Q is the total volume of commodities not only produced but realised, the total profit of the given commodity is: $\Pi = Q \times s = Q \times \lambda \times (e/1 + e)$. In this equation, the rise of e and Q can offset the decline of λ. But, if the mathematical limit is taken, $e/(1 + e)$ equals to 1. This implies that in the long run, the rise in the rate of surplus value plays less and less important role in offsetting a decline in λ and consequently in unit profit of commodity. Whether the total profit could rise is increasingly dependent upon the realised volume of use value.

13. In neo-Schumpeterian literature, the life cycle of any given product is described phenomenally in four phases: '*Introduction*: there are many product innovations as different options exist, but little is known about the nature of demand. *Growth:* there is increasing acceptance by customers, with a decreasing number of product innovations. Sales growth leads to standardization of technology, and there are cost-reducing process innovations. *Maturity*: the output ratio slows down, and competition through product differentiation increases; innovations concern improvements. Process innovations are labour-saving. *Decline*: declining sales. Attempts are made to escape saturation through changes in technology, and the use of labour-saving process innovations continues' (van Duijn, 1983, p. 133; also see Ch. 2).

14. The emergence of genetic inputs is considered by neo-Schumpeterians such as Carlota Perez (2002) as the very symbol of a technological revolution.

15. Also see Mandel (1995, p. 111) and Mandel (1975, pp. 144–145).

16. 'the emergence of a new expansionist long wave cannot be considered an endogenous (i.e. more or less spontaneous, mechanical, autonomous) result of the preceding depressive long wave, whatever the latter's duration and gravity. Not the laws of motion of capitalism but the results of the class struggle of a whole historical period are deciding this turning point' (Mandel, 1995, p. 37). As regarding Mandel is one of the most important contemporary Marxist economists, van Duijn (1983, p. 65) remarks: 'A true Marxist can never explain the long wave with the aid of purely endogenous mechanisms'.

ACKNOWLEDGEMENTS

The author thanks two anonymous referees and Professor Zarembka, whose comments helped to improve the article.

REFERENCES

Aglietta, M. (1976). *A theory of capitalist regulation*. London: Verso.

Baran, P., & Sweezy, P. (1968). *Monopoly capital*. New York: Monthly Review Press.

van Duijn, J. (1983). *The long wave in economic life*. London: George Allen and Unwin.

Freeman, C. (Ed.). (1996). *Long wave theory*. Cheltenham, UK: Edward Elgar.

Freeman, C., Clarke, J., & Soete, L. (1982). *Unemployment and technical Innovation*. Westport, CT: Greenwood Press.

Freeman, C., & Soete, L. (1997). *The economics of industrial innovation* (3rd edn). London: Pinter.

Gao, F. (2004). Product innovation and capital accumulation. *Modern Economic Research* (in Chinese), No. 4, pp. 3–10.

van Geldren, J. (1996). Springtide: Reflections on industrial development and price movements, translated in C. Freeman (Ed.), *The Long Wave Theory*. Cheltenham, UK: E. Elgar.

Gillman, J. M. (1957). *The falling rate of profit*. London: Dennis Dobson.

Heinrich, M. (1996 [1997]). Engels' edition of the third volume of "Capital" and Marx's original manuscript. *Science & Society, 60*(4), 452–466.

Kalecki, M. (1971). The problem of effective demand with Tugan-Baranovsky and Rosa Luxemburg. In *Selected essays on the dynamics of capitalist economy*. Cambridge: Cambridge University Press.

Kleinknecht, A. (1987). *Innovation patterns in crisis and prosperity*. London: Macmillan.

Kleinknecht, A., Mandel, E., & Wallerstein, I. (Eds.). (1992). *New findings in long-wave research*. New York: St Martin.

Lebowitz, M. (1976). Marx's falling rate of profit: A dialectical view. *Canadian Journal of Economics*, *IX*(2, May), 232–254.

Luxemburg, R. (1951). *The accumulation of capital*, translated by Agnes Schwarzschild, with an introduction by Joan Robinson. London: Routledge & K. Paul.

Mandel, E. (1975). *Late capitalism*. London: Verso.

Mandel, E. (1992). The international debate on long waves of capitalist development: An intermediary balance sheet. In: Kleinknecht et al. (Ed.), *New findings in long-wave research*. New York: St Martin.

Mandel, E. (1995). *Long waves of capitalist development: A Marxist interpretation*. London: Verso.

Marx, K. (1986). Economic manuscripts of 1857–58. In K. Marx & F. Engels (Eds.), *Collected works* (vol. 28). New York: International Publishers.

Marx, K. (1991). *Capital*, vol. 3, translated by David Fernbach, introduced by E. Mandel. London: Penguin Books.

Marx, K. (1993). *Grundrisse*, translated by Martin Nicolaus. London: Penguin Books.

Meng, J. (2001). *A treatise on the creative transformation of Marxist economics*. Beijing: Economic Science Publishing House.

Meng, J. (2012). How is the Golden Age of capitalism generated: A critique of two existing Marxist explanations. *Studies on Marxism* (in Chinese), No. 5, pp. 35–46.

Mensch, G. (1979). *Stalemate in technology* (English Trans.). Cambridge, MA: Ballinger.

Mensch, G., Weidlich, W., & Haag, G. (1987). Outline of a formal theory of long-term economic cycles. In T. Vasko (Ed.), *The long wave debate*. Berlin: Springer.

Minsky, H. P. (1986). Money and crisis in Schumpeter and Keynes. In H. J. Wagener & J. W. Drukker (Eds.), *The economic law of motion of modern society*. Cambridge University Press.

Nakatani, T., & Hagiwara, T. (1997). Product innovation and the rate of profit. *Kobe University Economic Review*, *43*, 39–51.

Okishio, N. (1961). Technical change and the rate of profit. *Kobe University Economic Review*, *7*, 85–99.

Perez, C. (2002). *Technological revolutions and financial capital*. Cheltenham, UK: Edward Elgar.

Quesnay, F. (1962). The "Dialogue on the Work of Artisans". In R. L. Meek (Ed.), *The economics of physiocracy* (pp. 203–230). London: George Allen & Unwin LTD.

Rosdolsky, R. (1977). *The making of Marx's capital*. London: Pluto Press.

Schumpeter, J. (1976). *Capitalism, socialism and democracy*. London: George Allenand Unwin.

Zarembka, P. (2003). Lenin as economist of production: A Ricardian step backwards. *Science & Society*, *67*(3), 276–302.